Research On Writing

Research On Writing
Principles and Methods

Edited by

Peter Mosenthal
Syracuse University

Lynne Tamor
*State University of New York
at Albany*

Sean A. Walmsley
*State University of New York
at Albany*

Longman
New York & London

RESEARCH ON WRITING
Principles and Methods

Longman Inc., 1560 Broadway, New York, N.Y. 10036
Associated companies, branches, and representatives
throughout the world.

Developmental Editor: Lane Akers
Editorial and Production Supervisor: Ferne Y. Kawahara
Manufacturing Supervisor: Marion Hess

Library of Congress Cataloging in Publication Data
Main entry under title:

Research on writing.

   "Based on discussions at the Conference on Writing
Research held at the State University of New York at
Albany in May 1980"—Pref.
   Includes bibliographies and index.
   1. English language—Rhetoric—Study and teaching.
2. Language arts. 3. Authorship. I. Mosenthal, Peter.
II. Tamor, Lynne. III. Walmsley, Sean. IV. Conference
on Writing Research (1980: State University of New
York at Albany)
PE1404.R43   001.54'3   82-15198
ISBN 0-582-28305-1   AACR2

Manufactured in the United States of America

Contents

Preface

During the past several years, writing has been resurrected as one of the basic skills; writing once again is viewed as a skill basic to functioning in school and in society. In education, there has been growing concern over a perceived lack of writing abilities in elementary, secondary, and post-secondary students. In the areas of business, government, and the armed forces, management has become increasingly concerned with the role that writing plays in effective communication within and between organizational hierarchies as well as between those organizations and clients, constituents, and the public.

In an attempt to understand writing, educators and management have turned to research for answers to old and new questions about writing. This interest has stimulated "pure" researchers in a number of disciplines to engage in a variety of writing-related research programs that are not necessarily restricted to resolving these practical questions. The programs reflect the parent disciplines of individual researchers and, therefore, represent different reasons for studying writing, pose different types of questions, use different methodologies, and apply different criteria to determine when a question has been adequately answered. Hence, it is sometimes difficult for the consumers of research findings—educators and management in particular—to recognize their own questions in research reports; research conducted within one discipline frequently fails to influence work within other disciplines even when significant overlap exists.

Books devoted to writing research have generally ignored the problem of this multiplicity of approaches. The books either discuss writing research from one field's point of view, or present a compendium of results from a variety of approaches. Underlying beliefs, assumptions, and methodologies are rarely made explicit, making integration of findings across projects and even comprehension of individual reports extremely difficult for many readers. The purpose of this book is to alleviate this problem by presenting explicit discussions of research principles and methods used by researchers actively working within a variety of disciplines.

In putting this book together, we have been more concerned with presenting the principles and procedures used by researchers in guiding their research than with presenting the particular findings generated by these principles and procedures. All of the contributors have reported specific results and conclusions elsewhere and most likely will continue to do so. They were asked to produce for this volume an essay describing the principles that govern their entire approach to generating research findings rather than a research report that might quickly become outdated.

The book is intended as a resource for anyone interested in research on writing. The contributors have presented their respective approaches clearly enough that graduate students in English, psychology, sociology, anthropology, linguistics, and education can understand approaches to writing research from disciplines other than their own. This book can, therefore, serve as an introductory textbook for courses in writing research. It is also intended as a source book for teachers, administrators, and others interested in obtaining an overview of several current approaches to research on writing that is derived from different disciplines. No less important, the book is intended for writing researchers themselves. Even within a discipline, discussions and publications tend to focus on research results. Researchers rarely reveal their underlying philosophies, goals, and methodologies for critical scrutiny, thereby obscuring disagreements and fostering misunderstandings. The contributors to this volume have risked critical scrutiny in the hope of providing a more thorough context for understanding their own work and of clarifying the similarities and differences among writing research programs developed by researchers with diverse backgrounds and goals.

In Part I, there are two chapters that describe very broad views of the entire research endeavor. Psychologists Carl Bereiter and Marlene Scardamalia identify six levels of inquiry, all of which play important roles in a cognitively oriented research program that explores the development of writing abilities in school-age children. Peter Mosenthal approaches the same problem from a somewhat more sociolinguistic perspective that has led to the development of a classroom competence model of writing.

Part II groups together four programs in which researchers undertake a series of relatively classical experimental projects, to explore a wide range of writing-related issues. Sarah Warshauer Freedman and Robert C. Calfee combine the concerns of college English with the methods of experimental psychology in a program that explores the processes used by readers in evaluating student compositions. Lynne Tamor and James T. Bond are also concerned with the evaluation of student writing, but for different reasons. Their backgrounds in developmental cognitive psychology and educational anthropology lead them to focus on the development of writing abilities in children, with a special emphasis on elicitation tasks and contexts. Victor Rentel and Martha King study children who are even younger and just beginning to write, and use longitudinal rather than cross-sectional methods. Finally, Robert Bracewell studies a range of ages from a more narrowly defined cognitive perspective.

The researchers represented in Part III use less formal, although no less careful, methodologies in their study of writing processes. All three chapters describe observational approaches, but with very different methods and goals. Like Freedman and Calfee, John R. Hayes and Linda S. Flower combine the concerns of college English and psychology, but they are interested in the composing processes of adult writers. They rely primarily on think-aloud protocols elicited during standard composing tasks. Lee Odell, Dixie Goswami, and Anne Herrington are also concerned with the composing processes of adults, but instead of students and professional writers, they study workers and their on-the-job writing performances. This focus has necessitated the development of alternative methodologies to those traditionally used in researcher-controlled settings and reflects a variation on the usual concerns of the English field. Educational ethnographers Christopher M. Clark and Susan Florio also study writing in nonexperimental settings, but their subjects are elementary school children and their setting is not the job but the classroom. In particular, their chapter describes the study of the role of the teacher in the student's writing process.

In Part IV, Sean Walmsley steps back from the current flurry of research on writing and examines the long tradition of interest in writing disabilities. He examines the roots of this work in remedial education and neurophysiology, and he raises questions about the current place for the notion of writing disabilities in the types of research described by the other contributors. Charles R. Cooper also examines a well-established literature in his review and analysis of approaches to text analysis. His survey covers classical methods from the fields of English and rhetoric as well as more newly developed procedures that incorporate ideas from linguistics and education.

Taken together, these chapters represent research derived at least in part from the fields of education, cognitive psychology, developmental psychology, English, linguistics, sociolinguistics, psycholinguistics, neurophysiology, anthropology, and ethnography. Although this is certainly not an exhaustive list of the fields that can or do influence writing-related research, it is large and diverse enough to offer insights into most of the research projects under way at the present time. It is not so diverse, however, that the reader will not see several threads of common concerns and approaches that tie the chapters together. These threads have deliberately been left implicit. Each chapter is intended to convey the underlying principles and methods of a research program in the language of the program's developers. In explaining their own work, some contributors do refer to the work of other contributors, but these discussions are not intended as general reviews or evaluations. We leave it to readers to make the comparisons and contrasts that are useful to their own purposes, unencumbered by any predetermined evaluative scheme we might have imposed.

This volume is based on discussions at the Conference on Writing Research held at the State University of New York at Albany in May 1980. The support of the University and the assistance of Carolyn Brown, Margie Byrd, Randie Davidson-Mosenthal, and Bonnie Walmsley were invaluable in running the conference and preparing the manuscript.

Peter Mosenthal
Lynne Tamor
Sean A. Walmsley

Part I

General Approaches

1

Levels of Inquiry in Writing Research

Carl Bereiter
Ontario Institute for Studies in Education
Marlene Scardamalia
York University, Toronto

This chapter is concerned with providing a systematic way of viewing the varied forms of inquiry into the process of written composition. Several motives lie behind this effort. On the one hand, we are impatient, as surely many others are, with the miscellaneous character of much writing research, with its orientation toward topics or methods rather than toward goals, and with its general lack of cumulative force. On the other hand, we think that in this era of competing methodologies there is a special need to promote tolerance and a free spirit of inquiry. Writing research is new and there is not much of it. It is not easy and there are, as yet, no magic keys to an understanding of it. Writing research needs to be varied without being unfocused, guided by theory without being dogmatic, progressive without being mindlessly trendy. To achieve such balance, it seems desirable for researchers to have conscious access to a scheme that allows them to conceive of their immediate activities within a larger pattern. In this chapter, we set forth such a scheme.

We conceive of research into the composing process as going on at six interacting levels. These levels, briefly described in Table 1.1 will be discussed in detail in the body of this chapter. Although it is possible for individual researchers to devote their careers largely to inquiry at one level, we conceive of inquiry as a whole: moving in a spiral course that starts at Level 1, moves upward and then returns to Level 1 to begin a new cycle—but with a heightened understanding acquired from the preceding cycle. The successive levels of inquiry are marked by movement that is (1) further and further away from the natural phenomena of writing

TABLE 1.1   Levels of Inquiry in Research on the Composing Process

Level	Characteristic Questions	Typical Methods
Level 1: Reflective inquiry	What is the nature of this phenomenon? What are the problems? What do the data mean?	Informal observation Introspection Literature review Discussion, argument, private reflection
Level 2: Empirical variable testing	Is this assumption correct? What is the relation between x and y?	Factorial analysis of variance Correlation analysis Surveys Coding of compositions
Level 3: Text analysis	What makes this text seem the way it does? What rules could the writer be following?	Error analysis Story grammar analysis Thematic analysis
Level 4: Process description	What is the writer thinking? What pattern or system is revealed in the writer's thoughts while composing?	Thinking aloud protocols Clinical-experimental interviews Retrospective reports Videotape recordings
Level 5: Theory-embedded experimentation	What is the nature of the cognitive system responsible for these observations? Which process model is right?	Experimental procedures tailored to questions Chronometry Interference
Level 6: Simulation	How does the cognitive mechanism work? What range of natural variations can the model account for? What remains to be accounted for?	Computer simulation Simulation by intervention

that are observed in their full context and (2) closer and closer to the psychological system viewed as a theoretical construct. Continual return to lower levels is, therefore, in part demanded by the need to keep renewing contact with phenomenal reality.

It should be evident, although it cannot hurt to emphasize the point, that higher levels of inquiry are *not* seen to be any way better than lower levels. Inquiry may be sophisticated or naive, superficial or profound, at any of the levels. Furthermore, understanding of the composing process does not emerge from inquiry at any particular level but rather through synthesizing knowledge gained in the course of spiraling through levels.

Why call them levels, then, the reader might ask, rather than something more neutral, such as phases, steps, or varieties? As we have already indicated, the levels are not merely sequential—in fact there is only a weak sequentiality to them—but they are ordered on a dimension of abstractness. The idea of levels has yet a stronger sense, however. It is possible for research to keep cycling between Levels 1 and 2, never going any higher. Indeed, the great bulk of educational research has tended to do this. We would argue that, although inquiry at Level 2 is not inherently inferior to inquiry at Level 4, a program of inquiry that never incorporates knowledge from levels higher than Level 2 is severely limited in comparison to one that incorporates Levels 1 through 4. In turn, such a program is limited in comparison to one that incorporates a level as high as Level 5. In this way, it is possible to compare research programs according to the highest level of inquiry they incorporate, but there is still no suggestion that the doing of Level 5 inquiry is in itself a more worthy intellectual endeavor than doing Level 2 or Level 3 inquiry.

THE SIX LEVELS OF INQUIRY

Level 1: Reflective Inquiry

Reflective inquiry does not involve seeking new information through empirical research. Instead, it involves reflection on the information one already has or that is available from ordinary experience. Reflective inquiry into the composing process has a long and honorable history, starting as far back as Aristotle's *Poetics*. Empirical scientists often disparage armchair analysis. Efforts to advance knowledge in fields like physics through purely reflective inquiry have, indeed, shown little accomplishment during two thousand years of earnest effort. With respect to the composing process, however, the reflective thinker has the benefit of access to an extremely important fund of information, the thinker's own experience as a writer. Many people who reflect on the composing process will also have had experience as teachers of writing, and all will have been exposed to numerous samples of the writing of others. Consequently, the armchair enquirer into the composing process is much better supplied with relevant knowledge than the typical armchair enquirer into astrophysics has been.

Some of the most influential contributions to our understanding of the process of writing and the process of learning to write have come from people who relied for material on their own experience as writers and teachers (e.g., Elbow, 1973; Moffett, 1968). In the present analysis, however, we are more interested in reflective analysis as part of a more comprehensive program of inquiry into the composing process. We see reflective inquiry as home base. It is the place from which other kinds of inquiry start; it is where inquiry keeps returning for fresh starts; it is where, finally, the knowledge gained through inquiry at other levels is consolidated into understanding. Thus we designate it as Level 1, not because it is the lowest (or the highest) type of inquiry, but because it is primary.

A sensitive discussion of the limitations of different kinds of Level 1 inquiry is provided by Emig (1971) as background to her ground-breaking venture to go beyond Level 1 in studying the composing process. We shall not dwell on those limitations here, leaving it to later discussion to argue the value of going to other levels of inquiry. It seems more important, at this point, to emphasize the significant role that Level 1 inquiry normally plays in empirical research. There is a caricature of empirical science frequently promulgated these days that depicts the empirical scientist as naively believing in objective truth and as disdaining intuition, introspection, everyday experience, common sense, ancient wisdom, and generalizations of any sort not based on statistical tests. This caricature is encouraged by the kinds of reports that appear in scientific journals. These reports seldom give any indication of the reflective thought that preceded or followed an investigation. But that is a characteristic of scientific journalism, not a characteristic of scientific inquiry. If you listen to empirical scientists talking shop informally, you do not hear them talking much about details of procedure or statistical tests; much less do you hear them trying to thrust objective truths on one another. In our experience, the overwhelming question that dominates at least 70 percent of the serious conversation among researchers on human behavior is, What is it really? What is the real process that our data hint at and that our theoretical models crudely represent?

This is Level 1 inquiry. It draws on knowledge and hunches of all sorts. Without it, empirical research can hardly move. There are, no doubt, some empirical researchers who fit the caricature, who do not mix Level 1 with other levels of inquiry. We think we know some. We call them hysterical empiricists—people who keep cranking out research according to a set method, frequently to amass support for a proposition that no reasonable person would doubt in the first place. These hysterical empiricists are capable of reflective analysis, but somewhere along the line they were miseducated into the belief that science requires putting reflection aside. True, science tries to go beyond the limits of what can be achieved through reflective inquiry. It does so to enrich reflection, not to replace it.

Level 2: Empirical Variable Testing

In the course of Level 1 inquiry, reflections inevitably make use of some premises that are testable matters of fact. In the course of reflecting on problems of writing instruction, for instance, premises like the following might come into play: the quality of student writing has declined in recent decades; students who read good literature write well; television watching encourages incoherent writing; many children do poorly because school writing assignments make them anxious. Although they are plausible, such premises could be factually wrong and, thus, could lead Level 1 inquiry astray. If one sets out to test such premises empirically, one has moved away from purely reflective inquiry to a different level, which we designate as Level 2.

Level 2 is called empirical variable testing because testing a premise empirically requires translating the premise into a statement about the relationships will be imperfect and thus reduce the force of the premise that students who read good literature write well, one has to specify a procedure for measuring "writing well" (such as teacher ratings) and for "reads good literature" (such as a score on a checklist of books read outside of class). Defining such variables may not be easy, and the result may not be any less controversial than the original premise that the variables were designed to test.

Level 2 research, in fact, is continually beset by a chorus of objections that render every empirical finding questionable. The variables may be challenged as not adequately measuring the thing intended (some good writers will score low on your measure of good writing). The empirical relationships will be imperfect and thus reduce the force of the premise (not every student who reads good literature will be a good writer, no matter how you measure the variables). It will be impossible to be sure that the observed relationship would also be found under other conditions and among other kinds of students. It will be impossible to deny that the implied causal relationship (for instance, good reading causes good writing) could result from some other untested variable (for instance, a literate home environment that encourages both good reading and good writing).

If the results of empirical variable testing are so inherently dubious, one may ask, Why do it? Level 2 inquiry, we believe, only makes sense as a supplement to Level 1 inquiry. It is not fair or reasonable to judge empirical variable testing against a standard of absolute certainty—to expect, for instance, that research on the relationship between good reading and good writing should finally yield us an answer that we can be as sure of as we are sure that two plus two make four. We should ask instead whether the research has given us a sounder factual basis for Level 1 reflection than we would have had without it—that is, whether the factual basis is sounder than we could achieve through informal observations, study of isolated cases, or commonsense assumptions. Not all Level 2 research passes this test, but much of it does.

It is too much to ask of any type of inquiry that it lead to error-free results, but a progressive form of inquiry should be capable of error reduction and that is where pure Level 1 inquiry fails. Level 2 inquiry, for all its limitations, does have the capacity, through a variety of experimental and analytical techniques, to diminish error. Therefore, it provides an essential supplement to—not replacement for—Level 1 inquiry.

A study of Scardamalia, Bereiter, and Woodruff (1980) will serve to illustrate on a small scale the role of Level 2 inquiry as supplementary to Level 1. Much advice to writers and much advice to teachers is premised on the belief that people write best about what they know best. This belief has a somewhat self-evident character about it in that, of necessity, people cannot write good pieces on topics about which they know nothing. Many of the commonplace beliefs that form the basis of Level 1 inquiry have this quasi-self-evident character—they are necessarily true in some sense or under some condition; and from this, their truth in general is assumed. But is the belief true across the relevant range of conditions? Is it true, for instance, across the range of topics about which a writer knows *something*, that the quality of composition increases according to the writer's familiarity with the topic?

The Scardamalia et al. (1980) study sought evidence bearing on this question. Elementary school children were interviewed to identify topics about which they claimed to know much or little. Then each child wrote two compositions, one on a high-familiarity topic and one on a low-familiarity topic. A variety of analyses failed to reveal any difference between compositions produced on the two kinds of topics. Most people to whom we have reported this finding have been reluctant to accept it. They have questioned the variables used in comparing the compositions. They have objected to our using the children's own nominations of familiar and unfamiliar topics (although we believe that if we had used experimenter-determined topics many of the same people would have objected to our not having left the children free to choose). They have questioned whether the same results would be obtained under different—for instance, more informal—task conditions. And they have suggested other variations of the experiment that would be needed to determine the generalizability of results.

These objections illustrate two points about Level 2 inquiry. First, the objections are quite legitimate and they illustrate the range of objections that can usually be brought against particular variable-testing studies. Second, the objections are at least partly motivated by an unwillingness to abandon a prior belief. If the study had shown that children produced markedly better compositions on more familiar topics, the study probably would not have provoked much criticism even though all the same criticisms would apply (along with the additional criticism that the study was only proving the obvious). This double standard, although troublesome at times, is on the whole quite sound. It reflects the fact that Level 2 findings are a supplement to, not a replacement for, Level 1 intuitions. One does not abandon an important belief grounded in common sense and ordinary experience simply because one empirical study has brought evidence against it.

On the other hand, a reasonable person will not ignore Level 2 results. At the very least, Level 2 findings that run against common knowledge should serve as signals that something is more complex than we had assumed. The Scardamalia et al. (1980) study, for instance, should at least provide a caution against assuming that a simple formula that relates greater topic familiarity to better expository writing holds universally. A good Level 2 study should, furthermore, establish its findings within a context that has some representative significance. Thus, the context in which Scardamalia et al. (1980) found the familiarity-quality equation to fail was not some bizarre situation never encountered in real life. It was well within the range of typical school writing contexts. To be sure, there may be other contexts within the typical range where the familiarity-quality equation does hold—but that remains to be established. Research that did establish it would add further increments to our knowledge about writing; it would not simply erase the previous finding.

Although Level 2 inquiry is a form of reality testing and looks for data that are representative of the real world, it can, nevertheless, be theoretically motivated and may even be motivated by quite abstract notions. In the Scardamalia et al. (1980) study, for instance, we were not motivated by the question of whether children should be encouraged to write about what they know. We were motivated by an interest in children's difficulties with self-directed memory search. We suspected that children lacked executive procedures for self-sustained search of memory. If this were true, it should also be true that children would have trouble developing content even on subjects about which they knew a lot, provided the search had to be carried out deliberately. This conclusion seemed at variance with commonly accepted knowledge; therefore, a Level 2 study that would test children's memory-search capabilities in a realistic context was required. The proposed Levels of Inquiry scheme, it will be recalled, has a spiral structure. In early stages, Level 2 inquiry is likely to be motivated primarily by issues of belief or practicality; at later stages, it is likely to be motivated increasingly by theoretical considerations that impinge on ordinary worldly knowledge.

Until recently, Level 2 inquiry has been the dominant mode of research in education and the social sciences. Much ingenuity has gone into devising ways to overcome its inherent weaknesses: methods of statistical control for variables that cannot be controlled experimentally, multivariate methods that deal with the redundancy among measures, factorial designs that make it possible to examine the independent and joint effects of person and situation variables. All of these methods, however, add additional sources of indeterminacy that, in turn, call for even more empirical studies.

The ultimate threat to all Level 2 inquiry is combinatorial explosion. If one considers all the variables that might impinge on a simple empirical outcome and all of the separate combinations of these variables that might act in distinct ways, one quickly generates a staggering number of needed empirical observations and the possible outcomes grow to an unmanageable complexity (Cronbach, 1975). We could easily spend the rest of our careers running variations on a content-familiarity study and have nothing to show for our pains but conclusions so loaded down with conditions and exceptions as to be utterly worthless.

How can one escape this combinatorial explosion? The answer seems to lie in higher levels of inquiry. Instead of pressing further into studying the conditions under which content familiarity does and does not correlate with various characteristics of compositions, we can try instead to find out how children actually use the content knowledge they have. How do they retrieve content from memory (Bereiter & Scardamalia, 1982)? How do they select what to include in their compositions (Scardamalia et al., 1980; Stein & Trabasso, 1982)? To what extent do they transform their knowledge to suit purposes of a composition as opposed to simply reporting knowledge as it is recalled (Bereiter & Scardamalia, in press; Flower, 1979)? Such questions are still questions about the relation between content knowledge and writing, but they reflect a different level of inquiry, a level that escapes the proliferation of empirical variables and their combinations because it is concerned with the structures and processes lying behind them.

Level 3: Text Analysis

Inquiry at Level 3 consists of trying to extract descriptive rules or principles by studying written texts. At the most general level, it embraces various analyses, for example, that of Halliday and Hasan (1976) aimed at uncovering a principle such as cohesion, which is applicable to all texts. It extends, however, to more specialized study, too, such as that of Stein and Trabasso (1982) in which common structures found in children's narratives are used as a basis for inferring the mental schemata that children use in understanding and generating stories. A rather different kind of analysis, still within the same sphere of inquiry, is that of Shaughnessy (1977), which aimed at inferring the rules that basic writers follow in coping with spelling, punctuation, and standard English syntax.

Text-analysis of this rule-seeking sort has its analogues in other fields of study—in the work of anthropologists like Levi-Strauss (1963), for instance, who infer the kinship structures of tribal peoples or in the work of ethnomethodologists who infer the rules governing different kinds of social exchange, including conversation (e.g., Wooton, 1975). Not all analyses done on texts qualify as Level 3 analyses however. In fact, most of the research involving counting and measuring T-units and frequencies of various sentence and text features is straight Level 2 empirical variable testing, which happens to use variables drawn from written texts. Level 3 inquiry is not the study of empirical variables that happen to be derived from texts. Level 3 inquiry approaches texts as complex phenomena that exhibit internal lawfulness, and it aims to understand that lawfulness.[1]

There does not seem to be much text analysis going on that is related to understanding the composing process. Perhaps this is because writing researchers have assumed that, in analyzing texts, one is necessarily studying product and that to study process, one must do something else. Such a belief is forcefully dispelled, however, by the work of de Beaugrande (1980; 1982) who draws heavily on text analysis for insights into the cognitive processes of composing.

There is a direct link between written products and the composing process. Whatever lawfulness is found in a text must reflect lawful behavior on the part of the writer because the physical properties of the text impose no requirements of lawfulness. One could keep piling up sticks at random until one accidentally produced a structure that stood up. This pile of sticks would, then, exhibit a structure that had no necessary counterpart in one's own mind. But in writing, whatever lawfulness appears must have its counterpart in the mind of the writer (provided, of course, there has been no response from a reader). The counterpart may not be obvious and may not be inferrable at all without supplementary information, but the product of writing is sure to remain an indispensible clue to process.

Much valuable research on composition can be done at Level 3. Especially needed are descriptions of rules used by children and unskilled writers at the whole-text, local, and sentence levels. Rhetorics and grammars typically give us rules of the skilled writer—and those, generally, not at a deep level. A typical writing handbook will devote page after page to rules for correct choice of pronouns, but it will never even mention the problem of choosing whether to use a pronoun or not. Overuse of pronouns seems to be one of the common traits of unskilled writing; yet, no writer is so unthinking as to use pronouns to the total exclusion of nouns. Research is needed to discover what rules less skilled writers actually use and how these rules differ from those of experts. Research on children's story grammars is an important kind of Level 3 inquiry, one that has only begun to be extended into other genres (see Bereiter & Scardamalia, 1982; Scardamalia, Bereiter, & Goelman, 1982).

Level 3 inquiry does have significant limitations however. First, there appear always to be different rule systems that can be used to account for the same observed regularities in text. There are different story grammars (e.g., de Beaugrande & Colby, 1979; Stein & Glenn, 1979) because there are many different sentence grammars. There is no way of determining from text analysis which, if any, of these grammars actually represent knowledge as it exists in the mind of writers. Independent evidence of the psychological reality of particular rule structures must be sought (Stein & Trabasso, 1982). Second, Level 3 inquiry does not yield insight into the composing process as such. It yields insight into the knowledge structures that direct the composing process, and this is vital for understanding the process; but it remains to find out how this knowledge is brought into play during the actual course of composing. To overcome these limitations—to establish the psychological reality of rule structures and to discover how they function in the composing process—inquiry at still higher levels is required.

Level 4: Process Description

Whereas Level 3 inquiry is a search for lawfulness and pattern in written texts, Level 4 inquiry is a search for lawfulness and pattern in the writer's thoughts while composing. Level 4 thus brings the investigator into more immediate touch with the composing process.

Level 4 inquiry faces a dramatic methodological problem that tends to overshadow other problems associated with inquiry at this level. The problem is, of course, that the writer's thoughts are not normally accessible to observation. Hypnosis and truth serums are possible ways around this obstacle, but they have not, so far as we know, been exploited in writing research. The two main ways that have been used are the clinical-experimental interview (Piaget, 1972) and the thinking-aloud procedure (Ericsson & Simon, 1980). The origins of the former in work with young children and of the latter in work with adults are probably not accidental. It has proved possible to get at least some adults to verbalize copiously while they carry out mental tasks and thus to obtain a rich record of things passing through their minds relevant to the on-going process. It has proved much harder to get children to sustain this kind of verbalization. To do so usually requires repeated intervention by the investigator and some external structuring of the task. In doing these things one is shifting over to the clinical-experimental method. In collecting thinking-aloud protocols, the investigator interacts little with the writer; the investigation may not even be present. In the clinical-experimental interview, the investigator interacts with the writer and tries to structure a task in which such interaction will be natural, but the investigator tries, nevertheless, to engineer the exchange in such a way that all the thoughts come from the writer, not from the investigator. An example of clinical experimental methodology is the study of evaluation and revision processes in children by Scardamalia and Bereiter (in press).

It is important, however, not to confuse Level 4 inquiry with the methods that are normally used to conduct it. Thinking-aloud protocols, for instance, may be used simply as a source of variables for Level 2 inquiry, and they may also be used in inquiry above Level 4. The defining characteristic of Level 4 inquiry is its search for a description of the composing process. Because most of the process is covert, Level 4 researchers tend to get involved in mind-reading problems of some sort, but this is a secondary phenomenon. Level 4 researchers could limit their study to the observable part of composing behavior, obtaining a valid, although necessarily limited, description of the process (e.g., Stallard, 1974). Or they could choose to study the process of group composition, in which case much more of the process would be externalized in the form of conversation (an example is presented in Bereiter & Scardamalia, 1982). In any event, the Level 4 investigator's job does not end with collecting and transcribing protocols any more than the Level 3 investigator's job ends with obtaining written texts. The main job is the search for lawfulness in the protocols.

Level 4 inquiry is relatively new in writing research and, indeed, in language research generally. It has generated enthusiasms and objections that are both (we think) somewhat misdirected—because, again, they tend to focus on the method of data collection rather than on the inquiry itself. The common objections have to do with the inevitable violations of naturalism that occur when one tries to gain access to normally covert behavior. How do we know that what a writer thinks under the unnatural conditions of thinking aloud or the clinical-experimental interview is what the writer would think while composing naturally? The criticism parallels one that could be leveled against a naturalist whose account of the behavior of apes was based entirely on watching them in zoos.

These objections, however, fail to take into account the difference between testimony and data. Writers' verbal reports should not be taken as presenting a picture of the composing process that one judges to be true or false and rejects if it is false. Rather, they should be taken as data (Ericsson & Simon, 1980) that the investigator uses, often in conjunction with other data, in constructing a description of the inferred process. Verbal reports, like any other kind of data, may be misleading; the issue, however, is not whether they are perfect but whether they lead to better process descriptions than can be produced without such data. Ultimately it is the investigator's description, not the subject's verbal report, that must be judged true or false.

Critics of thinking-aloud procedures frequently miss this point, but so do some enthusiasts, who seem to believe that thinking-aloud protocols offer direct insight into mental processes. A descriptive model of the composing process, such as that produced by Hayes and Flower (1980), is an intellectual construction based on inferred invariances in protocol data. It is not, like the naturalist's diary or sketchbook, simply a record of what was observed.

The fundamental limitations of Level 4 inquiry are similar to those of Level 3, but shifted to a different ground. There is a similar problem in establishing the psychological reality of the theoretical construction. Different models may be constructed that adequately describe patterns observed in protocol data. But what the actual organization of the composing process is within the mind of the writer is a question that cannot fully be answered through Level 4 inquiry. Instead, Level 4 inquiry produces possibilities, the testing of which requires inquiry at a higher level.

The other fundamental limitation of Level 4 inquiry is that it describes only one layer of the composing process—an extremely important layer, to be sure, but one that still leaves much of what is most mysterious about composing untouched. The layer it describes is the layer of conscious thought. It describes the flow of attention during composing, but it does not reveal why attention shifts when it does and where it does. It indicates processes of discrimination, evaluation, search, and recognition, but it does not describe the actual operation of these processes (Scardamalia et al., 1982). In effect, thinking-aloud protocols and clinical-experimental protocols display the *products* of these cognitive activities rather than the cognitive activity itself. Thus to a considerable extent, Level 4 inquiry, like that of Level 3, is a study of products. The differences are that at Level 4 the products are intermediate products, retained and further processed in the mind, rather than the final products that appear on the written page. This is an important difference, bringing us closer to, but not yet into, contact with the psychological system that generates composition.

Level 5: Theory-Embedded Experimentation

All levels of inquiry may be theory-guided in the sense that ideas, topics, or methods are inspired by some theory or other. The four levels of inquiry described previously, however, are all capable of thriving without theory. Although theory may often be invoked in interpreting results of inquiry at these lower levels, results can generally be understood and appreciated without a supporting theoretical context. In other words, inquiry at Levels 1 through 4 may proceed either bottom-up, by generalization from data, or top-down, by starting with a rational construction and testing it against data. The two remaining levels of inquiry, however, are ones that can only be entered top-down.

Level 5 research consists of testing a theoretical construction by testing its empirical implications. In a theoretically advanced field like physics, almost all empirical research is of this kind. For that reason, the lay person reading the procedures of an experiment in physics would seldom have any idea of the point of the experiment. With writing research, on the other hand, one expects to be able to infer purposes from procedures. This is normally the case with Level 2 research. As writing research becomes more sophisticated, however, we may expect studies to begin appearing that are incomprehensible except with reference to some theory or model out of which they are conceived.

We may perhaps best illustrate Level 5 inquiry by stepping aside from writing research to a related area where theory is better developed. Consider a study by Collins and Quillian (1969). Subjects were asked a variety of simple questions: Is a robin a bird? Is a robin an animal? Does a robin have wings? Does a robin have skin? The variable examined was the difference in time (measured in milliseconds) that it took subjects to answer these different questions. Notice that, without some further information, it would be impossible to figure out why the experiment was conducted. Even less would one be able to criticize the methodology—to argue that certain other questions should have been asked than the ones that were used, for instance. In fact, this experiment is of landmark significance because it provided evidence in support of a new model of memory organization. The model proposed a treelike structure. One implication of this model was that the time it would take to connect two items in memory (such as *robin* and *animal*) would depend on the number of branches that needed to be traversed in getting from one item to the other. The questions were constructed so that they would hypothetically require different numbers of branches to make a connection; therefore, what was really at issue in the experiment was whether the theory was strong enough to predict the pattern of differences in the time required to answer the various questions.

Level 5 research cannot be reliably distinguished from Level 2 research by considering studies in isolation. The same methods may be used at either level, and sometimes the variables studied at Level 5 will have both theoretical and commonsense significance. The study reported by Scardamalia et al. (1982) illustrates the importance of considering purpose in determining the level of inquiry at which to interpret a study. The experiment had children producing compositions either by writing, by dictating into a recorder, or by slow dictation, which made use of a scribe who took dictation at each child's previously observed writing rate. The study up to this point is easily viewed as a Level 2 investigation of how mode of production affects composing. Although slow dictation is not a normal mode of production, it reflects an effort, common in both Level 2 and Level 5 research, to separate variables—in this case, to separate the variable of speed from the variable of oral-versus-written production.

Another feature of the experiment is less obviously accounted for, however. When children finished their compositions, the experimenter, through a series of prescribed prompts, urged them to keep going and to write or dictate more and more. People who approach this experiment as a Level 2 investigation find this manipulation ridiculous, of course. They see it as having no ecological validity (that is, it has no counterpart in real life) and as so absurd that children can only be expected to rebel or generate nonsense. But our purpose was not the Level 2 purpose of empirical variable testing. Our purpose was to investigate a theoretical notion about how the language-production system must change when it shifts from being dependent on conversational exchange to being capable of functioning autonomously (Bereiter & Scardamalia, 1982). The experimental manipulation was designed to isolate one hypothesized aspect of conversational exchange (its activating function) from other functions. Because this isolation almost never occurs in nature, the experimental treatment was necessarily rather artificial. But no more realistic treatment—at least none we could think of—would have yielded the relevant information. (As it turned out, children did not rebel or generate nonsense and, as we tried to show in the cited document, the results were theoretically interesting.) A point we keep repeating throughout this chapter is that methods cannot be judged except in relation to purposes. This point becomes absolutely crucial in distinguishing between Level 2 and Level 5 inquiry.

Level 5 inquiry transcends many of the difficulties that plague Level 2 inquiry—the proliferation of variables, the endless succession of "yes buts" and "what ifs." The reason is Level 5 inquiry is primarily concerned with developing and testing rational constructions rather than with accounting for data. Thus, Collins and Quillian (1969) were not trying to account for all the differences in response time between questions, they were interested in investigating a theory of memory organization; therefore, their interest in the observed phenomena extended only insofar as it was relevant to the theoretical questions. Similarly, Scardamalia et al. (in 1982) were not interested in identifying all the factors that affect fluency in writing; they were interested in exploring a theory about what keeps the language-production system going in writing as compared to conversation.

We do not want to suggest that in doing Level 5 inquiry the investigator should be aloof from wordly concerns. Smart investigators are alert to opportunities for investigation at all levels all the time. Often, in the course of Level 5 injury, it is not the looked-for results that lead to theoretical modifications, but the incidental findings that are drawn from Level 3 examination of the texts or Level 4 examination of oral protocols. There is one danger in being too loose about Level 5 inquiry however; it is that good Level 5 research can easily degenerate into bad Level 2 research. All it takes is to start focusing on the procedure rather than on the theory. One could, for instance, start doing variations on the Scardamalia et al. (1982) study, trying different kinds of prompting to see which was most facilitative, testing whether girls behave differently from boys and so on. One would then be doing Level 2 research (but not very good Level 2 research) because the basic procedure is not a representation of real-life writing conditions.

Level 5 research has its problems, but they are the problems of theoretical research in general. It is highly inferential, and it is often possible to keep patching up a weak theory so that it survives no matter what the research turns up. We shall not try to discuss these problems here because there is a vast literature on the subject (e.g., Lakatos & Musgrave, 1970). Instead we shall note one particular limitation that points the way to yet a higher level of inquiry. Level 5 experimentation is good for testing crucial assumptions of theories or crucial differences between theories. This is important in theory development at points where major decisions must be made. But Level 5 inquiry does not tell us how good a job, on the whole, a theory does—how well it explains or represents the composing process. For this we need a form of inquiry in which a theory may be made in some sense to run—to function in a way that will let us assess its overall fit to reality. That is the role of inquiry at Level 6.

Level 6: Simulation

Simulation by computer has proved to be a useful method of inquiry for gaining understanding of a variety of mental processes, such as problem solving (Newell & Simon, 1972), chess playing (Newell, Shaw, & Simon,

1963), and language comprehension (Reddy & Newell, 1974). On the one hand, computer simulation serves as a way of testing process theories originally constructed at other levels of inquiry. Gaps or flaws in the theory emerge as unprogrammable operations or as deviant outputs. On the other hand, computer simulation serves as a variety of inquiry in its own right. It permits the rapid exploration of variations that would be difficult to explore with live subjects as well as the gradual development from a crude theory that accounts for only limited kinds or properties of behavior to a more elaborate theory that is able to account for more of the variety of actual human behavior.

At present there is only a limited scope for computer simulation in studying composition. This is because, with present-day artificial intelligence technology, computers fall too far short of human beings in the ability to produce language and to draw flexibly on large knowledge structures. Within these limitations, however, interesting work is going on in which computers create compositions by making choices among limited alternatives. Although this type of simulation cannot be said to model the *process* of composition, it does lead to a greatly enriched specification of the knowledge requirements of composition (Black, Wilkes-Gibbs, & Gibbs, 1982).

The idea of simulation is not limited, however, to simulation by machine. Role-playing, a frequently used therapeutic and educational technique, often involves one person simulating the behavior of another. It differs from ordinary acting in that novel, problematic situations are introduced and the role-player tries to behave as the designated person would behave. Thus it requires more than superficial imitation. It requires, in a sense, having a theory of the other person's behavior and operating according to that theory. The theory need not, of course, be understood in formal terms. It is usually tacit or implicit. Nevertheless it has the properties of a theory: it can be limited in scope or applicable to a variety of situations, it can yield confirmed or unconfirmed predictions, and it can be refined in the light of results

Some teachers of writing apparently develop a keen enough understanding of how their students write that they can produce compositions indistinguishable from those of their students. (This indistinguishability criterion is often employed in computer simulation studies to test the adequacy of a theory.) The process the teacher uses to generate a composition that will pass for the work of a typical twelve-year-old is not necessarily the same process used by the typical twelve-year-old, but at some important level it must be functionally equivalent. Therefore, if we could understand one process, we should probably have made a significant advance toward understanding the other.

The trouble with simulation on the basis of tacit knowledge, however, is that the process used by the simulator is no more comprehensible than the process being simulated. Thus, although the person doing the simulation may have an excellent working theory of the composing process, the theory cannot be communicated to anyone else.

There is another approach to using human beings as simulators that is more overt and that can result in communicable knowledge. If, instead of trying to write like a twelve-year-old yourself, you design a procedure that will cause other adults to write like twelve-year-olds, you will, perhaps have captured in the procedure some important principles that distinguish the composing processes of twelve-year-olds. If, in addition, you can use the same or a variant procedure to cause nine-year-olds to write like twelve-year-olds, you will even more surely have captured important insights into the development of the composing process.

The kind of simulation we have just described has recently started to be recognized as a potentially powerful method of inquiry (Brown & Campione, in press; Butterfield, Siladi, & Belmont, 1980), but there are few examples of its deliberate use. One impressive example is the work of Case and his coworkers (Case, Kurland, & Goldberg, in press) who tested a theory about the relation between speed of information processing and information-processing capacity. Studies were conducted to see whether by speeding people up or slowing them down to the rate of a target age group, their short-term-memory performance would be raised or reduced to that of the target age group. Simulation, it should be noted, is always partial or limited, and this is equally true whether one uses human beings or computers as the simulators. Just as the computer simulator does not expect the computer to watch television and exhibit sexual preferences, Case and his colleagues (in press) did not expect people to act in every way like the target age group but only to resemble them in the particular way that was relevant to the theoretical inquiry. Similarly, when we apply this method of inquiry to writing, we do not expect the writing of one group to resemble in every particular the writing of another group (although this might be a long-range objective once a comprehensive theory has been developed). Instead, one seeks to achieve limited, predictable changes through interventions that are focused in a theoretically interesting way.

The authors have experimented with a variety of simulations of this limited sort—not to boost the maturity of writing performance in a general way but instead to have particular effects that would show whether we were on the right track in our theorizing about development of the composing process. Many of these simulations are summarized in Bereiter and Scardamalia (1982). The most elaborate study is described in Scardamalia and Bereiter (in press). In this study, a model is proposed for the mental processes that go on in revision. A simplified procedure is introduced to enable children to execute these processes. The hypothesis is that children have the requisite competence to carry out the subprocesses in some fashion but that they lack an executive scheme for running the process as a whole. The results indicated that children who do not normally revise (except at the level of mechanics) can in fact carry out the more mature process. Evidence in support of the processing model did not, however, come from the revisions actually accomplished by the children. Their revisions were only marginally successful, for although it appeared that children were accurate in evaluating their writing at the sentence level, they lacked the additional skills needed to transform these evaluations into substantial improvements. Instead, the main evidence came from children's direct response to the new procedure. They reported that it enabled them to do things they did not normally do in writing, and their reports indicated that they were starting to attend to and question the kinds of things that mature writers attend to and question in revision. This points up a particular advantage that simulation using human beings has over simulation using computers. In addition to producing outputs that can be compared to other outputs, human beings—even young and naive ones—can provide a wealth of intelligent commentary that helps the investigator to figure out what is going on.

Although this kind of simulation has begun to be recognized as valuable, it still lacks a name. The authors call it simulation by intervention. Like other kinds of simulation, it is a way of investigating one process by trying to set into motion a second process that is hypothesized to be similar to the first process in some way and comparing the outputs of the natural process and the simulated process. Its special characteristic, however, is that the simulation is achieved by intervening in a natural process. This has a double-edged effect when contrasted to simulation by computer. On the one hand, simulation by intervention has greater scope because one does not have to understand or make strong assumptions about all the component processes to investigate one that is of particular interest. To simulate composition by computer, for instance, one must either build in a sentence-generating capability or else assume that sentence generation does not interact with the processes one is attempting to simulate. Neither of these is an attractive alternative. The choice can be avoided in simulation by intervention, however, by allowing sentence-generating capabilities to be as they are and to interact or not, as nature dictates, with the processes that one is attempting to simulate. On the other hand, simulation by intervention is more constrained in that the intervention, if it is to run, must be compatible with the subject's actual psychological system, whereas in computer simulation the new program need only be compatible with the system architecture one has selected. Thus, simulation by intervention provides both more freedom to explore partly understood processes and more frequent and stringent reality testing.

Because simulation by intervention frequently involves instruction or some other kind of facilitation, it is easy to confuse it with theory-guided instructional research. Students whom we have tried to initiate into research at this level often fall into this trap, believing that Level 6 inquiry consists of designing an instructional procedure inspired by theoretical notions and then seeing how it works. Level 6 inquiry is not that simple. An instructional procedure can work even though based on a wrong theory, and it can fail to work even though the theory behind it is valid. (One would not wish, for instance, to see the validity of Piaget's theory judged by the success of educational programs purportedly based on it.) Level 6 inquiry in writing research is concerned with investigating the nature of different composing strategies or composing abilities by trying to simulate them, and it is only indirectly concerned with how well a particular intervention works. Nonetheless, Level 6 inquiry does offer the most promise of yielding knowledge that can be put to direct use in instructional design.

LEVELS OF INQUIRY IN THE CURRENT CONTEXT

In this section we shall relate the Levels of Inquiry scheme to current trends in research methodology and conclude with recommendations for the conduct of writing research.

Important changes are going on in approaches to research on human behavior. There is no dominant movement but rather a variety of new tendencies stimulated, we believe, by the collapse of empiricism. Empiricism, as practiced by social scientists in the English-speaking world, consists of research programs confined to Level 1 and Level 2 inquiry. Empiricist theorizing consists of trying to establish sets of lawfully related variables that will account for observed variations in behavior (Cronbach & Meehl, 1955). Reasons for the collapse of this once-dominant approach to research are too numerous and complex to be discussed here, but a number have already been suggested in our discussion of Level 2 inquiry.

We expect that eventually a new dominant approach will develop that incorporates inquiry corresponding to all six of the levels we discussed into a coherent, integrative program. In the meantime we have a number of more limited approaches used by researches who emphasize inquiry at one particular level: there are linguists and ethnomethodologists who emphasize Level 3, a number of cognitively oriented researchers who emphasize Level 4, artificial intelligence researchers who emphasize Level 6, and a host of actual or would-be Level 5 researchers who urge us never to leave home without a theory. It is only in this last group that we sometimes see a tendency to carry their approach to an unhealthy excess. In the heyday of empiricism, it was common to insist that a student could not undertake an investigation without hypotheses, which meant predicting what all the results would be. We do not like to see this stifling orthodoxy carried over into the modern era in the form of insistence that every researcher have a theory, whether there is any basis for a theory or not. It should be clear that the whole thrust of the Levels of Inquiry scheme is toward explanatory theories. Because we hold theorizing in such high regard, we hate to see it cheapened into a routine procedure of formalizing one's preconceptions.

A conspicuous development in the last decade has been the rise of holistic approaches to research, approaches that insist on viewing natural behavior in its full context and that seek to break down the rigid division between observer and observed (Mishler, 1979). These new approaches, bearing labels like phenomenological, ethnographic, hermeneutic, and qualitative, are too diverse to put all in one pigeonhole but there does not seem to be any fundamental reason why writing research employing these approaches cannot usefully be described within the Levels of Inquiry framework—provided that the research is, in fact, concerned with understanding the composing process and is not limited to interpreting the experience of composing or the conditions under which it takes place.

At present, holistic methods appear to be used only at Levels 1, 2, 3, and 4. However, there are developments afoot in cognitive science that may provide the necessary theoretical tools for more phenomenological and contextualized inquiry at Levels 5 and 6 (Shaw & McIntyre, 1974; Shaw & Turvey, 1981).

Although holistic methods have much to offer in writing research, there is, on the other hand, a holistic ideology that poses an actual threat to writing research. The main feature of this ideology is opposition to any research (or instruction) that deals with less than the full act of writing carried out under natural conditions. One evident motive behind this ideology is to promote writing as a meaningful activity, but this laudable motive has gotten out of hand when it drives people to oppose any research procedure that they would not accept as an instructional procedure. It seems that advocates of this ideology make the same mistake that many researchers do. They confuse methods with purposes. To hold strictly to a holistic ideology would mean giving up any hope of understanding writing as a cognitive process. The Levels of Inquiry framework, we hope, will make it possible for concerned humanists of a holistic persuasion to see that various methodologies, ranging from naturalistic observation to esoteric laboratory procedures, can be combined into a coherent effort to understand how human minds actually accomplish the complete act of writing.

Within behavioral science as a whole, a shifting of paradigms seems to be taking place. But writing research is still in a preparadigm stage (Emig, 1978; Kuhn, 1970). There is no consensus about what needs explaining, what kind of inquiry will lead to explanation, or how one would judge whether something was or was not an explanation. Until there is a paradigm, one cannot have much useful methodological or theoretical controversy. And in fact we know of little theoretical controversy within writing research proper. Controversy that does occur is imported from other domains, such as sociology or pedagogy, where paradigms are better developed.

A research paradigm is not something that is proposed and agreed on. It emerges as investigators come to recognize common problems, to discover common ways of talking about them, and to agree on the relevance of certain kinds of data. The Levels of Inquiry scheme is, accordingly, not a paradigm nor even the outline of one. *It is a framework for the kind of interaction that should lead to a paradigm.*

Let us conclude by considering some practical points on which the ideas behind the Levels of Inquiry scheme may be helpful.

1. Much methodological controversy can be avoided as irrelevant and unnecessarily devisive. It makes no sense to compare participant observation with thinking-aloud protocol analysis, for instance, or either of these with laboratory experimentation, except when they apply at the same level of inquiry. Sometimes they do, and then there are real choices to make. But more often they do not, and then there is no ground for controversy.

2. There must be communication across levels. If inquiry at a certain level makes no contact with inquiry at any other level, then either it is badly off the mark or else everything else is.

3. The Levels of Inquiry scheme should be taken into account when planning writing research, but pigeonholing should be avoided. In planning our own research programs, we find the Levels of Inquiry scheme helpful in prompting us to consider such questions as: Are we ready to address this question at a higher level? Are we stuck in our efforts to design a Level 6 inquiry, for instance, because we lack some important knowledge that will require further inquiry at Level 3 or 4? Pigeonholing a particular study can be a mistake, however, because many studies provide opportunities for inquiry at more than one level and in some cases a study must do so to achieve its purpose. We customarily design every Level 5 or 6 study so that it will also help build up our understanding at Levels 3 and 4, and most of our time in planning, executing, and analyzing such studies is devoted to inquiry at Level 1.

4. The Levels of Inquiry scheme indicates the need for an interdisciplinary approach to writing research and suggests ways in which such an approach may be fruitful. We mean interdisciplinary here in the strong sense of having experts in different disciplines engaged in coordinated research toward common objectives. There is a soft sense in which the term is often used these days. It refers to taking into account knowledge from various disciplines in the course of Level 1 reflection, and perhaps even getting people from different disciplines together to share ideas in a joint Level 1 inquiry. Examples of successful interdisciplinary inquiry in the strong sense are rare in research on human behavior, however.

The most obvious need suggested by the Levels of Inquiry scheme is for people who are expert in studying written compositions on the one hand and people who are expert in studying thought processes on the other. People expert in both are surely few. The conditions for interdisciplinary research exist in that people with backgrounds in language and rhetoric communicate regularly with cognitive psychologists and have developed common interests in writing research. The interdisciplinary potentialities of this exchange have been little realized, however.

As we have already noted, there is little Level 3 research going on except in the area of grammar analysis in children's stories. Probably nothing is holding back progress toward understanding the composing process so much as this lack. We need to figure out the rules that children and novices use in composing. To a limited extent these rules are accessible to Level 4 inquiry (e.g., Bereiter, Scardamalia, & Turkish, 1980). But for the most part, they are unconscious, like rules of grammar (which, of course, are a subset of the rules we are interested in developing), and the most direct way to discover such rules is through analyzing texts. Just as Piaget has described child logic, we need to describe child rhetoric. This does not mean rating children's texts for this or that characteristic or enumerating the ways in which they differ from texts of mature writers; rather, it means working out a rule system that gives rise to texts like those children write. Such a child rhetoric (or collection of rhetorics) would greatly enrich research at all other levels, especially Level 6. It would also make possible the design of process theories strong enough to be testable.

5. Writing researchers are often under pressure to show that their work is leading toward improvements in the teaching of writing. Yet, research on the composing process is justified in the first place by a belief that significant improvements in teaching will depend on gaining a deeper understanding of the process, but gaining this understanding promises to be a long and difficult effort. The Levels of Inquiry scheme may help researchers explain where the research they are doing fits into a general program that does have performance change (at Level 6) as a planned outcome but that builds systematically on inquiry, most of which is not directly concerned with performance outcomes. Thus the Levels of Inquiry scheme may serve as an intellectually sound replacement for the now largely discredited notion of the basic-to-applied continuum.

NOTE

1. The distinction here is *not* the same as the distinction between sentence-level and text-level analysis even though, as a historical matter, most Level 2 research has used variables based on sentences or smaller units, whereas most Level 3 research has been concerned with text-level issues. It is quite possible to do Level 2 research using text-level variables, for instance, counting the number of cohesive ties. It is also possible to do Level 3 inquiry at the sentence level as illustrated by de Beaugrande's (1980) inquiry into what causes certain kinds of sentence fragments to be frequently mistaken for complete sentences by student writers. The difference remains that of either treating texts as exhibiting phenomena that are to be explained (Level 3) or as a source of variables whose relationships to one another or to other variables are to be tested (Level 2).

REFERENCES

Bereiter, C., & Scardamalia, M. Cognitive coping strategies and the problem of "inert knowledge." In S. S. Chipman, J. W. Segal, & R. Glaser (Eds.), *Thinking and learning skills: Current research and open questions* (Vol. 2). Hillsdale, N.J.: Erlbaum, in press.

Bereiter, C., & Scardamalia, M. From conversation to composition: The role of instruction in a developmental process. In R. Glaser (Ed.) *Advances in instructional psychology* (Vol. 2). Hillsdale, N.J.: Erlbaum, 1982.

Bereiter, C., Scardamalia, M., & Turkish, L. *The child as discourse grammarian.* Paper presented at the annual meeting of the American Educational Research Association, Boston, April 1980.

Black, J. B., Wilkes-Gibbs, D., & Gibbs, R. W., Jr. What writers need to know that they don't know they need to know. In M. Nystrand (Ed.), *What writers know: The language, process, and structure of written discourse.* New York: Academic Press, 1982.

Brown, A. L., & Campione, J. C. Inducing flexible thinking: A problem of access. In M. Friedman, J. P. Das, & N. O'Connor (Eds.) *Intelligence and learning.* New York: Plenum, in press.

Butterfield, E. C., Siladi, D., & Belmont, J. M. Validating theories of intelligence. In H. W. Resse & L. P. Lipsitt (Eds.), *Advances in child development and behavior* (Vol. 15). New York: Academic Press, 1980.

Case, R., Kurland, D. M., & Goldberg, J. Operational efficiency and the growth of short term memory span. *Journal of Experimental Child Psychology*, in press.

Collins, A. M., & Quillian, M. R. Retrieval time from semantic memory. *Journal of Verbal Learning and Verbal Behavior*, 1969, *8*, 240–270.

Cronbach L. J. Beyond the two disciplines of scientific psychology. *American Psychologist*, 1975, *30*, 116–127.

Cronbach, L. J., & Meehl, P. E. Construct validity in psychological tests. *Psychological Bulletin*, 1955, *52*, 281–302.

de Beaugrande, R. Psychology and composition: Past, present, future. In M. Nystrand (Ed.), *What writers know: The language, process, and structure of written discourse.* New York: Academic Press, 1982.

de Beaugrande, R. *Text, discourse, and process.* Norwood, N. J.: Ablex, 1980.

de Beaugrande, R., & Colby, B. N. Narrative models of action and interaction. *Cognitive Science*, 1979, *3*, 43–66.

Elbow, P. *Writing without teachers.* London: Oxford University Press, 1973.

Emig, J. *The composing process of twelfth graders* (Research Report No. 13). Urbana. Ill.: National Council of Teachers of English, 1971.

Emig, J. Hand, eye, brain: Some "basics" in the writing process. In C. R. Cooper & L. Odell (Eds.), *Research on the composing process.* Urbana, Ill.: National Council of Teachers of English, 1978.

Ericsson, K. A., & Simon, H. A. Verbal reports as data. *Psychological Review*, 1980, *87*, 215–251.

Flower, L. Writer-based prose: A cognitive basis for problems in writing. *College English*, 1979, *41*, 19–37.

Halliday, M. A. K., & Hasan, R. *Cohesion in English.* London: Longman, 1976.

Hayes, J. R., & Flower, L. Identifying the organization of writing processes. In

L. W. Gregg & E. R. Steinberg (Eds.), *Cognitive processes in writing*. Hillsdale, N. J.: Erlbaum, 1980.

Kuhn, T. *The structure of scientific revolutions*. Chicago: University of Chicago Press, 1970.

Lakatos, I., & Musgrave, A. (Eds.) *Criticism and the growth of knowledge*. New York: Cambridge University Press, 1970.

Levi-Strauss, C. *Structural anthropology*. New York: Basic Books, 1963.

Mishler, E. G. Meaning in context: Is there any other kind? *Harvard Educational Review*, 1979, *49*, 1–19.

Moffett, J. *Teaching the universe of discourse*. Boston: Houghton Mifflin, 1968.

Newell, A., Shaw, J. C., & Simon, H. A. Chess-playing programs and the problem of complexity. In E. A. Feigenbaum & J. Feldman (Eds.), *Computers and thought*. New York: McGraw-Hill, 1963.

Newell, A., & Simon, H. A. *Human problem solving*. Englewood Cliffs, N.J.: Prentice-Hall, 1972.

Piaget, J. *The child's conception of the world*. New York: Harcourt, Brace, 1972.

Reddy, R., & Newell, A. Knowledge and its representation in a speech understanding system. In L. W. Gregg (Ed.), *Knowledge and cognition*. Potomac, Md.: Erlbaum, 1974.

Scardamalia, M., & Bereiter, C. The development of evaluative, diagnostic, and remedial capabilities in children's composing. In M. Martlew (Ed.), *The psychology of written language: A developmental approach*. London: Wiley, in press.

Scardamalia, M., Bereiter, C., & Goelman, H. The role of production factors in writing ability. In M. Nystrand (Ed.), *What writers know: The language, process, and structure of written discourse*. New York: Academic Press, 1982.

Scardamalia, M., Bereiter, C., & Woodruff, E. *The effects of content knowledge on writing*. Paper presented at the annual meeting of the American Educational Research Association, Boston, April, 1980.

Shaugnessy, M. P. *Errors and expectations: A guide for the teacher of basic writing*. New York: Oxford University Press, 1977.

Shaw, R., & McIntyre, M. Algoristic foundations to cognitive psychology. In W. Weimer & D. Palermo (Eds.), *Cognition and the symbolic processes*. Hillsdale, N.J.: Erlbaum, 1974.

Shaw, R., & Turvey, M. T. Coalitions as models for ecosystems: A realist perspective on perceptual organization. In M. Kubovy & T. Pomerantz (Eds.), *Organization of Perception*. Hillsdale, N.J.: Erlbaum, 1981.

Stallard, C. K. An analysis of the writing behavior of good student writers. *Research in the Teaching of English*, 1974, *8*, 206–218.

Stein, N. L., & Glenn, C. G. An analysis of story comprehension in elementary school children. In R. O. Freedle (Ed.), *New directions in discourse processing* (Vol. 2). Norwood, N.J.: Ablex, 1979.

Stein, N. L., & Trabasso, T. What's in a story: An approach to comprehension and instruction. In R. Glaser (Ed.), *Advances in instructional psychology*. Hillsdale, N.J.: Erlbaum, 1982.

Wooton, A. *Dilemmas of discourse*. London: Allen & Unwin, 1975.

2

On Defining Writing and Classroom Writing Competence

Peter Mosenthal
Syracuse University

An important yet little understood question is, How do children acquire writing competence in classroom lessons? The question is important because children learn to write primarily in classroom lessons. Also, it is primarily in classroom lessons where children encounter the tasks that require them to write. One finds few tasks outside the setting of classroom lessons that require much writing; what writing tasks there are outside classroom lessons appear to require much less sophisticated responses than those tasks indigenous to classroom lessons (Scribner & Cole, 1981). Finally, it is in classroom lessons, more than in any other setting, that young children's success is defined by their ability to write. This will become increasingly true as states begin to require students to pass minimal writing-competency tests as early as the sixth grade.

Although some research (Britton, Burgess, Martin, McLeod, & Rosen, 1975; Doyle, 1981; Graves, 1975; King & Rentel, 1979; Loban, 1976) has focused on the question of how children acquire writing competence in classroom lessons, it has provided few adequate answers to the question. The major reason why few adequate answers have been forthcoming is that this research has been conducted in the absence of any leading paradigms[1] of writing (Mosenthal, in press-c). As Kuhn (1970) has noted, in the absence of any leading paradigm, all findings generated by studies are equally true or relevant:

> In the absence of a paradigm, all of the facts that could possibly pertain to the development of a given science are likely to seem equally relevant. As a result, early fact gathering is far more a nearly random activity than one that subsequent scientific development makes familiar.

Facts, at their most basic level, are nothing more than descriptive definitions that are assumed to be true or that have been shown to be true by the use of operational definitions and bridge principles (Rudner, 1966).[2] When there are no mutually agreed-upon criteria for establishing descriptive and operational definitions and bridge principles, there are no criteria against which one can test competing hypotheses of writing and writing acquisition (Kuhn, 1970; Stegmüller, 1976; Weimer, 1979); hence, there are no criteria for separating relevant from irrelevant facts. Because science typically advances by demonstrating the adequacy of one competing hypothesis over a second (Newell, 1973; Weimer, 1979), the absence of criteria for defining writing is a particularly significant limitation; understanding writing and classroom writing competence cannot be significantly advanced until adequate criteria for defining "writing" and "classroom writing competence" are established and competing hypotheses are tested.

Given the absence of criteria for defining these terms, the purpose of this chapter is to consider what criteria are possible for formulating descriptive and operational definitions of these terms and for formulating bridge principles that relate these descriptive and operational definitions. We begin with a discussion of descriptive definitions, operational definitions, and bridge principles. Second, a full context model of writing and classroom writing competence is proposed. Third, different sets of criteria for defining these terms are discussed. It is argued that the adoption of these different sets of ideological criteria entails different partial specifications of the full context model. Limitations of the different partial specifications are also considered. Finally, in the fourth section, a model of classroom writing competence is presented. The descriptive and operational definitions and the bridge principles of this model are discussed. The purpose of describing this model is to illustrate one solution to the problem of partial specification in writing research.

DESCRIPTIVE DEFINITIONS

These are two ways concepts of phenomena can be defined: by descriptive definitions and by operational definitions (Hempel, 1966). In formulating a descriptive definition of a concept, one can either list examples that illustrate this concept or one can list the distinguishing characteristics or distinctive features that render this concept unique. For example, consider the term *fruit*, which represents the concept of the phenomenon fruit. One way to formulate a descriptive definition of *fruit* is to list examples of what makes up the concept of fruit. In this instance, one might descriptively define *fruit* as apples, peaches, pears, oranges, and so on, until a representative set of examples of fruit has been given. In enumerating only a few representative examples illustrating a concept, one has formulated a partially specified descriptive definition; in enumerating the complete set of examples said to comprise a concept, one has formulated a fully specified descriptive definition of this concept (see Rudner, 1966).

One can also define fruit in terms of the characteristics that render this concept unique. For instance, one might define *fruit* as the developed ovary of a seed plant whose seeds are centrally contained, whose central seed containment is surrounded by a moist pulp, and whose moist pulp is surrounded by an identifiable skin. Using this type of definition, one can formulate a partially specified descriptive definition by enumerating only the representative characteristics of a concept that render this concept unique, say, in contrast to the phenomenon of vegetable. On the other hand, one can formulate a fully specified descriptive definition by enumerating the entire set of features that make this concept distinguishable from all plant seed encasements.

In the absence of any leading paradigms, one must confront the problem of how to formulate descriptive definitions of writing and classroom writing competence. Kuhn (1970) and Weimer (1979) have noted that paradigms specify criteria for selecting examples and features to be used in formulating descriptive definitions. In some instances, these criteria are clearly delineated. In other instances, there are no explicit criteria; one selects certain examples and features in formulating descriptive definitions simply because some authority associated with a paradigm has used these features or examples (Weimer, 1979). Given that there are no well-defined paradigms in writing research, there tends to be no consensually agreed-on criteria for selecting examples and features to formulate descriptive definitions of writing and classroom writing competence. In addition, there are few authorities who have developed well-defined descriptive definitions of these terms. Hence, until criteria for establishing descriptive definitions of these terms are explicitly identified or until some universally identified authority emerges with his or her descriptive definition of these terms, all descriptive definitions of these terms will remain arbitrary (e.g., there will be no well-established reason for selecting one descriptive definition over another), and all facts based on these definitions will remain equally relevant.

OPERATIONAL DEFINITIONS

In formulating an operational definition of a concept, one specifies two things: a procedure and a criterion (Hempel, 1966). The purpose of specifying a procedure is to make an event observable under a set of well-defined conditions. In identifying a criterion, one defines a condition brought about by the procedure's event; if this criterion is met, a phenomenon is said to have qualified for representation by the operational definition's concept term.

To illustrate how an operational definition works, consider the following examples. Assume one had a liquid solution and one wanted to know if this solution were an acid. One could operationally test this by first following the procedure of taking a piece of blue litmus paper and dipping it into the solution. If the operational criterion is met, that is, that the blue litmus paper turns red, then the solution is said to have been operationally defined as an *acid.*

Consider another example. Assume one wanted to define operationally *hardness* in geology. One operational definition of hardness might be: Begin with the procedure of scraping the edge of one rock across the surface of a second rock. State the criterion. That is, if the first rock produces a scratch on the second rock in conducting the designated procedure, then the first rock is said to be operationally harder than the second rock. Carry out the procedure. If the first rock does produce a scratch on the second rock, then, the first rock is said to be *harder.*

In research, operational definitions serve to validate or invalidate descriptive definitions. Just how operational definitions do this is found in our discussion of bridge principles. However, what is important here is that operational definitions, like descriptive definitions, are arbitrary definitions unless constrained by paradigms. And because there are no leading paradigms in writing research, there tends to be no consensual basis for selecting procedures and criteria to formulate operational definitions of writing and classroom writing competence. In addition, there are few recognized authorities who have developed well-defined operational definitions of these terms. Hence, until criteria for establishing operational definitions of them are explicitly identified and until some universally identified authority emerges with such operational definitions, all operational definitions of writing and classroom writing competence will continue to remain equally viable and the facts based on these definitions will be equally relevant.

BRIDGE PRINCIPLES

To formulate and test adequately a model of classroom writing competence, one needs to develop two kinds of principles: internal principles and bridge principles (Hempel, 1966; Mosenthal, 1976–1977a). Internal principles represent the criteria by which one selects features and examples for formulating a descriptive definition of a concept. Bridge principles, on the other hand, represent the criteria by which one selects procedures and criteria for formulating an operational definition.

The purpose of bridge principles is to indicate how features or examples in the descriptive definition are to be related to procedures and criteria in the operational definition (Hempel, 1966). The purpose of relating these two definitions is to relate theoretically posited features or examples in the descriptive definition that cannot be directly observed or measured to observable procedures and criteria (Bridgman, 1978). It is reasoned that if the procedures and criteria of an operational definition are met in the manner predicted by a descriptive definition, then the unobservable features and examples of the descriptive definition represent valid concepts and hence, relevant facts.

In terms of the operational definition of acid described, bridge principles would specify the reason why the litmus paper test was a valid operational test for some given descriptive definition of acid. Similarly, in terms of the operational definition of hardness described, bridge principles would specify the reason why the scratch test was a valid operational test for some given descriptive definition of hardness.

It is important to note that operational definitions are essentially constrained by two things: the features and examples mentioned in the descriptive definition and the bridge principles relating these features or examples to the procedures and criteria of an operational definition. As such, operational definitions by themselves have no meaning independent of the descriptive definitions that operational definitions render testable and the bridge principles that specify the relationship between descriptive and operational definitions.

Bridge principles, like internal principles, are usually implicitly or explicitly specified by the paradigms one adopts to define a phenomenon. In the absence of well-defined paradigms, bridge principles, like internal principles, are arbitrary, that is, there are no well-established reasons for choosing one set of bridge principles over another. Such is the case in writing research. Because few well-defined paradigms exist in writing research, the bridge principles used to relate descriptive and operational definitions of writing and classroom writing competence are equally valid. Hence, at this point, it is difficult, if not impossible, to determine which set of criteria for relating descriptive and operational definitions is the best set.

THE CONTEXT PYRAMID MODEL OF WRITING

It was noted earlier that a fully specified descriptive definition of writing and writing classroom competence was one that includes *all* the relevant features or examples said to distinguish these concepts from all others. Unfortunately, it is impossible to establish any absolute, fully specified descriptive definition of these terms, given the arbitrariness by which features and examples are selected for formulating descriptive definitions in writing. However, one may approximate a fully specified descriptive definition by identifying classes (Broadbent, 1973) of features and examples from which researchers have drawn to define writing and classroom writing competence.

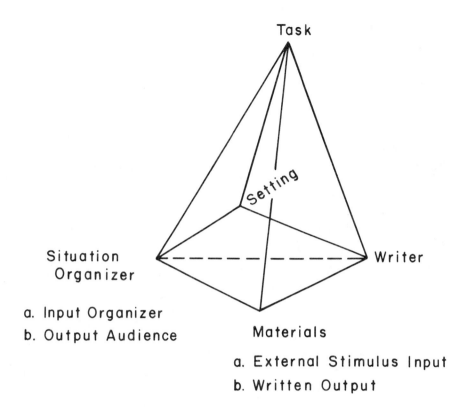

FIGURE 2.1   The Context Pyramid Model of Writing.

These classes can be represented in terms of a Context Pyramid Model of writing and classroom writing competence (Mosenthal, 1982a). This model, presented in Figure 2.1, is comprised of five contexts. Each of these contexts represents various classes of features and examples used to define descriptively a given context. For example, the writer context represents those classes of features and examples that define the uniqueness of a particular writer or groups of writers. In the writer context, one might descriptively define writers in terms of age, sex, background knowledge, IQ, reading ability, scholastic ability, grade level in school, and the processes writers use to produce written text.

There are two aspects to the materials context. One aspect includes all relevant features and examples of some physical stimulus that serves as input (i.e., materials as input). For example, such a stimulus might be the picture that the writer is describing or the selection of a text that the writer is trying to paraphrase. Significant features of a picture stimulus might include such things as what objects are in the picture, how these objects are arranged relative to one another, the features of these objects, and how these objects fill the picture space (see Mandler & Robinson,

1978). Significant features of the text that are to be re-called might include such things as the number of propositions (Kintsch, 1974), the theme (Meyer, 1977) or the episode structure (Stein & Glenn, 1979), or the type of relations between propositions (Frederiksen, 1977). A second aspect of the materials context includes all relevant features and examples of the writer's text output (i.e., materials as output). These features and examples are usually described in terms of linguistic variables.

The task context includes the features and examples characterizing some directive for writing. In addition, the task context includes specification of a criterion that defines whether a writer used the appropriate procedure and whether the writer achieved the appropriate goal specified by the directive. Directives representing the task context might be: Write a description about what you did last summer. Summarize this book. Write a short story about flowers.

There are two aspects to the situation organizer context. One aspect is the situation organizer as the person responsible for having the writer write. The second aspect is the situation organizer as the audience for whom the writer is writing. Although the situation organizer is usually both prompter for, and evaluator of, a writer's writing, this need not always be the case. Significant features of a situation organizer might include the age, sex, or authoritative power of the situation organizer.

Finally, the setting context is comprised of those classes of features and examples that are characteristic of where the writer writes and where the situation organizer prompts and evaluates the writer's writing. Hence, one might characterize different types of writing in terms of whether it was done in school or at home, in a group or individually, and the physical distance between the situation organizer and the writer.

To illustrate how the Context Pyramid Model approximates a fully specified descriptive definition of most writing situations, consider, for example, writing in an experimental situation and writing in a classroom situation. In an experimental situation the situation organizer context, both as prompter and evaluator, is usually represented by the experimenter. The materials context is often represented by a still picture or a motion picture. The writer context is represented by a person called a subject. The task context is represented by a set of precisely stated directives that the subject must follow in producing his or her written output. The setting context is represented by either a formal laboratory or an adjunct conference room in some school.

In a classroom situation, the situation organizer context is represented by the teacher and, in some cases, by the students themselves. The materials range from sights on field trips to pictures in basal readers and paragraphs in workbooks. The writer context is represented by a person called a student. The task context is represented by a range of teacher and material directives that are used to organize and conduct writing lessons.

The setting context is represented at one level by a classroom, at another level by a student working alone or in a group.

Meaning Sources and Writing Processes

Within the Context Pyramid Model, one can identify different meaning sources and writing processes. A meaning source represents a set of semantic information that could be used to produce meaningful written text output at some point in time (Mosenthal, 1982a). The four meaning sources include: meaning in prior knowledge, meaning in the external stimulus, meaning in the written text, and meaning in the social situation (Mosenthal, in press-a). Meaning in prior knowledge is the meaning source a writer brings to a writing situation; in short, this source is the set of semantic information derived from previous thought and experiences before a writing situation is encountered (Voss, Vesonder, & Spilich, 1980). Meaning in the external stimulus refers to the content of some stimulus about which a person may be writing. Meaning in the written text is the set of semantic information produced by the writer writing at some point in time. Three sources of meaning in the written text are: meaning in prior text, meaning in current text, and meaning in future text (cf. de Beaugrande, in press). Meaning in prior text refers to the semantic information a writer has produced sometime before the point of the writer's current writing. Meaning in current text refers to the semantic information that is being produced as the writer writes. Finally, meaning in future text refers to the semantic information that a writer will produce sometime after the writer's current writing. The fourth source of meaning is meaning in the social situation (Mosenthal, 1979; 1982a). This source of meaning is information derived from the interactions among the situation organizer, the setting, and the writer. In classroom lessons, this source of meaning often includes the interaction between students within the writer context (Skon, Johnson, & Johnson, 1981).

In addition to these sources of meaning, there are three types of writing processes indigenous to the Context Pyramid Model. Different writing processes refer to the possible ways a writer may recruit and integrate semantic information from the different meaning sources to produce written text. The three types of writing processes include: reproduction, reconstruction, and embellishment.

Reproduction refers to the process by which a writer produces written text by literally extracting features of meaning from a given meaning source or from a combination of meaning sources (Mosenthal, 1982).

Reconstruction refers to the process by which a writer produces written text by drawing inferences that are permissible interpretations of a meaning source (or a combination of meaning sources). For example, such inferences would include making both propositional (or logical) inferences and enabling inferences (Hildyard & Olson, 1978; Mosenthal & Na, 1980a, 1980b). Propositional inferences are those that are necessarily true or false by virtue of the logical form of the statement from which they are derived (Ackerman, 1978; Hildyard, 1979); for example, the inferences derived from three-term syllogism problems (Mosenthal, 1976–1977b) or factive statements (Mosenthal, 1978). Enabling inferences are those that must be drawn to make an event or a series of events cohesive and coherent and therefore comprehensible (Halliday & Hasan, 1976; Hildyard & Olson, 1978). In addition to these examples, one might include writing by analogy as a type of reconstruction (Schustack & Anderson, 1979; Sternberg, 1977; Verbruggel & McCarrell, 1977).

Embellishment refers to the process by which a writer produces inferences that have no identifiable antecedent in a meaning source or a combination of meaning sources. As such, embellishment tends to produce meaning source elaborations or distortions (Steffensen, Joag-Dev, & Anderson, 1979) that are derived seemingly independent of the content or structure of a given meaning source.

IDEOLOGIES OF PARTIAL SPECIFICATIONS

It is generally acknowledged (Hempel, 1966; Rudner, 1966; Weimer, 1979) that science serves two important functions: (1) it orders and simplifies the complexity of the world so that states and events can be made interpretable and (2) it enables one to predict future states and events based on known cause-and-effect relationships. Although both these ends are important, they unfortunately are often at odds with one another. Usually, as one simplifies, one reduces the number of causative variables identified; hence, one loses the power to predict accurately. And as one attempts to predict accurately by including more and more causative variables to account for a given effect, one complicates rather than simplifies.

One can restate these ends of science in terms of descriptive definitions, operational definitions, and bridge principles, which were discussed earlier. The principal way to maintain simplicity is to minimize the number of features and examples in formulating a descriptive definition of a concept. The ideal here is to specify just enough features and examples so that the partially specified descriptive definition closely approximates the fully specified descriptive definition; also, enough features and examples should be specified to insure that the concept defined by the descriptive definition has veridicality with the real-world phenomenon that the concept is said to represent.[3]

Following the dictum of good scientific procedures (Hempel, 1966; Rudner, 1966), one should have a corresponding operational definition for each set of cause-and-effect features and examples in the descriptive definition. Similarly, one should specify as many bridge principles as there are instances of descriptive features and examples being related to procedures and criteria in the operational definition. To comply with these dictums, the easiest way to achieve simplicity is by reducing the number of features and examples in the descriptive definition.

To achieve simplicity in their research, writing researchers have typically adopted the procedures of partial specification. These procedures serve to simplify the Context Pyramid Model so that a manageable number of features and examples, as well as procedures and criteria can be identified to define writing and classroom writing competence descriptively and operationally. These procedures of partial specification can be summarized as a set of directives (Mosenthal, in press-b):

1. Select one favorite context from among the five in the Context Pyramid Model; identify this context as the causative context.
2. Select a second favorite context from among the five in the Context Pyramid Model; identify this context as the effect context.
3. Establish a partially specified descriptive definition of writing and classroom writing competence by:
   a. selecting a set of features or examples representative of the causative context identified.
   b. selecting a set of features or examples representative of the effect context identified. (This completes the descriptive definition of writing and classroom writing competence.)
4. Establish operational definitions for:
   a. the set of features or examples identified in the descriptive definition as causative.
   b. the set of features or examples identified in the descriptive definition as effect.
5. State the bridge principles that relate sets of cause-and-effect features or examples in the partially specified descriptive definition to their respective procedures and criteria in the operational definition.
6. Adopt the following argument:
   a. if the partially specified descriptive definition is valid, then the operational definition is valid. (This premise comes from the bridge principles).
   b. if the operational definition is valid (as proven by analysis of statistical differences), then, the partially specified descriptive definition is valid (and the features examples of this definition are therefore facts).

What these procedures of partial specification mean is that, in formal experimental studies, researchers begin by constructing a partially specified descriptive definition of writing and, in some cases, classroom writing competence. If the study is at the level of merely discovering possible causative context features or examples, one is more concerned with identifying potentially significant features or examples that represent some causative context rather than with predicting the relationship between some set of features or examples of a causative context and those of an effect context. On the other hand, if the study is at the level of predicting the relationship between some set of features or examples of a causative context and those of an effect context, one may establish a partially specified descriptive definition of writing or classroom writing competence by presenting a model or a theory (Mosenthal, Davidson-Mosenthal, & Krieger, 1981; Mosenthal & Na, 1981).

Once one has arrived at a partially specified descriptive definition of writing and classroom writing competence (in procedures 1–3), one then establishes an operational definition of these terms. In so doing, as noted earlier, one attempts to link features and examples in the partially specified descriptive definition to observable procedures and criteria in the operational definition. Features and examples in the partially specified descriptive definition of a causative context are represented as independent variables; features and examples in the descriptive definition of an effect context are represented as dependent variables. In studies that serve primarily to order and simplify, the extent to which different causative context variables are shown to influence different effect context variables differentially represents one's level of success in identifying significant descriptive definition features and examples that are said to be representative of a fully specified descriptive definition. In studies serving primarily to test predictive validity, the extent to which causative context variables are shown significantly to influence the effect context variables according to a model's claims represents one's level of success of establishing a predictive model.

The important point is that in formal experimental situations, writing researchers never define writing, let alone classroom writing competence, in terms of either fully specified descriptive definitions or in terms of the complete Context Pyramid Model of Writing; they always define writing, and, if considered, classroom writing competence, in terms of partially specified descriptive definitions and simplified versions of the Context Pyramid Model. For example, in several studies of writing (Bereiter, Scardamalia, & Bracewell, 1979; Bracewell, 1980; Doyle, 1981; Menig-Peterson & McCabe, 1977; Mosenthal & Walmsley, 1979; Tamor, Bond, & Matz, 1980), the focus is on the task context; in these studies, writing is defined in terms of the relationship between task type and writing performance. In other studies (Bereiter, 1980; Bereiter & Scardamalia, 1982; Britton et al., 1975; Cartwright, 1969; Dupuis & Cartwright, 1979; Hunt, 1977; Kroll, 1978; Loban, 1976; O'Donnell, Griffin, & Norris, 1967; Rentel, King, Pappas, & Pettegrew, 1980; Voss et al., 1980), the focus is on the writer context; in these studies, writing is defined in terms of the relationship between various writer characteristics, such as age or background knowledge, and writing performance. Also in other studies, the focus is on the materials context; in these studies, writing is defined either in terms of the relationship between stimulus characteristics and writing performance (Golub & Frederick, 1970; Mosenthal & Walmsley, 1978, 1979) or in terms of written text characteristics (Mellon, 1969; Meyer, 1979). In still other studies (Clark & Delia, 1977; Crowhurst & Piché, 1979; Shaughnessy, 1977; Winterowd, 1975), the focus is on the situation organizer and, in some instances, the relationship between the situation organizer and the writer; in short, in these studies, writing is defined in terms of the relationship between the audience and writing performance or in terms of the interaction between the audience and the writer and this interaction's relationship to writing performance. Finally, in yet another group of studies (Britton et al., 1975; Florio, 1979; Graves, 1978; Odell & Goswami, 1980), the focus is on the setting context; in these studies, writing is defined in terms of the relationship between different setting characteristics and writing performance.

In addition to using partially specified descriptive definitions of writing and classroom writing competence, writing researchers also use partially specified operational definitions. In holistic scoring, some researchers (e.g., Cooper, 1977; Freedman, 1981) operationally define writing and writing quality in terms of what some situation organizer, as audience, arbitrarily decides what writing quality is. In primary-trait scoring, some researchers (e.g., Lloyd-Jones, 1977) operationally define writing and writing quality by arbitrarily selecting descriptive definition features and examples from the writer context, the task context, and the materials context. In this type of evaluation, a rater first considers whether these features and examples are present or absent in a writing sample; the rater then uses this consideration to make a judgment about the quality of this particular sample. In syntactic complexity analyses, some researchers (e.g. Hunt, 1977; Loban, 1976; O'Donnell, 1976) operationally define writing and quality of writing in terms of characteristics of the material context as output.

By reducing the number of contexts and, concomitantly, the number of features and examples used to formulate descriptive and operational definitions of writing and classroom writing competence, writing researchers do two things: (1) they reduce the number of potentially significant causative variables that may influence a writer's output; and (2) they restrict themselves to a particular type of writing in terms of meaning source and writing process.

For instance, by formulating a partially specified descriptive definition of writing with task as the causative context, researchers overlook the social situation as a source of meaning and the writing processes applied to this source of meaning. By formulating a partially specified descriptive definition of writing with the situation organizer as the causative context, researchers ignore prior knowledge, meaning in the stimulus, and meaning in both the written text and the writing processes applied to these sources of meaning. Similarly, by formulating a partially specified descriptive definition of writing with materials as output as the causative context, researchers overlook meaning in prior knowledge, meaning in both the stimulus and the social situation as sources of meaning, and the writing processes applied to these sources of meaning.

Although partial specification is common to all disciplines in science, most of these disciplines have paradigms that provide criteria that specify: (1) the contexts that are to be defined as causative contexts; (2) the contexts that are to be defined as effect contexts; (3) the features and examples of a causative and an effect context that are to be considered in formulating a partially specified descriptive definition of some phenomenon; (4) the procedures and criteria that are to be used in operationalizing the features and examples in a descriptive definition; and (5) the bridge principles that are viable for relating operational definitions to descriptive definitions. In short, paradigms provide criteria for conducting partial specification.

Given the absence of paradigms in writing research, an important question is, On what basis does partial specification in writing research proceed? Although there is no definitive answer to this question, it can be argued that partial specification is conducted on the basis of implicit ideology.

Partial Specification by Ideology Type

It has been argued that descriptive and operational definitions of writing and classroom writing competence represent only partially specified definitions; invariably, different descriptive and operational definitions of these terms represent different selections from among the universe of features, examples, procedures, and criteria of some fully specified definition of writing, such as the Context Pyramid Model. In short, different definitions of these terms represent partial specifications of the possible sets of features, examples, procedures, and criteria one could possibly use to define them.

An important function of paradigms is to provide established guidelines for conducting partial specification to formulate definitions of some concept. Given that there are no well-established paradigms in writing research, one is faced with the problem of identifying criteria for selecting different partially specified definitions of writing and classroom writing competence. In the following section, it is argued that criteria can be identified for conducting partial specifications in writing research by appealing to different ideologies.

Although different notions of ideology have been advanced (Bernier, 1981; Walmsley, 1981), these notions all share assumptions about goals. In turn, different assumptions about goals presuppose different contexts that are necessary for defining the achievement of these goals (Mosenthal, 1982a). In brief, an ideology is a world view of what should be the goal of a particular enterprise; each ideology defines achievement of its desired goal in terms of an optimal configuration of variables within or between contexts of the Context Pyramid Model. Because this chapter's primary consideration is classroom writing competence, the enterprise that will be specifically addressed is education.

Partial Specification from an Academic Ideology. As noted by Walmsley (1981), five types of educational ideologies can be identified: (1) academic, (2) utilitarian, (3) romantic, (4) cognitive developmental, and (5) emancipatory. In an academic ideology, the goal is to pass on from one generation to the next the knowledge, skills, and social and moral values of the culture that previous generations deemed important for succeeding generations to acquire. Researchers and practitioners who subscribe to this ideology attempt to define classroom writing competence in terms of behavioristic or Hulleanistic theories of behavior. These theories focus on the pairing of the "correct" response to a given stimulus or the generation of a response according to some authority's definition of correct (Mosenthal, in press-a). Hence, according to this ideology, writing competence is acquired by extensive practice in recognition, reproduction, and matching of "correct" responses to given stimuli or tasks.

In an academic ideology, researchers and practitioners use prescriptive grammars to define *classroom writing competence* operationally (Mosenthal, in press-c). Prescriptive grammars represent a set of conventional grammar rules that define *a priori* a set of well-formedness conditions; these conditions specify the proper conventions for spelling, punctuation, capitalization, usage, and syntactic form (Irmscher, 1976; Robins, 1967). For example, a prescriptive well-formedness condition might be the rule of when to use *who* or *whom* or when to capitalize the word *state*.

Perhaps the best illustration of how prescriptive grammars are used to define classroom writing competence operationally is on standardized writing tests (e.g., Educational Testing Service, 1975; Hackman & Johnson, 1976). In such tests, students generally are required to select a correct response from several options. The correct response is the one that most closely conforms to the well-formedness rule of some prescriptive grammar. Hence, such tests operationally define classroom writing competence as the ability to recognize the correct form of spelling, punctuation, and grammatical usage from among several options that comply or fail to comply with the specifications of some prescriptive grammar's well-formedness conditions.

The importance of prescriptive grammars in an academic ideology is that they define classroom writing competence as the ability to conform to an authority's established set of norms. In this regard, prescriptive grammars define this term in a way that establishes continuity between generations of language users in academia (Resnick & Resnick, 1977; Robins, 1967); by comparing what children write to what children should write—

as defined by some prescriptive grammar—one can assess the extent to which children have learned the conventions of academic language usage (Elley, Barham, Lamb, & Wyllie, 1976).

By defining classroom writing competence in the light of an academic ideology, researchers and practitioners limit their definitions to features, examples, procedures, and criteria derived from the materials as output context. Such definitions focus on how well students *reproduce correct linguistic form*; such definitions exclude consideration of the different meaning sources as well as how the different writing processes relate to these sources.

In terms of the tenets of good science mentioned earlier (i.e., simplification, ordering, and prediction), writing research conducted in terms of an academic ideology fails on all counts. First, given the large number of well-formedness conditions used to define classroom writing competence operationally, prescriptive grammars tend to confound rather than simplify. How many well-formedness rules of punctuation, capitalization, spelling, and syntax must students know before they are said to have classroom writing competence? Although the answer may be finite, the number, nevertheless, is extremely high.

Second, as Robins (1967) noted, different prescriptive grammars often make competing claims as to what constitutes proper well-formedness conditions. This, in part, stems from the fact that prescriptive grammars are somewhat arbitrary; there are as many "proper" prescriptive grammars as there are "proper" authorities who write prescriptive grammar texts. Each grammarian has his or her own arbitrary reason for identifying, selecting, and ordering his or her own set of well-formedness rules.

A third reason for this failure is this research does not establish an adequate descriptive definition of classroom writing competence. By failing to begin with a descriptive definition, all operational definitions of the term are completely arbitrary. In addition, there are no bridge principles for relating descriptive to operational definitions. Morever, in the absence of a descriptive definition relating some causative context to some effect context and in the absence of bridge principles, this research fails to provide any systematic means for testing predictions relating some causative context to some effect context under a set of well-defined conditions.

Partial Specification from a Utilitarian Ideology. A utilitarian ideology is similar to an academic ideology in that both stress the importance of cultural reproduction. However, the two ideologies make different claims of why cultural reproduction is important. The academic ideology stresses cultural reproduction for the purpose of inculcating conformity to societal norms; the utilitarian ideology stresses cultural reproduction for the purpose of teaching real-word survival skills. In short, in a utilitarian ideology, the goal is to pass on from one generation to the next the knowledge and skills necessary for survival in various real-life settings (Diehl, 1980; Scribner & Cole, 1981).

Several researchers and practitioners (Morris, Bransford, & Franks, 1977; Doyle, 1981) who subscribe to a utilitarian ideology attempt to define classroom writing competence in terms of what has been called levels of processing theories of behavior. In short, these theories argue that writers recruit different meaning sources and apply different writing processes to them, depending on the demands of an assigned task. Writers are said to have successfully met the demands of a task if they meet the task's criterion in some prescribed manner. What constitutes this prescribed manner is usually determined by some authority; the task typically is one that would be useful to survive in society (Bransford, Franks, Morris, & Stein, 1979), such as writing one's signature, letter writing, or filling out a job application. (In cases where the task serves no value for surviving in society but serves only some authority's end, this interpretation of levels of processing represents the academic ideology; see Craik, 1979).

Researchers and practitioners (e.g., Doyle, 1981; Odell & Goswami, 1980; Scribner & Cole, 1981) who adopt a utilitarian ideology formulate descriptive definitions of classroom writing competence in terms of the task and setting contexts of the Pyramid Context Model of Writing; in sum, classroom writing competence is defined in terms of the different procedures and criteria of the different types of tasks found in different settings.

Despite its practical appeal, writing research conducted under a utilitarian ideology is still in its infancy. Although descriptive definitions have been forthcoming, enabling one to distinguish among different types of writing tasks in different types of settings, few descriptive definitions have been proposed for defining the different linguistic outputs generated by different tasks. In addition, there have been few descriptive definitions formulated under this ideology that clearly relate the descriptive definitions of the task as causative context to the descriptive definitions of the materials as output as effect context. Moreover, there has been no systematic attempt in writing research, as there has been in reading research (Bransford et al., 1979), to relate writing processes to meaning sources according to different task demands. Finally, there has been no systematic attempt by research conducted under the utilitarian ideology to identify adequate operational definitions of the task and setting as causative contexts and materials as output as effect context; nor have adequate bridge principles been identified for relating descriptive definitions of the task, setting, and materials context to the operational definitions of these contexts.

Partial Specification from a Romantic Ideology. In a romantic ideology, the goal of education is to develop an individual's autonomy, self-worth, or self-ownership (Walmsley, 1981). This is achieved by enhancing an individual's self-understanding and an understanding of the world at large. Researchers and practitioners who subscribe to this ideology emphasize the importance of developing an extensive base of prior knowledge; consequently, endorsers of this ideology (Flower & Hayes, 1977, 1980; Voss et al., 1980) define classroom writing competence in terms of schema or top-down processing theories of behavior. Such theories argue that writers recruit and apply different writing processes as a function of how their background knowledge, or schema, is structured.

For example, in Voss et al.'s (1980) theory of writing, high-knowledge writers are said to compose differently from low-knowledge writers owing to differences in the respective problem spaces and differences in the ability to monitor the selected solution paths. Problem space refers to the quantity and quality of knowledge a person has of a particular topic, for example, one's knowledge of the rules and conventions of the game of baseball. Monitoring selected solution paths refers to the process of selecting different sets of information to solve a particular problem.

In sum, researchers and practitioners who adopt a romantic ideology formulate descriptive definitions of classroom writing competence in terms of the writer context; the salient descriptive features and examples of classroom writing competence include the quantity and quality of a writer's background knowledge about a topic and how the writer uses this background knowledge to solve problems dealing with this topic.

Writing research conducted under a romantic ideology primarily considers the meaning source of prior knowledge. In addition, this research focuses on how the writing processes of reproduction and reconstruction are applied to prior knowlege. Although this research acknowledges the importance of the task context in formulating descriptive definitions of classroom writing competence, no features or examples descriptive of the task context are operationally defined. Also, although this research does acknowledge the importance of meaning in prior text, current text, and future text by positing different problem-solving stages and strategies in the descriptive definition, it fails to consider meaning in social situation and the writing processes that relate to this meaning source.

In terms of the tenets of good science, research conducted under a romantic ideology generally meets the criteria of simplicity, ordering, and prediction. This research begins with a clearly articulated model that delineates and orders the features and examples of writing competence. In addition, the models in this research tend to describe clearly a cause-and-effect relationship that can be empirically tested.

In the work of Voss et al. (1980), the constraints under which posited cause-and-effect relationships transpire are specified clearly enough so that prediction is possible. In addition, prediction is made possible in the research of Voss et al. (1980) because they use predictive grammars that enable one operationally to relate characteristics of a writer's knowledge-domain input to characteristics of a writer's linguistic output.

Predictive grammars, such as those typically used in psycholinguistic research (e.g., Frederiksen, 1975, 1977; Kintsch, 1974; Mandler & Johnson, 1977; Stein & Glenn, 1979), first posit a set of ideal rules that describe what content should be present and how this content should be structured for a schema (knowledge domain) to be well formed (see Mosenthal, 1982b). For example in the Voss et al. 1980 study, a predictive grammar is first established to identify the well-formedness conditions of a high-knowledge schema for baseball. Writers are then given a recognition test to determine how many rules of the predictive grammar they know. On the basis of their performance, writers are operationally defined as being high-knowledge or low-knowledge writers. Next, writers are assigned a task to write about (either from prior knowledge or from prior text) a given topic (e.g., in the Voss et al. 1980 study, the particular topic was a half inning in a fictitious baseball game). The structure and content of the text generated by the writers is subsequently analyzed in terms of the well-formedness rules of the predictive grammar. The operational descriptions of text output yielded by this analysis is then matched against operational descriptions of the writers' initial inputs. (In Voss et al. 1980, this entailed comparing an operational description of what a writer wrote about in describing an inning of a fictitious baseball game to an operational description of what the writer knew about baseball.) By comparing the description of what a writer writes to the description of what a writer knows about a particular topic, one is able to determine which aspects of the prior knowledge meaning source the writer draws on and whether the writer reproduced or reconstructed these different aspects to create a written text.

The importance of using predictive grammars in writing research is that they enable one to define operationally some causative context as input, some effect context as output, and to test the validity of some cause-and-effect relationships hypothesized to exist between the causative and effect contexts. This use of predictive grammars thus enables one operationally to define features and examples assumed to represent both viable input and output in the definition of classroom writing competence. By using predictive grammars one can then test the extent to which some descriptive definition of classroom writing competence relates to some operational definition of this concept. If one has correctly identified the conditions under which a given operational definition will be met in a way that verifies a given descriptive definition, one is said to have achieved predictive validity.

In sum, by using predictive grammars, writing researchers operating under a romantic ideology have perhaps come closer to meeting the criteria of simplicity, order, and prediction than writing researchers operating under any other ideology. In part, this stems from the fact that research conducted under a romantic ideology best lends itself to using predictive grammars (Mosenthal, 1982b); the features and examples of schema as input and text as output can be descriptively and operationally defined in terms of linguistic characteristics (Hutchinson, 1974).

In addition, unlike writing research operating under other ideologies, research operating under a romantic ideology has a ready-made set of bridge principles; these bridge principles essentially have been developed in reading research. Frederiksen (1977) described these bridge principles when he noted:

> One strategy for investigating the nature of semantic knowledge is to investigate the semantic structure of texts under the assumption that a text's structure is a reflection of the knowledge structure of the speaker or writer who produced the text. The argument is that if a semantic distinction or structure is manifest in language, it must also represent an aspect of human memory structure.

In brief, these bridge principles are comprised of these assumptions:

1. The structure and content of a writer's schema are reflected in the structure and content of what a writer writes.
2. Linguistic grammars can be constructed that represent valid descriptive and operational definitions of a writer's schema and a writer's written output.
3. The processes writers use to relate their cognitive input to their written output can be psycholinguistically validated by matching descriptions of input to output.

By adopting these assumptions, writing researchers operating under a romantic ideology have eliminated one of the major problems underlying the research conducted under other ideologies—namely, the problem of selecting arbitrary bridge principles.

Partial Specification from a Cognitive Development Ideology. In a cognitive-developmental ideology, the goal is to nourish "the child's natural interaction with a developing society or environment" (Kohlberg & Mayer, 1972, p. 454) to promote intellectual growth throughout the development of the child. Researchers and practitioners who subscribe to this ideology generally define classroom writing competence in terms of Piagetian, neo-Piagetian (Case, 1978), or metacognitive (Brown, 1979, 1980) theories of behavior; these theories are based on the notion that children at different stages or levels of development qualitatively change in their ability to relate different writing processes to different meaning sources. In addition, these theories argue that children's ability at different stages or levels of development interact differently with different characteristics of task type or social condition. For example, at one stage or level of development, a child may be able to perform some tasks but not others or the child may be able to behave appropriately in some social situations but not in others.

Hence, when viewed from the perspective of a cognitive developmental ideology, classroom writing competence is said to be acquired by learning to assimilate and accommodate meaning in the various meaning sources with social condition and task demands. Assimilation and accommodation take place by learning how to apply the proper writing strategy to the proper information within or between meaning sources so that characteristics of the written text reflect the criteria for writing defined by some social condition or task.

Writing research conducted under a cognitive developmental ideology has been of two types: syntactic maturity studies and process studies. Syntactic maturity studies have focused primarily on the relationship between writer characteristics as input and linguistic characteristics as output (Hunt, 1977; Loban, 1976; O'Donnell et al., 1967). More specifically, these studies tend to define operationally the context in terms of chronological age and to define operationally the materials as output context in terms of some descriptive grammar (Mosenthal, 1982b).

Descriptive grammars, like prescriptive and predictive grammars, represent a set of rules that define a set of well-formedness conditions. However, what distinguishes descriptive grammars from prescriptive and predictive grammars is the manner in which the former grammar's well-formedness conditions are determined. In descriptive grammars, one first views a large sample of linguistic corpora; on the basis of this observation, one then determines what rules distinguish well-formed versus poorly formed linguistic output (Mosenthal, 1982b).

The descriptive grammar most commonly used in syntactic maturity studies is the one based on T-unit analysis. Hunt (1977, pp. 92–93) defines the T-unit as "a single main clause (or independent clause . . .) plus whatever other subordinate clauses or nonclauses are attached to, or embedded within, that one main clause. Put more briefly, a T-unit is a single main clause plus whatever else goes with it." Hunt also defines a clause as a subject (or coordinated subjects) with a finite verb (or coordinated finite verbs).

In an attempt to validate the concept of the T-unit as a descriptive definition of written output, Hunt begins with the assumption that, as school children mature, they tend to write longer T-units—length is measured as the mean number of words per T-unit. Hunt's second assumption is that, as school children mature, they tend to consolidate more sentence constituents into T-units, thereby increasing the number of dependent clauses per T-unit. Hence, Hunt's descriptive definition of classroom writing competence is comprised of two salient features. The principal feature of the writer as causative context is writer maturity; the principal feature of the materials as output as effect context is syntactic complexity. He operationally defines writer maturity in terms of the writer's chronological age; he operationally defines syntactic complexity in terms of the mean number of words and dependent clauses per T-unit in a given writing sample.

To relate his descriptive and operational definitions of classroom writing competence, Hunt (1977) posits this bridge principle:

> The T-unit length hypothesis is easy enough to prove true or false. All one has to do is get a representative sample from a school population of one age and compute the scores of the two samples. If the score for the older

group is larger, then that evidence tends to confirm the claim; if not, then the evidence tends to disconfirm the claim.

Using both free writing (Hunt, 1977) and rewriting tasks (Hunt, 1977), Hunt found evidence that appears to validate his claims. Following Hunt, a variety of other researchers (Dixon, 1972; O'Donnell et al., 1967; Loban, 1976; Potter, 1967) have used the T-unit as a basis for evaluating written output. The fact that Hunt's T-unit hypothesis has been confirmed has led some researchers to believe that more complex T-units represent better writing (i.e., represent better well-formedness) than less complex T-units. This assumption underlies the argument for sentence combining (Mellon, 1969; Strong, 1973).

On the surface, the research underlying syntactic maturity studies appears to meet two of the criteria for good science. First, because this research posits a very simple set of descriptive and operational definitions of classroom writing competence, it appears to meet the criterion of simplicity. Second, because it appears to be able to predict how syntactic complexity will vary as a function of age it appears to meet the criterion of prediction. In fact, however, this research achieves only simplicity; unfortunately, in its quest for simplicity, it renders the definition of classroom writing competence meaningless.

Consider first the criticism that this research oversimplifies the definition of classroom writing competence. It descriptively defines the writer context in terms of the feature writer maturity. As such, it fails to consider any of the writing processes writers apply to various meaning sources to produce a written output. In addition, this research descriptively defines the materials as output context in terms of the syntactic features of T-unit complexity. Hence, this research fails to consider any of the meaning sources to which writers apply writing processes to produce written text. By reducing the definition of classroom writing competence to the features of writer maturity and syntactic complexity, syntactic maturity studies have reduced the concept to the point of not studying competence but only performance.

Linguistic competence refers to what writers know in order to produce text; performance refers to what writers actually do in producing text. As noted in the discussion of predictive grammars, one of the most productive ways of studying classroom writing competence is by comparing the features and examples characterizing a writer's meaning source input to those characterizing a writer's meaning source output. Writing processes can be defined as those processes that transpired in creating similarities and differences between the meaning source input and output (Clark & Haviland, 1974; Frederiksen, 1977).

Unfortunately, because syntactic maturity studies rely on a descriptive grammar that is only capable of describing the syntactic form of some writer's meaning source output, such studies describe only writer performance. They provide little insight as to what form competence might assume during the course of writing; also, they provide little insight into the relationship between competence and performance and the nature of the processes relating competence and performance (Mosenthal, 1982b).

Consider next the criticism that syntactic maturity research fails to predict adequately. This criticism is related to the problem considered in the preceding discussion. For a theory of classroom writing competence, or of any psycholinguistic competence (Clark & Haviland, 1974; Hutchinson, 1974), to have predictive validity, it must be able to predict what features and examples of one or more meaning sources will be recruited under various conditions of written text production. In addition, this theory must be able to predict how writing processes will be applied to selected meaning source features and examples under various conditions of written text production. In short, for a theory of classroom writing competence to have validity, it must be able to predict how competence will be related to performance under a variety of conditions and how differences in written text output will vary as the relationship between competence and performance varies (Clark & Haviland, 1974; Frederiksen, 1977; Hutchinson, 1974; Mosenthal, 1982b).

Because syntactic maturity studies use only a grammar capable of describing performance, they are incapable of testing hypotheses relating writing competence to writing performance. Of course such studies are capable of testing the strength of the relationship between variables assumed to be related to writing competence and written performance. However, in using descriptive grammars, these studies can test these relationships only as correlations. Because findings of syntactic maturity studies are only correlational, the findings that writer maturity is related to syntactic maturity provides no more insight into the nature of classroom writing competence than the demonstration that height, weight, number of teeth, or shoe size are related to syntactic complexity (cf. Mehan, 1979).

In closing, it should be noted that some studies (e.g., Kroll, 1978; Rubin & Piché, 1979) have gone beyond more traditional syntactic maturity studies by further descriptively and operationally defining writer maturity in terms of Piagetian notions. Unfortunately, because these studies have also used descriptive grammars, they, too, have failed to provide any predictive insight as to how developmental differences in children's classroom writing competence is causally related to differences in classroom writing performance.

In contrast to syntactic maturity studies, another group of studies operating under a cognitive developmental ideology have been process studies (Bereiter, 1980; Bereiter & Scardamalia, 1978, 1982; Britton et al., 1975). The focus of these studies has been to identify how children acquire different writing processes in relationship to different writing tasks. In short, these studies have defined classroom writing competence largely in terms of the writing processes children acquire and are capable of using in the light of different tasks. Unfortunately, these studies have provided few insights into what constitutes the nature of meaning source inputs and outputs. Hence, these studies have provided few criteria for formulating internal principles describing the relationship between meaning sources and writing processes; in addition they have provided few well-defined bridge principles for testing the validity of their writing processes' features and examples.

Partial Specification from an Emancipatory Ideology. In an emancipatory ideology, the goal is to change the educational, social, and political structure so that the oppressed may forge a new, more egalitarian relationship with their oppressors (Freire, 1970; Walmsley, 1981). Proponents (e.g., Bowles & Gintis, 1976; Freire, 1970; Rist, 1970) of the emancipatory ideology claim that a principal function of schools in a capitalist society is to maintain the class distinctions of that society. These proponents thus argue the need to change the educational system so that class distinctions are eliminated and a more egalitarian society is established.

Researchers and practitioners who adopt an emancipatory ideology generally maintain that class distinctions develop as a function of teacher-student interactions. Their argument proceeds as follows. Teachers have lower expectations for lower socioeconomic status (SES) and lower IQ students and higher expectations for higher SES and higher IQ students. Because teachers teach to these expectations, they differentially interact with the lower SES/IQ students and the higher SES/IQ students, respectively. Based on this differential interaction, lower SES/IQ students and higher SES/IQ students develop different expectations about their respective abilities to succeed in school. Because students perform according to their differential expectations, lower SES/IQ students perform in a way that insures school failure; higher SES/IQ students perform in a way that insures school success.

Although there are different variations on the theme of the differential expectations hypothesis (e.g., Cherry, 1978; Doyle, 1979; Mosenthal, in press-a; Mosenthal & Na, 1980a; Rist, 1970), the point according to endorsers of an emancipatory ideology is that teachers rather than students are responsible for student failure and success; this failure and success, in turn, determines students' failure and success in later life. Those students who are programmed to fail in school are assumed to fill lower-class roles and positions; those students who are programmed to succeed in school are assumed to fill higher-class roles and positions.

Up to the present, few writing researchers have defined classroom writing competence under the assumptions of this ideology. However, because several reading researchers are now beginning to define classroom reading competence in terms of this ideology (see Mosenthal, in 1982a, for further discussion), there is the possibility that writing researchers, too, may begin to endorse this ideology.

Under this ideology, classroom writing competence is defined primarily in terms of the interactions between the situation organizer context and the writer context. The salient descriptive feature of the situation organizer context is the teacher's expectation for a student's performance; this may be operationally defined in terms of some sociolinguistic interaction pattern between the teacher and student, such as the type of prompts a teacher gives a student when the student makes an error during a writing lesson (Cherry, 1978; Mehan, 1979). The salient descriptive feature of the writer context might be the student's racial background, reading-group level, achievement level, SES, or IQ. Reading-group level might be operationally defined in terms of any number of informal classroom practices, such as the teacher's assignment of a student to a low-, middle-, or high-reading group. Achievement level, SES, and IQ might be operationally defined in terms of any number of standardized tests and questionnaires.

The bridge principles typically involved in research operating under an emancipatory ideology comprise the following assumptions. Certain teacher behaviors promote poor writing strategies in students; others promote good writing strategies. Poor writing strategies produce poor writing; good writing strategies produce good writing. In teachng lower SES/IQ students, teachers illustrate those behaviors that promote poor writing strategies; in teaching higher SES/IQ students, teachers illustrate those behaviors that promote good writing strategies. Hence, because lower SES/IQ students are taught (and subsequently use) poor writing strategies, they write more poorly, thus fulfilling the teacher's expectation that they are the poor writers and poorer students; because higher SES/IQ students are taught (and subsequently use) good writing stategies, they write better, thus fulfilling the teacher's expectation that they are the better writers and better students.

In terms of partial specification of the Context Pyramid Model of Writing, writing research conducted under an emancipatory ideology would focus primarily on the meaning source, meaning in social situation, and the writing processes that apply to this meaning source. What typically would not be considered would be meaning in prior knowledge and meaning in text as well as writing processes that can be applied to these two meaning sources. Because this research may sometimes focus on how teachers differentially structure different tasks for students of different SES, IQ, or achievement levels (Cherry, 1978), one could argue that task is an optional context that may or may not be considered in research operating under emancipatory ideology. The context that is most noticeably absent in this research is the materials context (Mosenthal, 1982a).

The principal shortcoming of research operating under this ideology is the inadequacy of the bridge principles typically assumed. Because this research (e.g., Cherry, 1978; Rist, 1970) fails to consider meaning in prior knowledge, meaning in text, and the writing processes that apply to these two meaning sources, this research never adequately defines either what is a good writing strategy or what a writing strategy is. In addition, the bridge principles typically involved in this research assume that the teacher is an authority of society, responsible for perpetuating class distinction. Yet, no attempt is ever made to compare what a teacher thinks is a good writing strategy and good piece of writing to the strategies students actually adopt and the pieces of writing students actually produce. In short, this research begins with the bridge principle assumption that differences are deficits and hence that there is no need to empirically test this assumption further.

COPING WITH PARTIAL SPECIFICATION

The preceding discussion suggests that to understand a concept like classroom writing competence, one must be able to answer three questions: What is it? What are the possible ways to define it? What ought to be the definition of it?

In an attempt to answer these questions, a Pyramid Context Model of Writing was first proposed. The purpose of this model was to illustrate the possible contexts from which one could construct possible, partially specified descriptive and operational definitions of writing and classroom writing competence. In discussing partial specifications from an ideological perspective, it was noted that to answer the question, What is classroom writing competence?, writing researchers have chosen one or two different contexts from among the set of possible contexts. This selection process, it was argued, always entails a different ideological assumption of what the goal of education should be (in other words, the selection of favorite contexts is always constrained by the assumptions of an identifiable ideology). Hence, the question, What is classroom writing competence?, is really the question, What ought to be the definition of classroom writing competence?, with the "ought to be" only implicitly stated.

What this ultimately means is that decisions of how to define writing and classroom writing competence are not purely objective decisions; they are also value decisions. This being the case, the question of partial specification is only half the question of which contexts to include and which to exclude (Mishler, 1979) in formulating partially specified descriptive and operational definitions of these two terms; the other half of the question is, Which ideology does one choose as the best framework for reducing the fully specified descriptive and operational definitions of writing and classroom writing competence to partially specified definitions?

Hence, in the absence of paradigms in writing research, researchers face two problems. They first face the crucial problem of deciding which ideology provides the best framework for defining writing and classroom writing competence. Once writing researchers have selected an ideology, they then must contend with the problem of determining which features and examples, procedures and criteria, and internal and bridge principles provide the best representation for understanding these terms relative to the assumptions of one's selected ideology.

There appear to be two ways these problems of partial specification can be resolved in writing research. First, one can resolve these problems by the acknowledgement of an authority in writing research (Weimer, 1979). What this means is that as different researchers posit different descriptive or operational definitions of writing and classroom writing competence, a few of these researchers will come to be regarded as the authorities (or experts) of how these terms should be defined. Other disciple researchers will begin to abide by the assumptions of the internal and bridge principles of these authorities' definitions. In abiding by these assumptions, disciple researchers will not attempt to challenge these authorities' assumptions; rather they will spend their efforts confirming these assumptions and demonstrating how the different authorities' definitions can be extended to new conditions. In time, enough disciple researchers will have abided by different authorities' assumptions so that distinct paradigms of writing research will have emerged. These paradigms may become disassociated with the authority and may become known only by the name of an authority's original theory, for example, behaviorism or cognitivism, or paradigms may become synonymous with the name of the authority, for example, Hulleanism or Piagetianism. This is the way most paradigms are formed (Kuhn, 1970; Weimer, 1979).

Under this type of resolution of the partial specification problem, disciple researchers adopt two types of assumptions when they buy into an authority's paradigm. First, they adopt an authority's assumptions about which descriptive and operational definitions (and their concomitant bridge principles) best define writing and classroom writing competence. Second, they adopt an authority's assumptions about which ideology provides the best framework for partially specifying the fully specified, descriptive, and operational definitions of these terms. Under this type of partial specification resolution, knowledge of a field is said to advance as more and more disciple researchers buy into an authority's paradigm and ideological assumptions.

A second way one can resolve the partial specification problem in writing research is to begin by positing a descriptive and an operational definition of writing and classroom writing competence that considers all the meaning sources and writing processes of the fully specified definition (i.e., the Pyramid Context Model of Writing). One can then study how different authorities, such as classroom teachers, reduce the fully specified definition and teach according to a partially specified definition of classroom writing competence that is representative of a given ideology. This approach to resolving the reduction problem has been adopted by Mosenthal (1981).

In addressing the question, How do children acquire classroom writing competence during lessons?, Mosenthal (1981) first attempted to redefine meaning sources and writing processes in terms of classroom literacy events. As the work of Doyle (1979, 1981) suggests, a literacy event during a classroom lesson consists of teacher tasks. A task is comprised of a goal, a procedure, and a criterion. For example, a literacy-event goal might be to increase children's ability to paraphrase newspaper articles. A literacy event set of procedures might involve students actually reading a given newspaper article, outlining the major points of the article, and then writing a paraphrase about the article. If students write the paraphrase in a way in which all the major points are included and all the minor points are excluded, the students may be said to have met the task's criterion.

As the work of Mehan (1979) suggests, a literacy event consists of a three-part sequence. First, there is the initiation phase. During this phase, the teacher begins by identifying one or more meaning sources to be used in the comprehension and production of text. Next, the teacher presents students with one or more tasks to be applied to these meaning sources; the tasks are usually presented in the form of directives and questions (e.g., the teacher saying, "Read [*directive*] this newspaper article [*meaning source*], make an outline of the major points of the article [*directive*], and write a paraphrase [*directive*] of this article from your outline [*meaning source*]"). The second part of the literacy event involves the student acting on some meaning source in response to a teacher's directive or question. In this phase, students generally apply one or more writing processes to one or more meaning sources to produce some type of verbal or written response. The third part of the literacy event involves the teacher's evaluation of how successfully students have met a task's criterion in responding to the teacher's directive or question. If a student correctly meets the task's criterion, the teacher may accept or praise the student's response (for example, by calling on another student for the correct response, or the teacher may prompt the student, providing the student with additional information that the student may use to revise his or her response).

During any literacy event, teachers may draw from a variety of meaning sources to initiate tasks. Similarly, students may draw from a variety of meaning sources to respond to a teacher's initiation. As noted previously, these sources of meaning include: (1) meaning in prior knowledge; (2) meaning in prior text, current text, or future text; and (3) meaning in social situation. Both the teacher as the situation organizer and students as writers have prior knowledge, which they bring to a given literacy event. Meaning in text may refer to: (1) the meaning in the guide the teacher uses for conducting a lesson, (2) the meaning in teacher's initiated verbal statements that serve to explain, or (3) the meaning in students' texts, for example, basal readers or workbooks. Meaning in social situation is the source of the meaning that teachers and students encounter in relating with one another in a particular setting, such as in a reading group.

Also, as suggested earlier, teachers and students may use a variety of processes for producing text; these processes include reproduction, reconstruction, and embellishment. In initiating lessons, teachers may reproduce basal-reader or writing-lesson guides by using the same tasks, task criteria, and task sequences as presented in the guides. Teachers may reconstruct these guides by using different but related tasks, task criteria, and task sequences as stated in the guides. Finally, teachers may embellish lesson guides by using different and unrelated tasks, task criteria, and task sequences.

Students may respond either verbally or in writing to a teacher's directives or questions by reproducing meaning (or abstracting out literal features of meaning) in prior knowledge and in different text meaning sources. Students may also respond by reconstructing the meaning in prior knowledge or in different text meaning sources by drawing inferences within the general constraints (i.e., organization and content) of one or more of these meaning sources. For example, given the compound sentence, "John walked into the room; the chandelier was beautiful," a student, in producing a written recall of this sentence, might reconstruct it by writing, "John was in the room with the chandelier, he saw the chandelier, and he thought the chandelier was beautiful." Students may respond by embellishing prior knowledge and text meaning sources, thereby drawing inferences that go beyond the general constraints of one or more of these meaning sources. For example, a student in producing a written recall of the above sentence, might embellish it by writing, "John saw the chandelier in cell 34 of Attica Prison."

Finally, students may reproduce meaning in social situations by adopting the identical task goals as the teacher and by attempting to arrive at the teacher's task criteria. Students may reconstruct meaning in social situations by adopting related but different task goals from those of the teacher and by attempting to arrive at task criteria that are related but different from those of the teacher. Students may embellish meaning in social situation by adopting different and unrelated goals from those of the teacher and by attempting to arrive at task criteria that are unrelated and different from the teacher's task criteria.

As this discussion suggests, the writing processes discussed in the first part of this chapter are assumed to represent a smaller subset of the larger set of meaning processes that students may apply to different classroom meaning sources in the different modes of responding (e.g., speaking versus writing).

TOWARD AN IDEOLOGICALLY UNBIASED MODEL OF CLASSROOM WRITING COMPETENCE

The preceding discussion suggests that there are a variety of ways students may produce written text. This presents the teacher with the problem of determining what is the most appropriate way a text should be produced;

in addition, this presents the teacher with the problem of knowing how to optimally organize task structures through initiations and evaluations so that students learn to respond and produce text appropriately, that is, so that students learn to meet the teacher's task criteria in a manner that the teacher desires.

The preceding discussion also suggests that there are a variety of ways that teachers may organize literacy events. This presents students with the problem of determing what the teacher thinks is the most appropriate way a text should be produced, and, concomitantly, this present students with the problem of knowing how to respond optimally so that the teacher's task goals and criteria are met.

To illustrate these problems, imagine a literacy event that involves the picture in Figure 2.2. Consider first the problem of writing about this picture from the student's perspective. Imagine that a teacher has given his or her students the directive to write a description about this picture from the point of view of the man. There are many ways students might respond to this task of writing about the current text of the picture: one student might respond by reproducing, "In this picture there is a man, a mouse, and a ladder"; another student might respond by reconstructing, "The mouse crawled out of his hole and onto the table; the man saw the mouse and was frightened"; a third student might respond by embellishing, "The

FIGURE 2.2 Picture Stimulus. (From Mosenthal & Na, 1981, p. 113. Copyright 1981 by the American Psychological Association. Reprinted/Adapted by permission.)

wife of the man in the picture wants a table for the living room; the man went into the the the basement to finish the table"; finally, a fourth student might respond by reconstructing in the light of prior knowledge, "This man has the same problem we have at home—mice in the basement." (See Mosenthal & Na, 1981, for further examples of writing about the current text of a picture.)

Now imagine a teacher giving these same students the second directive of writing a description from the perspective of the mouse. Students must again choose from among several options for producing a text. For example, they must decide whether they are to reproduce, reconstruct, or embellish the picture's current text further or whether they are to reproduce, reconstruct, or embellish the meaning in their first description (i.e., meaning in prior text). Also, they must decide how much meaning in prior knowledge to include in writing this description and whether they should reproduce, reconstruct, or embellish this meaning source.

In addition, students might be told that there will be a third assignment to describe this picture from yet a third perspective. In such an instance students might consider the problem of planning so that the meaning they are currently producing is somehow going to be in agreement with the meaning in their future text. Or students may consider the problem of revision so that the meaning that they produced (i.e., prior text) is somehow in agreement with what they are currently writing. (See Mosenthal et al., 1981, for further examples of rewriting from a second character's perspective.)

Consider next the problem of writing about the picture in Figure 2.2 from the teacher's perspective. The teacher must determine what will constitute an appropriate written response to the picture: Should the teacher ask students to write a description or a story about the picture? If the teacher asks students to write a description, the teacher must determine whether the uses of prior knowledge and reconstruction and embellishment of current text are appropriate meaning sources and what writing processes are to be included in the description. Furthermore, the teacher must determine what is the optimal form for organizing the meaning selected by students for describing this picture. (For further discussion of how one might define the organization of descriptive responses, see Mosenthal & Na, 1981).

If the teacher asks students to write a story about the picture, he or she must determine whether reproduction of current text is appropriately balanced against the reconstruction and embellishment of current text and against the reproduction, reconstruction, and embellishment of prior knowledge. Furthermore, the teacher must determine what is the optimal form for organizing the meaning selected by students into some type of narrative structure (Grueneich & Trabasso, 1979). (For further discussion of how one might define the organization of narrative responses, see Mosenthal et al., 1981.)

In sum, given that there are a variety of ways students may produce text and given that there are a variety of ways teachers may teach students to produce text in classroom lessons, an important question is: Do differences in the ways teachers teach writing (or written text production) influence the way students use meaning sources and meaning processes in classroom lessons?

To answer this question specifically and the larger question of how children acquire classroom writing competence in general, the author and his coworkers (Mosenthal, 1981; Mosenthal et al., 1981; Mosenthal & Na, 1981) have specified a descriptive definition of classroom writing competence based both on the notions of ideologies (Bernier, 1981; Walmsley, 1981) and classroom competence (Cherry, 1978; Mehan, 1979; Mosenthal & Na, 1980a, 1980b). Bernier (1981) has noted that how teachers conduct lessons reflects different ideologies or goals of education. These different ideologies reflect different interpretations of what constitutes an appropriate selection of a meaning source and writing process (Mosenthal, in press-a). The notion of classroom competence further suggests that because teachers have different notions of what constitutes appropriate use of meaning sources and writing processes, students learn to produce written text differently according to these notions of appropriateness.

For example, teachers who conduct literacy lessons that reflect a strong academic ideology stress cultural reproduction and conformity to authority (Walmsley, 1981). In stressing cultural reproduction, teachers emphasize conformity to their goals; moreover, they reproduce the basal-reader or writing-lesson guide and initiate tasks using directives and questions that focus primarily on current text. In addition, such teachers favorably evaluate students' reproduction of current text over other types of writing processes and meaning sources that students may select in producing written text (Mosenthal, 1981).

On the other hand, teachers who conduct literacy lessons that reflect a strong cognitive-developmental ideology stress the sharing of authority to nourish a child's interactive development with society (Walmsley, 1981). In stressing this interaction, cognitive developmental teachers emphasize the need to cooperate and to relate their goals to students' goals. Moreover, such teachers reconstruct as well as reproduce the basal-reader lesson guide. In addition, these teachers initiate tasks by using directives and questions that focus on prior knowledge, prior text, and future text as well as on current text. Moreover, such teachers favorably evaluate reconstruction and embellishment of prior knowledge and prior text as well as reproduction of current text (Mosenthal, 1982a).

Given these two ways that teachers might organize classroom literacy lessons, Mosenthal (1981) has made several predictions. If the manner in which teachers organize the social situation of classroom literacy events influences students' conceptions of what constitutes appropriate production of text, then, one should note the following differences. On the one hand, students in an academic teacher's class should produce more written text responses from a current text stimulus than from any other meaning source. In addition, these students should engage in the writing process of reproduction more often than they engage in reconstruction or embellishment. Also, because these students tend to conform rather than cooperate and because they pursue what the teacher defines as a goal rather than defining their own goal, they should be less likely to develop narratives with well-defined goal structures than students in a cognitive developmental teacher's class (Heider, 1958; Mosenthal et al., 1981). On the other hand, students in a cognitive developmental teacher's class should produce an equal number of text responses from prior knowledge and from prior text as well as from some current text stimulus. In addition, these students should be as likely to reconstruct and embellish some meaning source as they should be to reproduce some meaning source. Also, because these students tend to cooperate rather than conform and because they tend to accommodate the teacher's goal to their own goals, they should be more likely to develop stories with well-defined goal structures than students in an academic teacher's class.

These hypotheses were tested in Mosenthal's 1981 study. Based on this study, a brief account of how the author operationalized his descriptive definition of classroom writing competence is presented next.

Method

Identifying Teachers by Ideology Type. To identify two teachers whose ideologies were distinct enough so that possible differences could be demonstrated in student performance, the following procedure was used to select teachers as subjects. First, six fourth-grade teachers were observed and their reading lessons were taped. (Reading lessons were used because it was primarily during these lessons that students at this school engaged in writing activities.) The teachers taught the identical basal-reader lessons to three classroom reading groups. After three series of lesson observations for each teacher were made, the teachers' lessons were analyzed according to: (1) how frequently teachers reproduced, reconstructed, or embellished the basal-reader guide; (2) how frequently teachers asked questions or gave directions that required students to reproduce, reconstruct, or embellish a meaning source; and (3) how frequently teachers accepted, rejected, or prompted students' plausibly correct responses that were drawn from sources other than just from current text.

Teachers were said to reproduce the basal-reader guide if (1) they initiated a reading event using the identical task directive or question that was in the guide, and (2) they accepted only the guide's answer as the appropriate response. Teachers were said to reconstruct the basal-reader guide if (1) they initiated a reading event using task directives and questions not in the guide but that were related to the same task goal as was in the guide, and (2) they accepted as appropriate responses only answers that were similar in meaning source and comprehension process as those required to complete the task goal in the guide. In reconstructing the guide, the teachers typically gave tasks that supplemented and extended those tasks in the guide (e.g., proving additional words that illustrated how to divide CVCCVC[5] words, such as butter, into syllables). Teachers were said to embellish the teacher guide if they initiated a reading event that used task directives and questions that did not appear in the guide and that were unrelated to any identifiable task goal in the guide.

Teacher questions and directives were classified as reproductive if they literally or synonymously restated those in the teacher guide, they were classified as reconstructive if they reflected the same task goal as those questions and directives in the guide, and they were classified as embellished if they reflected novel task goals bearing no relation to those task goals in the guide. (This applied only to academic tasks and not to behavior tasks, which served to regulate students' bid-structure and general lesson-participation behaviors, Mehan, 1979).

Student responses were classified as plausibly correct if they were semantically acceptable, reproductive or reconstructive responses drawn from prior knowledge, prior text, or future text. To determine if certain student responses were derived from prior knowledge, students were interviewed after each day's lessons were completed. In individual sessions, an experimenter replayed segments of the lesson in which a student had given a response potentially drawn from prior knowledge. In each session, students were asked what had made them think of a particular answer. If students answered this question by relating their response to some prior experience or thought, the response was classified as having been drawn from prior knowledge. Responses that appeared to be wild guesses and that appeared not to be related to prior knowledge, prior text, or future text were not considered in the analysis.

The analysis for the six teachers' three lessons were computed by one scorer. On the basis of these analyses, one teacher was selected as most closely reflecting an academic ideology; of the six teachers, this teacher was the most likely to (1) reproduce the basal-reader guide, (2) ask reproductive questions and give reproductive directives, and (3) reject plausibly correct responses that were drawn from sources other than from current text.

In contrast, another teacher was selected as most closely reflecting a cognitive developmental ideology; of the six teachers, this teacher was most likely to (1) reconstruct the basal-reader guide, (2) ask reconstructive questions and give reconstructive directives, and (3) accept or prompt plausibly correct responses that were drawn from sources other than from current text.

To insure that these differences were reliable, seven more lesson sets were observed and taped over the course of the year. Again, in these lessons, the two teachers taught the same basal-reader lessons to three class-room reading groups. The frequency counts of distinguishing teacher characteristics were then refigured by adding the data from the lessons to the three lessons originally observed.

As a check for reliability, two raters independently classified the two teachers' lesson directives and questions as being reproductive, reconstructive, or embellished. There was 91 percent agreement between the raters. Most of the disagreement was over whether an embellished directive or question was academic or behavioral. In the case of the 9 percent disagreement, the raters discussed their differences until a consensus was reached.

The two raters then independently analyzed the two teachers' lessons into literacy events. There was 94 percent agreement as to what units of the lessons corresponded to literacy events. The raters usually disagreed as to what a literacy event was when it was unclear from the teacher's evaluation whether, in fact, an appropriate response had been given to a given task question. Again, in the case of the 6 percent disagreement, the raters discussed their differences until a consensus was reached.

Finally, the two raters independently scored the number of times teachers accepted, rejected, or prompted students' plausibly correct responses that were drawn from sources other than just from current text. Both raters listened to tape recordings of the student interviews as well as heard tape recordings of the lessons. In addition, both raters used the basal-reader guides in making their scoring decisions. There was 86 percent agreement between the raters in their scoring. Most of the disagreement came in the raters' attempts to determine whether an incorrect response was a creative guess that had no known meaning source or else was a response drawn from prior knowledge. In short, although the student interviews proved helpful, the interviews were generally not extensive enough to remove the ambiguity about 8 percent of the responses. Because there was no further way in which to remove the ambiguity from these responses, they were not included in the data analysis. For the remaining 6 percent of the disagreements, raters discussed these disagreements until a consensus for scoring was reached.

The resulting frequency counts of the ten observation sets for the two teachers revealed even stronger patterns of differences than had the frequency counts for the three observations (see Mosenthal, 1981, for the lesson profiles of the two teachers).

Subjects.   Sixty fourth graders from six different reading groups from the same school in upstate New York participated in the experiment.

Procedures and Materials.   After the tenth observation, the two teachers were asked to conduct the same set of writing lessons for each of their three reading groups. During the first lesson, the teachers administered a recognition test that assessed students' prior knowledge of baseball. This test was constructed following the principles and procedures used by Voss et al. (1980), in the construction of their baseball prior knowledge test.

During the second lesson, which occurred a day later, the teachers presented each student in the different reading groups with a series of thirteen pictures. The following sequence of states and actions in a baseball game were represented in this series of pictures:

1. Scoreboard showing that it was the bottom of the 5th inning: Visitors winning over Home, 3 to 0.
2. Two batters in a dugout.
3. A batter steps up to the plate.
4. The batter waits for a pitch.
5. The pitcher winds up.
6. The batter swings for strike 1.
7. The batter bunts foul for strike 2.
8. The batter hits the ball and begins to run for first base.
9. The shortstop drops the pop fly.
10. The shortstop overthrows the ball to the second baseman as the runner advances to second base.
11. The ball, thrown to the third baseman, hits the third baseman's foot and bounces off as the runner advances to third.
12. The runner slides across home plate as the catcher catches the ball.
13. The scoreboard shows 2 runs were scored by the home team in the bottom of the 5th inning; final score after 6 innings is Visitors 3, Home, 2.

The teachers then instructed the students to write a story about the picture sequence. Students were given forty minutes to complete the exercise.

During the third lesson, which occurred two days after the second lesson, the teachers instructed students to write everything they could remember about what they had written in their baseball picture-sequence stories.

During all three lessons, the teachers repeatedly emphasized the relationship between reading stories and writing stories. Their purpose was to insure that students perceived that the task of producing text had the same social-situation constraints as the task of comprehending text (cf. Mosenthal & Na, 1980a).

Scoring Students' Responses.   Two microlevel and two macrolevel analyses were performed. At the microlevel, students' compositions were analyzed in terms of proposition types, using the method developed by the author and his coworkers (see Mosenthal et al., 1981; Mosenthal & Na, 1981, for further details).

In sum, student compositions were first divided into simple sentences that were then divided into propositions following Kintsch (1974). For the narratives written in response to the picture sequence, propositions were classified as representing either (1) reproduction or reconstruction of prior knowledge, (based on how students completed the prior knowledge test about baseball, following Voss et al., 1980), (2) reproduction of the current text stimulus, (3) reconstruction of the current text stimulus, or (4) embellishment of some unidentifiable meaning source. For the narratives written as recalls of the original narratives, propositions were classified as representing either (1) reproduction or reconstruction of prior knowledge (again, following Voss et al., 1980), (2) reproduction of completed prior text, (3) reconstruction of prior text, (4) reproduction of the current text stimulus, or (5) reconstruction of the current text stimulus.

At the macrolevel, narratives were scored in terms of whether the student identified only an outcome, a goal causally unrelated to an outcome, or a goal causally related to an outcome (see Mosenthal et al., 1981, for further details). Also, narratives were scored in terms of how students represented the event structure of baseball as defined by Voss et al. (1980). In particular, the number of propositions by narrative were classified according to whether they represented (1) setting information, (2) goal state information, (3) game action information, or (4) nongame actions (see Voss et al., 1980, for further details).

Results. It was hypothesized that teachers who structured meaning in social situations differently would have different effects on how students used meaning sources and writing processes in producing written text. The results of Mosenthal's (1981) study showed that this was indeed the case. The results can be seen by comparing representative writing samples from students in the two classes. The first two samples below were written by students in the academic teacher's class, the second two samples were written by students in the cognitive-developmental teacher's class:

Sample I

People are having a baseball game. It is inning 5, the score is 3 to 0, the visitors in the lead. Players are waiting for their turn. Once again the empire call "Batter up!" and the next batter takes his turn. He waits for the pitcher to pitch the ball. When the pitcher pitched the ball, the player swings and misses. It is a strike. The pitcher pitches again, it is a low ball, so the player holds the bat down the ball hits the bat. The player dropped the bat and ran. An outfielder missed the ball. Another player threw the ball to another player and that player missed the ball. The player made a home run! At the end of the game the score was 3 to 2, the visitors won.

Sample II

This is a bace ball game. It is the 5th inning.

There are two people in the dugout. The empire calls batter up, so one of the player goes to bat. The batter whats for the pitch. The pitcher winds throughs the ball. The umpire called strike one.

The ball whent back to the pitcher the pitcher throughs the ball again the batter bunts, he got out.

The next batter came in. The batter swings, hits the ball it went in the out field the out fielder misses the ball.

The next batter came up to bat the short stop got the ball and through it and the batter made it to second bace.

Then the next batter was up he mad it to second bace. Then two men came in and the score was Visitors 3 home 2 visitors win.

Sample III

It's inning 6, the score is visitors 3, Home O. Even though they're losing the home team looks confident. The empire yells "batters up" and Butch steps up to base. He wents to make a run. He's ready now, the pitcher winds up the ball, shots, and Butch misses. "Strike one." Now He's really ready, the ball is pitched, and Butch bunts it. Too bad, its a foul. Butch is really mad now. The ball is pitched and he swings and hits it with all his might. The out fielder misses it, but picks it up and shots it to 2nd, and gets 1 guy out, Butch. But the other 2 players run home, with the last guy sliding into home.

The visitors won, better luck next time Home.

Sample IV

"Hello folks, here in foul territory, is Howard Cosell," Howard Cosell said. "The score stands 3 to 0 in the 5 inning. The Home Team, which is ABC, is up. Ron Howard and Henry Winkler are in the Dugout." Ron Howard steps up to the slate. You can tell he wants it bad. He gets ready for the pitch. For the NBC team the Pitcher, Richard Dawson, pitches the ball. Ron Howard swings, the catcher Mikeal Landon, catches the ball. The Umpire yells "SStrike I" The next pitch, Ron bunted the ball foul. On the next pitch wacked the ball to right field and Todd Bridges missed it, and threw it to high for first baseman Jack Klugman to reach it. He ran to get it and shot it to third where he now was. Third Baseman, Barbara Eden missed it and Robin Williams and Ron Howard ran home. "Safe" the Umpire yelled when the catcher caught the ball. "ABC won by 1 point this is Howard Corsell signing off" he said.

When asked to write a story about the picture sequence, students in the academic teacher's class reproduced the current text/picture stimulus more often than they reconstructed the current text/picture stimulus. In addition, they reconstructed the current text/picture stimulus more often than they reproduced or reconstructed prior knowledge. Students in the cognitive developmental teacher's class reproduced the current text/ picture stimulus more often than they reproduced or reconstructed prior knowledge. In addition, they reproduced and reconstructed prior knowledge more often than they reconstructed current text. Students in the academic teacher's class used current text (both in terms of reproduction and reconstruction) more often than did students in the cognitive-developmental teacher's class; students in the latter teacher's class used prior knowledge (both in terms of reproduction and reconstruction) more often than did students in the former teacher's class.

When asked to write a recall about what they had written as a narrative, students in the academic teacher's class reproduced the current text/picture stimulus more often than they reconstructed this meaning source. In addition, they reconstructed the current text/picture stimulus more often than they reproduced and reconstructed prior knowledge and prior text. Students in the cognitive-developmental teacher's class reproduced prior text and the current text/picture stimulus more often than they reproduced or reconstructed prior knowledge or reconstructed prior text. The writing process these students were least likely to use was reconstruction of the current text/picture stimulus. Students in the academic teacher's class used reproduction and reconstruction of the current text/picture stimulus more often than did students in the cognitive-developmental teacher's class. Students in the latter teacher's class more often reproduced and reconstructed prior knowledge and prior text than did students in the former teacher's class.

In devising and recalling narratives, students in the cognitive developmental teacher's class identified and developed a motive, or goal, for their narrative's central character more often than did students in the academic teacher's class. Also, the former students developed well defined goal states in describing the proceedings of their hypothetical baseball game more often than did the latter students.

A CRITIQUE OF THE CLASSROOM
WRITING COMPETENCE MODEL

In devising a classroom writing competence model, an attempt was made to formulate a partially specified descriptive definition that was ideologically unbiased and included all meaning sources and writing processes. Rather than beginining with a descriptive definition that was partially specified according to the assumptions of a given ideology, the study described began with the assumption that teachers behave in a manner that reflects a particular ideology (Bernier, 1981). On the basis of this ideology, teachers emphasize certain meaning sources and writing processes and de-emphasize others. Both statements apply to writing researchers too. Hence, teachers tend to teach (and researchers tend to research) writing and classroom writing competence from their own partially specified descriptive and operational definitions of these phenomena. In turn, students of different teachers (or different researchers) develop different notions of what writing entails in a manner that reflects their mentors' ideological bias for partial specification of writing and classroom writing competence.

In analyzing the proposed classroom competence model in the light of the heuristic scheme presented earlier, one notes that the favorite causative context of the proposed classroom writing competence model is the teacher, representing the situation organizer context. The favorite effect context is the student, representing the writer context. A proposed descriptive definition of this cause-and-effect relationship was based on the notions of ideology (Bernier, 1981) and general classroom competence models (Cherry, 1978; Mehan, 1979; Mosenthal & Na, 1980a, 1980b). The ideology of a teacher was operationally defined in terms of a sociolinguistic grammar of instruction. Students' use of meaning sources and meaning processes were operationally defined using two predictive grammars: one that compared the input and output of students' use of meaning in prior knowledge (following Voss et al., 1980) and one that compared the input and output of students' use of meaning in text (including the picture stimulus). The bridge principles used to relate the ideologies of the teacher to students' use of meaning sources and writing processes were similar to those used by psycholinguists (e.g., Frederiksen, 1977); it was assumed that differences in linguistic input and output structures and content represented real-time differences in teachers' and students' use of meaning sources and processes. Because the differences between students' use of meaning sources and writing processes were statistically distributed in a manner that was predicted by the descriptive definition, this suggested that there was some goodness of fit between this model's descriptive and operational definitions and, hence, this model's descriptive definition could be said to represent some fact about classroom writing competence.

In terms of the tenets of good science, this model succeeds fairly well in terms of predicting how teacher's ideologies influence students' writing performance. Unfortunately, to achieve this end, the model must posit complex operational definitions and, hence, is not adequate in terms of the criterion of simplicity. In short, simplicity is sacrificed for predictive validity. In terms of the criterion of ordering, the model posits that teachers are the most significant causative context responsible for the way children acquire language. This obviously is too simplistic a notion. Such a model fails to account for individual student differences and different achievement-group differences. In addition, the model posits no explanation of how teachers develop ideologies in the first place. In sum, the cause-and-effect explanation of this model's descriptive definition (in contrast to its cumbersome operational definitions) is too simplistic, too partially reduced.

In conclusion, to make this model more workable, the operational definitions need to be greatly streamlined; the descriptive definition used to be made more fully specified if the facts of this model are to have any relevance in this era of emerging writing research paradigms.

POSTSCRIPT

Questions of how one might better meet the tenets of good science are important; they are also questions that will ultimately produce better scientific facts. Yet, one might argue, the problem in writing research is not the need to produce facts but it is the need to understand the principles that produce these facts. As George Santayana once observed, never before has man known so many facts but so few principles. This is particularly true in writing research.

As this chapter has attempted to illustrate, there are two types of principles that serve to organize writing research: (1) ideological principles and (2) the principles of partial specification (i.e., internal and bridge principles). To advance writing research, it is necessary to advance understanding of both these principles. However, as has been suggested, it is not until writing researchers have a clear understanding of how principles of partial specification are related to ideological principles that writing researchers will be able significantly to advance writing research beyond the state where all facts appear equally relevant. As researchers, we must choose not only paradigms to answer, What is classroom writing competence? but also we need to entertain the vision of what are the possible ways to define classroom writing competence and, on the basis of this vision, to determine what ought to be the definition of classroom writing competence.

NOTES

1. A paradigm is a mutually agreed on set of criteria that enable one to separate relevant from irrelevant facts (Kuhn, 1970; Weimer, 1970).
2. These terms are defined in the next section of this chapter.
3. This specification procedure is similar to selecting a random sample assumed to be representative of a population in computing means and error variance.
4. For an excellent discussion of these theories, see Fodor, Bever, and Garrett (1974).
5. C = consonant; V = vowel.

REFERENCES

Ackerman, B. P. Children's comprehension of presupposed information: Logical and pragmatic inferences to speaker belief. *Journal of Experimental Child Psychology*, 1978, *26*, 92–114.

Bereiter, C. Development in writing. In L. W. Gregg & E. R. Steinberg (Eds.), *Cognitive processes in writing*. Hillsdale, N.J.: Erlbaum, 1980.

Bereiter, C., & Scardamalia, M. *Cognitive demands of writing as related to discourse type.* Paper presented at the annual meeting of the American Educational Research Association, Toronto, April, 1978.

Bereiter, C., & Scardamalia, M. From conversation to composition: The role of instruction in a developmental process. In R. Glaser (Ed.), *Advances in instructional psychology* (Vol. 2). Hillsdale, N.J.: Erlbaum, 1982.

Bereiter, C., Scardamalia, M., & Bracewell, R. J. *An applied cognitive-developmental approach to writing research.* Paper presented at the annual meeting of the American Educational Research Association, San Francisco, April 1979.

Bernier, N. R. Beyond instructional context identification: Some thoughts for extending the analysis of deliberate education. In J. L. Green & C. Wallat (Eds.), *Ethnography and language in educational settings.* Norwood, N.J.: Ablex, 1981.

Bowles, S., & Gintis, H. *Schooling in capitalist America: Educational reform and the contradictions of economic life.* New York: Basic Books, 1976.

Bracewell, R. J. *The ability of primary school children to manipulate language form when writing.* Paper presented at the annual meeting of the American Educational Research Association, Boston, April 1980.

Bransford, J. D., Franks, J. J., Morris C. D., & Stein, B. S. Some general constraints on learning and memory research. In L. S. Cermak & F. I. M. Craik (Eds.), *Levels of processing in human memory.* Hillsdale, N.J.: Erlbaum, 1979.

Bridgman, P. W. Operationism. In W. G. Hardy (Ed.), *Language, thought, and experience.* Baltimore University Park Press, 1978.

Britton, J., Burgess, T., Martin, N., McLeod, A., & Rosen, H. *The development of writing abilities (11–18).* London: MacMillan, 1975.

Broadbent, D. E. *In defense of empirical psychology.* London: Methuen, 1973.

Brown, A. L. Metacognitive development and reading. In R. J. Spiro, B. C. Bruce, & W. F. Brewer (Eds.), *Theoretical issues in reading comprehension.* Hillsdale, N.J.: Erlbaum, 1980.

Brown, A. L. Theories of memory and the problems of development: Activity, growth, and knowledge. In L. S. Cermak & F. I. M. Craik (Eds.), *Levels of processing in human memory.* Hillsdale, N.J.: Erlbaum, 1979.

Cartwright, G. P. Dimensions of written language of normal and retarded children. *American Journal of Mental Deficiency*, 1969, *73*, 631–635.

Case, R. Piaget and beyond: Toward a developmentally based theory and technology of instruction. In R. Glaser (Ed.), *Advances in instructional psychology* (Vol. 1). Hillsdale, N.J.: Erlbaum, 1978.

Cherry, L. A sociolinguistic approach to the study of teacher expectations. *Discourse Processes*, 1978, *1*, 373–394.

Clark, H. H., & Haviland, S. E. Psychological processes as linguistic explanation. In D. Cohen (Ed.), *Explaining linguistic phenomena.* Washington, D.C.: Hemisphere, 1974.

Clark, R. A., & Delia, J. G. Cognitive complexity, social perspective-taking, and functional persuasive skills in second-to-ninth-grade children. *Human Communication Research*, 1977, *3*, 128–134.

Cooper, C. R. Holistic evaluation in writing. In C. R. Cooper & L. Odell (Eds.), *Evaluating writing: Describing, measuring, judging.* Urbana, Ill.: National Council of Teachers of English, 1977.

Craik, F. I. M. Levels of processing: Overview and closing comments. In L. S. Cermak & F. I. M. Craik (Eds.), *Levels of processing in human memory.* Hillsdale, N.J.: Erlbaum, 1979.

Crowhurst, M., & Piché, G. L. Audience and mode of discourse effects of syntactic complexity in writing at two grade levels. *Research in the Teaching of English*, 1979, *13*, 101–109.

de Beaugrande, R. Text, attention, and memory in reading research. In R. J. Tierney, P. Anders, & J. Mitchell (Eds.), *Understanding readers' understanding*. Hillsdale, N.J.: Erlbaum, in press.

Diehl, W. A. *Functional literacy as a variable construct: An examination of attitudes, behaviors, and strategies related to occupational literacy*. Unpublished doctoral dissertation, Indiana University, Bloomington, 1980.

Dixon, E. Syntactic indexes and student writing performance. *Elementary English*, 1972, *49*, 714–716.

Doyle, W. *Accomplishing writing tasks in the classroom*. Paper presented at the annual meeting of the American Educational Research Association, Los Angeles, April 1981.

Doyle, W. Making managerial decisions in classrooms. In *Seventy-Eighth Yearbook, Part II; The National Society for the Study of Education*. Chicago: University of Chicago Press, 1979.

Dupuis, M. M., & Cartwright, G. P. *The writing of gifted children*. Paper presented at the annual meeting of the American Educational Research Association, San Francisco, April 1979.

Educational Testing Service. *The test of standard written English: Preliminary report*. Princeton, N.J.: Educational Testing Service, 1975.

Elley, W. B., Barham, I. H., Lamb, H., & Wyllie, M. The role of grammar in a secondary school English curriculum. *Research in the Teaching of English*, 1976, *10*, 5–21.

Florio, S. The problem of dead letters: Social perspective on the teaching of writing. *Elementary School Journal*, 1979, *80*, 1–7.

Flower, L. S., & Hayes, J. R. Problem-solving strategies and the writing process. *College English*, 1977, *39*, 449–461.

Flower, L. S., & Hayes, J. R. The dynamics of composing: Making plans and juggling constraints. In L. W. Gregg & E. R. Steinberg (Eds.), *Cognitive processes in wriing: An interdisciplinary approach*. Hillsdale, N. J.: Erlbaum, 1980.

Fodor, J. A., Bever, T. G., & Garrett, M. F. *The Psychology of Language*. New York: McGraw-Hill, 1974.

Frederiksen, C. Representing logical and semantic structure of knowledge acquired from discourse. *Cognitive Psychology*, 1975, *7*, 371–458.

Frederiksen, C. H. Semantic processing units in understanding text. In R. O. Freedle (Ed.), *Discourse production and comprehension* (Vol. 1). Norwood, N.J.: Ablex, 1977.

Freedman, S. W. Influences on evaluators of expository essays: Beyond the text. *Research in the Teaching of English*, 1981, *15*, 245–255.

Freire, P. *Pedagogy of the oppressed*. New York: Seabury, 1970.

Golub, L. S., & Frederick, W. An analysis of children's writing under different stimulus conditions. *Research in the Teaching of English*, 1970, *4*, 168–180.

Graves, D. H. *Balance the basics: Let them write*. New York: Ford Foundation, 1978.

Graves, D. H. An examination of the writing processes of seven-year-old children. *Research in the Teaching of English*, 1975, *9*, 227–241.

Grueneich, R., & Trabasso, T. *The story as social environment: Children's comprehension and evaluation of intentions and consequences*. Technical Report

No. 142 Urbana-Champaign: Center for the Study of Reading, University of Illinois, September, 1979.

Hackman, J. D., & Johnson, P. *Yale college freshman: How well do they write?* New Haven, Conn.: Yale University Press, 1976.

Halliday, M. A. K., & Hasan, R. *Cohesion in English.* London: Longman, 1976.

Heider, F. *The psychology of interpersonal relations.* New York: Wiley, 1958.

Hempel, C. G. *Philosophy of natural science.* Englewood Cliffs, N.J.: Prentice-Hall, 1966.

Hildyard, A. Children's production of inferences from oral texts. *Discourse Processes*, 1979, *2*, 33–56.

Hildyard, A., & Olson, D. R. Memory and inference in the comprehension of oral and written discourse. *Discourse Processes*, 1978, *1*, 91–118.

Hunt, K. W. Early blooming and late blooming syntactic structures. In C. R. Cooper & L. Odell (Eds.), *Evaluating writing: Describing, measuring, judging.* Urbana, Ill.: National Council of Teachers of English, 1977.

Hutchinson, L. G. Grammar as theory. In D. Cohen (Ed.), *Explaining linguistic phenomena.* Washington, D. C.: Hemisphere, 1974.

Irmscher, W. F. *The Holt guide to English* (2nd ed.). New York: Holt, Rinehart & Winston, 1976.

King, M. J., & Rentel, V. Toward a theory of early writing development. *Research in the Teaching of English*, 1979, *13*, 243–253.

Kintsch, W. *The representation of meaning in memory.* Hillsdale, N. J.: Erlbaum, 1974.

Kohlberg, L., & Mayer, R. Development as the aim of education. *Harvard Educational Review*, 1972, *42*, 449–496.

Kroll, B. Cognitive egocentrism and the problem of audience awareness in written discourse. *Research in the Teaching of English*, 1978, *12*, 269–281.

Kuhn, T. S. *The structure of scientific revolutions* (2nd ed.). Chicago: University of Chicago Press, 1970.

Lloyd-Jones, R. Primary trait scoring. In C. R. Cooper & L. Odell (Eds.), *Evaluating writing: Describing, measuring, judging.* Urbana, Ill.: National Council of Teachers of English, 1977.

Loban, W. *Language development: Kindergarten through grade twelve* (Research Report No. 18). Urbana, Ill.: National Council of Teachers of English, 1976.

Mandler, J. M., & Johnson, N. S. Remembrance of things parsed: Story structure and recall. *Cognitive Psychology*, 1977, *9*, 111–151.

Mandler, J. M., & Robinson, C. A. Developmental changes in picture recognition. *Journal of Experimental Child Psychology*, 1978, *26*, 122–136.

Mehan, H. *Learning lessons: Social organization in the classroom.* Cambridge, Mass.: Harvard University Press, 1979.

Mellon, J. C. *Transformational sentence-combining: A method for enhancing the development of syntactic fluency in English composition.* Urbana, Ill.: National Council of Teachers of English, 1969.

Menig-Peterson, C., & McCabe, A. *Structure of children's narratives.* Paper presented at the biennial meeting of the Society for Research in Child Development, New Orleans, March 1977.

Meyer, B. J. F. *Research on prose comprehension: Applications for composition teachers* (Research Report No. 2). Tempe: Department of Educational Psychology, Arizona State University, Spring 1979.

Meyer, B. J. F. The structure of prose: Effects on learning and memory and the implications for educational practice. In R. C. Anderson, R. J. Spiro, & W. E Montague (Eds.), *Schooling and the acquisition of knowledge.* Hillsdale, N.J.: Erlbaum, 1977.

Mishler, E. Meaning in context: Is there any other kind? *Harvard Educational Review*, 1979, *49*, 314–324.

Morris, C. D., Bransford, J. D., & Franks, J. J. Levels of processing versus transfer appropriate processing. *Journal of Verbal Learning and Verbal Behavior* 1977, *16*, 519–535.

Mosenthal, P. Bridge principles in an abridged reply to Goodman. *Reading Research Quarterly*, 1976–1977, *4*, 586–603. (a)

Mosenthal, P. Psycholinguistic properties of aural and visual comprehension as determined by children's ability to comprehend syllogisms. *Reading Research Quarterly*, 1976–1977, *12*, 55–92. (b)

Mosenthal, P. The new and given in children's comprehension of presuppositive negatives in two modes of processing. *Journal of Reading Behavior*, 1978, *10*, 267–278.

Mosenthal, P. Children's strategy preferences for resolving contradictory story information under two social conditions. *Journal of Experimental Child Psychology*, 1979, *28*, 323–343.

Mosenthal, P. *The influence of social situation on children's classroom writing.* Paper presented at the annual meeting of the National Council of Teachers of English, Boston, November 1981.

Mosenthal, P. On designing training programs for learning-disabled children: An ideological perspective. *Topical Issues in Learning and Learning Disabilities: Metacognition and Learning Disabilities*, 1982, *2*, 97–107. (a)

Mosenthal, P. Toward a paradigm of children's classroom writing competence. In B. A. Hutson (Ed.), *Advances in reading/language research* (Vol. 1). Greenwich, Conn.: JAI, 1982. (b)

Mosenthal, P. Reading research from a classroom perspective. In J. Flood (Ed.), *Advances in reading research.* Newark, Del.: International Reading Association, in press.

Mosenthal, P., Davidson-Mosenthal, R., & Krieger, V. How fourth graders develop point of view in classroom writing. *Research in the Teaching of English*, 1981, *15*, 197–214.

Mosenthal, P., & Na, T. J. Quality of children's recall under two classroom testing tasks: Towards a socio-psycholinguistic model of reading comprehension. *Reading Research Quarterly*, 1980, *15*, 504–528. (a)

Mosenthal, P., & Na, T. J. Quality of text recall as a function of children's classroom competence. *Journal of Experimental Child Psychology*, 1980, *30*, 1–21. (b)

Mosenthal, P., & Na, T. J. Classroom competence and children's individual differences in writing. *Journal of Educational Psychology*, 1981, *73*, 106–121.

Mosenthal, P., & Walmsley, S. *Picture and task effects on the quality of children's writing.* Paper presented at the annual meeting of the American Educational Research Association, San Francisco, April 1979.

Mosenthal, P., & Walmsley, S. *The quality of children's written discourse as a function of picture familiarity.* Paper presented at the annual conference of the Northeastern Educational Research Association, Ellenville, N.Y., October 1978.

Newell, A. You can't play 20 questions with nature and win. In W. G. Chase (Ed.), *Visual information processing.* New York: Academic Press, 1973.

Odell, L., & Goswami, D. *The nature and functions of writing in non-academic settings.* Paper presented at the Conference on Models and Processes of Writing, State University of New York, Albany, May 1980.

O'Donnell, R. C. A critique of some indices of syntactic maturity. *Research in the Teaching of English,* 1976, *10,* 31–38.

O'Donnell, R. C., Griffin, W. J., & Norris, R. C. *Syntax of kindergarten and elementary school children: A transformational analysis* (Research Report No. 8). Urbana, Ill.: National Council of Teachers of English, 1967.

Potter, R. R. Sentence structure and prose quality. *Research in the Teaching of English,* 1967, *1,* 1–17.

Rentel, V. M., King, M., Pappas, C., & Pettegrew, B. *Conjoining in children's oral and written texts: Developmental immaturity or developmental synergy?* Paper presented at the annual meeting of the American Educational Research Association, Boston, April 1980.

Resnick, D. P., & Resnick, L. B. The nature of literacy: A historical exploration. *Harvard Educational Review,* 1977, *47,* 370–385.

Rist, R. C. Student social class and teacher expectations: The self-fulfilling prophecy in ghetto education. *Harvard Educational Review,* 1970, *40,* 411–451.

Robins, R. H. *A short history of linguistics.* Bloomington: Indiana University Press, 1967.

Rubin, D. L., & Piché, G. L. Development in syntactic and strategic aspects of audience adaptation skills in written persuasive communication. *Research in the Teaching of English,* 1979, *13,* 293–316.

Rudner, R. S. *Philosophy of social science.* Englewood Cliffs, N. J.: Prentice-Hall, 1966.

Schustack, M. W., & Anderson, J. R. Effects of analogy to prior knowledge on memory for new information. *Journal of Verbal Learning and Verbal Behavior,* 1979, *18,* 565–583.

Scribner, S., & Cole, M. *The psychology of literacy.* Cambridge, Mass.: Harvard University Press, 1981.

Shaughnessy, M. *Errors and expectations.* New York: Oxford University Press, 1977.

Skon, L., Johnson, D. W., & Johnson, R. T. Cooperative peer interaction versus individual competition and individualistic efforts: Effects on the acquisition of cognitive reasoning strategies. *Journal of Educational Psychology,* 1981, *73,* 83–92.

Steffensen, M. S., Joag-Dev, C., & Anderson, R. C. A cross-cultural perspective on reading comprehension. *Reading Research Quarterly,* 1979, *15,* 10–29.

Stegmüller, W. *The structure and dynamics of theories.* New York: Springer, 1976.

Stein, N. L., & Glenn, C. G. An analysis of story comprehension in elementary school children. In R. O. Freedle (Ed.), *New directions in discourse processing* (Vol. 2). Norwood, N. J.: Ablex, 1979.

Sternberg, R. J. *Intelligence, information processing, and analogical reasoning: The componential analysis of human abilities.* Hillsdale, N. J.: Erlbaum, 1977.

Strong, W. *Sentence combining: A composing book.* New York: Random House, 1973.

Tamor, L., Bond, J. T., & Matz, R. D. *Instruction writing: A promising approach to the study and teaching of written composition.* Paper presented at the annual meeting of the American Educational Research Association, Boston, April 1980.

Verbruggel, R. R., & McCarrell, N. S. Metaphoric comprehension: Studies in reminding and resembling. *Cognitive Psychology,* 1977, *9,* 494–553.

Voss, J. F., Vesonder, G. T., & Spilich, G. J. Text generation and recall by high-knowledge and low-knowledge individuals. *Journal of Verbal Learning and Verbal Behavior,* 1980, *19,* 651–667.

Walmsley, S. A. On the purpose and content of secondary reading programs: An educational ideological perspective. *Curriculum Inquiry,* 1981, *11,* 73–93.

Weimer, W. B. *Notes on the methodology of scientific research.* Hillsdale, N.J.: Erlbaum, 1979.

Winterowd, W. R. *The contemporary writer.* New York: Harcourt Brace Jovanovich, 1975.

Part II

Experimental Approaches

3

Holistic Assessment of Writing: Experimental Design and Cognitive Theory[1]

Sarah Warshauer Freedman
University of California, Berkeley
Robert C. Calfee
Stanford University

During the past decade increasing attention has been given to the evaluation of student writing. Some states (e.g., California, Georgia, New York, and Texas) now require high school students to pass a writing-proficiency test that often includes a writing sample. The College Entrance Examination Board (CEEB) once again has a written essay in the English Composition Test. Essays are part of many college-level placement tests in writing (e.g., California and New Jersey's English Placement Tests), and many colleges and universities administer writing-proficiency tests to would-be graduates.

Assessment of a composition requires the judgment of a skilled evaluator; unlike objective multiple-choice questions, a writing sample does not have a single correct answer. At one time, schools relied almost exclusively on classroom teachers to judge essays, a task they performed as part of their regular duties in language arts and English composition courses. More recently, 'large-scale' assessments of essays have been used occasionally by the Educational Testing Service (ETS) and the CEEB. But these organizations have been frustrated by the expense of hiring readers and the difficulties of getting them to agree with one another. Consequently, they routinely supplement essay tests with multiple-choice items. Finally, essay assessments have served mainly for college placement—generations of graduate students in English have supplemented their income by reading essays to determine which college freshmen should take bonehead English.

The proficiency movement has brought with it a greater centralization of assessment and a greater reliance on the outcome of a single critical test episode. In earlier times, a student might do a poor job on an essay or the teacher might use poor judgment in evaluating it—no great matter because student and teacher were likely to engage in hundreds of writing encounters during the school years. Occasional mistakes by either party did not greatly influence the overall picture. The situation is quite different when a single test event is used to make significant decisions for the individual student.

How does an evaluator reach a judgment about a writing sample? This question is a central theme in this chapter. We shall not attempt a complete answer; rather, we shall show how a combination of cognitive theory and experimental design procedures can help to clarify our thinking about this question.

Because large-scale writing assessments generally rely on the *holistic scoring methods* developed by ETS in the 1950s and 1960s, we shall concentrate our efforts on this technique, one in which essays are given a numerical score that represents the rater's opinion of the overall quality of the essay. The rater is instructed to read the essay quickly and to score it as a whole without pondering the parts.

Understanding the process by which the rater makes a holistic judgment entails blending knowledge about human thought with a conception of the writing curriculum. It is not enough to know how people think in general. Instead, the focus must be on the very practical question of how skilled professionals critique a composition and then render a judgment. Some people are better than others at this task—their judgments are more consistent, and their explanations make more sense. Some contexts are more conducive than others to sound judgments—reading fifty compositions after a fully day of teaching may not be ideal. Some topics and writing tasks are more amenable than others to consistent scoring—if the student is not clear about what is expected or if the topic is trivial or misleading, the resulting composition may be such a motley that raters cannot render trustworthy judgments.

Given these sources of uncertainty—and we could add to the list—how are we to approach the question of how a rater reaches a judgment? One can simply announce that the question is academic, that common sense tells us we can rely on the experience and professional training of raters. Or one can resort to a variety of empirical techniques that measure the degree of interjudge consistency and that can be coupled with training procedures for enhancing the reliability of the ratings. Both approaches have practical utility; neither entails a particularly profound understanding of *how* rating is done, and thus neither can provide information for improving our rating procedure.

In this chapter, we shall illustrate and discuss a third option, one that takes as its central goal a cognitive analysis of the rating process and that uses the techniques of experimental design as its primary methodology. In the section that follows, we shall describe two studies by Sarah Warshauer Freedman that illustrate an experimental-design approach to untangling the web of variables that influence a person's judgment of a piece of writing. We shall next review basic principles for constructing such studies. We conclude the chapter by showing how cognitive theory provides a guiding framework for building an efficient and informative research design.

We should stress that, although our approach has the potential for advancing basic knowledge, it is grounded in a search for answers to practical questions. Properly conceived and executed, experimental research can lead to a better understanding of a theoretical problem and also tell what action makes best sense within the real world of writing assessment.

THE EFFECT ON HOLISTIC SCORING OF DIFFERENT FACETS OF THE RATING SITUATION

In planning the experiments described here, we have focused on the question, Which aspects of the rating process must one investigate to discover how expert evaluators reach judgments about student writing samples? The first experiment was designed as a preliminary study of the importance of three generic categories of factors that experts see as potentially important influences on how evaluators score essays: the essay, the rater, and the context (setting) for the rating. If holistic ratings are influenced more by the latter two sources than by the essays themselves, we might question the viability of the holistic rating approach. In other words, if the same essay received significantly different scores from different raters or received greatly different scores when rated by the same rater on one day rather than another, we would have to conclude that the procedure was not measuring the writer's performance in any trustworthy sense. On the other hand, if the essays themselves caused the evaluators to judge as they did, we would need to investigate more specifically how the essays exerted their influence to determine precisely how experts come to their evaluative decisions. Such knowledge could lead to definitions of good versus poor writing according to these experts, and such definitions could guide those of us who evaluate student writing.

Several considerations weighed on our minds in the planning of the first study. First, we wanted to examine specific factors that would be useful to practitioners within each of the three categories mentioned. For example, in examining how context might influence holistic scores, we were interested only in the contextual variations that were probable within and across large-scale assessments and that might substantially affect the scoring. Thus, we chose to examine such context variables as the time when the scoring occurred and the trainers who supervised the raters.

Second, to assure the trustworthiness of our results, we wanted to insure the greatest control possible, which we did by carefully separating the effects of the three categories (essays, raters, and context) and the subcategories (factors) within those three categories. If factors are not carefully separated, and if they are confounded, the researcher has difficulty interpreting the outcomes of the study. We shall show how we achieved this separation and control when we present the design of the study.

Third, to conserve time and energy, we needed to construct an efficient design, one that generated a great deal of information from a relatively small number of observations. Again, when we describe the design, we shall tell how we planned for efficiency.

The actual design of the experiment entailed two stages—the first was the selection of subcategories (factors) within each category, and the second was the arrangement of the various factors into an experimental plan. These categories and subcategories were the ones that we hypothesized could have a substantial influence on the score an evaluator awarded a composition. We shall next discuss how we selected our categories and describe the experimental plan.

The essay category contained three types of factors: topic type, topics within each topic type, and essays on each topic. First, two types of topics, similar to those used in large-scale assessments, were created. One kind required students to compare and contrast two quotations, for example:

> A Founding Father said: "Get what you can, and what you get hold: 'Tis the Stone that will turn all your Lead into Gold." A contemporary writer said: "If it feels good, do it."
>
> What do these two statements say? Explain how they are alike and how they are different.

The other kind of topic asked students to present their opinions on a controversial issue of the time, for example:

> Do you think the drinking age in California should or should not be lowered to 18? Give reasons for the position you take.

Second, within each topic type, four different topics were created along the lines illustrated above so that in all there were four quotation topics and four opinion topics. Third, with these topics as the stimulus, we asked eight students from colleges in the San Francisco Bay area to write essays on each topic, sixty-four writers in all. The topics were carefully distributed in each classroom to insure that a wide range of students wrote on each topic.

The rater category contained only one factor, the raters themselves. We selected as raters four highly qualified individuals of the sort that CEEB relies on. We were not interested in finding out how weak raters might undertake the task but rather in the extent of variation among good raters.

The category of context or environment in our design falls into two subcategories. One has to do with trainers; the other has to do with the time of the rating. Two trainers were selected to assist in the rating task. Their job was to establish specific criteria for each topic and to answer any questions that arose during the rating task. There were two time factors, the rating day and the rating session within a given day. The raters evaluated the essays on two Saturdays that were two weeks apart. Each rating day was divided into four sessions, within each of which a specific set of topics was judged (all of the essays on a particular topic were judged in the same session). Thus, the two factors related to time were the effects of long-term variation (the first and second Saturday) and the short-term trend within a day (the four sessions).

We have now described a total of seven factors: type of topic, specific topic within each type, essays on each topic, rater, trainer, rating day, and the rating session within each day.

The next task was to arrange these factors into a balanced and efficient design. Table 3.1 shows the plan that we created for this purpose.

TABLE 3.1 Balanced Sequential Design for Controlling Effects of Essay, Raters, and Time[a]. Each entry is a pair of raters assigned to read essays under conditions shown for that cell.

Trainer	Kind of Topic	Specific Topic	Weekend: First Saturday				Specific Topic	Weekend: Second Saturday			
			Session: I	II	III	IV		V	VI	VII	VIII
X	Quotation	A B		T, S		R, U	C D	R, S		T, U	
	Opinion	E F	T, U		R, S		G H		R, U		T, S
Y	Quotation	C D	R, S		T, U		A B		T, S		R, U
	Opinion	G H		R, U		T, S	E F	T, U		R, S	

The details about how we constructed this particular design are not as important as the concept of a balanced design and the notion that with a bit of care one can obtain a great deal of information relatively cheaply.

The design in Table 3.1 entails sixteen events, each of which consists of two raters reading a set of eight essays under a specified set of conditions. The letters R, S, T, and U are codes for the four raters. During

Session I on the first Saturday, for example, Raters T and U worked as a pair under the supervision of Trainer X to judge the eight essays written for topic F in the opinion category. Raters R and S were working at the same time on topic C in the quotation category under the supervision of Trainer Y.

By examining the plan in Table 3.1, one can see that each rater eventually read all sixty-four essays in a sequence that insured control over all the other factors in the experiment. Each rater worked an equal number of times with the other individuals with whom he or she was paired and an equal number of times with each trainer. The mirror-image quality of the paths taken by the raters through the eight sessions is characteristic of a well-controlled relationship between the various events and time; during each session, raters, trainers, and topics were so arranged that no systematic biases were present.

Each training session began with the trainer giving the two raters a packet containing two training essays and the set of eight essays that were to be judged during the session. The training essays covered the range of variation in the topic for that session. The two raters discussed the topic with the trainers, rated the training essays on the four-point holistic scale, and were aided by the trainer in reconciling any differences in judgment. Additional practice essays were available if further training was needed. As soon as the trainer thought the raters were ready, the raters read the eight essays in their packets and rated each on the holistic scale. The process worked quite well; interrater reliability as measured by the Cronbach alpha (Cronbach, 1970) was satisfactorily high ($\alpha = .84$).

To determine how each variable influences the holistic score, we used the analysis of variance (ANOVA) technique. This technique works particularly well for carefully balanced experimental designs such as the one in Table 3.1. Behavioral data are inherently variable. The researcher, in constructing an experimental plan, hopes to pin down the sources of variance in a systematic fashion. The ANOVA technique is a tool for measuring out the systematic sources of variation—the experimental design has been effective to the degree that the systematic sources of variance are large compared to the residual, or error, variance. We shall use ANOVA more or less, as a screening approach in examining the data from the design. From the ANOVA results, we can tell which of the factors in the design—essay factors, rater factors, and context factors—contribute substantially to variation in the holistic scores.

Table 3.2 shows the results of the ANOVA. The design is somewhat complex; therefore the table contains several sources (or potential influences on the score). We shall first discuss the list of sources, then the table headings, and finally the numbers in the table.

The sources of variance in the scores have been organized by the design categories. First are the essay factors—kind of topic, specific topics in kind, and essays on each topic. Because we were curious about the

TABLE 3.2   Analysis of Variance of Preliminary Study of Factors Affecting Rating Process

Source	Degrees of Freedom (df)	Mean Square	F Ratio
Essay			
Kind of topic	1	3.75	10.14*
Specific topic in kind			
Specific topic in quotation	3	.51	1.38
Essays in quotation	28	2.64	7.14*
Specific topic in opinion	3	3.89	10.51*
Essays in opinion	28	1.90	5.14*
Context			
Trainer	1	3.28	8.87*
Day	1	.09	.24
Session in day	3	.75	2.03
Rater			
Raters	3	.45	1.22
Interactions			
Kind by raters	3	.63	1.70
Specific topics by raters	18	1.46	3.95*
Residual	164	.37	—

* Critical values of *F* ratio:
   $F(1, 120, .01) = 6.85$
   $F(3, 120, .01) = 3.95$
   $F(20, 120, .01) = 2.03$
   $F(30, 120, .01) = 1.86$

extent of variation produced by each kind of topic, we calculated variance estimates separately for the topics and essays within each kind of topic. Next are the context factors—trainer, day, and session in day. These are followed by the rater category with its single factor.

We then isolated two interaction sources: Did raters vary in their judgments of the two kinds of topics? Did raters differ in their judgments of the specific topics within each kind? The last source in the table is the residual or leftover variation—this source gives a measure of the variance that is not controlled and that cannot be identified with any of the systematic factors in the design. It serves as the error term, a base line for judging the relative importance of the other sources of variation in the design.

We turn next to the headings of the table. The *degrees of freedom* (df) column gives a number that is a statistical index of the stability of the variance estimate for each source. For instance, the *kind of topic* source measures variance based on the single difference between quotation and opinion; thus, there is 1 df. By contrast, there are four specific topics within the quotation and opinion types, which yield 3 df for these two sources. In general, the df for a source are slightly less than the number of means being compared. There are thirty-two essays within the quotation and opinion types, and hence a large amount of information is available for estimating variation that is due to these sources. The details for calculating df are not important here—you should notice that whereas the kind of topic source has only 1 df, there are 3 df for specific topic and 28 df for the essays within each kind of topic—numbers that correspond roughly to the number of independent pieces of information about each source.

The mean square column shows the actual variance for each source. The higher the mean square, the more the particular source contributes to variability in the holistic scores. The F ratio column compares the mean square from each source to the error term (the residual mean square)—skimming this list shows where the action is. Thus, the kind of topic mean square, 3.75, is about ten times larger than the residual mean square, .37. To put it another way, variation in holistic scores that are due to the difference between the quotation and opinion topics is ten times larger than variation that is due to error of measurement. How large must the F ratio be for us to take it seriously? The answer to this question is found in tables of *critical F* ratios, which are in most statistics books. The footnote in Table 3.2 shows the critical F values that apply to our situation. For instance, if we compare a source with 1 df to an error term with 120 df, an F ratio as large as 6.85 will occur by chance less than once in a hundred times (a probability of .01). The actual F ratio for kind of topic, 10.14, is larger than the critical value of 6.85; therefore, we should take this source seriously. Our goal in this study was not so much to establish statistically significant results but rather to sort out sources of variation that are due to the different categories of factors and to determine the relative impact of the different categories on the rating process. The F ratios in Table 3.2 provide the essential information for achieving this goal; we should consider the statistical significance of each source, but the actual magnitude of the F ratio is more important for our purposes.

What do the results of the study tell us? The list of F ratios shows that several sources of variance in holistic scores are of substantial magnitude, most of them falling within the essay category. The kind of topic is highly significant, as are three of the four sources for specific topic and essays within topics. The large F ratio results for these sources suggest that it should be informative to graph the results for these factors, which we have done in Figure 3.1. There you can see a difference of almost 10 points favoring the quality of opinion composition over the quotation composition. There is also considerable variability in the judgments of specific topics within the opinion type. The general pattern in the graph reflects what is expected from the F ratios; the graph shows clearly the patterns of differences between topics. We have not graphed the results for specific essays within topics, but the F ratios in Table 3.1 indicate that there is considerable variation between the compositions by particular students within each of the topics.

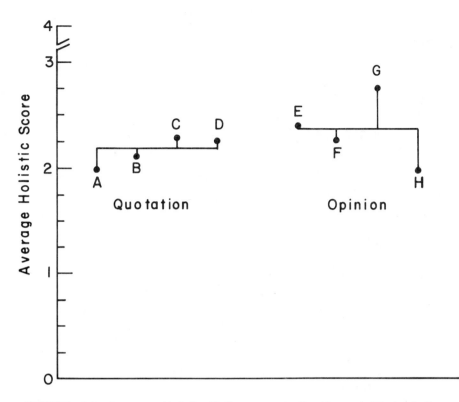

FIGURE 3.1 Average Holistic Ratings as a Function of Kind of Essay and Specific Topic.

Two other sources of variance are significant: the trainer effect and the rater in topic interaction. The trainer effect was unexpected. Both trainers worked together before the rating sessions to plan and standardize the training. They selected training essays on each topic and agreed ahead of time on scores for these essays. For the training, the trainers planned first to discuss the topic and then to present the training essays to the raters. After discovering the significant effect of the trainer on the variance in the holistic scores, we reviewed tape recordings of the training sessions, looking for differences in the training that might have contributed to the effect. We found that the two trainers approached the discussion of the topics differently. Trainer X simply presented the topic, and the raters discussed its meaning. Trainer Y asked the raters to discuss what they would expect from a good essay on the topic. During the discussion. Trainer Y reminded the raters that the students only had forty-five minutes to complete the task. Such a discussion might well have lowered the raters' expectations for a good essay and encouraged them to award higher scores. In any event, the raters did award higher scores under Trainer Y.

The rater in topic interaction, although significant, was not particularly large. It appears to have come about in the following way. During the discussion of the training essays, the trainers stuck to their agreed on scores but differed in how they handled the discussion about the scores. For example, in one case in which the trainers had previously agreed on a 2 for a particular essay, the two raters gave a 2 and a 1, respectively. Both trainers revealed that they had agreed on a 2 for the essay, but Trainer X said that they both thought the essay represented the low range of the 2s and that a 1 score was understandable. Given the same situation, Trainer Y said that 1s should be saved for the worst essays. Again, it was Trainer Y who elicited higher scores from the raters. Although we cannot fully determine the reasons for the training effect, it appears that subtle and not so subtle remarks can lead raters to score higher or lower, regardless of the training essays.

The important finding from this preliminary study is that the essays are the chief source of systematic variation. Of the total systematic variation among the ratings, more than 80 percent can be attributed to the essay category. There is some evidence that trainers may play an important supervisory role in setting a level of expectation, a finding with implications for the management of large-scale assessment projects. And within the essay category, it is important for assessors to note the effects attributable to individual topics. However, less than 18 percent of the systematic variance can be traced to these sources, and the findings suggest that skilled raters, when provided specific guidelines and supervised training, were able to rate a wide variety of compositions in a consistent and stable fashion. The most important influence on the rater's judgment was the individual essay. Thus, we could embark with confidence on the next phase of the research—an investigation of the analytic features of an essay that contributed to variation in the rater's response.

THE EFFECTS OF EXPERIMENTALLY VARIED FACETS OF A COMPOSITION ON HOLISTIC RATING

Given the results of the first study that showed that the individual essay affected the variance in holistic ratings more than any of the other factors in the design, we set out to examine how various qualities within the essay influenced the raters' decisions. We hoped to discover how our raters defined good writing and we wanted our findings to provide information that could help those involved in writing assessments. Accordingly, we wanted to address two issues that have not been considered by previous investigators who have studied how various facets of a composition relate to holistic scores (e.g., Grobe, 1981; Nold & Freedman, 1977; Slotnick & Knapp, 1971). First, we wanted to examine the relative influence of significant psycholinguistic categories on the holistic score; we were not content to limit ourselves to those few text variables that might be counted with relative ease and objectivity (e.g., T-unit length, words in unbound modifiers, percent of common verbs, and the like).

Using current theories of text analysis (de Beaugrande, 1980; Frederiksen, 1975; Kintsch, 1974), we decided to examine a set of factors in essays that were likely to have a systematic influence on the quality of a composition. These theories, which analyze texts hierarchically—propositional (idea development), schematic (organization), syntactic (sentence structure), and conventional (mechanics)—provided us with a framework for determining significant text variables in student essays.

The second issue that had not been considered in previous studies was the establishment of a causal relationship between the critical categories of the text and the score. Most past studies established correlations or associations by relying on post hoc analysis of already-scored essays to see which qualities could be used to predict the scores. A typical result from such studies is that longer essays receive higher scores. The problem with interpreting such findings is that length may or may not be an index of a significant psycholinguistic category such as idea development. Longer essays with fuller development of ideas may deserve higher scores than shorter essays, but longer essays padded with redundant information may deserve lower scores than their shorter counterparts. Correlational studies do not reveal why longer essays receive higher scores.

To test the extent to which each of the four categories of the essay—idea development, organization, sentence structure, and mechanics—caused raters to vary their holistic scores, we rewrote essays to incorporate strengths or weakneses within each category and then presented the rewritten essays to raters for holistic scoring. The raters, of course, were not told that the essays had been rewritten.

We wanted the rewriting to mirror actual strengths and weaknesses in student writing; thus, we followed a careful rewriting procedure. First, from the eight topics in the previous study, we chose the four essays that had received ratings closest to the average; this gave us plenty of room for making an essay better or worse. We rewrote each essay in several versions, representing various combinations of strengths and weaknesses in each category. For all rewritings, the main propositions (basic ideas) in the original essay were retained. Some rewritten essays were made stronger in every category; some were made weaker in every category; others were made stronger in some categories and weaker in others. The only rewriting not attempted was the combination of weak development and strong organization. It proved logically impossible to order illogical, underdeveloped thoughts! When finished, we had rewritten four essays on each of the eight topics in three versions each—one of the twelve versions on each topic keyed to each possible rewriting combination. In Table 3.3 are two rewritten versions of one of the original essays. The original essay was written in response to an opinion topic, the drinking age in California.

TABLE 3.3   Rewritten Versions of an Original Essay

Version I

The legal drinking age in California has been a conteversial issue for the past 10 years. Although arguements exist against the use of alcohol at any age, I feel that the right to purchase beverages should be an individuals *right* as an adult.

Opponents to the lowering of the drinking age have argue that the young adults would abuse the privelege, causing increases in social problems. But there are adults from every age group who abuse alcohol; why should 18 year olds be singled out? None of the States which already have the drinking age at 18 are experiencing any unusual difficulties from the new age group. I don't think this arguement of abuse is justified; 18 year olds have demonstrated their maturity.

This is in fact, the best argument in favor of reducing the age of drinking. The young adults have shown their maturity in the way they have conducted the other responsibilities given them at 18. This age group has participated in the election of governmental officials as well as fought in War for our country. There is no reason why, after having met the other responsibilities of adulthood, the 18 yr. old should not be allowed to drink.

While the imergence of maturity and decision-making abilities is a slow gradual process I feel that the majority of young adults have reached a responsible age at 18. The drinking age should be 18, when every other right of adulthood is given.

Version II

In the past, California alone has often been talked about having been one of the more liberal of the other states in the United States of America. I'd have to imagine that one of the bigger of the questions that revolves around when discussing the issue is whether eighteen-year-olds should be old enough to drink.

Opponents can probably argue some that the result of the lowering would make an increase in responsibility. The profit from the increase of the number of the sales that are made should seem to justify it.

It's true that there probably might be some kinds of people who would go and abuse this privilege, and their responsibility to other people. Just look at Watergate. It doesn't mean that all of a sudden a person is going to be completely old enough to automatically decide the things for himself.

Are the eighteen-year-olds any less mature than the eighteen-year-olds who happen to come from Hawaii, Montana, Maine, and New York? At that age, people are sent around to go and risk their own lives. I believe the legal drinking age should be a nationwide decision and law. I believe the legal drinking age should be lowered to eighteen.

You can see that Version I contains numerous mechanical problems (spelling and capitalization errors, missing apostrophes, and various kinds of incorrect punctuation), but the development, organization, and sentence structure are adequate. In contrast, Version II is mechanically correct, but it is weak in the other categories. The thesis is stated only in the last paragraph; pronoun references are ambiguous, yielding a sense of incoherence; paragraphs fail to develop their point; sentences are padded with unnecessary words, are often choppy, and have other structural problems. The first version was revised to be stronger in development, organization, and sentence structure and to be weaker in mechanics. The second version was made stronger in mechanics and weaker in the other three categories.[2]

Twelve raters with qualifications similar to those in the previous study were selected for the experiment. They were trained in groups of three to judge the set of essays on a given topic, which they were told had been written by college freshmen. Half of the essays were from the specially rewritten versions; the other half were originals, some of which had received high ratings, others low ratings. None of the raters remarked that the essays seemed unnatural.

After the training was completed for a topic, each rater received a packet containing the essays for that topic. The original essays were used to assess the interrater reliability; they again proved quite satisfactory (Cronbach α ranged from .86 to .96). After raters had finished the holistic ratings for their set of essays, they were asked to state for each essay the extent to which they thought that it was relatively strong in development, organization, sentence structure, and mechanics. No attempt was made to define these categories for the raters because we wanted to determine whether these categories were meaningful to them and whether they could independently evaluate these facets of the essay. In general, they were quite accurate in these judgments.

As in the first study, a highly efficient counterbalanced design was used to control the various categories of factors—the rewriting facets, the raters, and the order in which the various topics were rated. The basic principles were the same as those illustrated in the first study; details can be found in Freedman (1977, 1979).

Table 3.4 shows the ANOVA results for the second study. As in the first experiment, the sources are organized by the categories used to create the design. First, these are the four rewriting factors that were the focus of the study. Next on the list are several interactions that were selected as especially interesting—these measure the extent to which the effect of one of the rewriting factors varied from level to level of another rewriting factor. Below the interactions are several sources associated with the raters. First, there is the main effect of the raters themselves—this source measures variability that is due to overall differences in level of judgment (Did some raters give consistently higher or lower ratings than others?). Second, there are the interactions between raters and the rewriting factors. These sources measure individual differences in the effect of each rewriting factor—if all twelve raters reacted in a similar fashion to the contrast between the strong and weak versions along a particular dimension, the rater interaction with this factor would be small, and contrariwise.

The results in Table 3.4 support several important conclusions. First, three of the four rewriting factors strongly influenced the raters' judgments; development had the greatest effect, followed by organization and mechanics. Sentence structure was not a statistically significant factor, although the results were in the predicted direction. Second, although most of the systematic variability was attributable to the main effects, two interactions noticeably influenced the judgments. Both of the interactions

TABLE 3.4   Analysis of Variance for Holistic Scores: Rewriting Effects

Source	Degrees of Freedom (df)	Mean Square	F Ratio
Writing Factors			
Development (D)	1	9.86	31.70***
Organization (O)	1	5.20	16.70***
Sentence Structure (SS)	1	1.50	4.82
Mechanics (M)	1	5.04	16.21***
Writing Interaction			
D × SS	1	1.96	6.30
D × M	1	.99	3.18
O × SS	1	3.77	12.11**
O × M	1	6.16	19.78***
SS × M	1	.00	0
Reader and Reader Interactions			
Reader (R)	11	.45	
R × D	11	.26	
R × O	11	.18	
R × SS	11	.59	
R × M	11	.52	
Residual	31	.31	

** $p < .01$ 1, 31 df   F = 7.56   *F* is based on residual error variance.
*** $p < .001$ 1, 31 df   F = 13.29

involved the organization factor. If an essay was well organized, the ratings were clearly higher if the sentence structure and mechanics were also in good shape. However, if an essay had a weak organization, neither the sentence structure nor mechanics factors had much effect on the ratings. Finally, all of the rater sources were of roughly the same order of magnitude; individual differences were small among this sample of raters, who had been selected to be fairly homogeneous.

SOME FUNDAMENTALS OF EXPERIMENTAL DESIGN

The two studies described illustrate how the techniques of experimental design can serve as important tools for the systematic planning of research in the field of composition. Whether a project is primarily descriptive, correlational, experimental, or (more likely) a combination of these, the quality of the research depends in large measure on the coherence of the plan for identifying and controlling the factors that influence the phenomenon under investigation. In this section, we want to review briefly some important principles of experimental design (Calfee, 1975).

A design begins with a question that is clearly stated, precise, and answerable. The task of planning the design involves reflective and analytic thinking about the structure of the problem, about the parts of the process. Experimental design techniques provide a useful tool for implementing the planning process, but they also provide a guiding framework for analyzing the substance of a problem, as shown in our rewriting experiment.

Factors are the basic building blocks of an experiment. A *factor* is a dimension of systematic variation incorporated in the design to determine the effect of that dimension. One can distinguish three categories of factors—*treatment factors, person-classification factors* and *control (nuisance) factors.* A treatment factor is most often directly controlled by the experimenter (e.g., the rewriting of student texts). A person-classification factor is a dimension of individual differences that cannot be readily modified by the experimenter, but is instead controlled by the manner of selecting people (e.g., the experience of the rater). Control (nuisance) factors include variables that are not of particular interest to the experimenter but are incorporated in the design to avoid problems of interpretation (e.g., order of presentation of essays to raters).

When the researcher designs an experiment, many decisions must be made: the choice of factors to vary and to hold constant, the levels of each factor to include in the design, the manner of selecting subjects, and the planning of specific experimental procedures. During this decision making, three issues are of paramount importance—*variability, confounding*, and *interaction.*

Variability refers to the fluctuations in performance. Some variations reflect random, unpredictable changes; other variations reflect systematic, predictable changes. In designing an experiment, the aim is to maximize systematic variations and minimize random variability.

Confounding occurs when a factor varies in ways other than intended by the experimenter. For instance, in our second study, some papers were rewritten to have strong development, whereas others were rewritten to have weak development. If we had inadvertently changed the sentence structure while we were strengthening development, these two factors would have been confounded. In the first study, if we had not been careful in our assignment of topics to students, we could have confounded these two variables by assigning easier topics to less able students, and contrariwise. When a confounding exists, the results of the experiment are totally compromised. There is no way to determine whether a difference between treatments is due to the nominal factor (development), the confounded factor (sentence structure), or to both.

Interactions occur when the effects of a factor vary from one level to the next of a second factor. Interactions are not necessarily bad. Indeed, research questions can be designed to investigate specific interactions (Cronbach & Snow, 1977). When an experimenter suspects that two factors interact, however, additional care is required in the design, analysis, and interpretation of the study. The exact nature of the interaction must be described, and the intepretation must include discussion of the interaction. In our study, we found that organization interacted with both mechanics and sentence structure—these interactions were understandable and practically important.

The results of any single experiment are valuable only insofar as they generalize to a large set of situations. When interactions go undetected, the results can lead to false generalizations. For instance, if the organization had not been included in the design, one might have remained unaware of the circumstances under which the effects of sentence structure and mechanics are and are not of importance.

Interactions go undetected and confoundings occur most often because of inadequate designs. To be sure, it is impossible to include all potentially relevant factors of a research problem in a single study. Nonetheless, the goal in planning an experiment is to identify potentially significant interactions and confoundings and to build into the design those factors that are representative of the situations of interest.

Once the basic design has been formulated, there are numerous nondesign details, often referred to as experimental procedures, that have to be arranged. Whereas design decisions involve the selection of factors and levels of factors that are to be systematically varied, procedural decisions entail conditions that presumably remain constant throughout the experiment. For example, materials and techniques must be selected or developed, the experimental task and testing arrangments must be specified, the time and place of the study must be chosen. As with design decisions, procedural decisions should take into account the research question and the population to which the results are to be generalized.

Many experiments become flawed during the planning of procedures. These are often the last details to be worked out, and they often evolve in haste, with convenience and necessity serving as the chief criteria. When investigators have used up all of their options for systematic variation, they then settle on opportune ways of doing everything else, trusting that randomness will overcome bias and confounding.

It seems to us that a better practice in arranging the procedures for an experiment is to treat the procedures as part of the design process. That is, rather than selecting the materials, instruction, environment, and other procedural variables at the last moment by a cut-and-paste approach, the experimenter should also identify the significant dimensions on which the procedural facets of the study are to be chosen. This part of the design should be planned at the same time as the identification of the primary factors. The experimenter can then decide on the plan of the study from a broader vantage point—choosing which factors to vary and which to keep constant.

THEORY AS A FOUNDATION FOR DESIGN

Theory is generally heralded as a guide for research. Although no theory is perfect and although a theory may be little more than fuzzy thinking in disguise, even a bad theory is often better than none at all.

One of the virtues of a good theory is that it provides a simple understanding of phenomena that may otherwise appear quite complex. Herbert Simon, in *The Sciences of the Artificial* (1981), presents a general approach for creating theories of complex systems. According to Simon, the key to understanding a complex system is to discover how to divide it into simpler parts and how to arrange these parts in relation to one another. He introduces the concept of a decomposable hierarchy. A decomposable system is one in which each major part works more or less independently of every other part. "*Intracomponent* linkages are generally stronger than *intercomponent* linkages" (Simon, 1981, p. 106). There may be interactions between one part of the system and another (intercomponent linkages), but these are weaker than the interactions within a given subsystem (intracomponent linkages).

A hierarchical system is "composed of interrelated subsystems, each of the latter being, in turn, hierarchic in structure until we reach some lowest level of elementary subsystem" (Simon, 1981, p. 196). Linguists use the concept of a hierarchy when describing language as a complex system, with levels of semantics, syntax, morphology, and phonology each embedded within the other.

Simon's concept for the analysis of complex systems meshes quite well with contemporary thinking about cognition. Information processing models, which are used to represent complex thought processes, embody an effort to describe the surface complexities of human behavior by a relatively simpler representation of the underlying mechanism. These models, to the extent that they are well conceived, provide a reasonable basis for designing research and for dealing with the problems of practice. In the remainder of this section, we present a model of how a skilled rater evaluates a composition, discuss how our studies fit into this model, and suggest how the model can guide researchers in designing experiments.

An Information Processing Model of the Rater

The key to understanding how a person performs a complex task, following Simon's (1981) reasoning, is to try to identify the relatively small number of relatively separable processes that underlie the person's thinking for that task (Calfee, 1981). Figure 3.2 shows the three processes that we have identified as essential in rating a composition: (1) *read and comprehend text* to create text image, (2) *evaluate text* image and store impressions, and (3) *articulate evaluation*. The first two processes are receptive and handle the reader's (or the evaluator's) creation of a text image in working memory (WM). These internal receptive processes are followed by a productive process, the overt evaluation or judgment. In Figure 3.2, the open arrow at the top, from short-term memory (STM) *in* to WM and long-term memory (LTM), indicates the receptive nature of the reading and evaluative processes. The bottom open arrow, leading from WM and LTM *out*

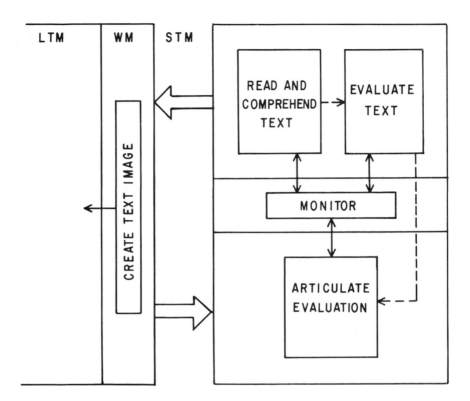

FIGURE 3.2   An Information-Processing Model of Rating a Composition.

to STM, indicates the productive nature of the articulation process. The next three sections provide details about the operation of each process.

Read and Comprehend Text to Build a Text Image.   To comprehend a text, the evaluator contructs an image in LTM. The image that the evaluator constructs is not identical to the text itself. The text is a concrete object in the "real" world, but it influences the evaluation process only through the image in which it is stored in the evaluator's memory. In principle, every evaluator stores a slightly different text image for a given text, but, for a homogeneous group of skilled evaluators reading a particular text under similar conditions, the similarities in their text images should be more important than the differences. Our studies supported this hypothesis.

Evaluate Text and Store Impressions.   As an image of the text is stored, the evaluator begins to make judgments about it. The evaluator makes decisions about what she or he thinks about the text-image—whether the evaluator generally likes the text, thinks it is well written, and so on. It seems reasonable that, as the text image is contructed, the evaluator also stores a set of impressions about that image. Our studies suggest that a homogeneous group of skilled evaluators not only stores similar text images but also shares common values about these texts—this conclusion is consistent with our research findings.

Articulate Evaluation. To articulate an evaluation, the evaluator usually gives either written or oral substantive comments and a numerical score or letter grade. The match between the internal decision and the extenal articulation of that decision may be more or less close. In a pedagogical setting, a teacher may think one thing about a student's paper but tell the student something different. For example, to avoid discouraging a student, the teacher may decide to give that student a softened version of a negative evaluation. However, in the experimental setting of our research, we think it likely that the scores accurately reflect the evaluator's internal decisions.

Relation Among Processes

How are these processes arranged? One hypothesis is that they normally occur in an ordered sequence. The skilled evaluator comprehends (i.e., constructs a text image) before making evaluative decisions about that text image, and it is only after making evaluative decisions that the evaluator articulates them. The broken arrow in Figure 3.2 shows the direction of the flow of these substages.

On the other hand, the operation may not proceed as three linear stages; the process may be recursive. After articulating part of an evaluation, the rater continues to read and does not necessarily withhold evaluation until all the text has been read. Rather, as bits of text are comprehended, they are judged. Furthermore, the evaluation of one section of text may change as one comprehends a subsequent section of text. The solid arrows leading in and out of the monitor allow for this possibility. Our studies did not let us decide between these two hypotheses, but current reading theory suggests that the recursive model is most probable.

What kind of evidence is needed to support the assumption that the three processes are "real," that rating is properly decomposed into the processes we have listed? If these parts are actually separable, Simon (1981) would say that they should act more or less independently of one another; he does recognize that there may be modest interactions among the parts. For example, an evaluator could store a text image but could come to different evaluative decisions about that text image, depending on the set of values applied; differing purposes for doing the evaluative could activate different values. To put it another way, values might slightly affect the text image, but they are much more likely to affect the evaluative decisions. For instance, when evaluators judge entries in a writing contest, they apply different values and come to different decisions than when judging the same texts to decide whether students should go into a remedial writing class. In the first case, a text might appear weak; in the second case, the same text might look strong. In these situations, creation of the text image is more or less independent of the evaluative decision making.

As an example of how evaluative decision making may be more or less independent of the actual evaluative statement, the audience is likely to affect articulation, over and above the covert evaluative decisions. If the evaluator is deciding on remedial placement and the audience is the teacher of the remedial class, the rater's statement may be different if the audience is the student writer.

Influences on Subprocesses

Given that reading, evaluating, and articulating are three separable processes, one can establish their independence by considering what factors could influence each process. If the processes are independent, then different factors will affect each process (Calfee, 1976c).

Figure 3.3 presents examples of factors that may uniquely influence the processes of reading, evaluating, and articulating. Along the sides of the figure you can see that these factors have been grouped into two categories: the personal characteristics of the raters and the characteristics of the task environment. Personal characteristics deemed likely to influence the rating process include (1) reading ability, (2) world knowledge, (3) expectations, (4) values, (5) the purpose of the evaluation, (6) productive ability, and (7) the audience for the evaluation. The task environment includes such variables as (1) time of day, (2) length of task, (3) type of text, (4) the physical environment, and (5) the kind of training and supervision provided.

If we consider the different personal characteristics that might influence evaluation, we can agree that the skilled evaluator of student writing should be a highly skilled reader. That person should know how to decode individual words, should have an adequate vocabulary to understand the text being read, should have an adequate knowledge of text structure to comprehend the text as a whole. And we assume that if the skilled reader has any difficulty within any level of text comprehension, the fault probably will be with the student writer; we also assume that any other skilled reader will have similar comprehension difficulties. Such difficulties should not be related to the reading ability of the evaluator.

The image of the text that the evaluator builds, we hypothesize, may also be influenced by the evaluator's stored world knowledge about the writer, the topic, and the situation in which the writing was performed. Recent research in reading comprehension has emphasized how important a role such world knowledge plays in the representation of a text or in the creation of the text image (e.g., Tierney & Cunningham, in press).

Expectations play a role in the following ways. If evaluators know that the writer is a college student, then in creating a text image, they will be

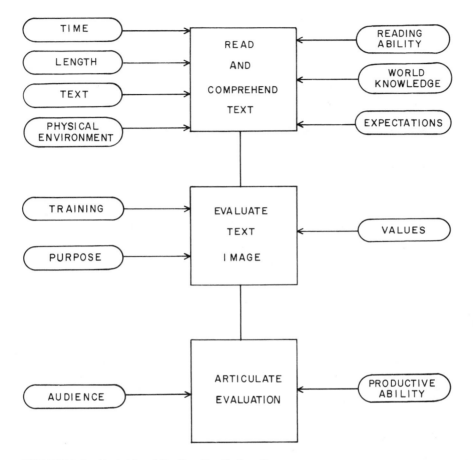

FIGURE 3.3   Variables Affecting the Rating Process.

likely to make certain inferences about the text based on that knowledge, inferences that will be different from those they would make if they thought that the writer was a professional writer or a young child. According to Grice's (1975) cooperative principle, if evaluators think a text is written by a professional and if they have difficulty comprehending a part of the text, they will blame themselves and try harder to make inferences to fill in the gaps in meaning. The evaluators, with these forced inferences, will build a different text image from one they might have built if they thought the text was produced by a student writer whom they would then blame for the comprehension difficulty (Freedman, in preparation). Likewise, if evaluators know that the writers had a forty-five-minute time limit during which to complete an essay, they might by more generous in filling in gaps in the text than if they thought the writers had an unlimited time to produce the text.

One can see that these three personal characteristics of the rater—reading ability, word knowledge, and expectations—could have a significant effect on the reading of the text and on the consequent text image that the reader will store in his or her LTM. And it is the nature of this text image that matters for the evaluation because it is the text image that receives the evaluation.

Figure 3.2 shows that we also hypothesize that other aspects of the task environment may influence the text image that the evaluator stores. If one is tired during an afternoon session, one may store a different image from when reading the same text bright and chipper in the morning. Most important, however, our first study suggests that the most significant influence on the skilled evaluator is the text itself. This finding leads us to propose that in a testing context where many personal factors are controlled, the skilled evaluator stores text images that primarily reflect variations in texts rather than, say, the time at which the reading occurred.

As we mentioned, the only potential influence on the evaluative decisions is one personal characteristic, the rater's values. Parts of the task environment may influence those values or the application of the values. For example, the first study we described showed that trainers may influence the rater to apply a certain set of values or to switch standards. Again, the only influence on the articulation of the decision is one aspect of the task environment, the audience for the evaluation. If the articulation is to be more than a number or a grade, then written and oral language skills (i.e. productive skills) may affect articulation.

Finally, notice in Figure 3.3 that evaluative decisions must be filtered through the raters' values. The articulation of those decisions must be filtered through the raters' perceptions of the audience and, if the articulation is substantive, must be filtered through the evaluator's productive abilities.

A BROADER PERSPECTIVE ON THE ISSUE OF DESIGN

In all areas of scholarly work, one encounters the tension between analysis and synthesis, between reductionism and holism (Shuy, 1981). Research on composition is especially prone to this tension. On the one hand, it partakes of the humanist tradition with its espousal of holism; on the other hand, it relies on the analytic methods of the social scientist. In this chapter we have taken a strongly analytic stance. In the research examples, in the review of experimental design, and in the cognitive model of the rater, our approach has been to break complex problems into a small number of easier-to-digest parts. We have emphasized Simon's (1981) concepts of decomposition and design because we see them as a bridge, as a compromise between extremes: "In the face of complexity, an in-principle reductionist may be at the same time a pragmatic holist" (Simon, 1981, p. 195).

The strength of Simon's argument is that it provides a technically adequate approach for combining analysis and synthesis in the study of complex systems.

We have emphasized experimental design procedures in this chapter for several reasons. First, they represent an elegant approach to design. Second, we think that they comprise a powerful but largely unused (or misused) tool. Third, these techniques are a good match to the emerging cognitive theories of human thought and behavior, theories that offer much to composition researchers.

Experimental design is not the only methodology suitable for research on composition of course. We agree with Graves (1980) that "depth needs to be added through different uses of case study, experimental, and ethnographic procedures *within the same study*" (p. 204). We think that the technical tools for achieving this goal exist (Calfee, 1976a, 1976c), and that a major task for the immediate future is to insure that English researchers possess the range of technical skills required in this demanding field. We do think that an important theme linking these various methodologies will prove to be the concept of *design*, a concept as important in ethnography as in experiment.

NOTES

1. In some sections of this chapter we relied heavily on four of our works: Freedman, 1979; Freedman, in preparation; Calfee, (1976a); Calfee and Piontkowski, in press. It should also be noted that although Freedman's studies form the basis for the discussion, for the sake of stylistic consistency we use the plural pronoun throughout. The work of Calfee in the preparation of this paper was supported in part by the Department of Education (NIE and OE/BEH) and the Center for Advanced Study in the Behavioral Sciences.

2. Freedman (1977, 1979) explains the procedures and the design for three rewriters who did the rewriting.

REFERENCES

Calfee, R. C. *Human experimental psychology*. New York: Holt, Rinehart & Winston, 1975.

Calfee, R. C. A proposal for practical (but good) research on reading. *Research in the Teaching of English*, 1976, *10*, 41–50. (a)

Calfee, R. C. Research perspectives from the behavioral sciences: Some new (and not so new) directions. In S. W. Lundsteen (Ed.), *Help for the teacher of written composition K–9: New directions in research*. Urbana, Ill.: National Conference on Research in English, 1976. (b) (Eric Document Reproduction Service No. 120731)

Calfee, R. C. Sources of dependency in cognitive processes. In D. Klahr (Ed.), *Cognition and instruction*. Hillsdale, N. J.: Erlbaum, 1976. (c)

Calfee, R. C. Cognitive psychology and education practice. In D. C. Berliner (Ed.), *Review of research in education*. Washington, D.C.: 1981.

Calfee, R. C., & Piontkowski, D. C. Design and analysis of experiments. In P. D. Pearson (Ed.), *Handbook of research in reading*, in press.

Cronbach, L. J., *Essential of psychological testing* (3rd ed.). New York: Harper & Row, 1970.

Cronbach, L. J., & Snow, R. E. *Aptitudes and instructional methods: A handbook for research on interactions*. New York: Irvington/Naiburg, 1977.

de Beaugrande, R. *Text, discourse, and process: Toward a multidisciplinary science of texts*. Norwood, N.J.: Ablex, 1980.

Frederiksen, C. Representing logical and semantic structure of knowledge acquired from discourse. *Cognitive Psychology*, 1975, *7*, 371–458.

Freedman, S. W. *Influences on the evaluators of student writing*. Unpublished doctoral dissertation, Stanford University, Stanford, Calif., 1977.

Freedman, S. W. How characteristics of student essays influence teachers' evaluations. *Journal of Educational Psychology*, 1979, *71*, 328–338.

Freedman, S. W. The registers of student and professional expository writing: Influences on teachers' responses. In R. Beach & L. Bridwell (Eds.), *New directions in composition research*. In preparation.

Graves, D. Research update: A new look at writing research. *Language Arts*, 1980, *57*, 913–919.

Grice, H. P. Logic and conversation. In P. Cole & J. Morgan (Eds.), *Syntax and semantics III: Speech acts*. New York: Academic Press, 1975.

Grobe, C. Syntactic maturity, mechanics, and vocabulary as predictors of quality ratings. *Research in the Teaching of English*, 1981, *15*, 75–85.

Kintsch, W. *The representation of meaning in memory*. Hillsdale, N. J.: Erlbaum, 1974.

Nold, E., & Freedman, S. An analysis of readers' responses to essays. *Research in the Teaching of English*, 1977, *11*, 164–174.

Shuy, R. A holistic view of language. *Research in the Teaching of English*, 1981, *15*, 101–111.

Simon, H. *The sciences of the artificial* (2nd ed.). Cambridge, Mass.: MIT Press, 1981.

Slotnick, H. B., & Knapp, J. V. Essay grading by computer: A laboratory phenomenon? *English Journal*, 1971, *60*, 75–87.

Tierney, R., & Cunningham, J. Research on teaching reading comprehension. In P. D. Pearson (Ed.), *Handbook on research in reading*. New York: Longman, in press.

4

Text Analysis:
Inferring Process from Product[1]

Lynne Tamor
State University of New York at Albany
James T. Bond
High/Scope Educational Research Foundation

Like that of most of the contributors to this volume, our research is motivated by the desire to answer a very practical question: How can teachers best foster the development of writing abilities in their students? We share the conviction that well-articulated and empirically supported explanatory theories will eventually provide the best foundation on which instructional approaches and methods can be based even though current theoretical inadequacies require that educational practitioners rely heavily on the less well-defined theories that are usually labeled intuition, common sense, and past experience.

Our approach, however, is different in a number of ways, the most immediately salient of which are our current focus on elementary school students and our emphasis on linking research on composing processes as closely as possible to research on written products (texts or compositions). Further, when we speak of processes, we refer not only to the cognitive operations resulting in the production of written texts but also to the role of affective factors within the total psychological system and to the surrounding social and physical environment that may influence the activity of that psychological system. As educators, we are fundamentally concerned with changes in the psychological system over time—some of which constitute learning—and in the factors that bring about those changes. Our long-term goal is thus the development of a theory that accounts for the cognitive operations involved in writing, the internal and external factors that influence those operations at any given time, changes in those operations over time, and the connection of those operations to specific features of resulting compositions.

THE THEORETICAL FRAMEWORK

We characterize our overall approach as a pragmatic approach to theory formulation and have summarized its procedures in Figure 4.1. That its ultimate goal is formulation of a comprehensive and rigorous theory is made clear by the bottom box toward which all efforts eventually lead. We consider the approach pragmatic for two reasons: first, because we are committed to using all available sources of information and inspiration; second, because we acknowledge the need to engage in curriculum planning and design before the theory has been developed. This is true both because schools and students cannot wait for significant progress on the theoretical front and because it is doubtful that significant progress will ever be made if research programs are divorced from direct involvement in classroom activities.

In the center of Figure 4.1 is the reference model, the organizing framework that coordinates even the most applied of our efforts with the

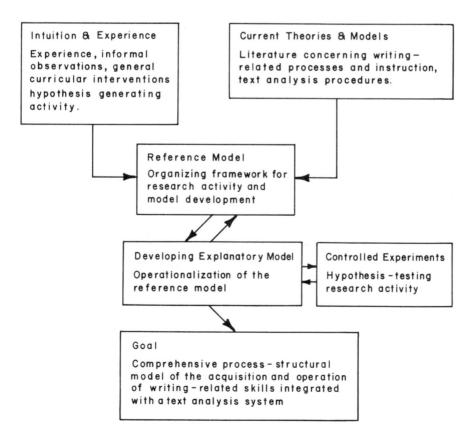

FIGURE 4.1   A Pragmatic Approach to Theory Formulation.

most theoretical and one that keeps us on a track, however convoluted, toward our ultimate goal. The reference model is quite general and is loosely based on the theory of cognitive development and processing developed by Pascual-Leone (1969; Pascual-Leone et al., 1978). It provides a language into which existing literature—included in the box labeled current models and theories—can be translated and thereby more thoroughly synthesized; it also provides a means for systematizing and analyzing the vast and tangled array of information and beliefs contained within the box labeled intuition and experience. To achieve the level of rigor and synthesis required in a comprehensive explanatory model, the reference model itself must conform to the principles governing the ultimate explanatory model. These principles are the major focus of this chapter and will be listed shortly.

The initial development of the reference model depended on two sources, both of which continue to shape the model as our research progresses. One of these is the existing literature, which includes both theories already subjected to empirical investigation as well as more tentative notions, anecdotes, introspections, and descriptions of classroom practice. The relevant literature included in the top right box of Figure 4.1 is not necessarily writing specific. For example, Pascual-Leone's general cognitive theory began in that location, although many of its premises and mechanisms have been appropriated by the reference model. Because the literature does not use consistent terminology and in fact does not represent uniformly compatible philosophies and basic premises, translation into the language of the reference model allows a level of synthesis that would not otherwise be possible. Not only are parallels between positions easily obscured by differences in terminology but also critical distinctions may be overlooked when the same label is applied to different constructs. This is most obvious with global terms like cognition and meaning, but can be at least as important when much narrower notions are under consideration.

The second source for development of the reference model was our own experience and intuition, represented by the top left box in Figure 4.1. This includes introspections on our own writing processes and their development, conclusions drawn from practical experience, and all the beliefs and impressions accumulated since early childhood. Much of this knowledge is relatively inaccessible to objective scrutiny; articulation of the reference model is a useful aid in retrieving and analyzing it. Intuition reconceptualized into a formal language can be subjected to disciplined examination and compared to the notions of others included in the box labeled current models and theories, or it can play a direct role in the development of an explanatory model. The attempt to translate intuition into the language of the reference model is often frustrating, but we believe it is vital in clarifying our underlying assumptions and biases, as well as in capitalizing on this important source of insight and information.

Because the primary purpose of the reference model is provision of a language for exploring writing-related constructs, processes, and mechanisms, it is best characterized as a descriptive model. Our ultimate goal, however, is an explanatory model that allows prediction of performance and development when causal factors are specified. The box labeled developing explanatory model represents a vital intermediate step toward reaching this goal. This step is an ongoing attempt to reconcile the ideas and constructs emerging through the reference model into a coherent explication of writing processes. The fact that the general cognitive model underlying the reference model is itself a generative, constructive model makes this transition natural if not always straightforward.

As the explanatory model develops, testable hypotheses are generated—hence the box labeled controlled experiments. Research results are used first to adjust, confirm, or extend the explanatory model as developed at the time. If, however, results do not conform to research hypotheses, adjustments to the reference model itself may sometimes prove necessary. Thus, theory building consists of refinement of the explanatory model—itself derived from the reference model—until it becomes the comprehensive, empirically supported model that is our goal.

It was a somewhat arbitrary decision to restrict the testing of the explanatory model to controlled experiments. In the future we expect to expand the empirical component of the theory-building program to include quasi-experimental and clinical studies. In all cases, however, the research will be designed to investigate well-articulated hypotheses formulated in the language of the reference model and representing predictions generated by the explanatory model. We expect that more exploratory research, especially classroom observations and informal curricular interventions, will continue to play a role in hypothesis generation. The results of such informal work enter the system via "intuition and experience" so that they can be reformulated within the reference model.

Clearly, the reference model is a critical element in our research program. The next section of this chapter will describe its governing principles. The various research efforts shaping or deriving from the reference model will be discussed only insofar as they clarify or demonstrate points raised with respect to these principles.

Principles Governing Construction of the Reference Model

The design of the reference model reflects seven principles established by our research group after extensive review of the literature, articulation of goals and priorities, and examination of our own experience and intuitions. These principles represent a strong and, perhaps, unique commitment to viewing all writing-related issues from the perspective of the individual writer's processing system. The only exception is a concern with the individual *reader's* processing system when examining text-analysis procedures. This is not to say that sociological and physical issues are ignored; rather, they are viewed through the filter of our more strictly psychological perspective. The seven principles can be summarized as following:

1. To be instructionally and theoretically useful, text-analysis procedures applied to compositions of primary school children should be based on variables linked to a well-defined model of writing processes.

2. Writing is best viewed as a communicative process that involves at least two parties, the writer and the reader. Text analysis must be explicit in distinguishing between reader-based and writer-based variables. Writer-based variables are necessarily inferential (reader-based variables may or may not be) and such inferences should be derived strictly from a well-defined theoretical framework. The cognitive model should allow for such inferences and should also account for the writer's representation of the reader and the influence of that representation, if any, on the writing process.

3. Any model of the writing process used in research and teaching of primary school students should be designed to deal with processual and structural changes attributable to both maturation (e.g., increase in mental processing capacity) and experience, educational and otherwise (learning). Both the text-analysis system and the cognitive model should distinguish between variables susceptible to educational intervention and those that are impervious to external influences.

4. Contextual and task variables influence the writing process and resulting texts only insofar as those variables are perceived by the cognitive system and affect cognitive operations. Hence, the cognitive model must be comprehensive enough to incorporate such perceptions and account for their influence on subsequent processing and resulting texts.

5. Any individual differences in processing or in texts must be attributable to differences in cognitive systems or processes (barring variations in physical production capabilities). To account for such differences, should they be found, the cognitive model must incorporate factors from which individual differences arise.

6. Both the text-analysis system and the cognitive model must be designed to differentiate between qualitative/descriptive differences in texts or psychological systems and differences in quality. It must not be assumed a priori that every dimension on which texts vary represents a continuum from bad to good, nor that every difference in cognitive processes necessarily represents a difference in level of skill or stages of development.

7. A text-analysis system must allow for simultaneous consideration of a range of text features. The effect of combinations of features on readers must be considered, and the cognitive processes leading to those combinations must be accounted for by the comprehensive model.

Integrating the Text-Analysis System with the Theory of Composing

In arguing for a link between text analysis and cognitive theory, we are not arguing that the rating process must be meshed with the writing process. Rather, we want to make sure that the criteria used by raters or analysts, whether human or electronic, reflect a viable conceptualization of writing processes. We do not require that the relationship between text features and process features be simple, only that it be well defined. For example, inclusion of T-unit length as an analytic variable does not require a unitary factor of syntactic maturity in the cognitive model; it does require that the model be able to account for observed differences in T-unit length. Thus, we view the development of a text-analysis system as an integral part of developing a psychological model of writing processes.

When we say that such an integrated approach is necessary for a useful analytic system (Principle 1), we speak from the perspective of educators interested in fostering the growth of writing abilities in primary school children. Utility defined by other disciplines—literary criticism or linguistics for example—may not require such a link. Because of this difference between the needs of various disciplines, we are wary of borrowing analytic systems from other disciplines for use in education-related endeavors, although such systems sometimes fortuitously fit with cognitively based notions of writing.

Writing as a Communicative Act

Defining writing as a communicative act that involves at least two parties does place a restriction on our research because those instances of writing in which writers have no intended readers (other than themselves) are excluded from consideration. We do not mean to imply that this type of personal writing is unimportant or unworthy of study. We do feel that research on personal writing faces enormous methodological problems because researchers have no grounds for eliciting or evaluating such texts, which may often be unintelligible to second-party readers. It is difficult enough to work with transactional writing, which as Britton points out is far too often pseudotransactional (Britton, Burgess, Martin, McLeod, & Rosen, 1975). We fear that research and instruction based on pseudopersonal writing could be theoretically misleading and pedagogically counterproductive.

Although our recent research has been confined to transactional and, alas, pseudotransactional writing, a focus on writers with intended audiences does not require such a limitation. Most expressive or poetic texts are also written for readers and can be judged from a reader's perspective. We have found, however, that it is easier to begin with transactional tasks because it is easier to define criteria by which explicitly communicative texts can be evaluated. In even the most mundane transactional text, more information is conveyed than the core message represented by traditional propositional analysis, but it is at least possible to determine which propositions that core message includes. In some tasks it is also possible to list the propositions that must be included if the text is to serve the writer's communicative purpose. In other types of discourse, such as fictional stories or poems, the researcher is deprived of this easy starting place. Propositional analysis becomes more difficult and no independent target content can be specified. Regardless of genre, however, our reference model prevents us from restricting attention solely to propositional content. We always assume that a written text conveys a larger message to the reader—readers may react to mechanical aspects, such as spelling, handwriting, or even the physical appearance of the page. Style, including register, syntactic complexity, and voice may also contribute to the total message received by the reader. Further, the reader may be influenced by the presence or absence of extraneous material that might make a text redundant, engaging, cryptic, boring, or confusing.

In the long run our focus on communication will require even more than the integrated process-product model we are proposing. By the logic that requires this integration, consideration of the reader's perspective during consumption or analysis of text also requires a cognitive model of reading that is parallel to that proposed for writing. In fact, the reference model does incorporate a general model of the reading process developed by one of the authors (Tamor, 1979). This model was constructed within the framework devised by Pascual-Leone and therefore uses language compatible with that used in our writing research. Far more work, however, remains to be done before the reading model can become part of the comprehensive explanatory model listed as the goal in Figure 4.1. For the time being we have chosen to refrain from research focused explicitly on reading, in part to keep our already grandiose goal to more manageable size, and in part because a number of reading researchers are currently engaged in solving relevant problems and our own emphasis is on the writer's role in the communicative act.

The communications view of writing has two major implications for our reference model, both of which are contained in Principle 2. First, the cognitive model must provide for the writer's construction of the communicative framework within which any given text is produced. That is, the writer's construction of audience and rhetorical context must be defined. The critical point here is that the researcher's construction of the communicative context must not be confused with the writer's construction—it is the writer's perceptions that affect the writing process, not the

researcher's. For example, the researcher may feel that a writer miscon-
strued his audience, but it was still the writer's notion of his audience
that constrained his composition. Second, a model of the composing process must contain the writer's notions about his or her reader, regardless
of what the researcher believes these notions could or should have been.
(Eventually, of course, instruction may be designed to enhance the writer's skills in this area, but that is another matter.) Similarly, it is necessary to separate the reader's reactions to texts from inferences about the
writer that may be drawn from those reactions. A notion like creativity is
an inference about a writer made by a reader. The text characteristics
leading to that inference must be isolated before a notion like creativity
can be incorporated into a model of writing processes or approached systematically in instructional settings. Further, different types of readers
can be posited, each linked to different, although not necessarily orthog-
onal, analytic systems. Differentiation of reader roles will be addressed
in a later section of this chapter.

The General Cognitive Theory

Principles 3, 4, and 5 differentiate our cognitive framework from that of
most researchers working from information processing and developmental perspectives. In general, our goal is to model the overall development
of writing-related structures and processes as well as text production in
specific-task contexts at specific points in that development. Discussion of
development can be divided into considerations of learning and maturation; discussion of processing can be divided into consideration of general
factors and those factors that are context or task specific.

Developmental Concerns. A maturational factor must be posited if
changes take place in the cognitive system over time that are independent
of specific experience. To maintain the possibility of one or more such
factors, the language of the reference model must provide a means for
discussing it and differentiating it from experience-induced change. Eventually not only the nature of this mechanism but also its very existence
must be established so that its role, if any, can be specified in the comprehensive explanatory model.

Any systematic change over time that is not attributable to maturation is by definition attributable to experience, and experience in turn
plays a role only when learning has taken place. Because the goal of
education is to ensure that certain types of learning do take place, any
cognitive theory to be used by educators must account for learning as
thoroughly as possible. There are two general issues to be considered;
these are the cognitive structures to be acquired and the factors that determine their acquisition. The reference model must provide a reasonably
detailed language for representing the nature of learning within the cognitive system.

Real-time Processing Concerns. With respect to processing at any given point in development, the reference model must provide a means for specifying a number of relevant factors that include at least the following:

1. *The operation of basic motivational drives and affective states.* It is generally accepted that general affective states, not necessarily related to the task at hand, may well influence task performance. For example, individuals who are preoccupied by problems at home may not perform in their "usual" way on a wide range of tasks, including writing. The same is true for someone who is angry, depressed, and so forth. The task context itself may also give rise to affective states that influence task performance. Test anxiety is a classic example of a context-induced influence on cognitive performance. Conversely, it may be possible to devise or capitalize on settings in which affective states enhance, rather than detract from, performance on a particular task. To take into account the influence of affect on cognitive processing, it is necessary to specify not only which affective factors influence performance but also how they exert that influence.

2. *The operation of expectancies concerning future events contingent on the outcome of the task at hand.* This notion is related to that raised in (1), but is more specifically related to motivation for performing any particular writing task. Although a task is intrinsically motivating at times, at least some motivation derives from expected results of engaging in or completing the task in most cases. In communicative writing tasks, writers may desire some specific actions or reactions from their readers that will produce some benefit for the writers themselves. In addition, young writers may want to please teachers or parents, be considered smart, or be able to do some other task for which the writing task is a prerequisite. Less positively, the students may wish to avoid incurring high expectations from teachers or parents or to avoid outperforming a friend or sibling. In many academic settings, a primary motivation for performance is avoidance of punishment for nonperformance. It is possible that these various motivations will result in significantly different performances even when other factors are held constant.

3. *The way in which task-relevant information is stored in memory.* Any cognitive task will draw on a wide variety of types of prior knowledge. To discuss the interaction of existing knowledge structures and the reorganization of structures needed to perform a particular task, some notion of the structure and function of the memory/knowledge system is necessary.

4. *The goals and strategies brought to bear on the task.* The goal of

performance in any task is set by the individual performing that task. That goal may or may not be congruent to the goal that the observer (researcher or teacher) believes that the individual has or should have. Once a goal has been set, some strategy or set of strategies is brought to bear to accomplish that goal. Definitions of goals and strategies is a joint function of motivation and affective state, prior experience, and perceived characteristics of particular tasks.

5. *The information processing constraints within the cognitive system.* Task performance may not be determined solely by the individual's knowledge structures and strategies. Additional constraints may be placed on performance by limits on the amount of information that can be processed at any moment. Such a limit might be viewed in terms of the size of working memory, attention span, mental processing capacity, and so forth.

6. *The linguistic knowledge and verbalization procedures in the cognitive system.* Strictly speaking, this issue was already covered in (3) because linguistic knowledge is a subset of all task-relevant knowledge. It is listed separately because there are times when it is useful to try to distinguish between linguistic and nonlinguistic knowledge even though the line between them is often blurred. By linguistic knowledge, we intend much more than some internal representation of phonology/graphology, syntax, and semantics. Sociolinguistic and other forms of language knowledge brought to bear in communication tasks are also included.

Task Contexts. Because we want our cognitive model to explicate performance on particular writing tasks in particular contexts, we need a system for describing tasks and contexts that is consistent with the cognitive model. This system must account for at least the following four dimensions along which written communication tasks may vary.

1. *General task setting: environmental parameters.* Such issues as the time and location where writing takes place; the physical surroundings; the identity of, the role played by, the director of activity (parent, teacher, researcher, peer) if any; and the non-task-relevant activities of others who are physically present are included in this category. The influence of such task characteristics may be on general affective state, goal setting, prior knowledge accessed, or amount of attention or processing capacity devoted to the writing task.

2. *General task definition: audience and purpose.* This dimension is concerned with the writer's general conception of the nature of the task at hand, both the ultimate text to be produced and the processes involved in creating that product. Answers to three

general questions guide the writer even though they may never be asked directly: What should the text accomplish? What should the text be like? How should I write the text? In many writing tasks, students are aware that their performance will be scrutinized and judged by readers who place themselves outside the communicative transaction. In addition to rhetorical specifications, the student's understanding of why this judgment is made, the criteria to be used, and the effect of resulting judgments on future events may all influence performance, especially by influencing general affective state and choice of specific goals and strategies.

3. *Definition of the particular task at hand: information to be conveyed and desired reader reaction.* The task that the observer believes is the one the student is attempting may or may not bear close resemblance to the task the student has actually set for himself or herself. To draw valid inferences from performance, it is vital that an observer be reasonably certain about the writer's actual intentions.

4. *Characteristics of the task itself.* Very specific qualities of tasks, even the size of the pencil or the kind of paper provided, may well have a significant effect on characteristics of the text eventually produced. Similarly, qualities of stimulus materials (including prewriting activities) may also have an impact on writing performance.

Integration of Task and Process Concerns. Concern with contextual and task characteristics expressed in Principle 4 is addressed by several of the process- and task-structure issues just listed. Task analysis is required to determine the task features that may influence the cognitive processes taking place during production of a written text. For example, in a writing task involving a report on a past event, the writing process is shaped by more than specifically writing-related structures and strategies. Memory of the event and strategies for retrieving information from memory play an important role. In fact, the composing strategies may well influence the memory-search strategies, and the content retrieved from memory may affect selection of particular composing strategies. A model that attempts to explain specific instances of writing performance will need a language that allows conceptual separation of numerous factors without artificially limiting the interactive potential of the hypothesized cognitive system.

In more technical language, the reference model must differentiate functional from structural distinctions. The same cognitive structure may function differently in different tasks without losing its own identity. Its structural definition will therefore remain constant, whereas its functional definition may change. In fact, the same structure might serve several different functions simultaneously. Conversely, the same function may be served by a set of structurally different cognitive units. Lack of clarity in the reference model may lead on one hand to the positing of redundant and unnecessary structures (including strategies) or on the other hand to obscuring critical distinctions. A confusion with obvious educational ramifications is failure to distinguish between strategic or operative knowledge and the content or figurative knowledge on which the strategies operate (Pascual-Leone, 1976a). Apparent differences in strategy may in fact be attributable to differences in content and vice versa.

Individual Differences

If task and context were to be held absolutely constant, could the researcher expect to elicit identical texts from two or more writers? Even though the question is hopelessly hypothetical, chances are no one would answer yes. However, if the answer is no, our goal of modeling specific performances by specific writers cannot be achieved without introducing the notion of individual differences (Principle 5). Such differences might be attributed to maturation or experience, both of which are taken into account in Principle 3. But we raise the possibility of a third source of individual differences when we ask the absurd hypothetical question, "If task, context, maturation, and experience were held constant, could a researcher expect to elicit identical texts from two or more writers?"[2] If the possibility of a no answer is to be entertained, then the third source of individual differences is global differences in cognitive systems, such as cognitive styles. The notion of such a source is controversial, but we would like our reference model to allow for the possibility that it exists.

When we have discussed our instruction writing task with other psychologists, they have frequently asked whether cognitive style—particularly, field dependence/independence—has a role in determining performance. In this task, writers are asked to provide instructions that would allow a reader to replicate a geometric design. It is possible, especially in the absence of task-specific training, that field independents would take a unit-by-unit analytic tack, whereas field dependents would produce a more holistic description. Either of these approaches could accomplish the communicative purposes of the task, but the content and organization of the texts might be quite different. So far, we have found almost no indication of holistic-analytic variation in the texts elicited, but this is by no means sufficient grounds for discarding the entire notion of systemic individual-difference factors. Having a reference model equipped to deal with the notion of such factors is necessary if the possibility of such influences is to be systematically examined.

Text Analysis

When we discussed the communications framework for studying writing, we pointed out the need to differentiate the role of the reader from the role of the writer. Principles 6 and 7 carry this point further and raise additional concerns. Both principles focus primarily on the text-analysis system, although they have significant ramifications for the general cognitive model as well.

It should be clear by now that we are not willing to make an a priori assumption that all mature writers are similar with respect to cognitive systems nor that there is a single continuum along which writing-related cognitive structures evolve. Principle 6 is designed to keep the text-analysis system similarly open to the possibility of alternative methods for achieving a single goal. Texts that vary widely in form or content may nonetheless accomplish very similar purposes, and quite different types of flaws may leave a reader with similar impressions of the writer's skill and knowledge. On the other hand, the notions of development and progress imply a concept of improvement, of moving from a less desirable state to a more desirable state. The general communications framework provides a means for defining desirability; that is, processes and texts can be compared with respect to the extent to which they achieve communicative goals. Within this framework, Principle 6 helps to maintain both positions by differentiating descriptive variables or factors from evaluative ones. Evaluative variables represent continua for which one pole is consistently more desirable than the other. As such, evaluative variables are at least ordinal scales. Descriptive variables, however, are nominal scales along which no context-free judgments of relative superiority can be made. Any construct introduced into the reference model, whether cognitive or textual, must be classified as falling into one of these two categories.

This distinction is not an easy one to make and indeed may be the most persistent conceptual problem plaguing text analysis at this time. It is most difficult to discriminate between features useful in simple categorizations of texts and features that can be used to rank order texts in terms of absolute quality. We do not believe that progress or development is necessarily limited to increases in quality, but we do believe that this distinction must be kept explicit.[3] For example, we are most suspicious of assumptions that long T-units are always better than short, that high vocabulary diversity is always better than low, or that adherence to conventional discourse structures (e.g., story grammars) is always better than deviation from them. Yet, all of these features have been used—sometimes by us—to infer differences in writing abilities among students. At the same time, we are unwilling to confine ourselves to those features that more clearly represent ordinal scales, such as spelling correctness, appropriateness of punctuation, and adherence to rules of sentential syntax. They simply do not reflect the many text characteristics critical to our communication-based perspective.

Principle 7 represents our commitment that the reference model be sensitive to interactions at every level of text analysis, from the most fine-grained to the most global. Even when considering clearly evaluative scales, the potential significance of interrelationships between textual variables is evident. An inverse relationship between spelling correctness and vocabulary diversity or between T-unit length and adequacy of punctuation is likely at some stages of development. Students may temporarily sacrifice spelling accuracy in an effort to expand their writing vocabularies, especially when encouraged to do so by some instructional methods. The complexities of intrasentence punctuation probably cannot be learned by writers until they have produced in writing the more complex sentences that require colons, semicolons, and even commas. Hence, one would not be surprised by periods during which T-unit length increased and punctuation correctness decreased.

A different sort of network of interrelationships may connect ratings of organization to a wide variety of more elemental text features. What exactly does it take to have a text deemed well-organized? How do inadequacies at any level detract from such a judgment? Even more complex are the factors determining judgments regarding qualities like persuasiveness, creativity, and entertainment value. In some cases these networks may prove to be content or task dependent, whereas in others they may be more universal.

The seven principles that govern the reference model are clearly difficult to satisfy. Consistent with our pragmatic approach, we have begun development of the tentative explanatory model before all the difficulties in the reference model have been resolved. However, eventual resolution will be a part of achievement of our ultimate goal; at that time, the reference model and tentative explanatory model will by subsumed by the comprehensive theory.

The Explanatory Model

Because we are interested in explaining and influencing the performance of individual students on writing tasks, the explanatory model must have the capacity to account for specific performances of specific individuals and at the same time allow for generalizations across individuals or tasks that have characteristics in common. Examples of across-subject generalizations might include investigations of age differences, sex differences, or curricular influences. Across-task generalizations, on the other hand, would involve examination of the performance of the same individuals on a number of tasks that have characteristics in common. Similarities might include genre, information content, audience, and purpose.

The theory of constructive operators developed by Pascual-Leone is designed to accomplish this for any cognitive performance, as well as account for developmental changes over time (Pascual-Leone, 1969). It is a model of the metasubject—the individual subject's "psychological organism, i.e., the 'silent organization' (cf. Scheerer, 1954) or his psychological machinery." It is intended to permit the researcher "to infer the metasubjective description of any environment or task, and the metasubjective process underlying the behavior which the subject produces in that task or environment" (Pascual-Leone, 1976a, pp. 111–112). Because this goal is a concise restatement of our own goals with respect to writing, the theory of constructive operators is an ideal foundation for our explanatory model of writing processes. Writing research that uses aspects of the theory has also been conducted by Scardamalia and her colleagues (e.g., 1977). Because the theory is too complex to elaborate in this chapter, we refer interested readers to numerous articles written by Pascual-Leone and his colleagues (e.g., Case, 1972, 1974a, 1974b; Pascual-Leone, 1969, 1976a, 1976b, Pascual-Leone et al., 1978).

For writing research, the linking of task, cognitive system, and performance is accomplished in part by the text-analysis system. Other indices of performance include think-aloud protocols (e.g., Flower & Hayes, 1980), records of the physical act of writing (e.g., Matsuhashi, 1982), and observations of students engaged in writing-related activities (e.g., Florio & Clark, 1980). Our emphasis on the communicative aspects of writing, however, focuses our attention on the communicative medium— the text itself. Although we do not discount the utility of other sources of performance data, texts have received our primary attention. (We have so far used at least two supplementary sources of data: observations and retrospective interviews.) Simply put, the text-analysis system is an integral part of the explanatory model because it is the production of text that we are seeking to explain.

Finally, Pascual-Leone (1976a) stated as one of his goals, "metasubjective description of any task or environment," committing himself to integration of a task-analysis system with the cognitive model. Both the intellectual demands of tasks and their context or environment must be described in terms that match the language of the cognitive model. For example, his task-analytic procedures include determining the dimensionality of each task, the minimum processing demand of the task at its most complex point. This task descriptor can then be matched directly with one of the constructive operators, mental power (Pascual-Leone, 1977). In tasks studied by Pascual-Leone, performance is analyzed simply, usually by rating each problem solution as a pass or a fail or by classifying solutions into a small set of independent categories. For writing, analysis of performance is more complicated, so that matching task analysis to performance analysis, as well as to the cognitive model, becomes a significant problem. Hence, our explanatory model includes three components: the task-analysis and text-analysis systems that constrain and are constrained by the cognitive model.

Applications to Research Problems

Virtually any writing-related issue could be approached within the conceptual framework we have outlined, although it might not suit a particular researcher's inclinations or purposes to do so. If, for example, study of classroom writing contexts were the major goal, the requirement that all contextual or environmental factors be translated into individual psychological terms might seem unnatural to investigators trained in such disciplines as sociology or anthropology. We argue, however, that external factors do not affect cognitive processes and their resultant performances directly. An external factor must be perceived by the cognitive system and will influence performance only insofar as that perception has consequences for cognitive processing. In other words, the cognitive system filters external stimuli, and only information passing through the filter actually influences the writing process. Study of environments, both social and physical, can be (and is) conducted without reference to such a filter, but eventually the filter must be taken into account if the researcher wishes to explain and predict the performances of individual writers performing specified tasks within specified contexts.

The applicability of the pragmatic framework is probably clearer for projects concerned directly with the analysis of cognitive processes or text analysis. Just as we argue that contextual considerations studied by ethnographers, sociolinguists, and others cannot be kept forever separate from cognitive considerations, we also argue that cognitive processes always take place within a context that impinges on those processes and cannot be ignored indefinitely. Texts, of course, reflect variations in both cognitive systems and task contexts. Even studies of the text-analysis process, such as those conducted by Freedman (1980), could be integrated into the comprehensive model, although further explication of the reading process would be necessary. In fact, such an integration would push the model to provide a broader and more realistic account of reading than is typical of most reading-specific models now under development.

The pragmatic approach to theory formulation does not dictate any specific line of research to its users. Any research question can serve as a starting point; the approach then guides the research program. Some tangents are made more salient than others, and the framework helps generate successive generations of empirical and theoretical undertakings. In the next section of this chapter we will discuss the goals and methods of the first generation of our own research program, the Ypsilanti Writing Research Project (YWRP). We will attempt to clarify its rationale and procedures with respect to both data collection and analysis, but we will not devote much attention to our findings because these have been, or will be, reported elsewhere.

THE YPSILANTI WRITING RESEARCH PROJECT (YWRP)

The YWRP initially approached the building of a psychological model of writing from an assessment perspective. This reflected both the research team's prior involvement in language-assessment work and a desire to influence the current intensive activity in the development and improvement of tests of writing abilities for students at all levels. The entire assessment enterprise seemed to us somewhat questionable (Bond & Tamor, 1979), and one goal of the study was either to develop and validate measures of writing abilities for elementary school students that could be used in large-scale evaluations (achievement or competency tests) or to demonstrate that such tests are a practical and theoretical impossibility. We intended to develop best-effort measures and then to study their properties in considerable depth. A second goal was documentation of the tasks we developed for use in research, regardless of our conclusions with respect to their use in large-scale assessment programs. This would allow teachers and researchers to have a sounder foundation for, and greater confidence in, the inferences they drew from student writing performances. Finally, it was hoped that the measurement procedures for both text elicitation and text analysis could be extended for use in instructional settings. A major emphasis was development of a text-analysis system that could be selectively used by teachers in responding to student writing and planning further instructional activities. All of these practical goals were inextricably bound to the theoretical goals laid out in the preceding section of this chapter. Task development and data analysis were directed by the reference model, and the ultimate goal of the comprehensive theory was viewed as the key to a truly consistent and integrated approach to curriculum development and writing assessment.

The YWRP Tasks

For the reasons mentioned earlier, we decided to restrict our first efforts to transactional writing. We felt that writing of fictional stories and other forms of expressive or poetic writing was problematic in standardized settings. In such writing, too much depends on getting a good idea, and it is impossible to know when one is reading a genuinely original, composed-on-the-spot story and when one has instead a retelling or variation on a favorite theme. Further, the complexity of stories can vary widely (as can many other features) without those variations representing any differences in quality, effort, or skill. Under such circumstances, comparative evaluations of text quality become extraordinarily difficult. Moreover, the inferences that can reasonably be made about the cognitive structures and processing strategies of the writer are quite limited. Although we were well aware that story writing is the foundation of many elementary school writing curricula, we believed that more might be learned in the short run from the study of other, more pragmatic, genres.

Transactional writing is writing with the primary purpose of transferring information between reader and writer. It may be intended to record, report, inform, persuade, instruct, inquire, or bring about any other sort of informational exchange. In natural contexts, the motivation for transactional writing is usually elicitiation of specifiable response from a particular reader, although on occasion other motives prompt the writing act (e.g., desire to document an event to protect one's legal rights). Too often, in school contexts, such writing falls into Britton's pseudoinformative or pseudoconative categories (Britton et al., 1975) because the teacher-reader is not an appropriate audience for the text and is unlikely to respond to the student's communicative intent. This need not be the case, however; in fact, the problem is no less serious for expressive writing in school settings.[4]

The advantages of transactional writing for research and evaluation are manifold, and many apply to instruction as well. Often, the information to be included in the text and the desired reader reaction can be specified a priori, greatly facilitating text analysis. One can check to see whether the necessary information has been provided, whether it is clear, whether extraneous information enhances or detracts from the effectiveness of the text, and so forth. In addition, task specifications can decrease the need to get a good idea, and the audience and communicative context can be defined quite concretely. Task demands can be controlled so that the intellectual demands and complexity of elicited texts are unlikely to exceed defined limits. Thus, many aspects of the text can be treated evaluatively when their counterparts in expressive writing could only be treated descriptively.

With respect to ecological validity, transactional writing compares favorably with other types. Few adults engage in writing stories or poetry, but nearly all those who ever write engage in some transactional writing. Odell and Goswami's work (1980) suggests the pervasiveness of transactional writing in many occupations. Adults also write transactional letters and informal messages to one another and to children. They are consumers of transactional texts when they read mail, newspapers, instruction manuals, information signs, and so forth. In secondary schools as well, students engage primarily in transactional and pseudotransactional writing. Only in elementary schools does expressive writing supersede transactional—and even that is not universally true. In interviews with the students in our YWRP sample, we found transactional writing to be a familiar experience for fourth and sixth graders. The students reported letter writing, informal message writing, and even instruction writing. Most frequently mentioned was persuasive writing, with relatives being the usual audience (requests for permission, gifts, and so forth). The students were also universally experienced readers of transactional texts, especially instructions.

In our study we investigated two forms of transactional writing that were quite different from one another and yet familiar to upper elementary school students: instruction and persuasion. Both forms were included in the battery used by the National Assessment of Educational Progress (NAEP); persuasive writing is also widely used in other tests and instructional settings. The choice of two different forms of transactional writing was intended to allow for investigation of the generalizability of inferences across types of writing. That is, to what extent are writing processes general enough that text characteristics in one task will correlate with text characteristics in the other task? The choice of instruction and persuasion, in particular, was guided by our interest in performance related to variations in the information processing demands of tasks: Persuasive writing requires the writer to generate and logically structure an argument from dissimilarly organized information in long-term memory, whereas the content and structure of instructions is generally (and specifically in the case of our task) determined by the task and represented episodically in memory.

The Instruction Writing Task

In our own earlier work, we had used a written-reporting task. Students are given a kit of materials (construction paper, pipe cleaners, tape, etc.) and are asked first to make something, then to write a report that would tell someone else with the same kit how to duplicate their constructions (Kittel, Smith, & Tamor, 1978). The task proved to be a useful evaluation tool for elementary school children and had considerable appeal among teachers and administrators, but it also had serious shortcomings.

An obvious problem is that the text analyst had no idea what the student had actually made, making it impossible to rate the texts for communicative success. Instead, texts could only be analyzed according to objective criteria, such as spelling, handwriting, fluency, T-unit length, vocabulary, and organization or on the basis of followability. The analyst could judge whether the instructions could be followed at all—whether materials and actions were clearly specified and steps logically sequenced —but could not detect all mistakes and gaps in the text. This same problem held for the instructional tasks included in the NAEP battery. For example, in a task asking the student to describe how to make or do something (i.e., anything), the reader (unless familiar with the specific process/ product about which the student has written) cannot determine whether the instructions are sufficient and accurate, only whether they are potentially followable.

A second problem is that some students set far more difficult tasks for themselves than others, depending on the complexity of their constructions. Students who merely clipped several pieces of paper together to make a book needed to explain far less than the students who made a model solar generator or fashioned a family of monsters using all available materials. Virtually every text variable could reasonably be expected to reflect differences in complexity, seriously confounding judgments about writing abilities.[5] Even the most articulate adult would have trouble explaining complicated cutouts and twisted pipe-cleaner sculptures without resorting to sketches or gestures.

The Instruction Writing Task (IWT) Design-Making Kit. We decided to revise the written reporting task to alleviate these problems without sacrificing the involvement we believed we had gained by having students engage in the activity about which they were asked to write. The IWT therefore utilized a standard materials kit and required students to replicate a standard geometric design. The kit consisted of a clear acrylic board and a black acylic board that were hinged along their short side to form a book. The clear board served as storage space for sixteen vinyl shapes, five of which were needed to replicate each standard design (Figure 4.2). The black board was marked with a grid of colored lines and served as background for the design. The vinyl shapes adhered easily to the acrylic boards. The boards could be laid flat while students were replicating the standard design or could be stood on edge during writing time to provide a clear view of the design and a partial partition around each student's work area. The clear board, which still had nine shapes stuck to it, provided an illusion of privacy while allowing the teacher or task administrator to monitor each student's activities without standing over anyone's shoulder. This allowed the adults present to take an unobtrusive role, an important aspect of the task because prior experience had led us to believe that hovering over a writer can have a significant influence on the quality and quantity of what is written.

The kits and standard designs were carefully devised to present a defined array of communications problems, none of which were unsuited to purely verbal solutions. Hence, problems parallel to those posed by pipe-cleaner sculptures were avoided but the task remained challenging. To guard against variation in performance owing to geometric vocabulary deficiencies, the clear storage board carried labels for square, rectangle, triangle, and circle, and the vinyl shapes were arrayed appropriately above them. This avoided problems encountered during pilot testing when some students confused the terms or were unfamiliar with them. The word box, for example, introduced great ambiguity when students used it to refer to a square, a rectangle, or a "quadrant," sometimes all within one or two sentences. No other technical vocabulary was necessary because the grid lines could be specified by their colors, but a few students did use words such as horizontal, vertical, and quadrant.

Our early fears that the IWT would seem too childish for some of the students were not borne out. Occasionally, distribution of the kits would be greeted by jeers of "Yuck, Sesame Street!" But such comments subsided as students became involved in their work. The only drawback of using materials with such high-interest value was that some students may have hurried their writing so that they would have time to create their own designs with the kits. In informal classroom work, we have encouraged students to work from original designs, a fruitful instructional application discussed by Tamor, Bond, & Matz (1980).

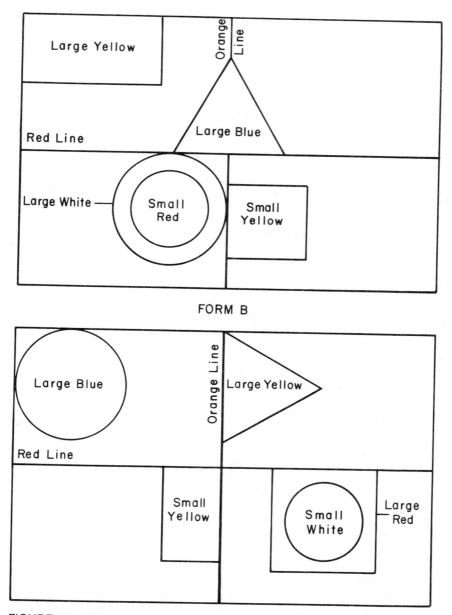

FIGURE 4.2   The Instruction Writing Task Target Designs.

Alternate Forms. Because we wanted to administer the IWT to some students more than once, alternate forms were used to avoid excessive boredom and practice effects. Figure 4.2 shows the two designs used, each involving five shapes and requiring thirty-one units of information to be provided to enable a reader to replicate the design reliably. In spite of our efforts to equate the designs along various dimensions, some text variables appeared to show small form effects. Preliminary analyses suggest two causes. First, the vast majority of students began their instructions with the shape in the upper left quadrant, and placement of the circle in Form B is easier to describe than placement of the rectangle in Form A. Instructions for placing the rectangle required more information and seemed to elicit longer T-units, a difference that persisted throughout the texts even though the shapes in both designs varied in difficulty or description. The second problem was that placement of the triangle in Form A seemed more difficult to describe than any other, even though other shapes required as many propositions for an adequate instruction. Because our data-collection design counterbalanced forms, these minor differences did not interfere significantly with our research. They did, however, indicate the difficulty of generating truly equivalent tasks and also raised further research questions.

Task Administration. The IWT had two distinct phases, one for design making and one for instruction writing. During the design-making phase, a board containing one of the two standard forms was displayed so that all students could see it clearly. The task administrator checked each student's design to make sure it was an exact copy. If not, deviations were pointed out with gestures and vague comments like, "Hmm, this isn't quite the same here." Words and syntactic constructions that could be used in the written instructions were avoided. The design-making phase generally took no more than 5 minutes.

The design-making phase served a number of critical functions in the IWT. First, many educators believe that hands-on constructive activity is a powerful motivator for young students and perhaps for older ones as well. It serves to focus attention and to generate a sense of commitment to the task. This belief should eventually be subjected to empirical test, but the other reasons for the design-making phase compelled us to keep it as a constant in our initial project. One of these reasons was that the act of exactly duplicating the design required each student to notice all the critical information he or she would have to convey, although perhaps not in a systematic, analytic, or conscious way. At some level, however, all writers knew, for example, that the large blue circle in the upper left quadrant just touched the top and side of the design board (Figure 4.2, Form A). A related motive was the hope that the act of duplication would help writers to appreciate the informational demands of the writing task. Although no one had serious difficulty in making his or her copy, it did require concentration and attention to detail. We hoped that this would demonstrate that far more was required than simple commands like, "put the red square on the board."

During the writing phase, each student worked independently and silently. The task administrator provided no assistance and did not read any of the work in progress. Whenever possible, task administrators tried to spend the time writing themselves while keeping an eye on the students. Students who seemed stymied by a spelling problem were not helped but advised to indicate their uncertainty—"so we'll know you weren't sure"—and to continue writing. Students were told to read their papers over when finished to make sure they were satisfied, but they were not further pushed to revise.[6,7]

The Persuasive Writing Task (PWT)

Instruction writing is a task that nearly everyone undertakes from time to time outside of school. Giving oral instructions over the telephone also shares many characteristics with our IWT, especially as the use of diagrams or gestures is not possible. Persuasive writing is equally a real-life skill and one with which students generally have had some experience. In oral language, persuasion is one of the primary themes of parent/child conversations, and it is also important in dealing with peers, teachers, and other adults. Written attempts to persuade may often be quite subtle, for example, when a child is angling for a particular Christmas present from Grandma—but they are not necessarily infrequent. It is not surprising that several states include persuasive writing in their competency test batteries, as did the NAEP.

Included in the NAEP battery was a task in which students were asked to write a letter to their school principal persuading him to make one change that would improve their school. Fictitious names for the principal, school, and student were provided, presumably to imply anonymity. Our pilot tests and task analysis suggested a number of difficulties inherent in this task that we attempted to overcome in designing our PWT.

We found that students' reactions to the assignment were strongly influenced by the state of their own schools, the style of the principal, and their relationships with him or her. Some students could think of nothing to change, a serious handicap in this task, whereas others felt that trying to persuade their principal would be futile. Confusion was introduced by the instruction to write to "your principal," followed by the provision of fictitious names. In fact, students were being asked to construct a fictitious principal and perhaps fictitious schools and personae as well. Our analysis suggests that all of this construction increased the intellectual processing demand of the task as well as making it singularly *pseudo*transactional and anomalous.

The YWRP Persuasive Writing Task (PWT). In designing our PWT, we wanted to provide a genuine audience of equal familiarity to all students and to overcome the problem of generating a topic. The English Composition Board at the University of Michigan had recently reported that television seemed to be a universally motivating topic for college freshmen, and pilot tests indicated it was equally suitable for elementary school students. We had some difficulty selecting an appropriate audience for persuasive letters about television but finally settled on the presidents of the three major networks. They are a rather remote audience, but we found the students to be quite comfortable with them. Students seemed to have a clearer notion of company presidents than of local station managers so that local individuals were psychologically more remote than presidents.

Efforts to develop topics involving genuinely familiar audiences uniformly ended in failure. Either we encountered the same problem described for the NAEP task—students varied in their attitudes toward, and knowledge of, any generally familiar audience—or we, the researchers, lacked sufficient knowledge of the audience to evaluate student responses. Few if any individuals were familiar to all students, and we wanted all students to write for the same audience. The network presidents were a compromise, but the best compromise we could come up with.

To overcome the problems that some students have generating topics and to stress the need to focus on recommending a single change, we provided students with a list of five potential topics and asked them to select one. All topics were generated by students of the same age range during group discussions. The issue of violence on television was excluded because we feared that students selecting it might reproduce arguments they had heard elsewhere rather than generate their own. If none of the five topics appealed, however, students were free to write on a topic of their own, and a few did write about violence. The suggested topics are listed in Table 4.1.

Table 4.1 Persuasive Writing Task Suggested Topics

Form A
1. All commercials should show products the way they really are and say only things that are really true.
2. Scheduled TV programs should not be interrupted by news specials.
3. There should be better programming for young people in the afternoon after school.
4. The networks should not have the same types of programs on at the same times.
5. There should be more sports programs made for young people.

Form B
1. TV commercials should be scheduled so that they do not disrupt the programs.
2. There should be more television shows about the subjects young people study in school which make those subjects more interesting.
3. Shows that young people like to watch should not be put on too late at night.
4. There should be more game shows made for children and young people.
5. There should be shows that teach people to do things they can do at home.

Alternate Forms. The only difference between forms of the PWT was the list of suggested topics. The original list of ten topics was sorted so that each form would include a similar range of ideas and would include some of the topics most frequently selected during pilot testing. Students were asked to write about a different change at the second task administration, and almost all of them did so.

Task Administration. The PWT was a more traditional writing task and lacked a phase comparable to the IWT's design-making phase. Students were simply asked to write their letters. Again, the task administrators offered no assistance and were as unobtrusive as possible. Exchange of information about programs and schedules among students usually did precede the writing time; we found that at least a few students in every group had memorized virtually the entire weekly television schedule so that provision of documents such as *TV Guide* could be avoided.

Task Contextualization

The differences between the IWTs and PWTs include aspects listed in the task-context section of the reference model—the audience and purpose are quite different, as are the more specific task definitions. Other contextual issues, especially the environmental parameters, could be held relatively constant. It is also possible to hold the general task—instruction or persuasion—constant while varying contextual features. To explore the influence of such variations on written texts, each of our tasks was embedded in two contexts. Both contexts were sufficiently standardized to allow for traditional assessment and research applications, but Level 1 was far more traditional than Level 2.

In the first level of contextualization, the tasks were presented with minimal explanation and discussion. Directions were given and writers were asked to rephrase them to ensure comprehension. Once the task administrator was assured that the directions had been understood, the writing phase began. In the second level, however, a prewriting discussion was introduced to develop more thorough task definitions as well as to increase involvement.

For the IWT, the discussion revolved around oral formulation of instructions for a second design presented by the task administrator, who followed the volunteered instructions as literally as possible and who, whenever there was an ambiguity, made a move leading to a mismatch with the target design. If the instruction was so vague that it suggested no clear action at all, then the task administrator merely expressed confusion. The discussion continued until fully adequate instructions had been generated for the target design. In the PWT, discussion was less structured and focused on what it takes to persuade an authority figure to make a change. The NAEP task of persuading a principal to make a change in the school was used in the prewriting discussion.

Other features also differentiated the two levels of contextualization.

In Level 1 of both tasks, test booklets were used and the tasks were presented as pseudotransactional because writers were told that the research team and their teachers wanted to see how well they could write. In Level 2, efforts were made to decrease the pseudotransactional features of the tasks. For the IWT, writers were given "technical" writing paper and were told that the research team would try to follow the instructions. They were also promised that papers would be returned so that instructions could be exchanged in the classroom. Stationery was provided in the Level 2 of the PWT, and students were told they would be helped to mail their letters. All of these promises were kept; in fact, *all* papers (Levels 1 and 2) were returned with as much class discussion as the teachers wished. All writers had an opportunity to mail their persuasive letters, regardless of contextualization level.

Because the two levels vary in several ways, observed differences in performance across levels are difficult to explain. We believe that the discussion is more powerful in the IWT than in the PWT; perhaps the differences in audience definition and writing paper are more salient in the PWT. Eventually it may prove useful to pick apart the various factors, but in this first project we were more concerned with discovering whether a traditional, testlike task would elicit texts significantly different from our best-effort versions. If differences were found—and they were— we wanted to see which text variables fluctuated and which remained constant.

Text Analysis

A major focus of the YWRP was exploration of the properties of text-analysis systems. Hence, the system used included a measure of virtually every characteristic we could think of or had read about. If the tasks prove useful for future research—and in fact they are currently being used in quite different projects—a much smaller analysis system will be used, depending on the documented properties of the text variables and the specific purposes of any given project.

To be consistent with our focus on writing as a communicative act, we have classified our full set of text variables according to the role played by the reader, human or mechanical, in assigning scores for each scale. Four general classifications are used, ranging from the mechanical reader, who need not comprehend the text to score it, to the omniscient reader, who not only reads with maximal comprehension but also knows what the writer intended to say. In between are the copy editor, who reads at a superficial level, and the interested reader, who represents the most realistic reader, one who seeks to receive the message being transmitted. All text variables are thus defined from the reader's perspective. Inferences about the writer drawn from text scores represent a second level of analysis, one based on the reference model or, even better, on empirically validated constructs in the explanatory model.

Mechanical Reader Variables. These variables can be scored by a computer that does not actually read the text, although sometimes human intervention is required to prepare the text for the computer. In the YWRP, the text-entry specialist prepared the text for computer processing in several ways, some of which could have been accomplished independently by a more sophisticated computer program. This specialist marked all misspellings, including those cases in which two or more words were run together with no separating spaces. Thus, the computer could then count the number of words and number of misspellings. From this, error rates could be computed as well as vocabulary diversity if desired. The specialist also divided the text into minimal utterances (MUs), a variation on Hunt's T-units that is designed to handle texts written by young writers (Hunt, 1977). This allowed calculation of average MU length, proportion of punctuated MUs, and proportion of MUs beginning with such connectives as then, so, or and. Actually, devision of texts into MUs (or T-units) does require reading with comprehension, as does full analysis of spelling errors, but once the text is prepared, no comprehension is required for scoring mechanical-reader variables.[8]

While entering the texts into the computer, the text-entry specialist also rated the text on scales concerning legibility and decodability. Some of these were also considered mechanical-reader variables, but others involved comprehensibility and fell into the next category.

Copy-editor Variables. Copy-editor variables are in fact the aspects of text generally attended to by copy editors (with the exception of spelling, which was classified as a mechanical-reader variable). They consisted of sentence-level syntax, including punctuation and capitalization, as well as adherence to the grammatical conventions of edited American English. Our scoring system focused on the following elements in a sentence: final punctuation, commas, and apostrophes; the grammatical features of nominal and pronominal reference; and semantic constraints on syntax. General grammaticality was also coded, and in a separate category instances of deviations from edited American English which are documented features of the spoken language of writers are recorded. These characteristics of usage were deliberately separated from more universal rules of English; they could of course be recombined for some purposes. Students in our sample represented three major American linguistic groups: mainstream colloquial English, urban black English, and Appalachian English. Because the three dialects coexist in the same community and share many features, texts were not sorted according to the writer's linguistic group membership. The usage features we recorded were predominantly variations in the verb system, subject-verb agreement, and means for marking possessives. Text analysts were provided with a very thorough description of the dialects in question, were trained in identifying usage errors, and had considerable prior experience with at least two of the three dialects.

Interested-Reader Variables. Readers who want to understand what the writer has to say may be impeded by problems recorded by mechanical readers and copy editors, but their primary interest lies elsewhere. For the interested reader, the goal is comprehension, and interested-reader variables record factors enhancing or detracting from comprehension. These include cohesion, organization (or text grammar), style, propositional context, and so forth. Although the first two sets of variables can be applied to any sort of text, task-specific scales are often necessary for interested-reader (and omniscient-reader) variables. For the IWT, many variables deal with the quality or followability of the instructions. In the PWT, several scales addressed the quality of the argument put forth: definition of the change requested, supporting reasons, anticipation of counterarguments, and the like. Even when a variable name seems equally applicable to both genres, logic, for example, it often must be operationalized differently.

Most of the scales used in the mechanical and copy-editor categories are based on quantifiable text features, either counts and proportions or summaries of counts and proportions. Some interested-reader variables can also be defined this way, but many cannot. A number of scales are what Cooper (1977) calls analytic and others are very close to Lloyd-Jones's (1977) primary traits. However, the method for measuring a variable is secondary to the factor it measures and the reader perspective represented by that factor.

Omniscient-Reader Variables. Particularly, but not solely, in school settings, readers may know—or believe they know—what the writer is trying to say. Often readers construct from what *was* said a notion of what the writer *must* have meant to say. Teachers and parents do this frequently and then assess the quality of the text by comparing it to the reader-constructed goal. This type of reading we have strenuously tried to avoid and does *not* represent our omniscient-reader perspective.

To "know" what the writer meant to say, the reader must have independent information apart from the text itself. Because we had no such information for the PWT, no omniscient-reader variables were measured for the persuasive letters. In scoring the IWT, however, the text analysts had before them the target designs and the full design-making kits. Although they could not know all of the writers' goals and intentions, they did know the core propositional content that had to be conveyed for the text to accomplish its stated purpose. The omniscient-reader variables (efficacy scales) matched the required content to the actual content of each instructional text. We had originally hoped to measure efficiency as well, but quickly discovered that efficiency is a slippery notion. Redundancy and the provision of information that could be presupposed sometimes enhance communication and sometimes detract from it. A simple measure of efficiency was obtained by comparing efficacy with length of text. Because the problem was not central to immediate research interests, we decided to attempt the development of more sophisticated measures in later projects.

Integrating the Text-Analysis System into the Reference Model. Our effort to tie the text-analysis system to the role of the reader is consistent with the second of our governing principles; it views writing as a communicative act that involves both a producer of text (the writer) and a consumer of text (the reader). All of our variables are defined in reader-based terms; writer-based inferences come later. We have also kept in mind Principle 6, which required differentiation of descriptive and qualitative variables by treating all variables as descriptive until the reference model and empirical evidence suggest otherwise. A case for the evaluative quality of most of the copy-editor and omniscient-reader variables may eventually be built, but many mechanical-reader and interested-reader variables may be fundamentally descriptive, at least when taken separately.

The third principle required differentiation between variables susceptible to educational intervention and those that are not. This principle calls for an empirical investigation and cannot be complied with a priori. However, it is important to note that just because a variable can be affected by educational intervention, that intervention should not necessarily take place. Particularly if the variable is descriptive, there may be little reason to design curricula to change it. An example may well be average length of T-unit, which, so far, we view as a descriptive variable that has an influence on communicative effectiveness only at the extreme ends of the scale. T-unit length has been shown to be easily altered by means of instruction, but the value of doing so is unclear.[9]

The seventh principle requires simultaneous consideration of a range of text features. This proves to be extremely difficult to accomplish in more useful ways than simple factor and regression analyses. This principle is closely tied to the first principle, which requires links between each text variable and the psychological model of the writing process. These two principles will most shape our long-term research program, with the remaining five serving largely to keep the program on track. Specific findings in the YWRP do help to link the text, task, and psychological components of our approach, but progress has been and will be slow.

YWRP Data-Collection Design

The YWRP is unusual in being a relatively large-scale study intended to test and extend a theory of writing that uses a classical experimental design. The sample comprised sixteen classrooms, each divided into four groups of students for writing workshops, yielding sixty-four subsamples, half at fourth-grade level and half at sixth-grade level. Each workshop group met four times: at the first three meetings writing tasks were presented; at the fourth meeting, papers were returned and discussed. The four workshop leaders were experienced teachers specially trained for the project.

Three major studies were included in the YWRP. A test-retest study was conducted in which the same task (PWT or IWT) was administered in two successive workshops, holding contextualization constant and counterbalancing alternate forms. This study was intended primarily to assess the stability of individual performances across time. A contextualization study also involved the administration of the same task (PWT or IWT) at two successive workshops, but the first contextualization level was used in the first workshop and the second contextualization level at the second workshop. This study allowed repeated-measures analysis of contextualization effects.

A third study involved comparing performance across tasks, holding contextualization level constant. Here, those variables that apply across genres could be investigated to see whether absolute scores and rank orders remain stable across tasks or whether they are task specific. In addition to checking each score independently, the stability of patterns of scores were also of interest. Could it be, for example, that T-unit length is more closely associated with more global ratings for persuasive writing than for instruction writing? If so, the variable is not strictly a matter of syntactic maturity because that sort of factor should be independent of specific task definition.

Additional Factors

The three major design factors in the studies outlined above are task (PWT or IWT), contextualization level, and trial (test or retest). Given a completely randomized design, the equivalence of the alternate forms could also be tested, although counterbalancing was used to preserve the validity of the central studies even if the forms proved not to be perfectly equivalent.

As mentioned earlier, subjects were drawn from two different grade levels, the fourth and sixth. Our psychological model predicted differences in processing between these two groups because of maturational factors. Such differences had already been reported by Scardamalia (1977) for a task similar to our PWT, the opinion essay. We hoped to show that this difference was not task-specific and to determine which text variables reflected it and which did not. Thus, grade-level comparisons were intended to test and to elaborate the explanatory model. As expected, some grade-level differences were stable across tasks, others were not. Those that were not were interpreted as reflecting experiential rather than strictly maturational changes (see Principle 3). Those that were consistent across tasks might still be experientially based, but in some cases our task analyses strongly suggested more general forces at work. Additional research will be required to substantiate this hypothesis.

There is a widespread belief that at least during elementary school, girls surpass boys in writing skills. Our theory offered no reason why this should be universally true, but suggested genre-specific differences attributable to experience and motivations. It may be that girls feel more free to let go in personal narratives or that boys tend to have more interest in, and experience with, science fiction. We saw no grounds for expecting sex differences in the PWT, but wondered whether boys might have more experience with technical instructions that would give them better strategies for the IWT. In fact, we found no sex differences above the copy-editor level; the only uniformly significant difference was in handwriting, where girls indeed scored higher than boys.

When we embarked on our study in 1978, a distinguished consultant informed us that he thought we were wasting our efforts. For young students, he said, writing ability is so closely connected to reading ability that scores on reading tests would tell us all we needed to know. We of course did not agree, but we did want to investigate the relationship between reading scores and scores on various text-analysis scales. Any complete analysis of the writing process will include consideration of reading; much of one's knowledge of edited American English and formal genre structures comes from reading; much linguistic knowledge required for one process is also required for the other, and rereading in an important part of composition itself. For these reasons our model led us to expect connections between measures of reading and writing, with strengths of association varying according to which measures were being compared. Because the writers in our sample were receiving relatively little instruction in writing in school and probably little at home as well, we believed that associations in our sample should be stronger than those we would expect for students receiving extensive support for the development of writing skills. This last hypothesis was not tested, of course, but it provided additional impetus for collecting reading achievement data for our sample.

Because reading was not a central focus in the YWRP, we did not collect the data ourselves. But the school district did administer Metropolitan Achievement Tests at both grade levels and made scores on the reading subtests available to us. We used these scores in forming (by stratified random assignment) workshop groups that, within the range for each classroom, were as heterogenous as possible. In a new study that is about to begin, a much more careful look at the role of specific reading skills on IWT performance will be taken. The focus will be on rereading during revision and the ultimate relationship of rereading to efficacy scores.[10]

All of the above factors—grade, sex, and reading ability—are subject characteristics. Additional subject variables that were recorded are workshop leader, classroom teacher, and school. Workshop leader is an important factor from the assessment perspective because systematic leader influences on performance would seriously weaken our tasks' utility in almost any context. Perhaps because of thorough training, no such differences were found. Teacher and school effects seemed likely because these variables represent a conglomerate of potential influences, including curriculum differences, attitude differences, and differences arising from variations in socioeconomic background. Because teacher- and school-related differences, if found, would be extremely difficult to interpret, these factors were not included in primary analyses. They are available for use in examining inconsistencies or anomalies in patterns of results however. Random division of classrooms into groups and random allocation of treatments across schools was intended to reduce the potential for teacher and school effects as much as possible.

Supplementary Data

The primary data source in the YWRP was the set of approximately 1,200 texts elicited from 451 writers. We also had access to all subjects' scores on the Metropolitan Achievement Tests. Two additional types of data were also collected. Workshop leaders filled out simple observation records for each writer during each workshop. This included information about general attitude, cooperation, time on task, and proofreading. Workshops leaders were also encouraged to write comments about any writer. After all texts were collected, the leaders conducted group interviews concerning the task just completed and the more general experience with writing, instructing, and persuading.

Both supplementary data sources served a dual purpose. First, they were intended to yield explanatory insight into text-related findings; second, they were to serve as exploratory research for further projects. Results were not fully integrated into primary analysis because of uneven quality (not all observation forms were complete and interview notes varied in depth and detail), but more important, because integration of data from such varied sources was a theoretical and statistical nightmare. Procedures for this type of integration are under development, but none yet lend themselves to our particular problem.

Summary of the YWRP

The YWRP included three major stages. The first was the development of tasks and scoring system and the creation of a data-collection design to allow testing a number of research hypotheses. This stage was greatly influenced by our general model-building effort. Indeed, the two efforts proceeded simultaneously, each shaping the other. The result was two tasks, one involving instruction writing and the other persuasion, a complex text-analysis system organized according to reader perspectives and an elaborate data-collection design. Three major substudies were designed to examine test-retest reliability, contextualization effects, and cross-genre comparisons. Other substudies ran across these, including a developmental comparison of fourth and six graders. Additional factors considered included sex, teacher, school, reading-achievement scores, and task administrator.

The data-collection stage was relatively short, involving a series of four writing workshops in each classroom. These were conducted by a team of specially trained teachers and proceeded strictly according to the plans from the first stage.

The data analysis stage is still continuing. Its first step was entry of all elicited texts into computer files. The text-entry specialist divided the tests into MUs, corrected all spelling errors,[11] and rated the texts for legibility and readability. This specialist was the only text analyst to work from handwritten originals. The computer then printed out two versions of each text, both without spelling errors. One presented the text as written. The other listed each MU separately along with a scoring grid. A team of four extensively trained text analysts scored each text directly on the computer printout. Every sixth text was scored by all four analysts to allow a check on interrater reliability. (Interrater reliability was uniformly high, ranging from .89 to .98). Data from the scoring grids was then entered into computer files for statistical analysis.

The data analysis stage is far from complete, but has already yielded many promising findings. The data base is so rich that fruitful analysis could continue almost indefinitely. So far, the IWT has received primary attention, although the PWT has been the subject of an independent study of scoring procedures (Tamor, 1981). The first analyses were variable-by-variable comparisons in the test-retest and contextualization levels sub-studies. Currently underway is the more difficult analysis of the inter-relationships between text characteristics. In addition, some attention has been paid to the influence of sex and grade-level differences. So far, the supplementary interview and observation data has been analyzed separately but not integrated with the text-based information.

EVALUATION

It has now been several years since our research team was constituted and began its initial planning phase. As time passes, our conviction that the time invested in development of the reference model and the pragmatic approach to theory formulation was well spent increases. The framework is broad enough to accommodate intellectual growth and position changes of individual team members and the reference model continues to provide a neutral means for examining differences of opinion or interpretation. Further, now that the first funded portion of the project has ended and the team no longer works together on a daily basis, the well-established conceptual framework is vital in coordinating data analysis and planning future projects. Enough information is available concerning the design of our tasks and scoring system that it is now time to move to studies that are either more practical—that directly address instructional questions—or more generally theoretical. The conceptual framework makes it possible for individual team members to capitalize fully on our past work when designing new projects and to re-examine that past work in light of new information.

Because the field of research on writing abounds with intriguing questions and methodologies, there is always a danger of serious fragmentation, of engaging in sets of small studies that, although individually informative, do not contribute to a deeper and more coherent understanding of writing in general. A clearly delineated framework can, we believe, prevent such fragmentation and instead provide the means for creating a total research program that is at least the sum of its parts.

Aside from guiding our own research, the pragmatic approach is also intended to aid in the assimilation of externally generated information to our explanatory model and, if necessary, in the accommodation of the model to that information. The greatest difficulty in using the approach in this way is the fuzziness with which constructs are frequently defined by researchers and theoreticians. The level of precision demanded by the reference model often requires that we select among various plausible interpretations of another researcher's ideas. Deferring such selections and maintaining two or more interpretations simultaneously is difficult, but it is undoubtedly just as problematic for researchers working without a reference model. The pressure for precision is a great help in examining our own ideas, intuitions, and impressions as well as in formulating theoretical questions to be posed to others.

A second more serious limitation on our approach is its commitment to defining all processes not only in psychological terms but also from the perspective of the individual metasubject. The approach would not be attractive to psychologists who focus on commonalities across individuals, let alone to sociologists and anthropologists. Further, the psychological position is developmental as well as metasubjective, demanding that the positing of any skill or knowledge structure includes an account of its acquisition and that underlying cognitive structures and mechanisms be inferred to explain performance. Many psychologists working from an information processing perspective reject the former constraint at least temporarily, and behaviorists or empiricists might reject the latter constraint outright.

Clearly, our particular approach is not for everyone. Difficulties arise not only from lack of universality of application but also from the fact that translation through the reference model is problematic for ideas developed within incompatible frameworks. Sociological theories, for example, do not necessarily map onto psychological theories any more than psychological theories inevitably map onto neurophysiological ones.

Things could not be otherwise, but we cannot imply that the translation process so central to our approach is always objective. The effort to reformulate a sociological—or even a social psychological—construct into our metasubjective reference language involves reworking that construct to the point that it may lose its former identity. This is a major theoretical problem in any interdisciplinary line of research. If, however, the reformulation is systematic, we believe it is better to do it than to ignore available information or leave it defined in terms alien to our entire approach. In fact, the effort to carry out reformulation is a fruitful theory-building endeavor in itself.

With respect to the specific principles governing the reference model, all seven have so far served us well. Perhaps the most powerful at this point is the commitment to differentiating between reader-based and writer-based text variables and between the various roles played by the reader. From a theoretical perspective, this principle has enormous implications for the psychological model of written communication and forces careful monitoring of the inferences drawn about that model from analyses of written texts. At the same time, it provides a useful tool in examining the feedback provided to student writers and for experimenting with the effects of feedback from teachers playing different reader roles.

The principle with which we have had the greatest difficulty is also concerned with text analysis, namely, the requirement that text variables be linked to the psychological model and that they be viewed and analyzed in psychologically plausible combinations. Difficulty arises in part from problems of statistical analysis, but more important, it arises from the incompleteness of the psychological model. This principle provides the link between two key components of the comprehensive model, the psychological model and the text analysis system. Compliance remains a critical goal, therefore, and the principle constantly influences research planning and interpretation of results. We cannot yet claim, however, to have specified the links between all variables in the text-analysis system and the constructs and processes in the psychological model. Indeed, full compliance with this principle can only come when the remaining principles have all been fully satisfied.

Our satisfaction with our general conceptual framework is greater than our satisfaction with the YWRP itself. Although we believe that the study was responsive to both our short-term assessment-oriented goals and our larger theoretical aims, it did have shortcomings. The size of the project was both a major strength and a serious drawback. Size was a strength because our methodological questions concerning reliability of measures and the interrelationships between text variables required large number of subjects if reasonable generalizability was to be achieved. This was especially true for text variables differing in rather subtle ways or between which expected relationships were predicted to be significant but mediated by intervening factors. Our practical questions about the feasibility of standardized assessment required extensive counterbalancing that could only be achieved with a large sample size.

The drawbacks to such a large study are obvious: the tasks of collecting, coding, analyzing, and interpreting data are enormous. Entering texts into the computer and coding them—a task assigned to a team of half-time assistants—took several months, followed by more months of entering codes into the computer; checking, organizing, and documenting data files; and creating higher order variables. Existing statistical packages in some cases proved inadequate or overly awkward so that programming time was also involved. As we said earlier, a great deal of our planned analysis is incomplete. In fact, so many substudies were built into the research design that fruitful analysis could continue almost indefinitely. Unfortunately, financial support for analysis of existing data is rare, and much of the analytic work is relegated to spare time at the present. One result of the study, however, will be simplification of the scoring system through the elimination of unreliable and redundant scales; therefore, future studies should require much less time for coding and statistical analysis.

As data analysis continues over long periods of time, with gaps of weeks or even months between analytic sessions, it becomes difficult for researchers to maintain their internal conceptualization of the project and their commitment. Both of these problems have been alleviated by the existence of the pragmatic framework, but they still cause significant problems. The analytic design and the data files have complex structures that must be partially relearned after interruptions. Hence, each analytic session begins with a reentry period during which analysis and interpretation proceed slowly with many false starts and blind alleys. Of course, it is possible to map out analytic plans in advance, but even when this is done, it takes time to reconstruct their rationales to interpret results. Even when commitment to the project goals remains high, time delays and wheel spinning take a toll on motivation.

This problem is exacerbated by the tantalizing findings that emerge as analysis proceeds. The temptation to initiate immediate follow-up studies is great, especially when such studies would enhance research reports and publications. Further, the feeling that critical factors were not measured is omnipresent in psychological research, but it is especially troublesome in large-scale studies. For example, the expected effects of contextualization level on IWT performance were found early on. But the two levels vary in several ways—for example, audience specification, prewriting activity, paper—and the next question concerns the relative importance of each of these variations. Surely reporting the general findings would be more satisfying if this question were to be addressed in a follow-up study. The original YWRP design was not faulty in this case; the primary goal was comparison of a traditional contextualization to a best effort, that comparison did reveal significant differences. It is painful, however, simply to add the new research idea to a list of future plans and return to analysis of the already-collected YWRP data.

If examples like the one just described were rare, there might be no harm in conducting a few small follow-up studies. Far from being infrequent, however, they are rampant, springing up in the course of virtually every analysis whether or not findings are statistically significant. Things should not be otherwise for researchers exploring a relatively new field, but restraint is vital. Too many writing researchers have file cabinets full of minimally analyzed data; in fact, new research questions arising during data collection sometimes attract a researcher so strongly that current data are never analyzed at all! A cogent conceptual framework laying out the goals, biases, and methods of a research program cannot entirely solve this problem, but it serves as a strong counteractive force to such momentary temptations. Just as important, careful examination of goals, biases, and assumptions prevents the researcher from being buffeted by each new idea, finding, or method appearing in the literature. It allows one to keep on track without wearing the blinders that are especially dangerous in a rapidly changing interdisciplinary field. The temptations to conduct new research before finishing the old and to be distracted or even derailed by external influences are especially great in large projects that take years to complete. Although we hope that the YWRP will achieve its full potential, we cannot yet claim that it has, and the outside temptations are very strong. For this reason, we will be reluctant to undertake so large a project again unless no set of smaller studies can achieve its objectives and those objectives are central to achieving our goals.

In summary, we find the support of a well-thought-out research framework and reference model so great that we would recommend developing such a framework to anyone intending to carry out a long-term research effort. The particulars of our pragmatic approach to theory formulation continue to serve us well and might prove equally useful to others working from a cognitive developmental or cognitve processing perspective. We hope that describing the framework will also clarify our perspective for those who do not share it, making it easier to isolate critical similarities and differences. The first empirical phase of our program, the YWRP, was greatly aided by the framework and was generally successful. At the present time, we are engaged in informal hypothesis-generating research and in smaller hypothesis-testing studies, both of which have places in our overall framework. Largely for practical reasons, we do not expect to embark on another large-scale study in the near future. Studies of all types—large/small, experimental/nonexperimental, qualitative/quantitative, text focused/process focused—have different but crucial contributions to make toward achieving our ultimate goal, which is a comprehensive explanatory model of writing processes with an integrated system for task and text analysis.

NOTES

1. This chapter reflects work largely carried out under a grant from the Carnegie Corporation of New York to the High/Scope Educational Research Foundation. The opinions expressed do not necessarily reflect the views of either institution. The authors acknowledge the contribution of the third senior member of their research team, Robert D. Matz, for his partnership throughout the project and especially for his major role in developing the text-analysis manual. They also wish to thank their research assistants, the staff of the High/Scope Data Processing Department, and other High/Scope staff for their assistance and support.

2. We call our question absurd because, practically speaking, one could not possibly control these variables. It is also absurd from the point of view of a believer in systemic differences because such differences would require that individuals presented with the same experiences would learn from them quite differently. Further, some theoreticians (e.g., Pascual-Leone, 1969; Witkin *et al.*, 1977) have suggested that systemic differences in older individuals may be, at least in part, the result of experiential differences during the first years of life. Hence, our question greatly oversimplifies a complex issue.

3. Certainly an area of growth that would not be visible in analysis of a single text, or even in many sets of multiple samples, is increase in the repertoire of high-level composition strategies. A more sophisticated development would be increase in the number of factors (including not only purpose and audience but also time available, quality of writer's knowledge, etc.) entering into the decisions determining *which* organizing strategies will be used. The research methodologies described by Odell, Goswami, and Herrington (Chapter 8) and by Hayes and Flower (Chapter 7) may be especially useful in exploring these issues.

4. There seems to be a widespread conviction that although transactional genres are plagued with problems of audience and purpose in school settings, expressive and poetic writing are not constrained by these factors. We are convinced that this is far from true and that our reference and explanatory models reflect this conviction. All of the task characteristics described under the task-contexts heading apply to any text written even in part for a second-party reader, irrespective of genre or mode.

5. This problem is not unique to the written reporting task. In any story-writing venture, for example, writers will vary in the complexity of their stories and hence set tasks of varying difficulty for themselves. Complex tasks introduce possibilities for error not posed by simpler tasks and also spread attention or processing capacity more thinly.

6. We anticipate that many readers will protest that these restrictions are unnatural and may not elicit every student's best effort; we do not in fact disagree. In standardized settings, whether for research or evaluation purposes, we see no wholly satisfactory solution to the problem of providing maximum support while eliciting individual and comparable efforts from each student. We selected our procedures in accordance with a desire to develop feasible assessment tools, but certainly hope to vary them in future research and curriculum-development projects.

7. We regret that the various task-design considerations discussed cannot be rephrased in the exact language of the reference model owing to the inadequate explication of the model that is provided in this chapter. It was no easy matter to accomplish this translation because our intuitive notions of motivation, knowing,

and the like, were fuzzy at best. In fact we can claim no more than a partial translation so far. The effort to make the translation, however, is one of the more productive elements of our method because it forces clarification and challenges assumptions. It also provides impetus for further research and unifies the wide range of writing-related concerns within a common conceptualization.

8. Text features impeding or enhancing the text-entry specialist's task in preparing the text for scoring of mechanical-reader variables are either recorded at time of entry or preserved and later picked up at the copy-editor and interested-reader levels. In any event, mechanical-reader variables can be treated as not directly reflecting the linguistic content of the text.

9. It may well be that training to lengthen T-units does result in better writing, but not because of longer T-units. Rather, the training may heighten many forms of linguistic and communication awareness.

10. This study is the doctoral dissertation project of Kathleen Scott, a doctoral candidate at the State University of New York at Albany.

11. Misspelled words were corrected but spellings were maintained in brackets. The computer could then print out the texts with or without the spelling errors. It could also produce lists of errors to allow a future spelling study. Because all text analysts except the text-entry specialist worked from printed text with no spelling errors, their judgments were not confounded by variations in handwriting, spelling, and legibility. Page formats were roughly preserved, however, including such devices as skipping lines between sentences and indentions.

REFERENCES

Bond, J. T., & Tamor, L. *Determining the validity and generalizability of writing tests.* Paper presented at the annual meeting of the American Educational Research Association, San Francisco, April 1979.

Britton, J., Burgess, T., Martin, N., McLeod, A., & Rosen, H. *The development of writing abilities (11–18).* London: Macmillan, 1975.

Case, R. Learning and development: A neo-Piagetian interpretation. *Human Development,* 1972, *15*, 339–358.

Case, R. Mental strategies, mental capacity, and instruction: A neo-Piagetian interpretation. *Journal of Experimental Child Psychology,* 1974, *18*, 382–397. (a)

Case, R. Structures and strictures: Some functional limitations on the course of cognitive growth. *Cognitive Psychology,* 1974, *6*, 544–573. (b)

Cooper, C. R. Holistic evaluation in writing. In C. R. Cooper & L. Odell (Eds.), *Evaluating writing: Describing, measuring, judging.* Urbana, Ill.: National Council of Teachers of English, 1977.

Florio, S., & Clark, C. *Naturalistic studies of the writing process.* Paper presented at the Conference on Writing Research, Albany, N.Y., May 1980.

Flower, L., & Hayes, J. *Protocol analysis as a window on the writing process.* Paper presented at the Conference on Writing Research, Albany, N.Y., May 1980.

Freedman, S. W. Writing and evaluation as independent processes. Paper presented at the Conference on Writing Research, State University of New York, Albany, May 1980.

Hunt, K. W. Early and late blooming syntactic structures. In C. R. Cooper & L.

Odell (Eds.), *Evaluating writing: Describing, measuring, judging.* Urbana, Ill.: National Council of Teachers of English, 1977.

Kittel, J. M., Smith, A. G., & Tamor, L. Evaluation of curriculum implementation and children's written language. *Annual Report, Cognitively Oriented Curriculum, Project Follow Through, 1977–78,* (Vol. II). Ypsilanti, Mich.: High/Scope Educational Research Foundation, October 1978.

Lloyd-Jones, R. Primary trait scoring. In C. R. Cooper & L. Odell (Eds.), *Evaluating writing: Describing, measuring, judging.* Urbana, Ill.: National Council of Teachers of English, 1977.

Matsuhashi, A. Explorations in the real-time production of written discourse. In M. Nystrand (Ed.), *What writers know: The language, process and structure of written discourse.* New York: Academic Press, 1982.

Odell, L., & Goswami, D. *Writing in the work place.* Paper presented at the Conference on Writing Research, Albany, N.Y., May 1980.

Pascual-Leone, J. *Cognitive development and cognitive style: A general psychological integration.* Unpublished doctoral dissertation, University of Geneva, Switz., 1969.

Pascual-Leone, J. Metasubjective problems of constructive cognition: Forms of knowing and their psychological mechanism. *Canadian Psychological Review,* 1976, *17,* 110–125. (a)

Pascual-Leone, J. A view of cognition from a formalist's perspective. In K. F. Riegel & J. A. Meacham (Eds.), *The developing individual in a changing world* (Vol. 1). The Hague: Mouton, 1976. (b)

Pascual-Leone, J. *Constructive problems for constructive theories: The current relevance of Piaget's work and a critique of information-processing simulation psychology.* Paper presented at the Invitational Conference of the Institüt die Pedagogik, Kiel, West Germany, 1977. Also in H. Spada & R. Kluwe (Eds.), *Developmental models of thinking.* New York: Academic Press, in press.

Pascual-Leone, J., Goodman, D., Ammon, P., & Subelman, I. Piagetian theory and neo-Piagetian analysis as psychological guides in education. In J. M. Gallagher & J. A. Easley (Eds.), *Knowledge and development* (Vol. 2). New York: Plenum, 1978.

Scardamalia, M. *How children cope with the cognitive demands of writing.* Paper presented at the National Institute of Education Conference on Writing, Los Angeles, 1977.

Scheerer, M. Cognitive theory. In G. Lindzey (Ed.), *Handbook of social psychology.* Cambridge, Mass.: Addison-Wesley, 1954.

Tamor, L. *Cognitive style and reading: The interrelationships of four cognitive styles and their influence on reading performance.* Unpublished doctoral dissertation, University of California, Berkeley, May 1979.

Tamor, L. *Holistic judgments of children's writing: Does the whole have any parts?* Paper presented at the annual meeting of the American Educational Research Association, Los Angeles, April 1981.

Tamor, L., Bond, J. T., & Matz, R. D. *Instruction writing: A promising approach to the study and teaching of composition.* Paper presented at the annual meeting of the American Educational Research Association, Boston, April 1980.

Witkin, H. A., Moore, C. A., Goodenough, D. R., & Cox, P. W. Field-dependent and field-independent cognitive styles and their educational implications. *Review of Educational Research,* 1977, *47,* 1–64.

5

Present at the Beginning[1]

Victor Rentel
The Ohio State University
Martha King
The Ohio State University

Several years ago we began a longitudinal study of forty-two kindergarten and forty-two first-grade children seeking to discover how their
text-forming strategies changed as they entered school and shifted from producing mainly oral texts to producing written texts. It is now four years
later. We have analyzed data from the first two years of the study and are
continuing to sort out and analyze data from the last two. More specifically, the text-forming strategies we wanted to study were those employed
by children to relate various layers of meaning encoded in texts and those
employed to build a rhetorical structure. Most earlier research on pri-
mary- and intermediate-grade children's writing, aside from the work of
Graves (1973, 1978, 1979), had focused on syntax (Hunt, 1965; Loban,
1963, 1976; O'Donnell, Griffin, & Norris, 1967) or phonology (Read,
1971). Of course, Hildreth (1963) had studied the development of
rudimentary aspects of children's writing from 3 to 6 years of age and
Wheeler (1971) had studied kindergarten children's beginning efforts to
write. Our purpose, however, was to describe how children come to grips
with the structure of texts rather than sentences or words and to describe
how children use cohesive ties to relate strands of meaning in their
spoken and written texts.

In an earlier work (King & Rentel, 1979), the authors sketched a
theory that attempted to account for several facets of beginning-writing
development. Briefly, we argued that several variables affect: (1) the way
children execute their communicative intentions, including what children
bring to writing in the way of oral language; (2) early concepts of the
functions of written messages; (3) children's exposure to, and their sense
of stories; (4) fundamental differences between written and spoken language; and (5) particular factors that influence production, such as mem-

ory, context, and audience. We noted that the decisions involved in an utterance entail different plans, depending on the unit being planned. Basing our arguments on Chafe's work (1977a, 1977b), we hypothesized three levels of planning that correspond to text units (schema, proposition, and category). These three levels included schematizing, propositionalizing, and categorizing.

The first level of planning, schematizing, involves interpreting knowledge to organize the flow of information so that all the pertinent meanings to be expressed and understood are included. The speaker's or writer's task is to plan chunks large enough to convey a coherent unit of meaning but small enough to constitute a unit of memory for particular instances and events.

The second level, propositionalizing, involves communicating appropriate detail by planning chunks small enough to be expressed in sentences. What is essential about propositionalizing is that proposition constituents be selected both in terms of how and which details are presented. That is, some details will be more salient to intentions than others, thus, necessitating a choice of what to include as new information relative to what has already been revealed. The planning problem is to factor out from the larger schema one or more details whose involvement in the larger chunk may be given a role or particularity of theme.

The third level of planning, categorizing, entails particularizing propositions into words and phrases. Some events or individuals, according to Chafe (1977a, 1977b), may be easier to categorize than others—be more codable—based on the possibility that natural categories are organized around prototypes (Rosch, 1973). Prototypes and members of the category nearest the prototype would be more easily coded than those more distance from the prototype, therefore leading to variations in precision and efficiency.

We further argued that fundamental distinctions between speech and writing (which we will explore in detail in the next section) would constitute the bases for expanding and refining these planning capabilities. Briefly, planning at each level would require realignment from the implicit, shared, dimensions of speech in situational contexts to the textual demands of writing where all meanings must be made explicit in the immediate text. We expected this realignment would be most clearly revealed through cohesion (Halliday & Hasan, 1976), language's major resource for linking elements of a discourse. Cohesion is a range of possibilities by which meanings in a text may be related through reference, substitution, ellipsis, conjunction, and lexical cohesion. These devices specify the nature of information to be retrieved when interpreting any particular segment of a text; at the beginning stages of writing development, children may assume that these devices reside in a context of situation rather than in their text. We expected that variations in context, content, audience, and purpose would affect the kind and distribution of cohesive resources children employed at all three levels of planning. In particular, the proportion of references to context of situation should decrease, whereas those confined to the text should increase as a function of learning to write. We expected that the need to embody relevant meanings within the written text, coupled with developmental increases in vocabulary (Clark, 1979), would lead to expanded use of lexical cohesion, which, in turn, would affect propositionalizing and categorizing. We argued, therefore, that an understanding of beginning-writing development necessarily should include an exploration of cohesion in children's oral and written texts.

Another major element of our theory was premised on young children's early writing intentions gleaned from their prior exposure to written texts and their sense of the purpose or function of writing. One kind of written text with which most children are intimately acquainted is the story. Given that a great deal of their experience with writing has been through stories, children are likely to assume that one of the major functions of writing is to tell stories. We anticipated that children incorporate this assumption into their understanding of general language functions (Halliday, 1973, 1975)—that is, the assumption that writing serves an ideational function (language's ability to characterize experience), and a textual function (language's ability to specify internally consistent relations within a text that is comprehensible without reference to anything outside the text). Our notion was that, for children, stories are prototypical texts that are clearly associated with writing whose function, form, and internal relations are reasonably well known to them. As a natural extension of this knowledge base, children will favor stories for schema planning in their early attempts to write. Of course, there are pragmatic considerations as well. Given that schooling is expected to produce literacy, language arts instruction almost guarantees that children will tell and write stories in the primary grades. Both schooling and their knowledge base incline children to plan schema in terms of familiar story and folktale structures. As children learn to make stories of increasing detail and complexity and as they acquire a deeper appreciation of the nature of written texts, their schema planning can be expected to become more formal, deliberate, and conscious. In the beginning of writing development, however, such planning is probably intuitive and unconscious.

In what follows we shall examine the role of cohesion and story structure in beginning-writing development. We shall then present one thread of our longitudinal studies, a two-year study of cohesion and the evolution of structure in children's oral and written stories.

CHILDREN'S ACQUISITION OF COHESION IN WRITING

One of the more important aspects of learning to write for children is to realign their text-forming strategies to suit the requirements of writing.

Texts, spoken or written, are embedded in and shaped by the contexts from which they arise. It is through language that individuals represent reality to themselves and express their personal meanings to others. Language is learned and functions in situational contexts that convey meaning to the participants. The social situation—the activity, purpose, participants, and mode of discourse as selected, acted upon, and interpreted by the language user—determines the character of a text, including the form, theme, and cohesive patterns employed.

Learning to talk occurs largely in contexts that involve face-to-face interaction, shared perceptual environment, intimacy, familiarity, and language that interacts with the ongoing action, frequently to the point of being ancillary to such action (Pettegrew, 1981). Indeed, it may well be that shared attention and joint action are necessary conditions for learning to talk (Bruner, 1975; Macnamara, 1972). Learning to write, however, occurs in contexts unsupported by a matrix of shared intimacy, familiarity, face-to-face interaction, and salience to ongoing events. Language associated with literacy is disembodied from a context of events (Donaldson, 1978; Francis, 1975) and is directed toward an abstract audience well beyond the range of an immediate perceptual environment. Cook-Gumperz (1977) and Halliday (1978) have observed that adult language can be distinguished from that of children by its very freedom from situational constraints and its capacity for indirect communication. The ability to emancipate language from situational constraints is dependent on learning the properties of texts associated with particular contexts (Hasan, 1973). What children must learn about writing is that the text itself is the relevant environment for establishing all meaning relations. In writing, unlike speech where attention may be directed always to intention and meaning, attention must be shifted not only away from situational constraints but also away from intention as well. In speaking and listening, as Cazden (1972, 1974) noted, attention is focused on meaning or intention, but with written language, the focus of attention must be shifted to means and to the form of language. This realignment is accomplished in large part within the formal context of schooling, where it may be assumed, although perhaps unconsciously, that textual functions are given dominant accent (Olson, 1977).

Another aspect of this realignment involves the distinction between oral and written discourse functions (Halliday, 1973, 1975). Halliday argues that spoken language essentially has an interpersonal function, whereas written language serves an ideational function. This latter function manifests the capacity to express through language the content of experiences as well as the fundamental relationships inherent within experiences not only of the external world but also of the mind as well. Olson (1977) makes a similar distinction. He, like Halliday, distinguishes text from utterance on the basis of function. Utterances serve primarily to maintain social relations, whereas texts serve the truth functions of language and specify the logical relations between sentences. One consequence of this specialization of function is that texts are highly conventionalized and premised on logical relations. Statements in texts are highly specialized. They explain and describe rather than regulate and maintain social or authority relations. They are statements coded for reflection rather than for action. Halliday has defined this specialized character of texts as the textual function of language.

Text refers to an internally consistent body of writing or speech that is interpretable without reference to anything outside the context of the discourse itself (Halliday & Hasan, 1976). Texts are semantic units encoded in sentences. They have meaning within themselves and in relation to the context of which they are a part. In other words, texts are embedded within and shaped by the social and linguistic contexts from which they arise. All texts occur in an environment that consists of what is happening within a social semiotic that has the language user at its core. But not all elements in an environment are equally important, either personally or linguistically; thus, any text produced is contingent on the context of situation (Halliday, 1973), the setting of relevant actions and events, the relationships among the participants in the discourse, and the medium of communication employed. All combine to produce a text of a particular sort.

The semantic relationships that are defined by a text comprise a kind of unity. It is this unity that distinguishes a text from random sentences that focus on the same topic. This unity of meaning Halliday and Hasan (1976) refer to as texture. They argue that it is achieved through cohesion—semantic relations that are established when one element of a discourse is interpretable only through some other element in the same text. A single instance of relationship between two such elements is known as a tie. Cohesion is the range of possible ties that may link meanings in a text. Halliday and Hasan (1976) set forth five distinct categories of cohesive ties: reference, substitution, ellipsis, conjunction, and lexis. We shall briefly define and illustrate these categories. Our definitions are based entirely on the work of Halliday and Hasan (1976), to whom we are greatly indebted. For a full treatment of cohesion, the interested reader should refer to their work.

1. Reference is a category of cohesive relations established through personal pronouns, demonstratives, and comparatives. All three depend for their interpretation on text elements to which they refer. The following excerpts from children's texts illustrate the nature of these relations. Italicized words denote the tie.

Personal pronouns:

Once there was a *bear* who lived in the woods. *He* was lonely. *He* had only a few friends.

Demonstratives:

One day the bear went to racoon's *house*. His friends were *there*.

Comparatives:

His friends were a squirrel, a racoon, and a deer. He had no *other* ones.

Frequently, in spoken language, reference is made to something in the context of situation—a reference likely to be understood by all present in the situation. But in written texts, failure to identify the referent results in confusion. When reference is made to something outside the text (exophoric reference), interpretation is difficult if not impossible. The next example, the beginning of another story, illustrates exophoric reference.

Exophoric reference:

They had no food. *They* had no bread. And then *the* little girl went out in *the* forest. (To whom does *they* refer? What girl? What forest?)

2. Substitution is a form of cohesive relationship that involves relatedness of form or wording. A linguistic "marker" replaces and stands for a word or group of words removed from the text. Ellipsis, its near cohesive relative, involves removing the presupposing item entirely, its interpretation being "understood." Both substitution and ellipsis can take place at the nominal, verbal, and clausal levels. That is, a substitution can replace a noun phrase, a verb phrase, or an entire clause. So also with ellipsis. The requisite noun phrase, verb phrase, or clause may be omitted. Examples of verbal substitution and clausal ellipsis follow.

Substitution:

The little girl said, "Stop boiling, pot, stop boiling." And it *did*.

Ellipsis:

Mr. Fox said, "But we want you to stay because you are our best friend.
    "Would you like to come with me?"
    So the fox said, "Why, yes." (I would like to come with you.)

3. Conjunction, another means to achieve cohesion, does not entail a presupposed relation but indicates instead how preceding text is to be linked semantically to what follows. These links fall into four categories: additive, adversative, causal, and temporal. In the following examples, conjunctions are italicized and their meanings will follow in parentheses.

Conjunction:

Once upon a time there was this little girl named Susie. *And* (additive) she lived in this old house with this dog.

Once there was a mother and a little kid. They was hungry.... *So* (causal) she went out to find berries. She looked in the forest *but* (adversative) did not find any.

She asked him to be a good little duck. *Then* (temporal) he went to bed.

4. The final category, lexical cohesion, is achieved through vocabulary relations, relations among word meanings. There are two categories of lexical cohesion: reiteration and collocation. Reiteration may occur as simple repetition or may be achieved through synonyms, antonyms, superordinate terms, or general terms, such as "thing." Collocation, on the other hand, is lexical choice that sustains "continuity of lexical meaning" (Halliday & Hasan, 1976, p. 320). Collocation is a cohesive relation stemming from lexical items that appear in similar contexts or that tend to share the same lexical environment. Pairs, such as hot and cold, man and woman; words from ordered sets, such as days of the week; members of the same more general class, such a pencil, pen, crayon, and other writing instruments; part to whole relationships, such as page and book; and proximity relations, such as bathe and tub illustrate these textual relations.

Lexical cohesion:

Once there was a tadpole who lived in a water tower. He thought that the water tower (reiteration) was the sea.

Once there was a little hamster named Dancer. Dancer ran all around the house. Then someone opened the door (collocation).

As children learn to compose both oral and written texts, one of the major tasks they must accomplish is to create texture—that is, a semantic unity among the strands of meaning they are attempting to weave into a coherent whole (Pappas, 1981). Because the overarching functions of writing and speech differ, the ways in which children employ cohesive ties, the particular ties they employ, and the kinds of relationships they attempt to establish when composing a text can be expected to vary from speech to writing. As children come to appreciate that the written text itself is the relevant environment for establishing all meaning relations, fewer references to context of situation (exophoric reference) can be predicted. But Bernstein's (1971) finding that lower-class children's texts reflect greater context dependence than do texts of middle-class children suggests differential rates of exophoric reference for these two populations. Given the relationship between social class and language variation (Bernstein, 1971; DeStefano, 1973; DeStefano & Rentel, 1975), text cohesion may vary as a function of dialect. Similarly, genre, context, and developmental level should entail variations in text cohesion. In short, by studying cohesive ties in the texts children produce as they mature, important patterns and way stations in development of writing ability may be identified.

THE ROLE OF STORIES IN BEGINNING-WRITING DEVELOPMENT

Stories also have a significant role to play in beginning-writing development. Children frequently tell stories, both old and new, as they create their first written messages. These stories constitute a familiar rhetorical structure around which children organize the flow of discourse into groupings large enough to represent a coherent unit of pertinent meanings but small enough to be constituted as a basic unit of memory for particular instances and events. Both Moffett (1968) and Britton (1970; Britton, Burgess, Martin, McLeod, & Rosen, 1975) have argued that the first tentative step children take toward writing is reflected in their ability to take over a conversation and maintain a topic independent of the prompting and feedback ordinarily found in dialogue. Britton argues that young children achieve their communicative intentions through speech but that writing at this stage in development serves another end, that is, its purpose is to create a tangible artifact, a drawing, or a display. Langer's (1953) notion of presentational symbolism, as distinguished from representational symbolism, would best characterize these aims. Children frequently tell a story as they produce these displays (Britton, 1970). This form of solo discourse between thought and action embodies both elements of dialogue that are less collaborative and elements of narrative that are maintained by distinct actions. The cues children use as they develop a text are found not in what an interlocutor said but in the previous text and in the ongoing constructive actions of producing an artifact. As Vygotsky (1962) noted, language without an interlocutor must be consciously directed and sustained to replace the dynamic guiding quality afforded by a conversational partner. Sustained speech may be one of the means children employ to sort out these distinctions between speech and writing.

There are, of course, other distinctions between speech and writing that children may come to appreciate through sustained speech. Gestures, prosodic information, and attributes of the discourse setting are all carriers of meaning in conversation. They afford redundant sources of meaning for the participants in a conversation—sources that are not explicitly realized in the spoken text. What children learning to write must grasp is how to take what is implicitly obvious in the context and render it explicit in text. Cook-Gumperz (1977) characterized this trait as the ability to appreciate language as a structure separate from action. Children must learn to place increased reliance on semantic and syntactic 'foregrounding' as dominant carriers of meaning. In short, they must learn to lexicalize and make explicit these alternative sources of meaning within the framework of some text structure (Cook-Gumperz, 1977; Doughty, Pearce, & Thornton, 1972; Ure, 1971). We shall now consider children's ability to appreciate language as structure.

At school age, children have learned the underlying structure of stories (Mandler & Johnson, 1977; Stein & Glenn, 1979). These structures appear to have nearly full representation in memory, for when asked to recall stories that have been randomly organized, children produce a stereotypical or canonically organized version of a tale. Further, there is some evidence that four- and five-year-old children's descriptions of common-event sequences, such as eating lunch at McDonald's (Nelson, 1978), rely heavily on schematic organization. This suggests a gradual acquisition of a story schema, beginning with scriptlike chronicles that continue to grow in structural complexity up to age ten and beyond (Botvin, 1977; Botvin & Sutton-Smith, 1977) and culminate in well-formed, episodically organized structures—that occurs in girls earlier than boys (Sutton-Smith, Abrams, Botvin, Caring, Gildesgaine, & Stevens, 1975; Dungan, 1977). If, indeed, memory for events and instances is so organized, then story schemata may constitute one of the fundamental cognitive bases for the rhetorical scaffolds employed by beginning writers.

Both Winograd (1979) and Halliday (1973) maintain that such discourse schemata do provide guides or models for integrating language into texts. One such pattern is narrative. Halliday (1973) argues that children develop conceptions of what language is and how it works—that is, 'relevant models' that represent a pattern of discourse. We think that such conventionalized models figure heavily in the design of children's beginning narratives and expect that fairy tales and folktales provide a rhetorical framework for beginning writers. But the extent to which such schemata guide production is not really known—however appealing or likely such a notion might be.

There is, of course, evidence that fairy tale and folktale elements are represented in the original stories children tell and write. Rubin and Gardner (1977) argue from their data that children starting at about three years of age, acquire a general frame for fiction, and then differentiate it into specific story genres. By four years of age children appear to have partially represented the 'frame' for fairy tales (Rubin & Gardner, 1977). By the time children are six, stock characters such as witches and fairies appear in their written and dictated stories (Applebee, 1978). Oral narratives produced by children demonstrate that action elements very much akin to Propp's functions, or plot units, do, indeed, characterize the organization and structure of children's fantasy narratives (Botvin, 1977; Botvin & Sutton-Smith, 1977).

Botvin and Sutton-Smith (1977) reported that many, but by no means the majority of their subjects, told fantasy narratives resembling the fairy tales analyzed by Propp (1968). Using a modification of Propp's morphological functions—generic descriptions of story characters' actions—Botvin and Sutton-Smith (1977) observed that the complexity of component action sequences in children's narratives increased in a direct relationship with age. Starting with nuclear diads, two logically related actions, children progressively expanded and elaborated these basic structures into fully embedded complex plots. It is not clear, however, what role, if any, familiar folktales and fairy tales played in providing these children with relevant models of fantasy texts and to what extent such models guided their early productions. Most plots that occurred in the narratives analyzed by Botvin and Sutton-Smith involved either a lack (a basic need, e.g., hunger) and its liquidation or involved a villainy (an act of depravity) and its nullification. These elements are identical to those posited by Propp (1968)—lack and lack liquidated, villainy coupled with villainy nullified. In Propp's morphology two additional pairings—(1) a struggle, usually between hero and villain, coupled with the hero's victory and difficult task, and (2) a test of the hero's authenticity paired with its solution—augment the obligatory functions of lack and villainy. This coincidence between children's narratives and the formal attributes of fairy tales, as set forth by Propp, suggests that, at some point in learning to compose, many (if not all) children employ a narrative schema that is quite similar to tales they have heard and read.

Fairy tales have a highly conventionalized plot structure (Propp, 1968). Favat (1977), who compared various popular tales—ranging from Perrault to the Grimms and H.C. Anderson—observed that these tales have an extraordinarily predictable structure and bear a striking similarity to their Russian counterparts analyzed by Propp. Even Propp (1968), speculating that fairy tales may have a common origin, made this observation:

> Yet one still feels inclined to pose this question: if all fairy tales are similar in form, does this not mean that they all originate from a single source? The morphologist does not have the right to answer this question. At this point he hands over his conclusions to a historian or should himself become a historian. Our answer, although in the form of a supposition, is that this appears to be so. However, the question of sources should not be posed merely in a narrowly geographic sense. . . . The single source may also be a psychological one. Much has been done by Wundt in this spere. But here also one must be very cautious. If the limitation of the tale were to be explained by the limited faculties of human imagination in general, we would have no tales other than those of our given category, but we possess thousands of other tales not resembling fairy tales. Finally, this single source may come from everyday life. (p. 106)

Other literary structuralists (Bremond, 1970; Dundes, 1964; Levi-Strauss, 1963; Maranda & Maranda, 1971; Todorov, 1971) have explored the constitutive principles that define the narrative form. Despite differences among them, their analyses bear certain fundamental similarities. They all identify a principle of order or 'succession' and both Propp (1968) and Todorov (1971) set forth a principle of transformation—although Propp did not incorporate the principle of transformation formally into his analysis of structure. These structuralists also identify elements or units that are indispensable or essential to the narrative. These elements generally include a beginning marked by some initial state of satisfaction or equilibrium, a complication or degredation of this initial state, a recognition of this change in state by the protogonist, an action that repairs or remedies the complication, and a restoration of equilibrium. None, however, completely fit the tales written for the enjoyment of children nor the tales written by children. Propp's (1968) analysis, however, does have the advantage of breadth and delicacy.

Hasan (1980) has argued that the stories children compose are a separate genre of fictional narrative that can be described in terms of five obligatory elements: (1) placement, (2) initial event, (3) sequent event, (4) final event, and (5) finale. She also proposed other nonobligatory elements found frequently in children's tales, such as rituals, attributions, habitual actions, and relations to characters. King, Rentel, and Cook (1980) compared Hasan's (1980) analysis of structure with Propp's (1968) and found that they correlated rather well (.65) when only obligatory elements were included in the analysis of narrative texts produced by six-years-olds. Leondar (1977), who also analyzed children's narrative texts, concluded that children at the age of five or six produce texts that include an initial state of affairs, an event that disrupts this state, a counteraction to reverse the disruption, and a restoration to the original state. Thus, the stories that children tell and write bear an appreciable resemblance—at least in terms of structure—to the various ways in which structure in fairy tales and folktales has been described. Leondar (1977) puts it this way:

> The constructive powers of the author and the reconstructive ones of the reader may be assumed to spring from a common source. On both counts, then, the development of narrative competence in early childhood invites examination. (p. 173)

Fairy tales, of course, comprise only one of the many genres of stories children encounter both in and out of school. Why should fairy tales and folktales be singled out as rhetorical models for beginning writers? First, the literature, as indicated above, provides evidence that young children's texts mirror many of the elements typically defined as elements of fairy and folktales. Second, when children retell stories, even stories in which the underlying grammar or structure has been violated, their retellings are biased toward a prototypical or canonical form (Mandler & Johnson, 1977; Stein & Glenn, 1979). Third, fairy tales and folktales delight and engage children unfailingly (Favat, 1977), and as Favat speculated, they probably do so because of their highly conventionalized structure. On these grounds, it is reasonable to assume that fairy tales in all probability are rather well represented in memory by school age. To the extent that they are, we expect that such tales are fundamental rhetorical guides for beginning writers.

But how do such guides function in the production of a text? Our notion is that abstract story elements provide a range of options for selecting and organizing events in a temporal sequence that reveals and emphasizes relations between and among characters and events (Leondar, 1977). They also provide a reservoir of states, complications, and repairs of an abstract sort (frames) to be propositionalized as events and roles (characters) to express the ideas contained in these frames (King & Rentel, 1979). The young storymaker must sustain a narrative in some cumulative way. Regardless of variety, the storyteller must produce a schema that contains both necessary and sufficient elements of a story. Such frames provide the basis for cumulating units, either additively or in parallel. Even with a minimum of rudimentary elements, through repetition, a narrative can be sustained indefinitely (Botvin & Sutton-Smith, 1977). Finally, particular sets of elements can be combined in parallel or in tandem to afford the storymaker opportunities for thematic variation; thus the storymaker can give dimension to a story in the making.

These various perspectives converge on the notion that conventionalized models of text figure in the design of children's narratives. But why study children's narratives? Why not study the entire range of discourse that children are capable of producing at school entry? First, even though rather sparse, there is at least a growing literature on the production of narrative texts by children at school age. The importance of having an existing literature from which hypotheses and methodology can be derived is self-explanatory. Economy alone is sufficient justification for focusing on a single genre, some of whose attributes and dimensions have already been characterized. Then, of course, with genre controlled, an important source of variation can be examined without need for further complicating an already complex set of logical and statistical comparisons. In addition, this existing literature has given rise to our expectation that children are more likely to produce texts of greater length and nuance in narrative form than in other discourse genres. Finally, of necessity, research in school contexts must conform to the ongoing life of a classroom. Our problem at the outset was to select variables and manipulations that fitted nicely into this context, yet constituted reliable and theoretically significant chunks of writing development to study. The structure of fictional narratives seemed to rest at the intersect of these points.

METHODS EMPLOYED TO STUDY COHESION AND STORY STRUCTURE

The overarching purpose of this study on cohesion and story structures that undertook to develop a longitudinal research paradigm for writing was to describe the transition children make from oral to written texts at the outset of schooling. Their use of cohesive devices was a major focus of the study along with their selection of particular story-structure elements. These two sets of variables were assumed to be fundamental text-forming strategies—the former as a means for tying various strands of meaning into a textured whole and the latter as a means for selecting and organizing elemental plot units into related sequences of action that featured varied temporal and character relations. Texts were elicited from children in three different discourse contexts: story retelling, dictation, and writing. The population we studied was stratified by sex, school, socioeconomic class, dialect, and grade. Two groups of thirty-six children randomly selected from each of the strata just noted were observed at three-month intervals for a period of sixteen months.

As noted earlier, the various status characteristics of this population —sex, socioeconomic class, grade, school location, and dialect—were expected to influence the production of narrative texts differentially in the course of writing development. The three discourse contexts imposed different but related task demands that also were expected to influence the structure and cohesion of texts children produced in each context.

Schools

To study writing at all, schools had to be found in which children were encouraged to write in grades 1 and 2, given our overall aim of investigating the transition from speech to writing. Schools with curricula of this sort are somewhat rare; we can only speculate why this is so. Our guess is that most educators (perhaps laypersons as well) equate learning to write with learning to produce correctly formed letters and correctly spelled words, at least in the beginning stages. Not surprisingly, factors bearing on the formation of texts appear to have little influence on decisions about the curriculum for beginning writing. First, research on this period of writing development has been slow to develop; thus, little basis has existed for incorporating activities and goals designed to encourage text-forming capabilities in the early writing curriculum. Second, the concern for, and emphasis on, spelling and handwriting are reasonable and well founded in children's needs and interests. Third, the scope and sequence of the curriculum for beginning writing traditionally has assumed a later start for both functional and creative writing. Considerable attention, therefore, has been devoted to locating, evaluating, and selecting schools where the curriculum has encouraged composing right from the beginning.

Subjects

A rather interesting finding by Bernstein (1971) shows that one characteristic of speech regulated by codes is the amount of exophoric reference in the texts of middle- and lower-class children. Bernstein argued that the texts of lower-class children reflected greater context dependence. As we argued earlier, learning to write inherently involves the ability to lexicalize meanings increasingly and to depend less and less on contextual sources of meaning. On this basis a decision was made to stratify our sample subjects by dialect and socioeconomic class. Other evidence suggested that a distinction must be made between geographic and socially constrained variation in language (DeStefano, 1973; DeStefano & Rentel, 1975) and that speakers of black English vary considerably in the number and kinds of forms they produce in varying circumstances (Carroll & Feigenbaum, 1967; Dillard, 1972; Labov & Cohen, 1967). This evidence supported the decision to stratify on socioeconomic class by dialect. Our final stratification decision rested on evidence that first-grade boys differed significantly from first-grade girls in the amount and kinds of information they incorporated in their retellings of stories (Dungan, 1977). Sex, therefore, also appeared to be a factor that required experimental control. This decision to control for sex was buttressed further by evidence that demonstrated that black females differ from black males in the number and kinds of vernacular forms they produce (Wolfram, 1969). Thus, subjects were selected on the basis of dialect, socioeconomic class, and sex.

One further stratification variable was incorporated in the designs for our various longitudinal studies. Grade level was included as another stratum, both to increase the potential generality of our findings and to provide opportunities to make cross-sectional comparisons between grade levels. The reasoning behind this decision was twofold. First, we had no way to estimate the variability of our population, either in terms of cohesive ties or in terms of the three story-structure variables that served as dependent measures in the study. We had neither a research literature nor very precise pilot data from which sample size could be estimated. The addition of thirty-six subjects increased our sample size to the level indicated as necessary by our crude pilot data. Second, longitudinal and cross-sectional studies of development have both inherent advantages and weaknesses. We hope to minimize the weaknesses of both research strategies and maximize their strengths. But the most important advantages to be gained by adding this grade-level comparison were greater external validity for our findings and potentially greater delicacy in our conclusions.

Determining Dialect Status. To determine that subjects spoke vernacular black English, three alternative screening techniques were considered: (1) technical detailed linguistic interviews (Fasold & Wolfram, 1970; Labov, Cohen, Robins & Lewis, 1968); (2) semi-informal interviews (Shuy, Wolfram, & Riley, 1968); and (3) sentence repetition tasks (Garvey & McFarlane, 1970; Politzer, Hoover, & Brown, 1974; Rentel & Kennedy, 1972). Given the inter- and intrasubject variability noted above, sentence-repetition tasks were employed because these tasks discriminate among subgroups with relatively high reliability on items where a difference exists between the form presented and a form habitually used by a subject and offered as a substitute (Garvey & McFarlane, 1970). In addition to the advantages of increased discriminability and reliability, sentence-repetition tests require less time and less exacting training for their proper administration. Ten structures from the Garvey and McFarlane scale with reliability coefficients greater than .55 were selected and included in our scale (four repetitions of each structure) for a total of forty items.

Subjects (twenty-four) were drawn from the first grade of an urban school, an elementary school so designated because of its open enrollment, open space, and open curriculum. This school was attended by children not only from a largely black neighborhood—with a socioeconomic status (SES) distribution that ranged from low class to lower middle class—but also from middle-class neighborhoods throughout this particular city. An additional sample (twelve) was drawn from the first grade of a suburban school with an SES distribution that ranged from middle to upper class. From the former population, twelve subjects were identified as vernacular black-dialect speakers—this was based on the revised measure of standard English proficiency noted above ($M = 21.67$; $SD = 5.99$). Subjects scoring ten or more on this measure were assumed to be vernacular black-dialect speakers.

Determining Socioeconomic Status (SES). During the first few weeks of the study (February 1979), SES was determined by the *Index of Status Characteristics* (Warner, Meeker & Ellis, 1949), a scale that rates occupation, source of income, house type, and dwelling area. Because Warner's occupation ratings are dated, we modified the *Index of Status Characteristics*, substituting instead Hollingshead's *Job Scale* and then adjusted weightings. Weighted totals of the four subscales comprised the SES score for each subject. The total scale had a range of 12 to 84.

All twenty of the vernacular speakers fell within the bottom quartile of the SES distribution, leading to the conclusion (at least within this population), that their dialect was socially constrained, that is, a sociolect (DeStefano, 1973). From this population, six boys and girls were drawn at random ($M = 71.00$; $SD = 8.51$). A random sample of middle-class subjects was drawn from both the same inner-city school and from the same suburban school (six boys and six girls from each) to contrast school and control for class and sex differences.

One of the most vexing problems in longitudinal research is subject mortality—the loss of subjects through moving, prolonged absence from school, or repeated unwillingness to participate in various experimental tasks. To compensate for the possible loss of subjects, two additional subjects were drawn randomly from each level of our stratified subject pool (dialect/socioeconomic class by sex, by grade, by school) for a total of twenty-four replacement subjects to be assigned as needed to any level of the research design. Data were obtained from these subjects, blind to their identity as replacements. In other words they were included in the study as if they were ordinary subjects. As expected, four subjects were lost during the sixteen-month duration of the study, two from each of two different levels of the population: Two lower-class, vernacular-speaking boys moved to another first grade in a different school as did two middle-class, nonvernacular-speaking girls from the first grade of the urban school. To obtain equal numbers of subjects in each cell, an important consideration for the statistical analyses employed in the study, two subjects were dropped randomly from the remaining levels of the design, leaving six subjects at each level.

Procedures

During the early weeks of the study, research associates worked in the classrooms with individuals and small groups of children. They read stories to the children; invited them to retell the stories or to tell other stories 'they knew,' and encouraged them to write, often providing such materials as colored paper, booklets, or flow pens. Children also were given the opportunity to dictate stories of their own composition, with the researcher acting as scribe. The oral story retellings as well as the dictated stories were frequently audiotaped to prepare the way for recording as a part of later data collection. These activities were carried out in the regular classroom or other available vacant rooms in the school. All children had the opportunity to hear stories, to retell stories, or to leave a dictation experience prior to the actual data collection for the study.

The language samples in the three modes were collected in March and October, 1979 and in May 1980. Seven research associates participated in the data collection; all of them had been working in the classrooms and were known to the children as visiting teachers. At least one associate worked regularly with each classroom and knew the children well. All researchers were trained in data-collection procedures.

Story-retelling data were usually collected on one day in each school, followed by the collection of dictation data, which required three or four days in each school. Every effort was made to fit the dictation and writing experiences into the ongoing life of the classroom. The writing was carried out in the classroom with the class teachers discussing the assignment with the children.

Story Retelling

Three very different folktales were chosen for the retelling experience. The quality of the story, reasonable length for retelling, and children's lack of knowledge of the tale were among the criteria that influenced selection.

Stories were read to small groups of four to six children who were told that they would hear one of the teacher's favorite stories and would be asked to retell the story to other teachers who had never heard the story. Children were taken to a small room away from the noise and bustle of the classroom, instructions were given, and the stories were read to the children, preserving as nearly as possible the technique ordinarily employed by the teacher. Pictures were viewed and comments from the children were accepted but not encouraged.

After listening to a story, each child was taken to a research assistant posing as a teacher who allegedly was unfamiliar with the story. A listener was available for each child, thereby controlling the elapsed time between listening and retelling. The research assistant reiterated the directions, including the "teacher's" alleged naive status regarding the story. Children were told that their retelling would be tape recorded for the purpose of presenting their rendition to other teachers who were interested in learning about stories. Children were neither interrupted nor aided while producing their texts so that nothing other than their productive, text-forming capabilities were obtained.

Dictated-Story Data

Over the sixteen months of the study, children dictated original stories during the same two-week period in which retelling and writing samples were obtained from each time interval sampled. Prior to each dictation, children were given opportunities to dictate original stories to research assistants as a way of familiarizing the children with procedures and establishing dictation as a commonplace classroom routine that involved being audiotaped. Children were instructed that stories were to be scribed (taken down) for them and that the stories were to be their very own rather than ones that they knew, had read, or had been told. They were also cautioned to avoid familiar television tales.

Research assistants wrote the dictated stories in manuscript form in full view of the children who were given every opportunity to observe and note the activities of the scribe. The purpose, of course, was to combine both oral and written contextual constraints. To eliminate background noise, dictations were elicited and taped in a room apart from the classroom. Children were told that their stories were to be placed in a classroom story collection and that the tape recorder would help to increase the accuracy of the scribe's transcription prior to typing the stories for the storybook collection. The scribe did not interrupt children once dictation began and attempted to write at the rate established by the children. Obvious retellings of familiar children's tales or television shows were discouraged and a new text was elicited.

Story-Writing Procedures

During the two-weeks observation period, an 'assigned writing' sample was collected from each subject. Every effort was made to make this activity a natural part of the ongoing work of the classrooms. But in some situations, particularly in the early collections in grade 1, the children were not accustomed to writing original stories; in fact, many did very little writing, and that which was produced was often copied from charts or the chalkboard. Therefore, in the beginning, it was necessary to develop with the teachers those conditions that would interest children and cause them to write a story within a period of one or two days. Emphasis was placed on writing stories; thus, children were given colored paper or paper folded into booklets to further establish the story context. Teachers discussed the writing assignment with the children and tried to link it to work and experiences in which the children were currently involved. Sometimes the discussion centered about stories, a wordless picture book, or a recent particular experience—a visit to the Big Bear Supermarket or a performance by a mime. The contexts were varied, but a first priority of the investigations was to work within the curriculum and constraints of each classroom.

Sessions for assigned writing were not limited in time. However, the norm was for the children to begin in early morning and continue for an hour or more, or until most children were finished. Anyone who was not finished and wished to do so kept his or her story to work on through the afternoon and next day. The researcher as well as the classroom teacher were available in the initial writing session and the researcher returned the next day to read through the produced stories with the child authors. This last step was essential because children were encouraged to use their personal, creative, or invented spellings. Occasionally, these renditions were beyond interpretation without the help of the child author. The exact word intended was essential for the cohesion and story-structure analysis as well as for the spelling coding.

As soon as the writing was obtained, two copies were made and the original was returned to the classroom if so requested by the teacher; however, in most instances, the original script was retained.

Preparing the Oral and Written Texts for Coding

Transcripts of the audiotaped retellings and dictations were first typed without punctuation, capitalizing proper nouns and the first-person singular pronoun. All recorded verbalizations were included in this transcript. Repetitions, filled pauses, corrections, false starts, and stutters were transcribed as well as interjections by the experimenter—usually an indication of interest, such as "yes" or repetition of a word or phrase following a long pause. Unintelligible text segments were indicated by ellipses points (. . .) and experimenter's interjections were noted by the code, IN.

Two research assistants then edited the transcripts with the aid of the recordings that had been made of the retellings, dictations, and oral readings of written stories. Children's texts were separated from the total recorded text of a session, with all text boundaries determined by two editors working in conjunction with one another. Filled pauses, unmotivated repetitions, and abandoned forms as well as asides and interjections were edited out of the final copy of these narratives. Two edited transcripts follow; first, a retelling; second, a dictation:

> once there was an old woman and her little girl and they were really poor and they only had [a little] a tiny loaf of bread and then every day the little girl would go out [to find] to the woods to find some nuts and berries. . . .

> . . .[um] the witch [um] went to feed the hogs then [um] the witch went to feed the chickens then the horses* did I say pigs
> did I say pigs*
> IN: **you said hogs**
> *oh then pigs* (she went to feed) she went to feed the pigs. . .

For the purpose of cohesion analysis, one further step was taken to prepare the texts for coding. Cohesion analysis at the intersentence level requires that sentences or sentencelike units of language be identified prior to coding. What constitutes a sentence in children's oral texts is often difficult to specify, as is the definition of a sentence in the absence of punctuation marks (Allerton, 1969; Crystal, 1976). Hunt's (1964) T-unit was selected as the operational definition of a sentence because of its known reliability in identifying complex clauses and because of the wide use of this segmentation procedure in other developmental research; thus, this afforded comparability with other language-development data. Texts were then segmented into T-units.

Story-Structure Coding and Analyses

Texts may be thought of as having fixed and variable elements. The purpose of text analysis is to characterize these two properties. Propp (1968) attempted to specify the fixed properties of Russian fairy tales according to the functions of the dramatis personae by focusing on what characters do rather than on who carries out actions or on how actions are accomplished. Functions abstractly represent actions; they are defined without reference to the character who performs them. A person who helps the hero satisfy a need can vary from tale to tale. The helper can be a witch, the hero's friend, or a stranger. The underlying action is the same. But because the action does take place within the overall set of actions that go to make up the tale, a given act can have different meanings. Someone who helps the hero obtain an agent necessary for satisfying a need renders a service far different from a person who helps lure the hero into a trap. Thus, identical acts can represent quite different functions. And quite different acts may have the same meaning. For example, a warning to a child not to go into the forest differs significantly from one given to a combatant in the course of a conflict. A function is always defined relative to its significance for the course of the action.

Functions, therefore, serve as fixed elements in a tale. They are the basic constituents of the story. Propp identified thirty-one functions; however, not all functions must occur in a single tale (see Table 5.1 for a list of these functions and their definitions). When functions do occur in a tale, they ordinarily do so in a particular order. Thus, order constitutes a second fixed element in a tale. Order grows out of the elemental logic of actions. Help cannot be given without some preexisting need for it or without some circumstances wherein the hero's plight is made obvious. The transfer of money must likewise be preceded by a clear need or a rendered service. Thus, order derives not from convention but from the logic of events and actions. Tales with the same functions and orders are most likely representative of the same genre. But too much should not be made of order. Even in Propp's analysis of Russian tales, he was forced to posit the notion of transformations to account for tales whose functions appeared in a noncanonical order. If the order of functions follows logically from the nature of the actions, then it is not necessary to preserve canonical order.

Subsidiary or minor tales may be embedded within or follow upon the major tale. Propp refers to these subsidiary tales as moves. The terminology is not critical; thus, we, too, in our study refer to all such subsidiary actions as moves. What is significant about them is that parallel, repeated, and sequential moves complicate a tale, giving rise to the question of how such subsidiary moves are to be coded and scaled. Propp, of course, solved the problem by bracketing moves, specifying two functions as the basis for assigning a bracket, villainy and lack. In addition, two pairings—struggle coupled with victory and a difficult task coupled with its solution—constitute mutually exclusive elements that distinguish villainy tales from seeker tales. A tale, conceivably, could contain both pairings, one pairing, or neither pairing. Their presence simply helps to distinguish between moves but in no way should be considered obligatory. What is obligatory is villainy or lack.

Functions may have a double meaning. For example, in *The Magic Porridge Pot* (Galdone, 1976), the mother lacks knowledge of the witch's interdiction, which, of course, she cannot help but violate. Both lack and violation of an interdiction were coded, for both meanings were inherent in the action that ensued. A text may also be vague in terms of the actions of a character—and a function, therefore, difficult to assign. For example, the text says: "Mother Goose was going out." But no further mention is made of her actions. Is this sufficient as a case of absention? Coding in these instances was governed by the principle of assigning functions on the basis of consequences. Did the tale proceed as if absention occurred? If so, then the meaning of the function was absention and so coded. If subsequent actions indicating Mother Goose did not go out, then absention was not coded. Questions of this sort were always resolved by defining the function according to its consequences.

TABLE 5.1   Propp's (1968) Functions and Their Definitions

---

1. Absention: One member of a family or other grouping leaves home.
   a. elders
   b. parents
   c. children
2. Interdiction: A restriction, obligation, imperative, request, or suggestion is addressed to the hero.
3. Violation: The interdiction is ignored or otherwise violated. Often the violation of an interdiction is accompanied by the introduction of a villain.
4. Reconnaissance: The villain attempts to observe and gather information about the victim.
5. Delivery: The villain obtains information about the victim, usually through a direct answer to the villain's deceptive inquiry or through a careless revelation.
6. Trickery: The villain attempts to deceive the victim in order to capture the victim or possess the victim's belongings or loved ones. The following means are most commonly employed:
   a. disguise and persuasion
   b. disguise and magic
   c. disguise and deception or coercion
7. Complicity: The hero unwittingly submits to deception, persuasion, or villainy, thereby aiding the villain, or through the hero's own action or inaction gives his adversary an advantage.
8A. Villainy: The villain causes harm or injury to a member of the group or family. The villainy may take one of the following forms:
   a. abduction
   b. seizure of belongings, magical agent or helper
   c. pillage
   d. enchantment
   e. injury
   f. victimize
   g. obdurate sacrifice
   h. murder
   i. torment
   j. war
   k. injustice
   l. despoiling
8B. Lack: One member of the group or family lacks or desires something. Desires may be personal, material, or ethereal. Common examples are:
   a. bride, friend, partner
   b. magical agent
   c. insight, rationality
   d. money, subsistence
9. Mediation: The villainy or lack is revealed either to the hero or by the hero. Mediation may be a:
   a. call for help
   b. request, command
   c. direct announcement
   d. banishment
   e. condemnation
   f. lament
10. Counteraction: The hero decides upon or agrees to a course of action.
11. Departure: The hero leaves home in quest of something or in response to an action or request. Departures are distinguished from other translocations by the pattern of ac-

tion that ensues. The most common accompaniment is the introduction of a donor or benefactor. But other subsequent actions are possible as well. A series of adventures, trials, dangers, and magical experiences may also accompany and follow a departure. To distinguish departures from naturally occurring or magical translocations, departures can be expected to occur only once within a move while translocations may occur without limitation on frequency, and ordinarily departures will be made from a locale such as home. Departures are integral to the developing action while translocations are not.

12. Preparation: The hero is prepared through interrogation, trial, testing, or observation to nullify the villainy or remedy the lack. Often a benefactor or donor is the instrument of this preparation.
13. Reaction: The preparation is either successful or a failure hinging on the hero's reaction to the preparation. Reaction and preparation are reciprocals. The range of preparatory tasks is almost unlimited but the hero either succeeds or fails to achieve a state of preparation necessary to nullify the villainy or remedy the lack. The remedy may be and often is achieved through magic but may also be gained through insight, knowledge, or strength of character.
14. Receipt: The hero acquires the agent or remedy through which the lack or villainy may be dispatched. Often the agent is magical, but may also be insight, knowledge, or inner strength.
15. Translocation: The hero transports or is transferred to a different location. The object of the hero's search or desires may be present in this location. The means of translocation may be extraodinary or even magical but there is no requirement that they be such.
16. Struggle: The hero and the villain join in combat. The range of contesting is considerable encompassing everything from open combat to dickering and persuasion.
17. Branding: The hero is marked by a wound or a binding for the wound.
18. Victory: The villain is defeated. Again the range of means is broad and, of course, related to the nature of the struggle. The villain may be killed, vanquished, banished, chastized, or merely outwitted.
19. Liquidation: The initial misfortune or lack is remedied. Ordinarily, the agent obtained earlier plays a pivotal role in liquidating the lack or achieving the victory. The agent employed, however, is not synonymous with a remedy. Particularly in the case of knowledge or insight acquired must this distinction be kept clear. The remedy is the changed state or condition of the hero—not the knowledge, or insight, or strength responsible for the change. The confusion that may arise on this point stems from failing to distinguish between generic and particular meaning. That is, particular cognition to the preparation. Reaction and preparation are reciprocals. The range of preparatory tasks is almost unlimited but the hero either succeeds or fails to achieve a
20. Return: The hero returns to the locale (home) where the action originated. This translocation will always be among the final ones in a move or tale.
21. Pursuit: While returning, the hero may be pursued by one or more persons or creatures.
22. Rescue: The hero is able to avoid his pursuers or is rescued from them.
23. Unrecognized Arrival: The hero arrives home unrecognized.
24. Unfounded Claims: A false hero makes unfounded claims.
25. Difficult Task: A difficult task is proposed to settle the opposing claims.
26. Solution: The difficult task is completed.
27. Recognition: The hero is recognized by virtue of performing the difficult task or by the brand acquired earlier.
28. Exposure: The false hero is exposed or the villain is revealed for what he is.
29. Transfiguration: The hero is given or acquires a new appearance.
30. Punishment/Rebuke: The villain is punished, and the hero is sometimes rebuked. The

hero may also be reprimanded for violating an interdiction or rebuked for a transgression. Both are intended though as gentle palliatives.
31. Equilibrium: A terminal state of harmony and union is achieved. Often this state is indicated by a marker such as "They lived happily ever after."

Genre Classification

After judges were trained and interjudge reliabilities were established, each protocol was classified as to its genre of discourse. For even though task instructions to the children had specified that they tell or write stories, many children produced other kinds of texts. Protocols thus were classified as follows:

1. *No text*—No utterance produced by the child.
2. *Statement/label*—A single word or phrase defining or describing something in the immediate environment. For example, "It was a duck" (or "desk").
3. *Composition*—A present tense depiction of a child's current experience. Compositions are closely identified with the circumstances in, and for, which they are produced, that is, completing a writing assignment for the teacher. To illustrate, "my mom is nice. I go to school. My mom loves me."
4. *Interaction*—A text with many elements of a dialogue that has an implied listener with whom an experience is being shared. For example, "First, you draw a circle. Then you draw a line. Then you make another line here."
5. *Chronicle*—Narrative that parallels real events in a child's life, yet expressed in a story frame with conventions, such as, "Once a little girl and boy went to Disneyland." Characters, actions that parallel nonfictive experience, and thematic unity characterize these texts.
6. *Tale*—Narrative that sets forth events and circumstances that may reflect real life but without essential dependence on historical fact. It has thematic unity, conventional story markers, and fictional characters as well as fantastical events. It is fictive in nature.

Following genre classification, chronicles and tales were coded and scored for Proppian functions by five judges blind to subject identity but aware of context variations because there was no way to conceal these differences entirely—retellings, of course, being about the same well-known stories. Only retellings and dictations were compared. Despite instructions to the contrary, many children failed to produce chronicles and tales in the writing context, thus precluding comparisons with a measure that presumed a story genre. As reported earlier, interjudge reliabilities were moderately high. Still, occasional coding problems and questions arose. Two judges resolved such questions and assigned a function as agreed. It should be noted that in scoring the retellings, no attempt was made to assess recall. Only the functions found in the children's texts were scored, regardless of whether or not a counterpart for a given function could be found in the tale the children had heard. The present study sought only to compare 'packaging' and production of functions. Studies of the role of memory and comprehension in production are under consideration for later analyses.

Selecting Stories for Retelling

In selecting stories for retelling, a main concern was to find stories that were not known to our subjects but that would likely interest them. Our subjects varied greatly in their experiences with traditional literature—from one group who seemed to have some acquaintence with almost all stories considered to another group whose background was meager. Selecting stories became more of a problem than originally anticipated.

Most Russian fairy tales were too long and complex for some of our subjects at the beginning of the project. We looked for well-formed and artfully illustrated folktales, especially recently published ones or new versions of old tales. To heighten interest we chose to use picture books, but this decision constrained our choices of stories.

Three very different stories were eventually selected for story retelling—a modern fable, a folktale, and a Russian fairy tale. These included Preston's (1974) *Squawk to the Moon, Little Goose*; Galdone's (1976) *The Magic Porridge Pot*, and the Zemachs's (1976) *Salt: A Russian Folk Tale.*

Squawk to the Moon, Little Goose is a story of lack that has embedded within it three brief tales of villainy that provide the trebling element found in many folktales. The story also contains folktale features of trickery and Little Goose's refrain, "Good's good and bad's bad."

In Proppian analysis, the tale has two moves:

a   (beginning situation)
2   (interdiction) coupled with 1 (absention)
8B (lack; maturity and insight) and 3 (violation of interdiction)
. . .
6   (trickery) coupled with 7 (complicity)
8A (villainy)
10 (counteraction)
11 (departure)
12 (preparation)
13 (reaction)
15 (translocation)
8A (villainy)
9   (mediation)

10 (counteraction) coupled with 14 (receipt)
18 (victory) coupled with 19 (liquidation)
. . .
20 (return)
30 (punishment 1 rebuke)
31 (equilibrium)

    The Magic Porridge Pot is one version of the magic pot tales that exist in several different cultures. It is especially appealing to children because it is the mother who uses the magic pot without permission and as a result creates a huge problem that the daughter solves. Actually *The Magic Porridge Pot* is two tales conjoined by an interdiction given in the first and the violation of the interdiction in the second. In Propp's terms it is a tale with two moves:

a   (beginning situation)
8B (lack) joined with 11 (departure)
9   (mediation)
12 (function of donor) and 2 (interdiction)
14 (receipt of magic agent) and 15 (transference)
19 (lack liquidated) and 31 (equilibrium)

    The final state of happiness in the first tale provides the beginning for the second:

1   (absention)
8B (lack) and 3 (violation of interdiction)
20 (return)
19 (lack liquidated)
31 (equilibrium)

    Salt: A Russian Folk Tale is a story of the younger brother, "the fool," succeeding in making his fortune while his two older brothers turn to villainy and fail. It is a tale of lack—lack of status and success—that, although rich in detail, is shorter and somewhat more complex than *Squawk to the Moon, Little Goose*. Both *Salt: A Russian Folk Tale* and *Squawk to the Moon, Little Goose* differ considerably, however, from *The Magic Porridge Pot*, which is a fairly straightforward and brief story with a slight ironical twist in the second move. Both *Salt: A Russian Folk Tale* and *Squawk to the Moon, Little Goose* contain parallel action and multiple embedding. Although *Squawk to the Moon, Little Goose* embodies the simple but clear moral ambiance of a fable for children, *Salt: A Russian Folk Tale* has all the atmospherics of a true Russian fairy tale. Thus, each story constituted a rather different experience for each retelling.

Data Analyses

Both multivariate and univariate analyses of variance were employed for cohesion and story-structure analyses. Proportions of the five kinds of cohesive ties and number of story functions, function types, and moves served as dependent variables in a wide variety of complementary comparisons designed to probe changes in these text-forming characteristics that stem from developmental, production-mode, school, constitutional, and socioeconomic sources. The purpose of these analyses was to tease out differences and relationships that accounted for differences in texts. Detailed descriptions of these procedures may be found in King, Rentel, Pappas, Pettegrew, and Zutell, (1981) and in King and Rentel (1982) along with full presentations of findings.

Cohesion in Beginning Writing

Over the first sixteen months of the study, the latter half of first-grade and all of second-grade children increased their use of lexical cohesion dramatically, irrespective of social or linguistic background (King & Rentel, 1981). On the average, children increased the proportion of lexical cohesion in writing from roughly 18 percent to nearly 50 percent of cohesive ties employed. In addition to lexical cohesion, children used conjunctions proportionately more, and a wider range of them, thus adding approximately 5 percent more conjunctions to their texts every 4 months. Lexical devices appeared to link meanings at the level of both propositionalizing and schematizing. Beginning texts, like the one that follows, depended heavily on additive conjunctions, repetition, and synonymy to link propositions. Note also this example:

(1) Once there were these *bombers.*
(2) *And they* tried to destroy this bridge.
(3) *And they* had *airplanes* and *bombers.*

In (3), the ultimate referent for *they* lies outside the text, but in (2), *they* refers back to *bombers.* Such use of reference, both exophoric and endophoric (that is, reference outside and within the text), marked children's early productions. About 34 percent of the total ties in children's beginning texts referred to something or someone outside the text, but this percentage declined swiftly to 3 percent by the second month of grade 2 and remained at that level throughout the year. Thus, children, regardless of class, sex, dialect, or school, increasingly confined reference ties to their texts. Both substitution and ellipsis were employed sparingly.

These overall developmental differences in use of cohesion are illustrated by the text below. This excerpted text is from a sample of writing collected at the end of the second grade. The excerpts are from a much longer text but are presented with intervening units omitted to convey a sense of how various cohesive devices are employed over large spans of text to link presupposed meanings.

(1) Once there was a little *hamster* named *Dancer.*

.
.
.

(8) *Dancer ran* all *around* the *house.*
(9) Then someone opened the door.

.
.
.

(10) *She skitter-skattered out* of the *house.*

.
.
.

(14) *When she* was *outside, she* made lots of *friends.*

.
.
.

(18) *Toby,* the *tomcat,* was *her* best *friend.*
(19) *She* met Bom Bom, the *bird,* and Tommy, the *tiger.*

First, there are the lexical ties: around, out, outside (collocation); house, door (meronymy or part-whole relationships); ran, skitter-skattered (synonymy); friends, friend (reiteration); and tomcat, bird, tiger (hyponymy or coclassification). The conjunctions then and when (both temporals), have replaced the word and (an additive conjunction) as the means of linking grammatical units. The pronouns she and her refer consistently within the text to Dancer, the hamster.

Children appear to have discovered the versatility of lexical ties as a means for establishing textual relevance through synonyms, antonyms, hyponyms, meronyms, and reiteration. Coupled with their dramatic increase in the ability to establish identity of reference within a text (at the end of second grade), children tied schemata together with relations of identity and similarity. Decreases in exophoric reference indicate that they understood that the text must be the relevant environment for all meaning relations. Lexical cohesion, conjunction, and reference were used also to link adjacent propositions. And, as evidenced by the enormous increase in lexical cohesion found in their texts, the children clearly grew in their ability to establish relations at the level of categories. By the end of second grade, they had acquired a wide range of cohesive options and a reasonably well-organized set of systematic options for using them. Their reference ties were routinely endophoric. They employed substitution and ellipsis infrequently; conversely, they were unhesitant in their use of conjunction. In short, so far as cohesion is concerned, their transition from oral to written texts, although not complete, was well under way by the end of second grade with few initial differences among populations remaining.

Story Structure in Beginning Writing

Earlier we argued that action elements similar to those identified by the Russian structuralist, Vladimir Propp, were often found in children's fictional narratives (Applebee, 1978; Botvin & Sutton-Smith, 1977; Rubin & Gardner, 1977). Based on this evidence as well as on evidence that the story recalls of children's skew toward a prototypical or canonical story form (Mandler & Johnson, 1977; Stein & Glenn, 1979), we hypothesized that these action elements provide relevant discourse models for beginning writers. We argued that fairy tale and folktale models influence the production of stories in three ways. First, the young storymaker must sustain a text in some cumulative way. The storyteller must produce a text containing the necessary elements of a genre. Just a relative handful of such units would provide children with a flexible cumulative basis for creating story plots, a genre most children know well.

The key to sustaining a text is repetition. Any function or group of functions may be repeated until sufficient volume has been created. For children, sustaining a text without the interactive support of a conversational partner is itself a challenging task. Simultaneously, the struggle to imagine and create elements of a plot, characters, texture, and a consistent narrative stance coupled with the mysteries of spelling, handwriting, and spatial organization also make enormous demands on processing capabilities. Potentially, repetition of functions can restrict the range of action units to be managed. This simplifies the problem of text formation. Plot, character relations, narrative stance, and texture may be held in check while continuing to maintain a story line. More attention can be devoted to the actual production of a written artifact without sacrificing important narrative intentions. The following excerpt from a beginning second grader illustrates this use of repetition:

(1) Once there was a wicked old witch
(2) her name was treetop
(3) now she was a very very wicked old witch
(4) she lived on witch main street
(5) one day when she was walking down she saw a little girl
(6) and she said in her mind that she was going to eat her
(7) so the next day she took a little walk and saw the girl
(8) the girl said do you think she is going to eat me
    .
    .
    .
(13) so the next day when she took her walk her mom came with
     her...

Once setting information has been established in lines (1) through (4), the repetition of the functions departure and villainy (potential) sustain this text throughout the remaining units. Repetition of any given function or combination of functions thus provides a means for sustaining a text. Having this capability would provide children with an important asset in helping them make the transition from face-to-face oral-text production to solo written production.

Second, the availability of underlying abstract functions provides a limited range of options from which an almost limitless variety of stories can be generated. Particular sets of options serve as defining features for such a genre as the fairy tale. This ability to specify genres constitutes an important advantage of functions over more abstract story grammars. In addition, functions, linked as they are to the actions of characters, define not only the relations between a protagonist and events that make up a plot but also have the potential for defining relations among characters and thus the capacity for specifying multiple relations with events.

Third, logical pairings, such as lack and lack liquidated or villainy and villainy nullified, comprise nuclear combinations or 'diads' that Botvin and Sutton-Smith (1977) have described as basic building blocks in the development of narrative competence. These pairings, when combined in tandem, in parallel, or when embedded one within the other, afford the storymaker opportunities for thematic reflection, permutation, and variation. The principal advantage to be gained through such pairings is that of dimensionality. Using pairings such as these, children would possess the ingredients to create rather complex stories without making excessive demands on memory.

Very substantial differences among discourse contexts for all three story-structure variables demonstrated that production was clearly affected by input factors and the availability or, perhaps, accessibility of information stored in memory. Retelling texts contained roughly twice as many functions and function types as dictated texts and about four to five times as many functions and function types as written texts. Both retellings and dictations contained significantly more moves than written stories. Quite obviously and expectedly, producing a written text makes enormous demands and places severe restrictions on composing capabilities. Over an observation period of sixteen months, only a significant overall effect for function types was obtained. When each discourse context was analyzed separately, however, significant effects for all three dependent variables were obtained only for the writing context. In the retelling context, just function types increased significantly over observations; in the dictation context, no significant differences were obtained over observations for any of the dependent variables.

The finding that number of function types increased significantly over observations for both the retelling and the writing context suggests that developmental increases in the ability to comprehend and recall stories are accompanied by corollary increases in production capabilities. Recalling that the stories children retold at Observation 1 and at Observation 3 contained an equal number of function types, the differences observed in their retellings over this sixteen-month period cannot be attributed to input stories. Thus, either comprehension and recall abilities increased significantly over this period or production abilities improved significantly. Probably both kinds of ability increased concomitantly. Given the findings for writing, certainly there was a real increase in production capabilities. Correlations between retellings and written texts on number of function types ranged from low (.34) at Observation 1 to moderate (.53) at Observation 3; thus, these two tasks increasingly shared variance associated with an expanding range of function types. It seems reasonable to conclude that the same developmental factors that were responsible for differences in retellings over observations were also responsible for the wider range of function types found in children's written texts over this same period of time. The variable, function types, is presumably rooted in exposure to folktales and fairy tales or their fantasy counterparts found in television cartoons and serials as well as motion pictures.

Some appreciation of how much the children's tales came to bear a clear resemblance to traditional folktales and fairy tales can be gleaned from the following story written by a child at the end of the second grade.

Unit	*Function*
(1) Once upon a time there was a bunny named Benjie	Setting
(2) and she had magic powers	Magical agent
(3) one day she was walking in the woods	Departure
(4) and a boy bunny appeared	"
(5) and they went together for a walk	Translocation
(6) and a man appeared with a big net	Reconnaisance
(7) and he got the two bunnies and went in a big ship	Villainy
(8) poor bunnies	
(9) they were caught now	
(10) but right then the girl bunny tripped the man	Struggle
(11) and they got free once again	Villainy Nullifield
(12) so the boy bunny thanked the girl bunny for saving him	Reward
(13) the boy bunny asked the girl bunny to marry him	Equilibrium (Propp's wedding)
(14) and she said yes	"
(15) so they had six baby bunnies	"
(16) and they lived happily ever after	"

The resemblance between this second-grader's story and a fairy tale is a strong one. The range of functions included in this tale exceeds the range of functions typically produced by late second graders. Yet, in other respects, such as length, cohesive ties, number of functions and complexity, this story is fairly typical of texts written by children near the end of the second grade.

The evidence we have obtained about the role of stories in beginning-writing development is far from decisive. It does provide weak but plausible grounds for believing that the comprehension and representation of stories in memory constitute rudiments of a rhetorical schema for composing stories during the beginning phases of writing development. Over time, children in our sample increasingly built narrative structures predicated on functionlike action units. As they wrote longer stories, they included more functions and a greater range of function types in their tales. The correlation between story length as measured by number of T-units and number of functions over observations ranged from .61 at Observation 1 to .92 at Observation 2 and to .70 at Observation 3. Correlations between text length and the range of function types, as might be expected, closely paralleled those for number of functions: Observation 1, .54; Observation 2, .90; and Observation 3, .75. Both sets of correlations indicated that functions and function types were measuring the same, or nearly the same, underlying capability relative to text length. But function types appeared to be a somewhat more sensitive developmental indicator than functions. These correlations with length suggested that as texts increased in length, they manifested greater breadth and range of storymaking capabilities and increased sustaining power on the part of the developing writers we studied. We think that familiarity with stories played a substantial role in this development.

LONGITUDINAL STUDIES OF WRITING DEVELOPMENT

The structure in which scientific knowledge is created is relatively straightforward and simple. The scientist merely asks, "How are two things related?" "Under what conditions do they affect one another?" "What is a reasonable explanation of these relationships and effects?" The scientist's logic, attitudes, and traditions of peer review are his or her major defenses against error. Aside from the ways in which conditions and things are controlled, scientific methods differ mainly in nuance. At the heart of the enterprise is reasoning of the form, "if p, then q." At the end is an empirical test of the validity of the scientist's explanations. The most creative aspect of science is determining what p and q are.

Longitudinal research is one method for asking questions and submitting them to empirical tests. Its advantage and disadvantage is that things come to the researcher in their natural states where both things and their relationships are difficult to sort out. Because a necessary first step in science is to determine what to observe, that is, to delineate the dependent variables of the phenomenon under study, some consideration must be given to how these variables are to be selected. Our arguments, of course, led to the selection of cohesive ties and elemental functions in fairy tales as variables salient to the transition from spoken to written texts. But aside from the arguments given, were there other reasons of a different nature that influenced our selection? Both cohesion and story structure promised to be sensitive to the sorts of manipulations permissible in the ongoing life of classrooms—sensitive because we could reliably observe them in the protocols children produced and we had a fairly full grasp of their theoretical significance. The conditions for learning to write were very clearly defined by the existing curricula in the schools we studied. Obviously, we had little choice in that matter. But we could establish or easily devise ways of assessing a child's status with respect to these variables and thus characterize the emergence of the ability to write under specified conditions. These conditions we attempted to describe fully and clearly.

The factors that influence learning to write are enormously complicated and highly interactive. Unraveling the sheer number and kinds of interactions, ranging from contextual to constitutional contingencies, as they accumulate over time is a staggering problem. Our initial aim was to separate relevant independent variables from this flux. We had little or no hope of determining causes. What we did have, however, were children whose histories and achievements typically differ dramatically—poor inner-city black children and affluent suburban white children—and in that inner-city magnet school, a population of affluent middle-class white children. By focusing on their emerging histories through successive, well-timed observations that incorporated ever-so-slight manipulations, we hoped to ensnare rather large global attributes at first. Subsequent studies, designed to sift the data from these observations through finer and finer analyses, will provide us with a fuller, more complete picture of the factors that contribute to growth in writing ability. As stated earlier, we have identified the following global characteristics: school, grade, sex, SES, dialect, and discourse context.

Most of our original developmental hypotheses were confirmed. Very early in the process of schooling, the children in our study appeared to grasp the notion that in writing all meanings must be confined to their texts. As predicted, they relied heavily on lexical cohesion, conjunction, and reference to link propositions in their texts. Their ability to write longer complex stories was predicated on gains in their ability to comprehend and recall stories. These findings, however, do not constitute adequate evidence for drawing strong inferences about schematizing, propositionalizing, and categorizing as fundamental mechanisms of production. Such evidence can only come from tightly controlled laboratory studies. Instead, our data provided careful, detailed descriptions of important developmental trends and differences in writing and in the transition to writing.

Currently, we are investigating how developing patterns of cohesion contribute to text coherence by probing how chains of reference ties and lexical ties throughout the text intertwine at grammatical intersections in sentences (Hasan, 1978, 1980). In companion studies, we are attempting to determine how these relationships combine with narrative stance or point of view as cocontributors to text coherence—again, within a developmental framework.

The ultimate purpose of any kind of educational research, of course, is the compilation of knowledge necessary to guide educational theory and practice. The goals of educational research, regardless of type, are to minimize harmful or wasteful experience and maximize the probability of optimal development for each student. When all goes well, there even may be the potential in educational research for making contributions to basic knowledge. Research on writing shares these purposes and goals. Like educational research in general, research on writing shares many of the fundamental difficulties encountered in school-related inquiry.

Not the least of these problems is that of obtaining reliable and representative samples of data. Most learning contexts and all school settings are complex interactive social entities. We would like to propose two safeguards against errors arising from these difficulties. First, to the extent possible, that observations or measures of attributes of writing be set within the fullest theoretical backing available. Where theoretical backing is weak or lacking, then the most stringent protections available should be applied to the analysis of data and great care taken to restrict generalization. Second, that multiple measures or observations within varying contexts be taken, that is, sampling of several sorts from the population of situations where writing is likely to occur. Our work thus far has demonstrated to us that there is an ebb and flow to writing development linked intimately to situations and population groupings. And there are individual eddies in this swirling current. There is an old and familiar nursery verse that begins, "Monday's child is..." and ends with "Sunday's child is..." We have learned to expect this variability in each child.

The major drawback of our research, as in all longitudinal research, is the inability to draw strong causal inferences from our data. It is not possible, in any sense, to do more with our data than describe the status of our various populations at given points in a developmental trajectory. The value of longitudinal data is the control exercised over within-subject differences. Stable differences among subjects can be identified in a way that is reasonably free of this within-subjects' error. The power of our data and of longitudinial research in general is its firm link with reality and its potentially strong developmental effects. These links and effects can blaze a trail for more compelling and causally persuasive experimental research. In this sense, longitudinal studies of writing development constitute a productive approach to theory and inquiry—longitudinal research can and often does serve as an important source of reasonable experimental hypotheses. And, at a very practical level, longitudinal studies set out clear developmental beacons that teachers may follow in shaping their expectations for curricula and instruction.

NOTE

1. This is part of a larger study by M. King, V. Rentel, C. Pappas, B. Pettegrew, & J. Zutell, *How Children Learn to Write: A Longitudinal Study*, published by The Ohio State University Research Foundation in 1981. This study was made possible by two grants, NIE G–79–0039 and G–79–0137; awarded to the co-authors of this chapter. The opinions expressed in this chapter do not necessarily reflect the position, policy, or endorsement of the National Institute of Education.

REFERENCES

Allerton, D. J. The sentence as a linguistic unit. *Lingua*, 1969, *22*, 27–46.

Applebee, A. N. *The child's concept of story: Ages two to seventeen*. Chicago: University of Chicago Press, 1978.

Bernstein, B. *Class, codes and control* (Vol. 1). London: Routledge & Kegan Paul, 1971.

Botvin, G. J. *The development of narrative competence: A syntagmatic analysis of children's fantasy narratives*. Unpublished doctoral dissertation, Columbia University, 1977.

Botvin, G. J., & Sutton-Smith, B. The development of structural complexity in children's fantasy narratives. *Developmental Psychology*, 1977, *13*, 377–388.

Bremond, C. Morphology of the French folktale. *Semiotica*, 1970, *2*, 247–276.

Britton, J. *Language and learning*. Harmondsworth, England: Penguin, 1970.

Britton, J., Burgess, T., Martin, McLeod, A., & Rosen, H. *The development of writing abilities (11–18)*. London: Macmillan, 1975.

Bruner, J. S. The ontogenesis of speech acts. *Journal of Child Language*, 1975, *2*, 1–19.

Carroll, W. S., & Feigenbaum, I. Teaching a second dialect and some implications for TESOL. *TESOL Quarterly*, 1967, *1*, 31–40.

Cazden, C. B. *Child language and education*. New York: Holt, Rinehart & Winston, 1972.

Cazden, C. B. Play and metalinguistic awareness: One dimension of language experience. *Urban Review*, 1974, 7, 28–39.

Chafe, W. L. Creativity in verbalization and its implications for the nature of stored knowledge. In R. O. Freedle (Ed.), *Discourse production and comprehension* (Vol. 1). Norwood, N.J.: Ablex, 1977. (a)

Chafe, W. L. The recall and verbalization of past experience. In R. W. Cole (Ed.), *Current issues in linguistic theory*. Bloomington: Indiana University Press, 1977. (b)

Clark, E. U. Building a vocabulary: Words for objects, actions, and relations. In P. Fletcher & M. Garman (Eds.), *Language acquisition.* London: Cambridge University Press, 1979.

Cook-Gumperz, J. Situated instructions: Language socialization of school-age children. In S. Ervin-Tripp & C. Mitchell-Kernan (Eds.), *Child discourse.* New York: Academic Press, 1977.

Crystal, D. *Child language, learning and linguistics.* London: Edward Arnold, 1976.

DeStefano, J. S. Black English. In J. S. DeStefano (Ed.), *Language, society and education: A profile of black English.* Worthington, Ohio: Charles A. Jones, 1973.

DeStefano, J. S., & Rentel, V. Language variation: Perspectives for teachers. *Theory into Practice,* 1975, *15*, 328–337.

Dillard, J. L. *Black English: Its history and usage in the United States.* New York: Random House, 1972.

Donaldson, M. *Children's minds.* Glasgow: Fontana/Collins, 1978

Doughty, P., Pearce, J., & Thornton, G. *Exploring language.* London: Edward Arnold, 1972.

Dundes, A. *The morphology of North American Indian folktales.* Helsinki: F. F. Communications, No. 1965, 1964.

Dungan, R. *Prose memory of good and poor first-grade readers: Effects of repeated exposures.* Unpublished doctoral dissertation, The Ohio State University, Columbus, Ohio, 1977.

Fasold, R. W., & Wolfram, W. Some linguistic features of negro dialect. In R. W. Fasold & R. W. Shuy (Eds.), *Teaching standard English in the inner city.* Washington, D. C.: Center for Applied Linguistics, 1970.

Favat, A. *Child and tale: The origins of interest* (Research Report No. 19). Urbana, Ill., National Council of Teachers of English, 1977.

Francis, H. *Language in childhood: Form and function in language learning.* London: Paul Elek, 1975.

Galdone, P. *The magic porridge pot.* (Illus. P. Galdone.) Boston: Houghton Mifflin, 1976.

Garvey, C., & McFarlane, P. A measure of standard English proficiency of inner-city children. *American Educational Research Journal,* 1970, *7,* 29–40.

Graves, D. *Children's writing: Research directions and hypotheses based upon an examination of the writing process of seven-year-old children.* Unpublished doctoral dissertation, State University of New York at Buffalo, Buffalo, N.Y., 1973. (ERIC Document Reproduction Service No. ED 095 371)

Graves, D. We won't let them write. *Language Arts,* 1978, *55,* 635–640.

Graves, D. Andrea learns to make writing hard. *Language Arts,* 1979, *56,* 569–576.

Garvin, P. L. Operations in syntactic analysis. In *On linguistic method: Selected papers.* The Hague: Mouton, 1964.

Halliday, M. A. K. *Explorations in the functions of language.* London: Edward Arnold, 1973.

Halliday, M. A. K. *Learning how to mean: Explorations in the development of language.* London: Edward Arnold, 1975.

Halliday, M. A. K. *Language as social semiotic.* London: Edward Arnold, 1978.

Halliday, M. A. K., & Hasan, R. *Cohesion in English.* London: Longman, 1976.

Hasan, R. Code, register and social dialect. In B. Bernstein (Ed.), *Class, codes and control* (Vol. 2). London: Routledge & Kegan Paul, 1973.

Hasan, R. *Cohesive harmony.* Paper presented at the annual meeting of the International Reading Association, St. Louis, May 1980.

Hasan, R. The texture of a text. In M. A. K. Halliday & R. Hasan (Eds.), *Text and context: Aspects of language in a sociosemiotic perspective.* Tokyo: Sophia University, 1978.

Hildreth, G. Developmental sequences in name writing. *Child Development,* 1936, *7,* 291–302.

Hunt, K. W. *Differences in grammatical structures written at three grade levels: The structures to be analyzed by transformational methods* (Cooperative Research Project No. 1998). Tallahassee, Fl.: U.S. Office of Education, 1964. (Report)

Hunt, K. W. *Grammatical structures written at three grade levels* (Research Report No. 3). Urbana Ill.: National Council of Teachers of English, 1965.

King, M. & Rentel, V. Research update: Conveying meaning in written texts. *Language Arts,* 1981, *58,* 721–728.

King, M., & Rentel, V. Toward theory of early writing development. *Research in the Teaching of English,* 1979, *13,* 243–253.

King, M., & Rentel, V. *The transition to writing: Cohesion and story structure.* Columbus: The Ohio State University Research Foundation, Columbus, Ohio, 1982.

King, M., Rentel, V., & Cook, C. *The influence of story structure on children's oral and written texts.* Paper presented at the annual meeting of the American Educational Research Association, Boston, April 1980.

King, M., Rentel, V., Pappas, C. C., Pettegrew, B. C., & Zutell, J. *How children learn to write: A longitudinal study.* Columbus: The Ohio State University Research Foundation, 1981.

Labov, W., & Cohen, P. *Systematic relations of standard and nonstandard rules in the grammar of negro speakers* (Project Literacy Report No. 8). Ithaca, N.Y.: Cornell University, 1967.

Labov, W., Cohen, P., Robins, C., & Lewis, J. *A study of the non-standard English Negro and Puerto Rican speakers in New York City (Vol. 1): Phonological and grammatical analysis.* (Cooperative Research Project No. 3288). Washington, D.C.: U.S. Office of Education, 1968.

Langer, S. K. *Feeling and form.* New York: Charles Scribner's, 1953.

Leondar, B. Hatching plots: Genesis of storymaking. In D. Perkins & B. Leondar (Eds.), *The arts and cognition.* Baltimore: The Johns Hopkins University Press, 1977.

Levi-Strauss, C. *The structural study of myths.* New York: Basic Books, 1963.

Loban, W. *The language of elementary school children* (Report No. 1). Urbana, Ill.: National Council of Teachers of English, 1963.

Loban, W. *Language development: Kindergarten through grade twelve* (Research Report No. 18). Urbana, Ill.: National Council of Teachers of English, 1976.

Macnamara, J. Cognitive basis of language learning in infants. *Psychological Review,* 1972, *79,* 1–13.

Mandler, J. M., & Johnson, N. S. Remembrance of things parsed: Story structure and recall. *Cognitive Psychology,* 1977, *9,* 111–151.

Maranda, E., & Maranda, K. *Structural models in folklore and transformational essays.* The Hague: Mouton, 1971.

Moffett, J. *Teaching the universe of discourse.* Boston: Houghton Mifflin, 1968.

Nelson, K. How young children represent knowledge of their world in and out of language: A preliminary report. In R. Siegler (Ed.), *Children's thinking—what develops?* Hillsdale, N.J.: Erlbaum, 1978.

O'Donnell, R., Griffin, W. J., & Norris, R. C. *Syntax of kindergarten and elementary school children: A transformational analysis* (Research Report No. 8). Urbana, Ill.: National Council of Teachers of English, 1967.

Olson, D. R. The languages of instruction: The literate bias of schooling. In R. C. Anderson, R. J. Spiro, & W. C. Montague (Eds.), *Schooling and the acquisition of knowledge.* Hillsdale, N.J.: Earlbaum, 1977.

Pappas, C. C. *The development of narrative capabilities within a synergistic, variable perspective of language development: An examination of cohesive harmony of stories produced in three contexts—retelling, dictating, and writing.* Unpublished doctoral dissertation, The Ohio State University, Columbus, Ohio, 1981.

Pettegrew, B. C. *Text formation: A comparative study of literate and preliterate first-grade children.* Unpublished doctoral dissertation, The Ohio State University, Columbus, Ohio, 1981.

Politzer, R. L., Hoover, M. R., & Brown, D. A test of proficiency in black standard and nonstandard speech. *TESOL Quarterly*, 1974, *8*, 27–35.

Preston, E. M. *Squawk to the moon, Little Goose.* (Illus. B. Cooney). New York: Viking, 1974.

Propp, V. *Morphology of the folktale* (Lawrence Scott, trans.). Austin: University of Texas Press, 1968.

Read, C. Pre-school children's knowledge of English phonology. *Harvard Educational Review*, 1971, *23*, 17–38.

Rentel, V., & Kennedy, J. Effects of pattern drill on the phonology, syntax, and reading achievement of rural Appalachian children. *American Educational Research Journal*, 1972, *9*, 87–100.

Rosch, E. On the internal structure of perceptual and semantic categories. In T. E. Moore (Ed.), *Cognitive development and the acquisition of language.* New York: Academic Press, 1973.

Rubin, S., & Gardner, H. Unpublished notes from a presentation at a conference on research in literature held at Buffalo, N.Y., 1977.

Shuy, R. W., Wolfram, W., & Riley, W. K. *Field techniques in the urban language study.* Washington, D.C.: Center for Applied Linguistics, 1968.

Stein, N. L., & Glenn, C. G. An analysis of story comprehension in elementary school children. In R. O. Freedle (Ed.), *New directions in discourse processing* (Vol. 2). Norwood, N. J.: Albex, 1979.

Sutton-Smith, B., Abrams, D., Botvin, G. J., Caring, M., Gildesgaine, D., & Stevens, T. The importance of the storymaker: An investigation of the imaginative life. *Urban Review*, 1975, *19*, 1–13.

Todorov, T. The two principles of narrative. *Diacritics*, 1971, *4*, 37–44.

Ure, J. Lexical density and register differentiation. In G. E. Perren & J. L. M. Trim (Eds.), *Applications of linguistics: Selected papers of the Second International Congress of Applied Linguistics* (Cambridge, 1969). London: Cambridge University Press, 1971.

Vygotsky, L. S. *Thought and language*. Cambridge, Mass.: MIT Press, 1962.

Warner, W. L., Meeker, M., & Ellis, K. *Social class in America*. New York: Stratford Press, 1949.

Wheeler, M. E. *Untutored acquisition of writing skill*. Unpublished doctoral dissertation, Cornell University, Ithaca, N.Y., 1971.

Winograd, T. A. A framework for understanding discourse. In M. A. Just & P. A. Carpenter (Eds.), *Cognitive processes in comprehension*. Hillsdale, N.J.: Earlbaum, 1979.

Wolfram, W. *A sociolinguistic description of Detroit Negro speech*. Washington, D.C.: Center for Applied Linguistics, 1969.

Zemach, H., & Zemach M. *Salt: A Russian folk tale*. (Illus. M. Zemach) New York: Farrar, Straus & Giroux, 1977.

6

Investigating the Control of Writing Skills[1]

Robert J. Bracewell
McGill University

This is a book on principles and methods of writing research. The reader probably has approached this book with some misgivings, which seems to me a sensible thing to do, for reading (or indeed writing) even a chapter on such a topic is a hazardous business. The problem is that people treat things labeled as principles or methods so seriously, when a commonsense knowledge of how research progresses indicates that principles and methods should be treated simply as tools to be used in the construction and criticism of theories and data. Who now remembers details of the principles and methods of the introspectionist psychologists? What is remembered is that their theoretical apparatus was abandoned because their data were not sufficiently replicable.

The danger of advancing principles and methods is that they each become enshrined in their own way, thereby losing their heuristic function of helping to direct inquiry in an area. *Principles* become canonized in textbooks, presumably to be memorized and recalled by students as good things to know. My favorite example is Bruner's six benchmarks of cognitive development. Bruner (1966) offered a number of thoughts about the nature of intellectual growth that he felt were important to keep in mind when evaluating theories of development. It is clear that these thoughts were presented somewhat tentatively:

> Probably the best way . . . is to set up some benchmarks about the nature of intellectual growth against which to measure one's efforts at explanation. My own list would include the following . . . (which) will do as a minimal list—or perhaps it is too long, for quite plainly several items on the list overlap. (p. 26).

Yet, a few years later we find these reflections tabularized in current text-books (e.g., Gage & Berliner, 1979, p. 154; Owen, Blount, & Moscow, 1978, pp. 50–51). My own guess is that Bruner, too, realized the usual fate of such proposals; nevertheless, his qualifications did not save them from sanctification.

Those *methodologies* that are adopted by the research community often undergo a type of functional ritualization. Within the research community generally, this is most often seen with data-analysis methods, such as factor-analytic techniques. But, more specifically, within the educational research community, the technique of sentence combining provides an example of ritualized method in the area of writing research itself. Research and practice on sentence combining developed out of educators' interest in transformational-generative grammar as a model of language production (Mellon, 1969). Here we have an experimental method in widespread use, for which the original theoretical basis and rationale have been proved unnecessary (O'Hare, 1974), and which, although undoubtedly influencing writing behavior, has effects of indeterminate validity (Marzano, 1976). In spite of these problems, we have seen a proliferation of sentence-combining studies, most of which have addressed essentially peripheral issues, such as the duration of the effect of practice rather than how such practice fits with the process of composing.

The danger of unwarranted doctrine is a major one in an emerging and potentially lucrative area, which writing research currently is. So the reader is advised to render reverence to those things that deserve it and to treat principles and methods to the healthy criticism that all secular activities merit. In particular, the methods for investigating the control of writing skills that I describe in this chapter should be treated with some irreverence. Not only are they educationally rather bizarre but they also are not the final word on how to investigate the writer's control over the pen. If the only outcome of this chapter is to stimulate the reader to develop alternatives for such investigations, then this effort will have achieved a modest success.

The chapter is divided into three sections. The first is concerned with the issue of writer's control over the mental activities involved in composing and with a method for assessing such control. The second deals with some initial results from studies of such control. The third section considers three of the implications of these results for research and instruction in writing.

THE CONTROL OF WRITING PROCESSES

By control of writing processes I mean the deliberate manipulation by the writer of whatever mental and physical activities that lead to the production of text. Of course the production of text does not require deliberate control of writing activities for either the skilled or unskilled writer; but I shall present the position that the ability to do so when necessary is the hallmark of the expert.

Before we begin one may ask, Is it worthwhile writing a chapter on such a topic when just about everybody would acknowledge that such control is indeed a good thing for a writer to have? Those with some knowledge about writing and its development would grant this but would advance as more worthy of consideration such issues as the possible developmental constraints on learning to write and the overcoming of writing blocks and apprehension. After all, children simply do not do very much writing (Applebee, 1981; Fillion, 1979; Graves, 1978), and any methods or principles for increasing their output should take precedence over issues of secondary importance, such as how to control writing once one is able or willing to do it. But those with more knowledge still would bring together some facts that implicate control as a crucial issue in the development of writing skills. It is true that children (and most adults) do not do much writing; moreover, when they do, they display few of the activities of expert writers, such as planning, note taking, and so on. Curiously however, when asked to do things that experts do, such as planning, what unskilled writers do is to compose text in complete sentences (Bereiter, Scardamalia, Anderson, & Smart, 1980). So, infrequent writing is not due to an inability to produce text; it must be due to something else. As the facts briefly touched on above suggest, the causes of infrequent writing are complex. But two things are clear. First, children can express themselves in writing; somewhat surprisingly (because children are usually very fond of expressing themselves), they do not do very much writing. Perhaps part of the reason for this puzzling juxtaposition lies in an ability to write that is paired with an an inability to exercise a great deal of control over the processes of writing.

The issue of control of writing processes addresses for a specific area a general issue that is of increasing importance in education, namely, the control by the student of various mental activities and strategies that increase learning. Within education this issue is often talked about in terms of study skills, awareness of comprehension failure, and learning how to learn. Within cognitive psychology, it is talked about under the rubric of metacognition, a buzzword that has begotten many little metas— metalinguistics, metamemory, metacomprehension, and so on. Such terms, even though they seem to proliferate and have little more than descriptive status, do point to an important generalization (dare one say principle?) about learning. Generally, the better grasp students have of their abilities and strategies for learning, the quicker they are able to acquire new knowledge and skills.

It is worthwhile to elaborate on what is meant by grasp of learning abilities and strategies to resolve part of the considerable confusion at the theoretical level and in the interpretation of data in this area. This confusion is well represented in the field of metacognition, and the discussion presented here focuses on this area and its terminology; but similar problems exist in the related areas of educational research. For example, How can we adequately characterize learning-how-to-learn abilities? What methods can we devise to identify their use by the learner?

Metacognition is a term used to refer to two different types of behavior (Brown, 1978; Brown & Campione, 1980; Flavell & Wellman, 1977). The first is the learner's ability to take stock of his or her own cognitive resources and task demands. A typical example would be a learner's knowledge that a list of facts grouped by categories is easier to learn than an ungrouped list. Of course, such metacognitive knowledge might not be used by a learner. This brings us to the second aspect of metacognition, the use of these abilities and strategies in a learning situation. For example, in learning a list of facts, the student would try to impose some classification on them to aid acquisition.

The criterion for the first kind of behavior, labeled metacognitive knowledge, is quite straightforward, that is, the possessor of such knowledge should be able to *state verbally* characteristics of learning, knowing, or task structure that influence performance on the task (Brown & Campione, 1980). The reason verbalization is used as a criterion is that saying what is metacognitive about a task requires deliberate choice from among all the things that might be said about a given task. In other words, the assumption is made that the learner must exercise control over the selection of knowledge relevant to the task. Certainly, it seems unlikely that such knowledge can be faked, for example, by rote memorization. In addition, the verbalization criterion permits a reasonable separation between metacognitive knowledge and cognitive knowledge because tests of invariant aspects of metacognition may be operationalized by examining stability of metacognitive responses across different tasks that vary in cognitive content.

This straightforward method for assessing metacognitive knowledge contrasts with criteria for assessing the other type of metacognitive behavior. This second type is concerned with the use of metacognitive knowledge in carrying out cognitive tasks, which for ease of reference I shall call metacognitive skill to differentiate it from metacognitive knowledge. As criteria for the presence of metacognitive skill, various activities have been proposed, such as checking, planning, selecting, monitoring, and inferring (Brown & Campione, 1980); self-interrogation and introspection (Brown, 1978); and monitoring and interpretation of ongoing experience (Flavell & Wellman, 1977). Although adequate operationalizations for most of these activities can be specified, one runs into considerable difficulty in deciding whether they are adequate criteria for distinguishing metacognitive from cognitive activity. All the above activities are certainly candidates for indices of metacognitive skill, especially planning, self-interrogation, monitoring, and checking, but others occur also in the course of cognitive activity. For example, the use of language (and all metacognitive tasks are language tasks) requires inferring, selecting, and interpretation of ongoing experience. How are we to separate the metacognitive use of these skills from the simply cognitive use?

The chameleonlike quality of metacognitive skill is illustrated in statements about its characteristics. In earlier characterizations, the conscious regulation of cognitive activity was emphasized:

> Metacognition refers, among other things to the active monitoring and consequent regulation and orchestration of these processes in relation to the cognitive objects on which they bear, usually in the service of some concrete goal or objective. (Flavell, 1976, p. 252),

> The processes described as metacognitive are the important aspects of knowledge... in the domain of deliberate learning and problem solving situations, conscious executive control of the routines available to the system is the essence of intelligent activity. (Brown, 1978, p. 79)

More recently, metacognitive skills have been characterized as including nonconscious regulation of cognitive activity as well:

> They (metacognitive skills) are also not necessarily statable as a great deal of selecting, monitoring, inferring, etc. must go on at a level below conscious awareness. (Brown & Campione, 1980, p. 13)

In part, this extension of the domain of metacognitive skill to include nonconscious regulation represents acknowledgment of the complex nature of the phenomena of intelligent behavior. Flavell and Wellman (1977) succinctly summarized this complexity in considering the possible relationship between memory and metamemory behavior:

> Paradoxically, metamemory in the sense of present, conscious monitoring of mnemonic means, goals, and variables may actually diminish as effective storage and retrieval behaviors become progressively automatized and quasi-reflexive through repeated use and overlearning. The metamemory-memory behavior link of the older child is not thereby extinguished, of course. However, the need for it to become clearly conscious may well diminish as the behaviors it once mediated become more self-starting. (pp. 28–29)

It is probably true that the need for conscious monitoring declines with experience on a task; nevertheless, this extension of metacognitive skill does vitiate the theoretical usefulness of the term because it considerably obscures whatever it is we mean by the learner's use of abilities and strategies for learning. Consider as a concrete example the results of a comprehension study by Brown and Smiley (1977). In this study, primary-grade children did two tasks with short stories that they read. The first was simply to retell the story in their own words. Analysis of the retellings demonstrated that children included important information and deleted nonessential information. The second task was an editing task in which children were to underline important information in a story. That is, the children were asked to use deliberately the knowledge of what was important in a story that they had displayed on the retelling task. Their performance on this latter task was substantially inferior to that on the former, with consistent differentiation of important and unimportant information only beginning to emerge with older children. A reasonable speculation on these results is that children tacitly used their knowledge of story structure on the retelling task but were unable to access this knowledge deliberately for the editing task. With respect to metacognition, should we say that the children displayed metacognitive skill on the retelling task but not on the editing task? If so, does it make sense to maintain a distinction between metacognitive and cognitive skill when tacit use of knowledge in the absence of its deliberate use can be demonstrated in many skill areas? With such a definition would metacognitive skill serve to differentiate the novice from the expert or the intelligent from the unintelligent?

My own preference is to reserve the term metacognitive skill for those behaviors that reveal the deliberate and conscious manipulation of cognitive skills. For those phenomena where there is a discrepancy in the use of cognitive skills on similar tasks, as in the Brown and Smiley study (1977), we should turn to other constructs, such as accessibility to knowledge and strategies (Brown, 1980) and automaticity of cognitive processes, both to account for the data and to endow the term metacognitive skill with more than merely descriptive status.

The reason that constructs such as accessibility and automaticity emerge as important in this area has to do with our increasing knowledge of learner characteristics, task demands, and the acquisition of skill. On the one hand, because of capacity limitations in working memory, certain subskills of more complex cognitive skills are not simply acquired but, in the course of acquisition and practice, are also automated in the sense that the subskill may be used without demanding attentional capacity. The nature and significance of such automated acquisition is being examined for reading (e.g., Kolers, 1975; LaBerge & Samuels, 1974) and for arithmetic (e.g., Groen & Parkman, 1972; Groen & Resnick, 1977). On the other hand, especially for complex cognitive tasks, such as reasoning and writing, that depend on the development of a strategy for effective performance, the deliberate control of certain subskills is required. Although the acquisition of such control has received less attention from researchers, primarily because study of strategy-dependent skills is fairly recent, the importance of control is recognized in mathematical problem solving (Greeno, 1976) and in writing (Bereiter & Scardamalia, 1982; Bracewell, 1980).

In writing, the ability to control deliberately certain subskills is particularly important for two reasons. First, writing is a language skill that is acquired on the basis of a well-developed skill, namely oral language, that has many already automated subskills. Much of the acquisition of writing skill requires not the learning of novel subskills but the assuming of control by the writer over already automatized language subskills. Second, writing is a type of problem solving—a skill that requires the construction of a solution that in its particulars is unique for a given task. One definition of a problem is a task that does not yield to routinized procedures for its resolution. In constructing solutions to writing problems, the writer must have conscious access to writing subskills that range from vocabulary to genre levels.

Given that control ability is essential for writing skill, one is still left with the problem of identifying whether a writer has it. This is essentially a problem of identifying metacognitive skill, which has been characterized above as the deliberate and conscious manipulation of cognitive skills. What we need is a criterion comparable to the verbalization criterion for metacognitive knowledge; that is, a type of behavior whose presence would make it reasonable to infer that deliberate, as opposed to tacit, use was being made of a cognitive process. The criterion proposed as an index of metacognitive skill is the production of both optimal and nonoptimal outcomes for a given task. When the task is writing, this means that the metacognitively skilled writer should be able to produce both good and bad versions of text on the same topic. In a close parallel to the assumption made for the verbalization criterion, the assumption for the optimal/nonoptimal criterion is that the production of such outcomes requires deliberate[2] manipulation of writing processes from among all the possible processes that could produce text on a given topic. For logical reasons outlined below, particular attention is paid to the structure of nonoptimal productions in analyzing the texts. To date, the method has been used to examine writing skills, primarily at the sentence level; however, the method should be readily extendable to examination of writing skills at discourse levels.

STUDIES ON THE CONTROL OF WRITING PROCESSES

Study 1: Children's Manipulation of Simple Sentences

Every child who writes displays a variety of syntactic and language forms, as indicated by variability in number of words per sentence; use of different syntactic structures, such as coordinate and dependent clauses; and so on. We have carried out a number of studies on children's ability to manipulate syntactic form and to use conjunctions appropriately when writing (Bracewell, 1980; Bracewell & Scardamalia, 1979). The writing skills we were interested in were rather elementary, of the kind that would lead to the following different surface structures for the same content:

Ernie has a dog. Grover has a cat. Grover has a canary. Grover has a dog.

and

Ernie has a dog; but Grover has a cat, a canary, and a dog.

In keeping with the elementary nature of the task materials, the children who participated were at the beginning stages of learning to compose, being in grades 2, 4 and 6 (approximately ages seven, nine, and ten respectively).

The variability of language form seen in children's writing is in some sense controlled because children by and large do write grammatical sentences. But the production of a variety of grammatical and other language forms does not by itself indicate *deliberate* control over the cognitive processes that lead to these forms. Many of the factors that govern these processes appear to operate at an intuitive level. Sometimes, as is the case with oral language, these factors can be isolated (e.g., rules of conversation, Grice, 1975, and linguistic and extralinguistic cues from other speakers); but often, as is the case with children's writing, these factors must be inferred (e.g., Bereiter's 1980 "associative strategy" in producing text). At the same time, the achievement of deliberate control over language form is an important objective for the writer because it is only with such control that one is able to communicate reliably the full range of one's ideas and intentions to different readerships. The deliberate fitting of form to meaning is closely related to what Hirsch (1977) labels semantic integration—the coordination of meaning that forms the basis of readable prose.

In writing, the burden of making decisions about appropriate ways to express ideas falls on the writer. To make such decisions, writers must possess metalinguistic skill. That is, they must be able to generate and to analyze at will different ways of relating content and to select the best language form for achieving these relationships. But the fact that variability of language form in writing is often produced nondeliberately brings us face to face with a methodological problem. By what methods can we differentiate intentional variation in children's writing from variation produced by nonintentional factors? Of course, this is a particular case of the problem of differentiating metacognitive from cognitive skill. In Study 1, the method used in assessing children's deliberate control of language form was based on the criterion proposed earlier for assessing metacognitive skill, namely, the production of optimal and nonoptimal outcomes for a given task. Specifically, each child was asked to write up the same information in ways that the child considered to be both good and bad.

Tasks and Materials. Asking children to produce optimal and nonoptimal (in this case, 'best' and 'worst') write-ups is a decidedly odd request that leads to a number of problems. Apart from the fact that few, if any, children ever do something where an important goal is to perform *poorly*, there are issues of task definition. The first concerns how to tell children that what we are interested in is deliberate manipulation of syntax rather than all the other aspects of writing that can be optimal or non-optimal, like handwriting, spelling, grammar, semantic content, and so on. Obviously, simply telling children to manipulate syntax is not sufficiently informative. Showing children examples of the various ways that the same ideas can be put together in sentences would appear more adequate. But this leads to a second issue that is concerned with not restricting the task definition so much that it becomes simply a memory task rather than metalinguistic. If the experimenter, in attempting to orient children toward syntax, simply told them a good and a bad way to put together ideas in sentences, then the subsequent writing task could become merely a memory task where the goal was to recall the surface structure of the examples.

In an attempt to navigate between Scylla and Charybdis, we had the children carry out a 'read-and-choose' task before they did the writing task. In this prior task, children read different ways of writing up the same information, thereby (we hoped) orienting themselves toward syntactic aspects of writing. But instead of the experimenter designating which sentence write-ups were 'good' or 'bad', the children chose those write-ups they themselves thought were good or bad. One of the reasons for having children do this was to engage their own abilities to evaluate ways of expressing information and to attempt to avoid strategies in which memory for a particular sentence surface structure was used. This 'read-and-choose' procedure was carried out as follows. First, children were presented with a matrix of content words and four different ways of writing up the matrix content in sentences. An example of these matrix and sentence materials is presented in Table 6.1. The matrix consists of content words and a title that serves to organize the words into four simple propositions (e.g., Ernie has a dog. Grover has a cat.) The different ways of writing up the matrix content were not selected randomly but were ordered by an increasing degree of coordination among the propositions achieved by the use of syntactical rules, conjunctions, and cohesive relations. In the sentence items of Table 6.1, the degree of coordination increases from top to bottom. Sentence item (1) contains four propositions expressed as simple sentences. Because no relationships are expressed among the propositions, this item was assigned a coordination level of 0. Sentence item (2), in which the use of *and*, signals a coordination of the related set of propositions about Grover, was assigned a coordination level of 1. Sentence item (3), which contains in addition a coordination signalled by *but*, the word, between the first proposition and the latter three, was assigned a coordination level of 2. Sentence item (4), which contains these coordinations plus the relationship to the superordinate term, *pets*,

TABLE 6.1   Language Materials Used for Syntax Manipulation Study

Example of matrix materials, read-and-choose task:
   Title: Who has what pet?

Who	Pet
Ernie	dog
Grover	cat
Grover	canary
Grover	dog

Example of sentence materials, read-and-choose task:
1. Ernie has a dog. Grover has a cat. Grover has a canary. Grover has a dog.
2. Ernie has a dog. Grover has a cat, a canary, and a dog.
3. Ernie has a dog; but Grover has a cat, a canary, and a dog.
4. Ernie has a dog; but Grover has three different pets, a cat, a canary, and a dog.

Example of matrix materials, writing task:
   Title: Who has what pet?

Who	Pet
Bert	hamster
Kermit	goldfish
Kermit	turtle
Kermit	hamster

From Bracewell and Scardamalia, 1979.

was assigned a coordination level of 3. Matrices and associated sentences were designed for four different topics. Each topic used vocabulary familiar to grade-school children.

To do the 'read-and-choose' task, the child first read the title and words of the matrix. The sentence items, typed on individual slips of paper, were placed in front of the child in random order. The child then read these items pointing out the similarities and differences in wording and structure among them. This analysis included counting the number of sentences in each sentence item. This child then chose which items he or she considered the best and the worst written. The order of selecting best and worst was counterbalanced across children. Specific instructions were, "Point out for me the one that you think is the best (worst) written one. Which one sounds the best (worst) to you when you read it? In which one are the words put together in the best (worst) way?" The child read aloud each item after choosing and then was asked to justify the choice.

The use of this task prior to writing accomplished a number of purposes. First, it oriented the children to the syntactic aspect of writing that was the focus of the task. Second, the use of an ordered set of sentence items provided a metric for assessing the child's sensitivity to syntactic coordination of content. Third, the choice of well and poorly written sentences together with the child's justification for each choice provided an assessment of metalinguistic knowledge against which metalinguistic skill in manipulation-language form could be compared.

Immediately following the read-and-choose task, each child wrote 'best' and 'worst' sentences, using a matrix on the same topic as that used on the reading task but with different content words. An example of such a matrix is presented in the bottom section of Table 6. 1. After reading the title and words of the matrix, the child wrote a sentence item using the content. Instruction order conformed to that used on the reading task; that is, students who had chosen best and worst written items wrote a best sentence item and then a worst sentence item. Those who had chosen in the worst-best order wrote a worst item and then a best item. Verbal instructions that paralleled those used on the reading task were, "Put together the words of the matrix in a sentence or sentences so that what you write sounds like the best (worst) one you picked out before.' Coordination levels for the possible selections on the read-and-choose task are presented in Table 6.2. The assignment of coordination levels for written productions followed a procedure like that outlined above for the sentence items of the read-and-choose task. That is, assignment of a level was determined by the maximum number of relationships expressed for any one of the four basic propositions. For example, the production "Ernie has a dog. Gover has a cat. Grover has a canary. Also Grover has a dog." was assigned a coordination level of 1 because the last proposition is signalled by the conjunction, 'also,' as being related to previous propositions.

TABLE 6.2   Mean Coordination Levels for Tasks and Instructions

	Task	
	Read	Write
Grade 2 Students[a]		
Instruction		
Best	1.25	0.94
Worst	1.15	0.82
Grade 4 and 6 Students[b]		
Instruction		
Best	2.04	1.41
Worst	0.15	0.46

[a] Square root of (MSe/n) = .17 (for subjects as error term).
[b] Square root of (MSe/n) = .06 (for subjects as error term).
From Bracewell and Scardamalia, 1979.

Results and Discussion.   Before examining the results, let us speculate on what one might expect if the student had full metacognitive control over language skills. First, on the read-and-choose task, one would probably find a difference in coordination level between sentence items selected as best and worst. One might expect, in addition, that the coordination level of best-sentence items would be higher on the average than the coordination level of worst-sentence items, although this might not be the case for all students' selections—certainly one can think of contexts in which a lower degree of coordination would be more appropriate than a higher degree. Second, on the writing task, one would find that the degree of coordination achieved in the student's own productions would be the same as those selected on the read-and-choose task. That is, the coordination level of the best-written item would be the same as that coordination level of the item chosen as best and the coordination level of the worst-written item would be the same as that chosen as worst.

The coordination levels of children's selections and productions did not, of course, show such a straightforward pattern. The pattern that was found was a much more intriguing one that throws some light on the control of syntax in writing, has important implications for how we evaluate children's writing, and raises many more researchable questions about how children acquire control over their writing skills.

Let us deal with the data from grade-2 children first.[3] The average coordination levels for these children are presented in the top half of Table 6.2. Here we see that the average coordination levels of different tasks and instructions hovered around Level 1. In fact, there were no statistically significant differences among the means. This uniformity of coordination levels together with a comparatively high degree of unsystematic variability in selections and productions, both within and across second-grade children, suggests that these children were not able to exercise metalinguistic skills on either the read-and-choose or the writing tasks.

Now, let us turn to the data from grade 4 and grade 6 children. The average coordination levels for these children, which did not differ across grades, are presented in the bottom half of Table 6. 2. The principal finding for these children was an interaction effect of tasks and instructions. For both the read-and-choose and the writing task, coordination levels for best instructions exceeded those for worst instructions, but this difference between best and worst was attenuated for the writing task. Coordination level for best writing was less than that for best choices; coordination level for worst writing was *greater* than that for worst choices. This pattern for grade 4 and grade 6 children, when considered together with other data from this study, suggests a number of things about children's control of syntactic form in writing.

First, the clear differentiation in coordination levels between best and worst sentences on both reading and writing tasks together with children's comments on their choices and productions, implies metalinguistic skill and metalinguistic knowledge. This is most evident for data from the read-and-choose task. At the same time, the differences in coordination levels between the reading and writing tasks raise questions about the relationship between the metalinguistic knowledge and skill for these data. On the read-and-choose task, metalinguistic skill was implied not only by the differentiation in coordination levels but also by the finding that coordination level for best choices was not at ceiling. The children were not selecting best sentences in an unreflective manner based on some global impression of sentence complexity. Most children thought that the Level 1 or Level 2 sentence items were the best write-ups. As one child put it in rejecting the Level 3 sentence item. "You don't have to say they're different pets, everybody already knows that." The making of deliberate choices is also implied by the rational justifications the children offered for their choices. Children who chose the 0 Level item (four-sentence) as worst cited the use of four sentences as being poor, saying further that they did not like the repetition of the subject noun (i.e., Grover). When choosing a more coordinated sentence item as best, they said that they liked the use of such words as "and" and "but" as well as the way the words were "put together in one (or two) sentences." Children's ability to comment in this way on their choices also implies metalinguistic knowledge (albeit of a fairly rudimentary kind) about how words can be put together to make effective sentences; however, the role that this knowledge played in helping children to make choices is unclear. It is possible that the knowledge implied by the justifications determined sentence-item choice; on the other hand, such knowledge may have been adjunctive, an epiphenomenon of the metalinguistic skills used in making choices. Evidence that the latter possibility more accurately describes the status of these justifications is provided by the intermediate coordination levels found on the writing task, particularly by the higher coordination levels found for worst productions compared with worst selections. Those children who were attempting to write four simple sentences for a worst version were aware that this was their goal and, having written, were quite confident that they had produced four sentences. When asked to count the actual number of sentences in their write-up, those children who had produced less than four sentences (for example by coordinating Grover propositons) showed considerable surprise that their production had not met their stated objective. This disassociation between goals and actual performance, of which the children became aware only after examining their productions, makes it unlikely that overt knowledge about sentence structure was governing their productions. It appears that these children were in something of a transition period with respect to metalinguistic knowledge about sentence structure—one in which the ability to talk about sentences requires the perceptual support of already-written sentences. Of course the emancipation of such knowledge and the development of the ability to apply it in the course of sentence production emerges as an important educational issue.

Second, the attenuation of coordination levels for best and worst write-ups compared with those found on the read-and-choose task indicates that the children could not exercise full control over syntactic production processes. The most important results are those found for worst write-ups as compared with worst selections. The children's worst write-ups, which by and large were to be simple uncoordinated sentences, contained a significant degree of coordination. This finding rules out a simple explanation of writing and reading differences based on capacity limitations in working memory and differential task difficulty. Such an explanation can account for the pattern of data for best write-ups—writing is a more capacity-demanding task than reading. In attempting to compose sentences, children hit a capacity limitation for coordinating information; hence, the coordination level achieved for writing was less than that for reading. But the pattern of the data was reversed for worst write-ups. The simplest strategy for producing worst write-ups would have been to write a series of single simple sentences. But this is not what significant proportion of the children did. In coordinating propositions when attempting to write worst sentences, grade 4 and grade 6 children used what appears to be a logically more, not less, capacity-demanding strategy.

Third, the differences between what was intended and what was produced on the writing task suggests that the cognitive processes of sentence production were largely automatic, in the sense that they operated without (and sometimes despite) conscious attention. Of course the observation that we can do things without having to attend to them, especially in the domain of language, has been noted and discussed by many investigators. Given a limited capacity-processing system for attention, the results could scarcely be otherwise. But the nature of automaticity implied by these results is stronger—namely, that children were *unable* to pay attention to their production processes. The strength of these automatic processes is illustrated by results of a variant of the matrix task carried out with grade-4 children (Bracewell, 1980). This variation emphasized memory for surface structure. Children simply were asked to find the four sentence write-ups from among a group of sentence items, like those in Table 6. 1, and then were asked to write up information from a different matrix in four simple sentences. All children were able to identify the four sentence items easily (that is, the item with 0 level coordination), and the request to write such an item frequently led to astonishment that adults could be interested in such a simple and mundane task. Nevertheless, the degree of coordination found in children's productions was the same as that found for worst productions on the above task.

It is one thing not to have to pay attention to carry out a task, it is quite another not to be able to do so. The writing difficulties children experienced on these matrix tasks were not related to writing activity per se but to the purposeful control of writing activity. Of course the data gathered on these simple tasks essentially amounts to a demonstration of automaticity of syntactic production processes, although they are perhaps all the more striking because of the simplicity of the tasks and materials. In further research two important directions to pursue are (1) the investigation of such a phenomenon on true composing tasks, where children select a topic and provide content themselves and (2) the investigation of how children learn to pay attention to, monitor, and eventually control such automatic processes. For both directions, the use of optimal/nonoptimal production strategies is likely to be an important aspect of the research methodology.

Study 2: Recognition and Production of Grammatical Errors

Difficulties in the manipulation of syntax that suggest automatic-writing processes are not limited to beginning writers. We have found evidence for such processes with older writers when investigating the control that secondary-school students were able to exercise over syntactic structures that are considered to be grammatical errors (Bracewell & Kress, 1979; Kress & Bracewell, 1981). A list of the errors examined together with an example of each (the erroneous structure is underlined) is presented in Table 6. 3.

Such errors, although distressingly familiar to most English educators, are noteworthy in a number of ways. First, these are errors primarily because of convention. Which is the 'correct' form and which is the 'incorrect' form is arbitrary and not derived from rational analyses. Certainly, it is the rare instance, especially when embedded in text, that such errors lead to a problem in understanding. Second, for some students such errors are very difficult to overcome. Nor is this afflicted group of an insignificant size in the secondary schools—the appearance and reappearance year by year in English curricula of instructional units on 'major grammatical errors' testifies to the extent of the difficulty of mastering

TABLE 6.3   Common Grammatical Errors

Error Name	Example
1. "Be" plus adverbial clause	A hangover is when someone has had too much to drink.
2. "Sense" verb plus adverbial clause	I see how Tom Lewis has been expelled from school.
3. Reason plus "because" clause	John is unable to sit still. The reason is because he wants to leave.
4. Fragment sentence	The C. N. Tower, which is the world's tallest free-standing structure.
5. Fused sentences and comma splice	You can still go almost everywhere by subway there are many stops.
6. Redundant preposition	Valley Hill is the town in which we used to live in.
7. Pronoun case	Don't tell anyone our secret; this is strictly between you and I.
8. Pronoun number agreement	Everyone has to listen to their own conscience.
9. Past modal plus "of"	Couldn't you of told me he was having trouble?
10. Faulty pronoun reference	All through the rock concert it was really fantastic.
11. Faulty parallelism	He was not only stubborn, but he was also shy.
12. Dangling participle	Being just six years old, my mother took me with her when she plowed the field.

From Bracewell and Kress, 1979.

such conventions as well as to the intransigence of their associated errors. Third, in spite of the fact that failures to follow such conventions interfere little, if at all, with communication, much of the hue and cry over writing skills raised by the public and by higher education authorities focuses on such errors. This focus, whether one agrees with it or not, makes the teaching of these writing conventions of practical importance to English educators. The fact that errors on these conventions are difficult to overcome, despite (in most cases) a quite regular surface structure, makes them of theoretical interest to those of us who study writing processes.

A common workbook exercise on grammatical errors at the secondary-school level is one that presents a list of sentences and requires students to find and correct the errors contained in the sentences. Students often achieve a considerable measure of success doing such tasks, yet continue to produce erroneous grammatical structures in their own compositions. This transfer failure from the workbook to composing suggests a problem of control of writing processes. It is not that such students lack knowledge of grammatical errors, it is that they lack sufficient control over their writing activity to be able to apply it when it is appropriate. Specifically, they lack the ability to control those syntactic production processes that lead to the production of grammatical errors.

The lack-of-control explanation for grammatical errors can be tested by using the optimal/nonoptimal strategy. In an optimal task the objective would be to write the conventionally correct structure and avoid making an error. In a nonoptimal task the objective would be to write the incorrect structure, thereby deliberately making an error. If the lack-of-control explanation is correct, then the following hypothesis can be made about the data pattern from these two tasks. On the optimal task, because they have difficulty controlling syntactic processes, students should make at least some grammatical errors. On the nonoptimal task, again because of difficulties controlling syntactic processes, students should be unable to make deliberately those errors that they produce on the optimal task.

Tasks and Materials. Public opinion to the contrary, the occurrence of grammatical errors in the writing of secondary-school students is an infrequent event. The majority of sentences that students write are grammatically correct, and it is the troubled student, indeed, who on the average commits more than one syntactic faux pas for every ten sentences written. Moreover, students do not habitually make a large number of different types of error; an individual student's problems usually are limited to one or two conventions. In carrying out research of this kind, such infrequency of errors leads to problems of amassing a data base sufficiently large to test a hypothesis. To increase the amount of data available for analysis, two special features were incorporated into the research design. The first had to do with selection of the students who contributed data. These were sixteen grade 11 students (aged fifteen to seventeen years) who had voluntarily enrolled in a remedial writing class because of difficulties they were having with writing, which included making grammatical errors. Although such a selection restricts the potential generality of our results, we thought it worthwhile at the beginning to cast our control hypothesis on what was likely to be fertile ground. In the course of their studies, the students were taught to recognize and correct most major grammatical errors, including those listed in Table 6. 3.

The second feature had to do with the operationalization of the optimal production strategy. For grammatical conventions, the optimal strategy consists of producing the correct syntactic structure and avoiding an error. The most naturalistic method of gathering data on students' error patterns when the objective is to produce conventionally correct syntactic structures would be to search their prior compositions. To gather sufficient data, a search of compositions written over many months would have had to be made, a lengthy time period that raises its own problems about stability of processes that lead to errors, possible learning effects, and so on. To avoid these problems, we decided to test students' production of syntactic conventions by using a paper-and-pencil test called *The Diagnostic Writing Test* (Kress, 1978). The test consists of sentence items that the student must complete either by adding or rearranging words to make a grammatically correct sentence. The items have been derived from examples of errors that previous students have made in their writing. For example, one of the items designed to test for the error of the redundant preposition is:

Valley Hill is a town in which ——————————————— .

A correct completion for the item would be:
    Valley Hill is a town in which we used to live.

An incorrect completion, in which a redundant preposition is used, would be:
    Valley Hill is a town in which we used to live in.

The errors tested were those listed in Table 6.3; an example of one test item for each error is presented in Table 6.4. On the diagnostic test, there were three different sentence items for each error. The items were presented a fixed random order.

For nonoptimal productions, students were asked to produce sentences containing syntactic errors. An assessment of students' ability to produce deliberately the errors about which they had been taught was made by having the students carry out the Competitive Proofreading exercise from the Scardamalia and Bereiter writing exercise handbook (1979). In this exercise, students write a composition in which they purposely bury some of the errors that they have learned. They make two copies of the error-filled composition. On the one that they keep, they

TABLE 6.4 Grammatical Errors and Sample Items from *The Diagnostic Writing Test*

Error Name	Sample Item
1. "Be" plus adverbial clause	A hangover _____ when someone has had too much to drink.
2. "Sense" verb plus adverbial clause	I see _____ Tom Lewis has been expelled from school.
3. Reason plus "because" clause	John is unable to sit still. The reason is _____ he wants to leave.
4. Fragment sentence	The C. N. Tower, which is the world's tallest free-standing _____ .
5. Fused sentences and comma splice	You can still go almost everywhere by subway _____ . (many, there, are, stops)
6. Redundant preposition	Valley Hill is the town in which _____.
7. Pronoun case	Don't tell anyone our secret; this is strictly between you and _____.
8. Pronoun number agreement	Everyone has to listen to _____ own conscience.
9. Past modal plus "of"	Couldn't you _____ told me he was having trouble?
10. Faulty pronoun reference	All through the rock concert _____ was really fantastic.
11. Faulty parallelism	He was not only stubborn, but _____ shy.
12. Dangling participle	_____ just six years old, my mother took me with her when she plowed the field.

From Kress, 1978.

underline the errors; the other copy is given to another student, whose task it is to proofread the composition, locating and correcting as many of the inserted errors as he can. The task is competitive in that the author receives points for the number of errors that the proofreader is unable to find and correct. Thus, from this exercise, it is possible to obtain a record of which language structures that author thinks are grammatical errors. The Competitive Proofreading exercise allows the student to select which errors to bury in his or her composition. This selection procedure, as opposed to a procedure in which students would be told which errors to try to make, was used because we were interested in assessing the grammatical errors that students themselves felt capable of making. To avoid possible contamination, the diagnostic test was administered one week after the proofreading task. It is possible that certain of the items of the diagnostic test are memorable enough that they could have been copied from memory on the proofreading task rather than generated by the student.

Results and Discussion. The terminology we use to refer to the possible outcomes on the two tasks is based on the intentions of the students for each task. On the diagnostic test, students attempted to avoid grammatical errors. Hence, a properly completed item is referred to as *correct*, an item in which the grammatical error is made is referred to as *incorrect*. On the proofreading task, students attempted to place grammatical errors in their texts. Hence, an error properly made on this task is referred to as a *success*. A word or string of words marked on the proofreading task that was not, in fact, an error is referred to as a *failure*. Thus, *correct* and *incorrect* refer to the diagnostic test; *success* and *failure* refer to the proofreading task.

Our hypothesis was that, because of lack of control of the syntactic production processes, those grammatical errors that a student made on the diagnostic test should have been the ones that he or she failed to make on the proofreading task. A corollary of this hypothesis is that those grammatical errors that the student succeeded in making on the proofreading task should have been the ones completed correctly on the diagnostic test. Errors successfully made on the proofreading task indicate control over those syntactic production processes responsible for the particular error. Hence, on the diagnostic test, the student should have been able to control the processes and avoid making that error. In brief, incorrect completions on the diagnostic test should have been paired with failures on the proofreading task; correct completions on the diagnostic test should have been paired with successes on the proofreading task.

The extent of this pairing can be evaluated by constructing a cross-classification table of the outcomes on the two tasks. This cross-classification is presented in Table 6.5. The rows of the table present the outcomes for the Diagnostic test; the columns present the outcomes for the proofreading task. The entries within the cells of the table are totals of outcomes taken across students and across error types. For example, if a student was successful in making a particular error on the proofreading task and then completed items for that error correctly on the diagnostic test, a score of 1 was entered in the top left-hand cell of Table 6.5.

Generally, the pattern of results presented in Table 6.5 confirmed the hypothesis. When students completed items of an error set correctly on the diagnostic test, they tended to bury successfully that particular error on the proofreading task (19 versus 3 outcomes); when students completed items of an error on the diagnostic test incorrectly, they tended

TABLE 6.5   Outcomes for Optimal and Nonoptimal Writing of Grammatical Conventions

	Proofreading Task (Nonoptimal Operationalization)	
	Success	*Failure*
Diagnostic Test (Optimal Operationalization)		
Correct	19	3
Incorrect	1	8

From Bracewell and Kress, 1979.

to fail to make that error on the proofreading task (8 versus 1 outcomes)[4]. A direct statistical evaluation of this pattern cannot be made because each count for the outcomes in Table 6.5 does not necessarily come from a separate student. Thus, the assumption of independence of events for chi-square tests of association is questionable. A related relationship can be evaluated statistically, however—namely, whether individual students showed greater response pairing than nonpairing on the two tasks. That is, for individual students, did the number of outcomes in which incorrects were paired with failures and corrects paired with successes exceed the number in which corrects were paired with failures and incorrects with successes? The answer to this question is yes; for thirteen of the sixteen students, the number of pairing responses exceeded the number of non-pairing responses (by a binomial test $p < .01$, $p = q = 0.5$). Of seven students who failed to make errors on the proofreading task, the number of failure-incorrect pairs exceeded the number of failure-correct pairs for six of the seven. Of twelve students who successfully made errors on the proofreading task, the number of success-correct pairs exceeded the number of success-incorrect pairs for ten of the twelve. An additional factor that is useful in evaluating the data pattern of Table 6.5 concerns the number of different types of errors for which a pairing tendency was observed. Pairing outcomes were found for eight of the twelve error types: "sense" verb plus adverbal clause, reason plus "because" clause, redundant preposition, pronoun case, pronoun number agreement, past modal plus "of," faulty pronoun reference, and faulty parallelism. To summarize, the pairing effect was a general one, obtained from a majority of students on a number of different grammatical conventions.

One of the major results of this study is rather remarkable: Students demonstrated that they were capable of making a given grammatical error (e.g., faulty pronoun reference) by inadvertently making the error on the diagnostic test; however, when attempting to make the error deliberately on the proofreading task, they were unable to make the error. In most cases, students were able to produce an error deliberately only when they also avoided making that error on the diagnostic test. The pattern of results is one that would be expected if students possessed metalinguistic skill only over some grammatical production processes, whereas other processes operated in an automatic way that is not subject to metalinguistic skill.

Of course, an automaticity interpretation is not the only one that can account for the pairing effect. An alternative explanation can be based on the possibility that what students think is an error and what is usually scored as an error do not correspond. For some types of error, students may overgeneralize the language structures considered to be erroneous; for others, they may undergeneralize. By making some reasonable assumptions about the frequency of such noncorrespondence, it is possible to generate a pairing pattern very much like that found in Table 6.5

(Bracewell, unpublished research note, January 1981). One problem with such an explanation is that it does not account for the difficulty that many students experience in learning these conventions, which have a quite regular and seemingly salient surface structure in many cases. In other words, one would still have to account for how the overgeneralizations and undergeneralizations arose in the first place. Evidence that would discriminate between the two interpretations and that would considerably strengthen the automaticity interpretation would be to demonstrate that students could recognize and correct errors on workbook exercises but that on production tasks, they would continue to make the same error when composing and also be unable to produce an example of it deliberately. Such a test has not yet been carried out.

RESEARCH AND EDUCATIONAL IMPLICATIONS

The information yielded by the technique of asking students to produce both optimal and nonoptimal kinds of writing has important educational implications for language and writing research and instruction, of which I shall mention three.

The first concerns the definition of metalinguistic awareness and its measurement. A major focus of metalinguistic research has been on the relationship between reading ability and knowledge of words, syllables, and phonemes. This area is too large to review in detail, and in any case quite competent reviews already exist (Ehri, 1979). But even a cursory glance at the recent literature makes one wonder whether our insights into the development of metalinguistic awareness and its relationship to reading have progressed much beyond the seminal formulations of the Russian psychologists (Elkonin, 1971; Vygotsky, 1962). It appears that there is a positive relationship between metalinguistic awareness and reading skill, but the exact nature of the relationship remains a mystery. In part this mystery is to be expected because of the complex cognitive nature of reading; but in part our difficulties lie in an inadequate specification of what we mean by metalinguistic awareness. We do not possess the conceptual foundation to tell us why, for example, having a child tap for each word of a sentence is an adequate test of word awareness, or why counting phonemes of a syllable is an adequate test of phoneme awareness. One can sense the unease with this lack of definition in the various alternative explanations advanced for successful or partially successful performance on such tasks—prosodic cues in the case of word identification and articulatory movements in the case of phoneme counting. But such alternatives do not resolve the problem of inexplicitness.

The critique of metacognitive awareness presented in the introductory section applies equally to metalinguistic awareness at word, syllable, and phoneme levels. Questions about metalinguistic knowledge as assessed by statability criteria are obviously inappropriate given the verbal skills of children this age. In any case, what one is interested in is how metalinguistic knowledge is used by the child. The question then is how to assess metalinguistic skill. It is here that the optimal/nonoptimal criterion provides a standard. Performance requiring metalinguistic skill is one in which the child can achieve both optimal and nonoptimal outcomes with the same materials. For example, can the child segment a sentence into words in two different ways? At first glance, such a task may seem odd or pointless; but performance in which a child always segments a sentence into conventional word segments does not reveal whether performance is linguistically or metalinguistically based in the same way that application of categorization skills in a metamemory task is equivocal concerning meta versus memory skills. Because of the conventionality of English word segmentation, successful performance on such a task is certainly suggestive of metalinguistically based performance, but other linguistic knowledge may also serve as a basis. The issue in how to differentiate the two.

Generally, tasks intended to tap metalinguistic skill do not permit examination of a broad enough range of behavior from the child to allow such a differentiation. In particular, the tasks are too recogitory, requiring the child to respond to presented language sequences. This restriction of methodology to receptive tasks is curious given the fascinating results reported for about a decade concerning invented spellings by children (Chomsky, 1971, 1979; Read, 1971, 1975). The very nature of the phenomenon reported, namely that orthography progresses naturally from highly variable and idiosyncratic to regular and conventionalized, would appear to make it an obvious candidate for accounts based on an emerging rational analysis by the child of problems involved in recording language, and the need for systematic as opposed to unsystematic variation in language representation. It seems likely that in these manipulatory— indeed, essentially play-like—activities (Cazden, 1974), the child begins to experience and to master the variations possible for representing language. Awareness of such possible variation provides a basis for selecting or at least appreciating principles of language representation, such as separating words with a space, which are correlated with reading skill. As the two studies reported in this paper indicate, a better picture of children's metalinguistic skills is obtained from tasks that examine the variation children are able to achieve in their own productions. It seems likely that more progress will be made in this area when the methodologies used capitalize on the promising results found for invented spellings and are expanded to include assessments of variability in children's productions.

A second implication may be called substantive in that it provides a rationale for the meager amount of writing done by students in many North American schools (Applebee, 1981; Fillion, 1979; Graves, 1978). Both the matrix and the syntactic error studies suggest that the students themselves are aware of this gap (although this latter finding is more evident in the matrix studies). If such results are borne out in further studies, then one reason for low writing output may be simply that students find composing self-defeating (Bracewell, 1980). It is a punishing situation when you wish to do certain things in writing—things that you are given ample evidence can be attained in the materials you read—yet fail to achieve them in your own composing. And everybody tends to avoid punishing situations. In fact, a number of studies have indicated that the production of text is not a problem for beginning writers once the perceptual motor components of composing have been overcome. When the writing situation is properly developed (i.e., children select a topic with which they feel confortable and they write for a trusted adult who values their output) children have little difficulty producing text (Bereiter & Scardamalia, 1980; Scardamalia & Bracewell, 1979). The problem for beginning writers is one of controlling and manipulating this output to achieve a satisfying product. Such findings suggest that simply encouraging children to do more writing in schools is more likely to exacerbate than to ameliorate any anxiety children feel about their writing unless instructional means are found for helping children manipulate their texts.

The third implication of these results concerns instructional methodology. At present, many instructional methods for writing can be characterized as discrimination training (Bracewell & Kress, 1979). Following the common model-analyze-write procedure, teachers usually begin by presenting an example of text (e.g., a common grammatical error) to students. Teachers and students then anyalyze the text in order to determine and give verbal labels to distinguishing features of the language form. Having determined these features, the students are usually set to a writing task that requires use of the language form. The rationale for this procedure is quite straightforward. By learning to recognize distinguishing language features students should be able to apply them (or avoid them in the case of errors) in the production of their own texts. The problem with this method is that it seems not to be very effective. The automaticity interpretation offered in this paper suggests why this should be so. The model-analyze-write procedure addresses and seeks to foster knowledge about writing. But what needs to be cultivated is not just knowledge but the mental processes that underlie the activity of writing. Instruction on writing should be oriented toward the doing, not the facts, of writing.

To make this maxim more concrete, let me give an example of an instructional task that focuses on writing activity rather than on writing knowledge. The task is presented in Table 6.6; dubbed the "Uh-oh Prediction Exercise," it is intended to foster awareness of cognitive processes involved in a worrisome point of punctuation, that of the use and misuse of commas.

In the course of playing this game, students develop a feeling for the types of sentence structures that lead inevitably to a comma. The ability

TABLE 6.6 "Uh-oh" Prediction Exercise for Comma Use

---

1. Students are taught some point of grammar or punctuation. Henceforth, commas will be used to illustrate.
2. Students are divided into teams of four.
3. The teacher begins writing a sentence on the board. He or she may write one word or several.
4. Each group, in turn, is asked to supply, within five seconds of being asked, a next word for the sentence. Any team that cannot produce a word to continue the sentence loses 2 points.
5. The moment a comma is perceived to be inevitable—because of the way in which the sentence is developing—the person who notices yells, "Uh-oh!"
6. The group, one of whose members has said, "Uh-oh!", must finish the sentence, putting in the comma(s) and explaining the applicable rule. The team gets 2 points for a successful completion; it loses 2 points for an unsuccessful completion.
7. Any other team in the class may then gain 2 or more points by showing that there is a way to complete the sentence without using any commas.
8. The teacher begins a new sentence.

From Kress and Bracewell, 1981.

to predict a comma is a far more useful skill than the ability to explain where a comma ought to be used, because the prediction task has a better chance of leading to the actual *use* of a comma while the student is writing.

Prediction tasks need not be so complicated nor is their use limited to instruction or writing conventions. Many exercises that are presently in use could be made into prediction tasks with only minor alterations. Sentence-combining techniques (O 'Hare, 1975), for example, lend themselves very well to this sort of adaptation (e.g., "What will I have to be careful about if I try to combine 'George arrived late' and 'George is thankful the class has not yet begun' and 'because' into one sentence?") Another good prediction task is one in which students must complete correctly a sentence begun by the teacher. The dangling participle, famous in song and story, might very well be examined by asking students to finish a sentence beginning, "Having replaced three of the wheels during a fifteen-second pit stop, —————————————————————————— ."

Generally, the objective of such prediction tasks is to recruit automatic language processes by requiring a sequence of activities over time that parallels the time sequence of the language production process. Conducted as a group exercise, a prediction task would provide feedback to the students on their predictions, and because the predictions derive from the language process, on the language process itself. Note how the prediction task differs from the analysis of a model. In the latter, all the language is given to the student. Although the student must read the model, this reading may not involve the language production processes that produce the error in the student's writing.

This is not to say that perceptual discrimination methods should be abandoned in teaching writing. But what is required is some additional procedure, such as prediction tasks, that will permit the hookup between knowledge of language structures and the processes that produce them. It seems likely that it is only process-based instructional methods that will lead (in the jargon of cognitive psychologists) to student writers with metalinguistic skills or, in more straightforward terms, to student writers who are able to control their composing skills.

NOTES

1. The research reported in this paper was supported by grants from the Alfred P. Sloan Foundation, the Ontario Institute for Studies in Education, and the Social Sciences and Humanities Research Council of Canada. Preparation of the paper was supported by grants from the Faculty of Graduate Studies, McGill University and Le Programme de Formation de Chercheurs et d'Action Concertée, Quebec. I thank Mark Aulls and Carl Frederiksen for their critical comments on an earlier draft of the chapter.

2. It is important to note that what is being proposed is an index of deliberate and conscious decision making, not a definition. Definitions in this area would involve us in philosophical issues concerning the concept of intention that certainly will not be resolved in the near future, if ever. In proposing the optimal/nonoptimal criterion, I assume only that it is unlikely, not impossible, for successful performance to be achieved in the absence of deliberate manipulation of cognitive skills.

3. Coordination level results were assessed by a series of analyses of variance. All effects reported were significant ($\alpha < .05$) by minimum quasi-F statistics that used child and matrix topic as random variables. Each child in grades 4 and 6 completed reading and writing tasks for three different topics. There were no differences between grade 4 and grade 6 performance. Pilot testing revealed this to be too lengthy a procedure for grade 2 children. Consequently, these children completed reading and writing tasks for only two topics—hence, the separation between analyses and results of grade 2 and those of grades 4 and 6.

4. Table 6.5 presents data relevant to an evaluation of the lack-of-control hypothesis. Additional data obtained from these tasks suggest that information processing demands resulting from the syntactic complexity of the particular sentence that a student was attempting to write also affected error production. Complete results are presented and discussed in Bracewell and Kress (1979).

REFERENCES

Applebee, A. N. *A study of writing in the secondary schools*. Paper presented at the annual meeting of the American Educational Research Association, Los Angeles, April 1981.

Bereiter, C. Development in writing. In L. W. Gregg & E. R. Steinberg (Eds.), *Cognitive processes in writing*. Hillsdale, N. J: Erlbaum, 1980.

Bereiter, C., & Scardamalia, M. From conversation to composition: The role of instruction in a developmental process. In R. Glaser (Ed.), *Advances in instructional psychology* (Vol. 2). Hillsdale, N. J.: Erlbaum, 1982.

Bereiter, C., Scardamalia, M., Anderson, V., & Smart, D. *An experiment in teaching abstract planning in writing.* Paper presented at the annual meeting of the American Educational Research Association, Boston, April 1980.

Bracewell, R. J. *The ability of primary school children to manipulate language form when writing.* Paper presented at the annual meeting of the American Educational Research Association, Boston, April 1980.

Bracewell, R. J. Writing as a cognitive activity. *Visible Language*, 1981, *14*, 400–422.

Bracewell, R. J., & Kress, F. *Taught but not learned: Some reasons why students have difficulty correcting their grammatical errors.* Paper presented at the Twelfth Annual Conference of the Canadian Council of Teachers of English, Ottawa, May 1979.

Bracewell, R. J., & Scardamalia, M. *Children's ability to integrate information when they write.* Paper presented at the annual meeting of the American Educational Research Association, San Francisco, 1979.

Brown, A. L. Knowing when, where, and how to remember: A problem of metacognition. In R. Glaser (Ed.), *Advances in instructional psychology* (Vol. 1). Hillsdale, N. J.: Erlbaum, 1978.

Brown, A. L. *Learning and development: The problems of compatibility, access, and induction* (Technical Report No. 165). Urbana-Champaign: Center for the Study of Reading, University of Illinois, March 1980.

Brown, A. L., & Campione, J. C. *Inducing flexible thinking: A problem of access* (Technical report no. 189). Urbana-Champaign: Center for the Study of Reading, University of Illinois, January 1980.

Brown, A. L., & Smiley, S. S. Rating the importance of structural units of prose passages: A problem of metacognitive development. *Child Development*, 1977, *48*, 1–8.

Bruner, J. S. *Toward a theory of instruction.* Cambridge, Mass.: Harvard University Press, 1966.

Cazden, C. Play with language and metalinguistic awareness: One dimension of language experience. *International Journal of Early Childhood.* 1974, *6*, 12–24.

Chomsky, C. Approaching reading through invented spelling. In L. B. Resnick & P. A. Weaver (Eds.), *Theory and practice of early reading* (Vol. 2). Hillsdale, N. J.: Erlbaum, 1979.

Chomsky, C. Write first, read later. *Childhood Education*, 1971, *47*, 296–299.

Ehri, L. C. Linguistic insight: Threshold of reading acquisition. *Reading Research: Advances in Theory and Practice*, 1979, *1*, 63–114.

Elkonin, D. B. Development of speech. In A. V. Zaporozhets & D. B. Elkonin (Eds.), *The psychology of preschool children.* Cambridge, Mass.: The MIT Press, 1971.

Fillion, B. Language across the curriculum: Examining the place of language in our schools. *McGill Journal of Education*, 1979, *14*, 47–60.

Flavell, J. H. Metacognitive aspects of problem solving. In L. B. Resnick (Ed.), *The nature of intelligence.* Hillsdale, N. J.: Erlbaum, 1976.

Flavell, J. H., & Wellman, H. M. Metamemory. In R. V. Kail, Jr. & J. W.

Hagen (Eds.), *Perspectives on the development of memory and cognition*. Hillsdale, N. J.: Erlbaum, 1977.

Gage, N. L., & Berliner, D. *Educational psychology*. New York: Rand McNally, 1979.

Graves, D. *Balance the basics: Let them write*. New York: Ford Foundation 1978.

Greeno, J. G. Cognitive objectives of instruction: Theory of knowledge for solving problems and answering questions. In D. Klahr (Ed.), *Cognition and instruction*. Hillsdale, N. J.: Erlbaum, 1976.

Grice, H. P. Logic and conversation. In P. Cole & J. J. Morgan (Eds.), *Syntax and semantics* (Vol. 3): *Speech acts*. New York: Academic Press, 1975.

Groen, G., & Parkman, J. M. A chronometric analysis of simple addition. *Psychological Review*, 1972, *79*, 329–343.

Groen, G. & Resnick, L. B. Can preschool children invent addition algorithms? *Journal of Educational Psychology*, 1975, *69*, 645–652.

Hirsch, E. D. *The philosophy of composition*. Chicago: University of Chicago Press, 1977.

Kolers, P. A. Memorial consequences of automatized encoding. *Journal of Experimental Pyschology: Human Learning and Memory, 1*, 689–701.

Kress, F. *The diagnostic writing test*. Unpublished manuscript. North York Board of Education, Toronto, June 1978.

Kress, F., & Bracewell, R. J. Taught but not learned: Reasons for grammatical errors and implications for instruction. In I. Pringle & A. Freedman (Eds.), *Teaching writing learning*. Ottawa: Canadian Council of Teachers of English, 1981.

LaBerge, D., & Samuels, S. J. Toward a theory of automatic information processing in reading. *Cognitive Psychology*, 1974, *7*, 293–323.

Marzano, R. J. The sentence combining myth. *English Journal*, 1976, *65*, 57–59.

Mellon, J. C. *Transformational sentence-combining: A method for enhancing the development of syntactic fluency in English composition*. Urbana, Ill.: National Council of Teachers of English, 1969.

O'Hare, F. *Sentence combining: Improving student writing without formal grammar instruction*. Urbana, Ill.: National Council of Teachers of English, 1973.

O'Hare, F. *Sentencecraft*. Lexington, Mass.: Gage, 1975.

Owen, S. V., Blount, H. P., & Moscow, N. *Educational psychology: An introduction*. Boston: Little, Brown, 1978.

Read, C. Pre-school children's knowledge of English phonology. *Harvard Educational Review*, 1971 *41*, 1–34.

Read, C. Lessons to be learned from the preschool orthographer. In E. H. Lenneberg & E. Lenneberg (Eds.), *Foundations of language development*. New York: Academic, 1975.

Scardamalia, M, & Bereiter, C. *A cognitive approach to writing instruction: Cognitively based writing activities*. Unpublished manuscript. Ontario Institute for Studies in Education, Toronto, September 1978.

Scardamalia, M. & Bracewell, R. J. *Local planning in writing*. Paper presented at the annual meeting of the American Educational Research Association, San Francisco, April 1979.

Vygotsky, L. S. *Thought and language*. Cambridge, Mass.: The MIT Press, 1962.

Part III

Observational Approaches

7

Uncovering Cognitive Processes in Writing: An Introduction to Protocol Analysis

John R. Hayes and Linda S. Flower
Carnegie-Mellon University

Writing is a marvelously complex activity that allows writers great freedom of choice at many levels—from the choice of topics to the choice of tenses. Writing research is also a complex activity that allows the researcher great freedom of choice in research method and level of analysis—from the study of the highest levels of planning to the lowest levels of linguistic structures. The recent, very exciting surge of research on writing has involved many methods. The developmental research of Bereiter and Scardamalia (1980, 1982) and of Graves (1979) has already yielded exciting results and seems certain to continue to do so. Odell's (Odell & Goswami, 1980) method of collecting retrospective reports from adult writers also seems extremely promising. Gould (1978) and Matsuhashi and Cooper (1978) have focused on the pauses observed during writing. Our own preoccupation has been with protocol analysis.

In this chapter, we shall discuss the place of protocol analysis in the arsenal of available writing-research methods. In addition, we shall try to differentiate protocol analysis from other closely related methods with which it is sometimes confused.

To provide context for this discussion, we must first say something about the nature of writing. We cannot fully appreciate the relations among the research methods without first discussing the subject matter to which they are applied.

A COGNITIVE-PROCESS THEORY OF WRITING

The theory sketched here identifies four key features of writing that promise to provide broad explanatory power in accounting for the way people behave as they write. The four features, to be discussed in detail, are: writing consists of distinct processes, writing processes are highly embedded, writing is goal directed, and writing stimulates the discovery of new goals.

Writing Consists of Distinct Processes

The act of composing is best described not as a sequence of stages but as a set of distinguishable processes that the writer must orchestrate in the act of writing. Our model of composing, shown in Figure 7. 1, specifies how these processes are organized. Notice that the model specifies three main elements that must interact:

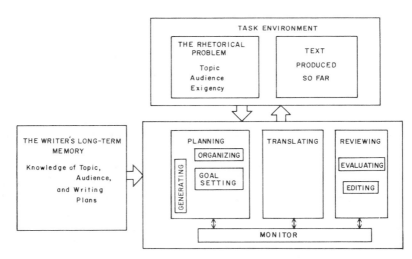

Figure 7.1 Structure of the Writing Model. (From Lee W., Gregg and Erwin R. Steinberg (Eds.), *Cognitive Processes in Writing.* © 1980 by Lawrence Erlbaum Associates, Inc. Reprinted with permission.)

The Task Environment. This includes everything outside the writer's skin, including the assignment or exigency for writing, the audience, and eventually the written text itself. It is important to note that no matter what rhetorical problem is actually presented to the writer, what finally matters will be the problem the writers represent to themselves in the act of composing (Flower & Hayes, 1980).

The Writer's Long-term Memory (LTM). The writer's LTM includes not only the writer's knowledge of the topic but also the writer's knowledge of writing plans, conventions, genre, rhetorical problems, and so forth.

Again, what counts in writing is not what the writer may be said to know but what he or she is able, or chooses, to draw from memory during the act of composing.

The Writing Processes. The writing processes are the major thinking processes that writers employ in complex ways during the act of composing.

Planning is generating content, organizing it, and setting up goals and procedures for writing. We see Planning as a very broad activity that includes deciding on one's meaning, deciding what part of that measuring to convey to the audience, and choosing rhetorical strategies. In short, it includes the whole range of thinking activities that are required before we can put words on paper. It is important to note that (1) planning goes on throughout composing and (2) the plan may not be encoded in a fully articulated or even in a verbal form. (Plans may be visual images.)

Translating is the act of expressing the content of Planning in written English. Although one can reliably distinguish when writers move from Planning (which may produce notes and doodles) to translating (the attempt to produce prose), this does not mean that writers have a fully formed meaning that they simply express in words. Rather, writers have some more or less developed representation encoded in one form. The act of translating this encoded representation to another form (i.e., written English) can add enormous new constraints and often forces the writer to develop, clarify, and often revise that meaning. For that reason, the act of translating often sends writers back to planning. Often these processes alternate with each other from one minute to the next.

Reviewing is the act of evaluating either what has been written or what has been planned. When the evaluation of a text or a plan is negative, reviewing often (but not invariably) leads to revision.

Some reviewing is undertaken self-consciously, either in the midst of composing or at the end of a draft. For example, the writer may decide to suspend other writing activities and read the text systematically to evaluate it. Some reviewing, however, seems to occur quite automatically—unexpectedly interrupting ongoing composing processed when an error or mismatch is spotted.

The Monitor is the executive of the writing process that determines when to switch from one writing process to another, for example, when one has generated enough ideas and is ready to write. The monitor may function differently from writer to writer and from writing task to writing task. Some people move into translation as soon as possible in writing a paper, whereas others will not write a word until they are reasonably certain that planning is complete. Further, a writer undertaking an easy task, for example, a short letter, may do little or no planning before writing the first sentence, whereas the same writer undertaking a difficult task, for example, a philosophical treatise, may plan for months before writing a word.

Writing Processes are Highly Embedded

Writing processes are not constrained to occur in a fixed sequence, such as plan, translate, review. Rather, the writer uses the processes as if they were tools in a tool kit to be applied in any order the job demands. For example, while reviewing, a writer may discover an inadequate transition between sentences. To remedy this situation, the writer may call in the planning and translation processes to insert new sentences into the text that will smooth the transition.

Writing Is Goal Directed

A major part of composing is spent in developing both global goals for affecting an audience and developing ideas and more local goals and plans that guide the act of writing. Both the quality and quantity of these goals appear related to the ability of the writer. They provide logic and coherence to the entire process even when writers perceive their own experience as chaotic and unpredictable.

Writing Stimulates the Discovery of New Goals

Writers not only implement goals by creating networks of supporting subgoals but also, at times, they discover major new goals through insights triggered by the act of writing. Writing to achieve one objective, then, may lead spontaneously to new goals and perhaps to a radical redirection of the writer's efforts.

The conditions under which these new goals are created suggests a relation to the phenomenon of incubation (Simon, 1966). The new goals depend on intensive preparation, that is, on knowledge gained during earlier writing efforts (Wallas, 1926), and they appear—welcome but unexpected—while the writer is pursuing a different goal. Thus, although writing is a goal-directed activity, it is not necessarily constrained by the goals the writer starts with. An important aspect of the writer's creativity is the ability to create new goals during writing.

The four features of writing that we have discussed are described in greater detail together with their supporting evidence in other publications (e.g. Hayes & Flower, 1980a, 1980b). We have summarized them here because they have provided us, and we hope they will provide others, with a springboard for further research.

METHODS FOR STUDYING WRITING

Writing research methods can be divided quite naturally into two groups: The input-output methods and the process-tracing methods. The relationship between the two methods can be understood as follows. When we use input-output methods to study writing, we act as if the writing processes were occurring in a locked room—a room we are forbidden to enter or to look into. We put writers, writing assignments, and reference books (inputs) into the room, and we receive the finished text (the output) at the door. However, we never try to observe directly the processes that occur in the room. Rather, by varying the inputs and observing their effects on the output, we try to infer what the intervening writing processes must have been.

In contrast, when we use process-tracing methods, it is as if, in addition to the information above, we have a window that allows us to look into the locked room and observe some of the processes by which input leads to output.

Input-output Methods

Many of the standard procedures of experimental psychology are of the input-output type. Consider experiments on verbal memory for example. Subjects are presented lists of words under various conditions (the inputs) and are then asked to remember them (the output) at some later time. The psychologists, of course, do not observe memory processes directly. Rather, they try to infer them from the relations between input and output. An excellent example of an input-output study in the field of literature is Lowes's (1927) famous study of Samuel Taylor Coleridge. Lowes was able to demonstrate a striking relation between what Coleridge read in the three or four years before writing "Kubla Khan" (the inputs) and the images the poet presents in the poem (the outputs). On the basis of this relation, Lowes was able to draw important inferences about Coleridge's process of invention.

In an impressive sequence of studies, Bereiter and Scardamalia have examined the impact of the writer's developmental stage (input) on the written output and have derived a number of important inferences about writing processes (Bereiter & Scardamalia, 1980a 1980b; Bereiter, Scardamalia, & Bracewell, 1979).

Process-Tracing Methods

There are four categories of process-tracing methods we shall need to consider:

1. In *behavior protocols*, we record what subjects *do* while they perform a task, but we do not ask them to report their thought processes verbally.
2. In *retrospective reports*, we ask subjects to tell us how they performed a task after the task has been completed.
3. In *directed reports*, we instruct subjects that we are interested in certain aspects of task performance and ask them to report only on these aspects *while* they are performing the task.

4. In *thinking-aloud protocols*, we instruct subjects to report on anything they are thinking while performing the task.

These methods have a long history of application, both in psychology and in English. Introspectionist psychologists (see Humphrey, 1951) trained subjects to report on well-specified aspects of their mental states while performing a variety of tasks. Thus, the introspectionists used directed reports.

Ruger (1910) studied the solution of mechanical puzzles by watching people as they solved them and by recording the running comments of the subjects as they worked. Ruger's method, then, combined behavioral and thinking-aloud protocols. Claparéde (1971) strongly advocated use of thinking-aloud protocols to study problem-solving processes.

In both psychology and English, retrospective reports have been used to shed light on creative processes (Plimpton, 1965). Ghiselin (1952) has compiled numerous retrospective reports by artists, musicians, and writers about their creative processes. Emig (1971) has pioneered the use of process-tracing methods in the study of writing. Perl (1978) and Pianko (1979) have also made valuable contributions to the study of writing through process-tracing methods.

There has also been a long history of controversy surrounding these methods. In this section, we shall discuss the reasons for and against using process-tracing methods.

There are three very compelling reasons for wanting to use process-tracing methods.

1. Process-tracing methods tell us about process in a much more direct way than do input-output methods. For example, we can pinpoint students' difficulties much more readily if we watch while they are struggling with problems than if we try to infer the problems from errors they have made in their final answers.
2. Because the data they yield are rich, process-tracing methods offer us valuable opportunities for scientific exploration. For example, thinking-aloud protocol of a writer at work may yield fifteen pages of comment for every page of written text. Reading through the protocol is an occasion for discovering many things about the writing process that we did not suspect beforehand.
3. There are some aspects of process that are difficult to observe without process-tracing methods. For example, process-tracing methods show us that the order in which writers generate the ideas for writing a paper is quite different from the order in which these ideas are presented in the finished paper. If we look only at the finished paper, that is, the output, it may be difficult or impossible to study the order of idea generation.

Criticisms of Process-Tracing Methods

Although behavioral protocols have generally been favorably received, a number of concerns have been voiced about the other process-tracing methods. These concerns center on the use of verbal reporting. Four major objections have been raised to the use of verbal reports as data:

1. Such reports are not valid because people are not conscious of their cognitive processes.
2. Even if people were aware of their cognitive processes, reporting them verbally would distort them.
3. Verbal reports are incomplete.
4. Verbal reports are not objective and, therefore, cannot be used as scientific data.

Nisbett and Wilson's (1977) widely read review, "Telling More Than We can Know: Verbal Reports on Mental Processes," provides a good starting point for our discussion of the first two of these objections. Looking at experimental studies of attitude change, Nisbett and Wilson found that often the subjects in these studies were not aware of certain affective and perceptual processes, particularly ones that lead to judgments and changes in attitude. Nevertheless, when asked, for example, "Why did you choose that detergent?" or "Why did you fail to use contraceptives?" these subjects were able to provide causal explanations based on reasonable inferences without necessarily consulting or knowing their own processes. Furthermore, these inferences about the causes of their attitude change were often wrong. In other words, although subjects were able to report the result of their decision processes and give an after-the-fact rationale for it, they were often unaware of the process itself. Therefore, asking a writer why he or she followed one train of thought rather than another may produce a reasonable but fabricated answer. Nisbett and Wilson concluded that subjects are generally not aware of their own processes. Rather, when they are asked to describe their mental processes, they describe what they believe their mental states should have been— not what they actually were.

Nisbett and Wilson's claims have been analyzed in a careful review of the literature by Ericsson and Simon (1980). Ericsson and Simon confirmed Nisbett and Wilson's (1979) claims for some kinds of verbal reports but not for others. In particular, they found that Nisbett and Wilson's claims did not apply to concurrent verbal protocols. Ericsson and Simon (1980) have proposed a model of verbal reporting that is consistent with all of the data reported in the literature, including that reviewed by Nisbett and Wilson (1977). They postulate that when subjects perform a task (e.g., mental multiplication) in their usual way, some of the information involved in performing the task, but typically not all of it, is attended to and enters short-term memory (STM).

If subjects give a concurrent verbal report of their mental process-es—that is, if they try to say how they are performing the task *while they are performing it*—the consequences will depend on the nature of the task and on the nature of the report.

Ericsson and Simon (1980) specify three experimental situations in which verbalizing could go on:

1. In the first situation, the subjects report only information to which they normally attend while doing the task. The feature that distinguishes this situation is that the information is already in verbal form before it is reported. Imagine, for example, that the subject is trying to solve the anagram CLEAM. The subject might report, "Let's see, meals, no. Alms, no. Calms, CAMEL!" These proposed solutions are already in verbal form before they are reported. A number of studies have shown that merely adding audible expression to such verbal information has no observable effect on the performance of the task.

2. In the second situation, the subjects are also reporting only information to which they would normally attend while doing the task. However, in this case, the information is not already encoded in words. It may be encoded as visual images, motor images, or in some other form. As an example, imagine trying to describe over the phone what you were doing while buttoning a button. The monologue might proceed as follows: "Well, first I'm taking hold of the button with the thumb and forefinger of my right hand, and the button hole with the same two fingers of my left hand. Then I sort of open up the button hole with my left thumb and. . . . Clearly, describing this action while doing it is going to take longer than just doing it. In any task where reporting requires subjects to translate nonverbal information into verbal form, doing the task with a verbal report may be slower than doing the task without one. However, there is no evidence in situations of this kind that verbal reporting changes the performance of the task in any other way. That is, even though processes are slowed down, their course and sequence are unchanged.

3. In the third situation, subjects are asked to report information to which they would not normally attend in performing the task. They may be asked, for example, to report on their motives or to justify their decisions. To understand the effects that this sort of reporting could have on task performance, imagine that you are participating in a study on long division. The experimenter wants you to divide 248 into 1336 in your head and to tell him or her every time you notice an odd number. Your report might go something like this: "248 into 1336 is about 5, so 5 times 248

is—oops, 5 is an odd number—now where was I? Is there something important about odd numbers in this problem? Oh, yeah, 5—that's an odd number—well. . . ." Asking subjects to report information to which they would ordinarily not have attended in performing a task can seriously disrupt task performance.

The situations described involve people giving concurrent verbal reports—thinking aloud while they are performing the task. If, however, subjects give retrospective accounts after the performance, the Ericsson and Simon (1980) model would predict that much of the information brought into memory during performance would be lost. And the longer the interval between performance and report, of course, the larger the amount of information that is likely to be lost.

One of the most pervasive factors causing loss of information from memory is interference—a fact may be confused with other information either before or after presented, and, hence, lost. A second factor that may be especially important in forgetting that is associated with writing tasks is the Zeigarnik effect discovered by Gestalt psychologists. Essentially, the Zeigarnik effect is the tendency for people to forget goals and subgoals once they have been accomplished. Investigation of the Zeigarnik effect was triggered by an observation made by a group of Gestalt psychologists in a Berlin restaurant. Impressed by their waiter's success in remembering their orders, they were surprised that when they questioned him after they had paid their bill, he no longer had any memory of what he had served them.

During writing protocols, we have observed writers struggling mightily with word choice and word order in writing a particularly difficult sentence. When we asked them later about the difficulties they had had with that sentence, they denied them. "It just came to me," they said, "no problem." The writers were not lying. It is just that the delicate structure of goals and subgoals erected to construct the sentence was destroyed when the goal was accomplished. The Zeigarnik effect acts to clear way information when it is no longer needed.

The social situation involved in being an experimental subject may well affect the kind and the amount of information people will report. Subjects participating in studies typically try to be cooperative. Their cooperativeness may sometimes have unfortunate side effects when they are asked about information that they have forgotten or failed to notice. For example:

1. Subjects often try to please experimenters. If asked, "Did you do any planning?" or "Do you usually outline when you write?" subjects will say, "Yes," meaning, "If you think I should have, I did."

2. When subjects do not know the answer to a question, they may well try to help the experimenter by figuring out what the answer should be. Nisbett and Wilson (1977) found that when people chose among identical clothing items on a rack, they showed preferences for certain positions. When subjects were asked why they made a particular choice, they never referred to the position preference of which they were unaware. Instead, they gave the sorts of reasons that one would expect to be important in such decisions—imagined differences among the identical items.

3. To understand their own behavior, subjects will probably draw on conventions or schemas they know about. If they believe in incubation—and know the term—they may well think they used it. We shall never know whether it actually occurred or not. If they experience incubation but do not know the concept, chances are it will not be reported.

As we noted, the Ericsson and Simon (1980) model not only accounts for the literature they surveyed but also for the literature surveyed by Nisbett and Wilson (1977). Most of the studies cited in the Nisbett and Wilson review either involve retrospective reports or ask the subjects to report information to which they would not normally attend in the course of performing the task. Accurate reports of mental processes would not be expected in such studies. In fact, none of the studies reported by Nisbett and Wilson violates the predictions of the Ericsson and Simon model (1980).

Verbal protocols have been subject to some undeserved criticism because they have been confused with other methods of verbal reporting. Nisbett and Wilson's (1977) criticisms of verbal-reporting methods are appropriately applied only to some of the methods. Retrospective reports are likely to lose information and directed reports are likely to distort the process being studied. However, thinking-aloud protocols have neither of these problems. Ericsson and Simon (1980) found no evidence that thinking-aloud protocols change the course or structure of the task being studied. Rather, they concluded that thinking-aloud protocols reveal the structure of psychological processes quite accurately.

A common criticism of protocols is that they are incomplete. In fact, they *are* incomplete. Many of the psychological processes on which we depend every day are completely unconscious and therefore will not appear explicitly in thinking-aloud protocols. For example, when we read, we are conscious of the topic being discussed and sometimes of style, but we are never conscious of the processes by which we retrieve the meanings of the words we see on the page from memory.

Some processes are conscious at times and unconscious at other times. For example, some processes may enter consciousness only when they encounter difficulties. We may be unaware that we are doing grammatical analysis as a part of reading except when we run into especially difficult sentences. Some processes may be conscious when we first acquire them, but they become unconscious as we become more expert. For example, inexperienced writers may be very aware of their efforts to take the audience into account, whereas experts who exercise the same processes may do so so automatically that the processes are no longer conscious.

It is interesting that verbal protocols are singled out for criticism on the grounds of incompleteness because protocols, although not complete, are characteristically *more* complete than most of the other methods with which they are compared. For example, a protocol of a writer in action typically provides us with many more clues and with clearer clues to writing process than does the most careful input-output analysis (e.g., analysis of the text that the writer produces).

Summary of Criticisms and Replies

In concurrent verbal reporting: (1) if the subject is reporting memory traces that are verbal, then reporting appears neither to change nor to slow down task performance; (2) if the subject is reporting nonverbal memory traces, then reporting may slow task performance but does not appear to change its course or structure; (3) if the subject is asked to report information to which he or she would not normally attend while performing the task (e.g., "Tell me every time you think of an odd number"), then reporting may modify the usual sequence of mental processes involved in performing the task. In *retrospective reporting*, subjects are likely to forget some of the information about processes that was available during task performance. If subjects are asked to report on information they have forgotten, as they may be asked to do in *retrospection*, or to report on information they have not noticed, as they may asked to do in *directed reporting*, they may invent answers that do not describe the processes that actually occurred. Although they have been criticized for incompleteness, protocols typically provide more complete information about processes than do other methods.

THE ROLE OF PROTOCOL ANALYSIS IN WRITING RESEARCH

Having discussed the theory of writing and the theory of verbal reports, we are now in a better position to evaluate thinking-aloud protocols as a method for studying writing and to discuss their place among other writing research methods.

Whether we should use protocols or some other method to investigate a particular research problem depends on the nature of the problem and on how well we understand it. Protocols are expensive. For each page of text, there may be twenty pages of protocol, and analysis of those twenty pages typically requires a great deal of work. Protocols are appropriate only if the advantages they provide us in extra information justify that work.

Thinking-aloud protocols share the three advantages of process-tracing methods we have already mentioned, that is:

1. They provide direct evidence about processes.
2. They yield rich data and thus promote exploration.
3. They can detect processes that are invisible to other methods.

These advantages can be particularly important in the study of writing. Because writing involves a complex integration of processes and because writing extends over considerable periods of time, it presents special problems for analysis by input-output methods. When an activity consists of a complex mixture of processes, it is very difficult to figure out through input-output analysis what each process is contributing. This is what Minsky (1963) calls the credit assignment problem. The problem is that the same output might have been caused by many different combinations of processes. Thus, direct observation, that is, observation that bridges the gap between input and output, is important for determining which combination of processes *actually* occurred.

Research on writing is still in an early stage of development. We are now enjoying, or suffering through, a period of exploration. The territory we are discovering is new, and our current crude theories provide only the most primitive of charts to guide us. Later, as the shape of the new territory is revealed, our theories can take more definite form. We shall be able more frequently to formulate precise hypotheses, which we can test with narrowly focused and powerful experiments. At present, narrowly focused experiments are relatively inefficient because, without strong theoretical guidance, they often miss their intended targets and reveal nothing. In contrast, protocol studies which are less narrowly focused, are well suited for exploring unknown territory. Because the data they provide is rich, protocols frequently reveal important processes we did not set out to find.

In some cases, it is desirable to mix methods. For example, we may want the economy of a narrowly focused input-output study so that we can collect large amounts of data to establish a particular fact with confidence. In addition, we may want the richness of a protocol study to be sure that we understand the relation of the fact to a broader range of processes in which it is embedded. Mixing methods in such cases would involve dividing the subjects into two groups. The larger of the two groups, consisting of most of the subjects, would be run by the more economical input-output method. The smaller group would be run through the same experimental procedures as the larger group, but in addition the procedures would include thinking-aloud protocols.

In summary, protocols can provide us with a valuable window onto our thought processes. Although the scope of that window is not infinite, it is wider than most of the other windows available.

REFERENCES

Bereiter, C., & Scardamalia, M. *Cognitive coping strategies and the problem of "inert knowledge."* Paper presented at the NIE–LRDC Conference on Thinking and Learning Skills, Pittsburgh, October 1980.

Bereiter, C., & Scardamalia, M. From conversation to composition: The role of instruction in a developmental process. In R. Glaser (Ed.), *Advances in instructional psychology* (Vol. 2). Hillsdale, N. J.: Erlbaum, 1982.

Bereiter, C., Scardamalia, M., & Bracewell, R. J. *An applied cognitive-developmental approach to writing research.* Paper presented at the annual meeting of the American Educational Research Association, San Francisco, April 1979.

Claparéde, E. *Scientia*, 1917, *22*, 353–368.

Emig, J. *The composing processes of twelfth graders* (Report No. 13). Urbana, Ill.: National Council of Teachers of English Research, 1971.

Ericsson, K. A., & Simon, H. A. Verbal reports as data. *Psychological Review*, 1980, *87*, 215–251.

Flower, L., & Hayes, J. R. The cognition of discovery: Defining a rhetorical problem. *College Composition and Communication*, 1980, *31*, 21–32.

Ghiselin, B. (Ed.). *The creative process.* New York: New American Library, 1952, (Mentor Books) 1952.

Gould, J. D. *Composing letters with computer-based text editors* (RC 8446, No. 36750). Yorktown Heights, N.Y.: IBM Research Center, 1978.

Graves, D. H. *The growth and development of first grade writers.* Paper presented at the annual meeting of the Canadian Council of Teachers of English, Ottawa, May 1979.

Hayes, J. R., & Flower, L. S. Identifying the organization of writing processes. In L. W. Gregg & E. R. Steinberg (Eds.) *Cognitive processes in writing.* Hillsdale, N. J.: Erlbaum, 1980. (a)

Hayes, J. R., & Flower, L. S. Writing as problem solving. *Visible language*, 1980, *14*, 388–399. (b)

Humphrey, G. *Thinking.* London: Methuen, 1951.

Lowes, J. L. *The road to Xanadu.* Boston: Houghton Mifflin, 1927.

Matsuhashi, A., & Cooper, C. *A video time-monitored observational study: The transcribing behavior and composing processes of a competent high school writer.* Paper presented at the annual meeting of the American Educational Research Association, Toronto, March 1978.

Minsky, M. Steps toward artificial intelligence. In E. A. Feigenbaum & J. Feldman (Eds.), *Computers and thought.* New York: McGraw-Hill, 1963.

Nisbett, R. E., & Wilson, T. D. Telling more than we can know: Verbal reports on mental processes. *Psychological Review*, 1977, *84*, 231–259.

Odell, L., & Goswami, D. *The nature and functions of writing in non-academic settings.* Paper presented at the Conference on Models and Processes of Writing, State University of New York, Albany, May 1980.

Perl, S. *Five writers writing: Case studies of the composing process of unskilled college writers.* Unpublished doctoral dissertation, New York University, June 1978.

Pianko, S. A description of the composing process of college freshmen writers. *Research in the Teaching of English*, 1979, *13*, 5–22.

Plimpton, G. (Ed.) *Writers at work.* New York: Viking, 1965.

Ruger, H. The psychology of efficiency. *Archives of Psychology*, 1910, *15*, 223–239.

Simon, H. A. Scientific discovery and the psychology of problem solving. In R. G. Colodny (Ed.), *Mind and cosmos: Essays in contemporary science and philosophy* (Vol. 3) Pittsburgh: University of Pittsburgh Press, 1966.

Wallas, G. *The art of thought.* New York: Harcourt, Brace, 1926.

8

The Discourse-Based Interview: A Procedure for Exploring the Tacit Knowledge of Writers in Nonacademic Settings

Lee Odell
Rensselaer Polytechnic Institute
Dixie Goswami
American Institute for Research
Anne Herrington
Rensselaer Polytechnic Institute

According to Michael Polanyi (Polanyi & Prosch, 1975), much of our knowledge is personal and tacit. We acquire this knowledge not so much by memorizing rules or reading textbook explanations as by repeatedly engaging in a given acitivity or, in Polanyi's terms, "dwelling in" a particular action. For example, we develop our skill as writers not by studying rules, but by continually writing. Further, it is likely that we do not consciously formulate much of this knowledge as a set of premises or maxims, but instead internalize it as inexplicit functional knowledge that we shall use and expand upon each time we write. Polanyi argues that this knowledge is characteristic of all activities, whether physical—such as riding a bicycle—or mental—such as solving a difficult chess problem. Polanyi also claims that tacit knowledge exists at a number of levels. Most significantly for our purposes, Polanyi cites the example of oral communication. At the lowest level, we have learned a phonological system (although most of us could not readily explain how it works), and at the highest level, we have learned to become sensitive to rhetorical or interpersonal context; we have inferred from experience how to vary our style of expression according to the audience we are addressing. This knowledge includes our understanding of both the contexts in which we speak and the strategies that are appropriate for a given context.

A number of sociolinguistic studies of oral language have confirmed the influence of social context on speech. In a review of research on language acquisition, Cazden (1970) stresses the situational relativity of children's speech and cites research evidence that shows the influence of such situation-specific factors as topic, task, and speaker-listener relationship. Labov (1970) cites the influence of these same factors on stylistic shifts, and he asserts that "there are no single-style speakers . . . every speaker will show some variation in phonological and syntactic rules according to the immediate context in which he is speaking" (p. 16). A similar conclusion appears to hold true for writing. Discourse theorists and teachers of composition (Booth, 1975; Gibson, 1969; Kinneavy, 1980) argue that writing does not exist in a vacuum, that a writer's purpose and knowledge of audience and subject shape the stylistic and substantive choices the writer makes. This point of view receives some support from several recent studies that show that certain groups of writers vary syntax according to the rhetorical context, the audience, and purpose for which they are writing (Crowhurst & Piché, 1979; Rubin & Piché, 1979).

By studying the ways that rhetorical context influences writing, researchers have begun to confirm assumptions that are widely held but that have not been subjected to careful testing. Moreover, results of these studies help justify pedagogical and evaluative practices recommended by Lloyd-Jones (1977), Moffett (1968), and others. However, studies of written language are limited in two respects. For one thing, composition researchers have carried out their work in classroom or experimental settings. With few exceptions (e.g., Scribner & Cole, 1978), researchers have not studied the writing people do as a part of their daily lives in nonacademic settings. Moreover, few researchers have attempted to understand the tacit personal knowledge that writers bring to bear on their writing tasks. Thus, existing research tells us, for example, that the syntax of student writing addressed to a teacher may differ from the syntax of student writing addressed to a close friend. But this research is not likely to help us understand the tacit knowledge the writers brought to bear on these tasks. We cannot determine what assumptions writers made or what background knowledge they had concerning the audience, the topic, and the strategies that might be appropriate for achieving their assigned purpose with a given audience.

These limitations seem important. We know (Goswami, 1978; Van Dyck, 1980) that some workers in nonacademic settings frequently have to write for diverse audiences and purposes. We have reason to think (Knoblauch, 1980; Odell & Goswami, 1982) that some of these workers possess detailed, useful information concerning the occupational and rhetorical context for their writing. We believe that much of this information may be tacit knowledge. That is, having derived it through repeated experience, writers can use it without having to formulate it consciously each time they write. We also believe that this knowledge may be of interest to both theorists and teachers. Consequently, we want to raise a methodological question that will occupy the rest of this chapter. How can researchers get at the tacit knowledge of people who write in nonacademic settings? What methodology will enable writers to make explicit the knowledge or strategies that previously may have been only implicit?

Our answer to these questions is illustrated in the following letter from a business executive to a sales representative. This letter, part of a larger sample collected from this executive, has been modified so that at five points it indicates both the original text and an alternative the writer might have chosen. In three of these instances (1, 4, and 5), the writer was asked to consider using an alternative form for each of the following: addressing his reader (1), asking the reader to perform an action (4), and referring to himself (5). At two other points, the writer was asked to consider deleting an introductory, context-setting statement (bracketed passage at 2) and a passage that elaborates on a general term (bracketed passage at 4). In all five instances, the alternatives were, in fact, reflected in some other piece of this executive's work-related writing. To elicit information concerning the writer's tacit knowledge about the rhetorical context for the letter, an interviewer asked, in effect, two basic questions: "Here you do X. In other pieces of writing, you do Y or Z. In this passage, would you be willing to do Y or Z rather than X? What basis do you have for preferring one alternative to the other?"

When asked about the first alternative, the form used in addressing his reader, the writer was not willing to use "Dear Mr. Bunch" rather than "Dear Ron":

> ["Dear Mr. Bunch"] is a possible alternative, but I was trying to establish with "Dear Ron" that I've talked to him a number of times and I feel that we're on some sort of a personal basis and that's what I was trying to establish. It's a business letter but I didn't want to make it so stiff.

The writer also declined to omit the context-setting phrase, "Pursuant to our conversations over the past few months . . ."

> I do want to get the point in about the fact that we've talked about this a couple of times in the past. He was, quite frankly, chasing the daylights out of me to get this account. We've been talking on and off and it's been generally at his initiative and, now that we've made a positive decision, I want to recall that to him, if you will, in such a subtle way as to further make him do the job.

In these two excerpts from his interview, the writer gives us information about his actual and his desired relationship with Ron Bunch. He reveals that he has had frequent personal contacts with Ron Bunch, contacts that Bunch had initiated. His comments also suggest he is trying to

27 September 1979

Mr. Ronald R. Bunch
Marketing Corporation
100 Southward Island
Clearwater, Florida 33500

Subject: SALES REPRESENTATIVE CONTRACT

(1)   Dear Ron:
       Dear Mr. Bunch:

(2)   [Pursuant to our conversations over the past few months and in line with our need and desire for professional sales coverage in Florida], I am happy to report that you have been chosen to represent the PDS portion of the Acme Amalgamated product line.

(3)   As a result, I have enclosed two copies of our sales representative agreement covering PDS products. [This agreement has an 11/1/79 effective date and you will receive 5% commission on the listed products for all invoices dated 11/1/79 and beyond. This, of course, includes all new orders received on or after this date plus all orders presented in house.]

(4)   [Please sign . . .
       You must sign . . .
       It is imperative that you sign . . .]
       both copies of this contract and return one to us for our records.
           Ron, it is indeed a pleasure to have you as part of our sales team, and I am excited about the prospects for the future.

(5)   [I am looking forward to . . .
       We are looking forward to . . .
       Amalgamated Products is looking forward to . . .]
       a long and mutually beneficial relationship.
           If there should be any questions in this matter, please call me.

                                                              Sincerely yours,

                                                              J. F. Moon
                                                              Product Manager
       JFM/d
       Enclosure

---

maintain a rather delicate relationship with his reader. The writer wants to avoid the formality that characterizes some employer-employee relationships, yet he retains the rather authoritative role of someone who is responsible for seeing that another carries out a job as effectively as possible. Furthermore, the writer's comments imply at least two rhetorical strategies. The first is commonplace enough, that is, the writer uses the reader's first name to establish or confirm a personal relationship and to create a tone that is not too stiff. The second strategy seems somewhat less obvious. The writer subtly reminds the reader of his previous expressions of interest to enhance the reader's motivation.

In discussing the alternatives for paragraphs three and four, the writer expresses his sense of what he may and may not assume to be true of his reader. He is unwilling to delete the details about the sales agreement (3), in part because he cannot be sure about his reader's prior experience:

> I want it understood up front what we are going to pay commissions for and when we are going to start paying the commissions. The important part of any relationship is the beginning. And I don't want anything inferred or assumed. I want the facts clearly stated. . . . [This arrangement] may be different from what he has been accustomed to in the past.

Yet, in discussing ways to phrase a request (4), the writer assumes that he and his reader share a certain amount of common knowledge. He refuses to accept the alternative, "It is imperative. . .," because he believes that the reader will recognize the importance of the request the writer is making:

> Obviously, it is imperative that he sign both copies but I don't think I would choose that particular type of phrasing for it. We're dealing with a professional sales representative and we're supposed to be professionals; it's implied that both copies have to be signed before it's valid. "Imperative" would seem like too strong a word in this particular context. . . .

A moment later in his interview, the writer reveals a strategy for evaluating an alternative, a strategy that entails asking himself how he would react to a given phrase in a particular context (4):

> If I heard that, "it is imperative that you sign . . ." something that obviously is going to be done, my response would be nervousness, or some other thought.

In commenting on the fifth alternative [the form he will use in referring to himself (5)], the writer seems, at first, to be guided only by a simple stylistic rule:

> You should basically stay away from too much of "I, I, I" in a business type of letter. That's a mistake.

Yet, he immediately goes on to relate his preference for "We are looking forward. . ." because of his sense of his relationship to his company and his reader. The writer points out that using "I" in this context implies that the reader is:

> Dealing one to one with me as opposed to me as a representative of Amalgamated Products as a whole. He understands perfectly well what's going on here, but [using I] is a little bit presumptuous on my part.

We cannot, of course, argue that the business executive consciously considered the relationship between himself, his company, and the reader while he was actually writing his letter. Although we did not observe the executive's composing process, we would expect that several of the alternatives mentioned previously were chosen with little or no apparent deliberation. Indeed, because the executive was an experienced writer and this was not a terribly unusual task, we assume that the task of writing this letter was eased somewhat by knowledge that the writer may not have explicitly formulated while writing the letter, knowledge about the subject, the audience, and the strategies that were most likely to prove effective.

Information about this knowledge is interesting, because in part, it may help us test discourse theorists' claims about ways in which considerations of audience and purpose are important for writers. Furthermore, this information has practical implications. For example, the Ron Bunch letter and interview transcripts are from a study conducted by David Lauerman and his colleagues (personal communication) at Canisius College in Buffalo, N.Y. As part of their effort to design an advanced composition course for students in business, Lauerman and his colleagues have collected an extensive writing sample from executives in several different businesses and have interviewed these executives using the procedures we have described. As a result of this work, Lauerman is able to create writing tasks that actually reflect some of the rhetorical demands students will encounter in their careers. Further, interview materials from the study frequently serve as a basis for class discussion. For example, students are frequently given a piece of writing comparable to the Ron Bunch letter. Students are asked to decide which alternatives seem most appropriate to them and then compare their choices and reasoning with those of the original writer.

To summarize our argument thus far: (1) our interview procedure can be used with writers in diverse settings, writers whose ability may vary widely; (2) interviews with these writers enable them to tell us about the tacit knowledge they bring to writing tasks they encounter every day; (3) information about this knowledge is of interest to both theorists and teachers.

This series of claims raises a number of questions:

How does one justify studying the writing people do routinely? Would we not elicit more information if we designed more challenging experimental tasks that would tax their composing skills more severely than a routine task?

How valid is interview data? Can we have any confidence in the observations that writers make well after a given piece of writing has been completed?

Why should researchers, rather than writers, determine what features of a text are discussed in an interview?

How significant are the features we have selected for writers to comment on?

How does our research methodology relate to the 'compose-aloud' procedure used by several other researchers?

ROUTINE OF EXPERIMENTAL TASKS

Because they are interested in studying writers' underlying composing processes, such writing researchers as Flower & Hayes (1980), have made extensive use of experimental tasks that are designed to pose unique and unexpected demands for a writer. Their rationale is that to do such tasks, writers would have to draw on their full repertoire of composing strategies and not rely on "stored problem representations" that they have developed for routine tasks. Because such experimental tasks are designed to avoid familiar, natural contexts, they are not suitable for our purpose, which is to probe a worker's store of knowledge of the rhetorical context for writing done on the job. Consider, for example, an experimental task, such as "Write about abortion, pro and con, for *Children's Digest*, which is read by ten- to twelve-year-olds." This task might elicit information about strategies a social services administrator would use to solve unique tasks for which he or she has no context, and perhaps elicit as well information about global strategies the administrator uses. But it would not elicit information about the contextual knowledge that shapes that administrator's writing on the job or about how global strategies are combined with task and context-specific knowledge to compose a particular piece.

RELIABILITY OF INTERVIEW DATA

One answer to this question is suggested by Atlas (1979). In reviewing widely reported techniques for studying writing, Atlas concluded that the validity of interviews "depends heavily on the accuracy of the subjects' self knowledge; for this reason, interview data is probably best treated as weak evidence, suggestive but not conclusive" (p. 36). Our response to this criticism depends on the use to which an interview is being put. If a researcher is using an interview to determine what went on while a writer was engaged in the process of composing, we agree with Atlas. When experience is transferred from short-term memory (STM) to long-term memory (LTM), we assume that it is simplified and restructured; it seems unlikely that LTM can retain the full complexity of mental activity attendant on the moment-by-moment process of composing. Further, we agree with Polanyi and Prosch (1975) that some tacit knowledge is so internalized that it becomes unconscious and inaccessible. However, we are not using interviews to obtain information about mental processes. We are using interviews to identify the kinds of world knowledge and expectations that informants bring to writing tasks and to discover the perceptions informants have about the conceptual demands that functional, interactive writing tasks make on them. Research on verbal reports as data confirms that informants can report reliably on such socially learned information, which has been tacitly transformed into functional plans they apply when writing (Smith & Miller, 1978).

Later in this chapter, we shall argue that our interviewing procedures are particularly well suited for eliciting this sort of information. But the validity of this information is subject to at least two other criticisms. It may be that an interviewer will bias a writer's response by the kinds of questions he or she asks simply by deciding to ask about one feature of a text rather than some other feature. Further, there is the chance that interviewees will mislead researchers and themselves if only by allowing feelings or preconceptions to influence their statements. There may be no way to satisfy completely the first of these criticisms. The very act of observing any phenomenon may alter that phenomenon. However, we have devised interview procedures that will help an interviewer be as non-directive as possible (Odell & Goswami, 1982). Furthermore, we are inclined to trust interviewees' statements. For one thing, interviewees rarely respond to our questions with abstract precepts about good writing. Instead, they usually talk specifically about the interpersonal and occupational context in which their writing exists. It may be that any single one of these statements is suspect, that at any given moment an interviewee may mislead himself or herself or the researcher. But we have some evidence that interviewees' statements seem to vary according to the type of job they hold. We find patterns in the statements of workers in one group that differ from patterns in statements by workers in another group. This blend of consistency within groups and variations between groups leads us to believe that interviewees' responses are not simply individual writers' whims or misperceptions, and are not governed solely by our intrusion as interviewers or by some bias in one interview technique.

SELECTION OF TOPICS FOR INTERVIEWS

As we have noted, our interview procedures require the researcher rather than the writer to decide which feature of the text will be discussed. We know, of course, that a finished, edited text gives no clue as to what parts of the text required extensive deliberation and what parts were written quickly with little conscious effort. Consequently, it is quite possible that the interviewer will fail to ask the writer about matters that occupied large parts of the composing process. This possibility raises two further suggestions: perhaps the writer should identify at least some of the matters to be discussed in the interview; perhaps the interview should not be based solely on the finished text. In response to the first speculation, we must point out that we are interested in knowledge that may not be consciously learned or applied. If this knowledge is not at the front of a writer's consciousness while composing, it seems unreasonable to expect the writer to identify points at which he or she has relied on that knowledge. As to the second suggestion, we agree that there may be times when observation of a writer's composing process can enable a researcher to ask questions about, for example, points at which a writer made and crossed out several false starts. Or it might be possible to base an interview on the revisions a writer makes in successive drafts of a piece of writing (see Cooper & Odell, 1976). Yet these strategies may tell us only part of what we want to know. Insofar as, for example, revision entails tacit knowledge, we might profit from interviewing writers about their revising. But this knowledge is almost certainly functioning when a writer does not have to stop, deliberate, and revise. Indeed, we believe that the transformation of contextual knowledge into tacit plans is what enables large parts of the composing process to proceed with little conscious effort; tacit knowledge is not limited to those parts of a text that require revision.

This last assertion raises a series of questions. If many parts of a text may have allowed a writer to use his or her tacit knowledge, how will researchers decide about what parts of a text they will ask questions? How can researchers be sure they are not ignoring important parts of a text? What basis does one have for assuming that a given feature of the text is significant?

SIGNIFICANCE OF TOPICS SELECTED

In trying to decide what parts of a text we would ask writers to comment on, we made several assumptions. The first was that writers, like speakers, are not univocal; that is, they are capable of varying the language, syntax, and content of their writing. Consequently, we gathered samples of writing from each person we interviewed, materials representing the full range of written tasks that the person typically did as part of his or her job. We examined these writing samples, looking for variations, trying to identify the alternatives that were part of each writer's repertoire. Our next assumption was that many of these alternatives might have been chosen with little or no conscious deliberation, that a particular locution or bit of information may have seemed so routine or so uniquely appropriate that a writer might not recognize it as a choice. Finally, we assumed that if we asked writers to consider alternatives (alternatives that were evident in other materials he or she had written), we might create a cognitive dissonance that would enable a writer to become conscious of the tacit knowledge that justified the use of a particular alternative.

Having identified alternatives to discuss with writers, we still cannot provide a completely satisfactory answer to the second question we raised earlier; we must acknowledge that there may be other features of a text that will provide as much information as, or perhaps more information than, those features we have chosen. As soon as researchers direct their attention in one direction, they blind themselves, at least temporarily, to information that might be available if they were to look in another direction. But we can mitigate this problem if we ask writers about a variety of features in a given set of texts and if we are willing to ask about different kinds of features when we are dealing with different sorts of texts. For example, in a study of writing in a welfare agency, Odell and Goswami (1982) interviewed administrators about their letters and memos, texts that involved many of the same alternatives as were illustrated earlier in the letter of Ron Bunch. However, caseworkers in the welfare agency rarely wrote letters and memos; instead, they were most likely to write reports of their meetings with clients. In interviewing caseworkers about these reports, it was necessary to consider a different set of alternatives. In place of asking about the form used in addressing a reader or the way they signed their name to a letter or memo, the researchers asked about such decisions as whether to refer to a client informally (by just using his or her first name), formally (by using Mr., Mrs., or Ms.), or impersonally (by referring to the client as *client*); whether to include/exclude information about the caseworker's actions during a meeting with a client; or whether or not to refer to the client's actions.

On the face of it, some of the alternatives discussed in our interviews seem rather insignificant. For example, in our interviews based on letters and memos, we have asked writers about the way they signed their name. We assume that writers may spend very little time trying to decide whether they should use their full name or just their first name. Yet questions about such an apparently simple matter as this can provide a great deal of information. When we read a collection of one administrator's writings, we noticed that she had several different ways of signing her name: M. Smith, Margaret Smith, Meg Smith, and Meg. In one of our interviews we asked her if she would be willing to sign her name on a particular letter as Margaret or Meg Smith rather than M. Smith. Here is an excerpt from her reply:

> This [letter] is going to a permanent file. I am looking to the years to come. Someone coming back. . . . It makes no difference whether I am male or female making this decision. [What matters is that] I am a grade A supervisor. They have to know where he is placed and who evaluated him. But I don't use Margaret Smith for this reason: I want to be neuter.

In commenting on the way she signed a memo, the administrator remarked that she preferred the signature Margaret Smith (rather than M. Smith) because:

This is not a formal little note. . . . I'm sharing some information, so I put Margaret. I use that M. when I don't want the reader to know whether I'm male or female.

In yet another interview, this writer noted that it was unusual for a woman to hold a high administrative post in the agency where she worked. She remarked that she sometimes felt her writing carried more weight when a reader did not know whether the writer was a man or a woman. Thus, our inquiry into an apparently simple matter elicited a great deal of information about the writer's understanding of her status in the agency and about one of her strategies for accomplishing her work.

We want to make a similar claim for the other alternatives used in interviews with workers in the welfare agency. All of these alternatives elicited information about writers' knowledge of the rhetorical and occupational context for their writing. Further, writers' comments about these alternatives reflected writers' knowledge of ways to vary style and substance to achieve particular effects. For example, the Ron Bunch interview illustrates that the questions about form of address (1), form of command/request (4), and form of reference to self (5) reveal the writer's knowledge of how to establish the desired writer/reader relationship, the professional context, and the conventions within that context. In short, although an isolated feature (e.g., form of address or elaboration) may seem insignificant, it is a sensitive indicator of writers' complex understanding of the rhetorical context and ways for them to achieve their purpose within that context.

COMPOSING ALOUD

Flower and Hayes (1980) have shown the usefulness of asking writers to compose aloud, to verbalize the thoughts and feelings that accompany their efforts to complete a piece of writing. Although composing aloud was not used in the study of writers in a welfare agency (cited earlier), we realize that this procedure has enabled some writers to comment on the rhetorical context for their writing. Consequently, we asked four welfare workers (two administrators and two caseworkers, all of whom participated in the study by Odell & Goswami, 1982) to do some composing aloud. One administrator did two composing-aloud tasks. Each of the other participants did four such tasks. As we analyzed their work on these tasks, we gained some understanding of both the uses and limitations of the composing-aloud technique. One argument for the composing-aloud methodology is that it can be an excellent way to get at the generating, planning, and organizing activities that make up a large part of a writer's composing process. Moreover this procedure sometimes can give a good record of what Britton has called, "shaping at the point of utterance" (Britton, Burgess, Martin, McLeod, & Rosen, 1975). In some of the composing-aloud protocols we have collected, we can observe a writer reflecting on the accuracy of a particular phrase or debating the wisdom of including a given bit of information. Here, for example, is a transcript of a case worker composing aloud while writing a report of her visit with a child in a foster home:

Writes	I found him watching his shows on television. He is a delightful five-year-old child with blond . . .
Interrupts/	
Speaks	Not, it's not blond, it's sort of dirty blond. Well, let's see . . .
Writes	He is a delightful five-year-old child. Long lashes, cute, tall slender . . .
Speaks	That's what I wrote about him. Tall and slender.
Writes	He is a delightful five-year-old with long [eye] lashes . . .
Speaks	. . and very intellectual looking?
Writes	. . . intellectual looking in his corrective lenses, in his glasses.
Reads	He is a delightful five-year-old with long lashes and very intellectual looking in his glasses.
Speaks	That doesn't sound right. No, cross all that out.
Writes	He is a delightful five-year-old.

Another example of composing aloud comes from a protocol in which an administrator was writing a memo to advise lower level supervisors that their workers were not following the correct procedure for filling out a particular form. The draft this administrator wrote during her composing-aloud session began with a request:

Please advise all workers that Form 189–B . . . is somewhat confusing to workers. This form should be used only when . . .

Apparently this request was very important to the administrator. She revised it considerably for her final draft. And almost half of the comments in her protocol concern this request. Although she was writing this request, she made the following comments, over a period of several minutes:

No, ah, let's see. How do we word this one so that they don't get uptight? Can't demand, can't ask, just. . . . Ah, let's see. Do we advise them of the incorrect usage? Ah, oh dear. *Writes*: "Please remind. . . ." Oh, Lord, how to be tactful? Let's see, what do I want to do? I want to tell them that they . . . why they use form 189–B and that they're doing it wrong.

In these comments, the administrator mentions concerns that also appear in the interviews we had conducted over a year earlier: How are my readers likely to react to what I am going to say? How can I create a persona that will cause as little undue stress as possible?

Our first example of composing aloud suggests that this procedure elicits certain types of information that cannot be obtained through the interview procedure we have described. The second example suggests that, for some writers, composing aloud elicits some of the same types of comments we encountered in our interviews. Having acknowledged these values of the composing-aloud procedure, we want to suggest some of its limitations. The most obvious limitation is that not everyone feels comfortable composing aloud. In one study, Cooper and Odell (1976) tried to get professional writers to compose aloud. Of the eight writers involved, only one gave a detailed report of the thoughts, feelings, and questions that attended his effort to write a draft. Most of the other writers simply read aloud the words they wrote on the page, responding briefly or not at all to our requests to "tell us what you are thinking as you write." With workers in the department of social services, results were somewhat more encouraging. All four provided at least some useful information while composing aloud in response to this request, "Write a description of your job for readers of *Seventeen* magazine." But when asked to compose aloud while doing her normal day-to-day writing tasks, one writer did nothing more than write and read aloud as she wrote. As we have noted, other writers provided somewhat more information. But when compared to their comments on their reasons for choosing one alternative in preference to another, this information seems relatively limited. Consider the writing of the administrator who was writing the memo about the correct use of form 189–B. When we examined a collection of her memos and letters, we realized that her writings were likely to vary in several ways:

The way she addressed her reader.

Whether she included introductory, context-setting material at the beginning of her writing.

The way she referred to herself.

Whether she shifted level of abstraction to elaborate on a given statement.

The way she phrased a command or a request.

Whether she concluded a memo or letter with a phrase inviting further communication (e.g., if you have any questions . . .").

The way she signed her name.

In her composing-aloud protocol, this writer commented on one of these variations—the way she wanted to phrase a request. Her comments touch on issues that also appear in her interviews. However, during her composing aloud, she makes no comment at all on other types of choices (listed above), even though our interviews led us to believe that these choices were not trivial for her. This administrator was the person, cited earlier, who had very definite notions about the usefulness of signing her name M. Smith, Margaret Smith, or Meg. Interestingly, the memo about form 189–B was signed M. Smith. Yet, the composing-aloud protocol did not contain any reference to a matter that, as we have seen, is quite important to this writer. It seems, then, that this writer constructed through experience a plan based on a quite complex knowledge of possible reader biases. Once that plan was formulated, the writer did not need to reconstruct it for each writing and thus did not need to attend to it or verbalize it. That a decision of this sort may not be made consciously for each piece does not diminish its importance, but it does suggest why it will not likely be revealed in a composing aloud protocol, which is more suitable for eliciting information about global processes, not about the specific knowledge and plans applied to familiar tasks.

We cannot make too much of this single omission from one composing-aloud session. Yet, the problem we have described consistently occurs in the composing aloud of the two caseworkers. From each of these caseworkers, we have three transcripts of their composing aloud while writing reports of their meetings with clients. None of these protocols contains any comment on types of choices that appear in the writing of every worker in their unit. Given this fact, one might wonder whether these choices are, in fact, as important as we have suggested. After all, if a choice were really important, would not a writer comment on it during the composing-aloud process? We agree, of course, that points mentioned when a writer composes aloud are worth our attention. When a writer deliberates over, say, a phrase, it seems reasonable to assume that the phrase may represent a significant rhetorical decision. But it does not seem reasonable to assume that composing aloud will enable a writer to comment on all the important choices he or she must make. As we know, the composing process is complex; in writing a sentence, a writer has to decide on a number of matters, ranging from the syntactic form in which a proposition may be cast to the appropriateness of expressing that proposition to the intended audience. Given this range of decisions, many of which must be made almost simultaneously, and given the limitations of STM, it is surely inevitable that a written text will entail significant decisions that cannot be remarked upon when one composes aloud.

In suggesting that composing-aloud protocols might omit important information, we raise a criticism that may be made of any research methodology, ours included. It is unlikely that a single methodology—in effect, a single perspective—will ever tell us all we need to know. Consequently, we think researchers should look for ways that several existing methodologies might be brought to bear on the same topic. For example, we think composing-aloud protocols might complement the information derived from our interviews. Composing-aloud protocols may be useful, for instance, in differentiating between that to which experienced versus inexperienced workers consciously attend when they write. We speculate that inexperienced workers—because they do not yet have the same knowledge of the rhetorical context and the way to manipulate language to achieve their purposes within that context—would have to devote more attention to constructing that knowledge when they write each piece. The composing-aloud protocols should reflect this difference and also provide information about how inexperienced workers build that knowledge. Composing-aloud protocols might also be a source of information about the strategies a writer uses to solve the unique problem presented by each writing task, more specifically the way context-specific knowledge is combined with more global-writing strategies to solve these problems. Such information about what writers know and how they use this knowledge, information derived from discourse-based interviews, and composing-aloud protocols could serve as a useful heuristic, particularly for inexperienced workers.

In suggesting one way research strategies might complement each other, we are making this assumption: Researchers in our field need a repertoire of research strategies, a repertoire that includes interviews, composing aloud, analyses of written products, and videotaping writers while they are writing. Our goal in this chapter is to add to that repertoire.

REFERENCES

Atlas, M. A. *Assessing an audience: A study of expert-novice differences in writing* (Technical Report No. 3, Document Design Project). Pittsburgh, Pa.: Carnegie-Mellon University, 1979. Contract No. NIE–400–78–0043.

Booth, W. The rhetorical stance. In W. Winterowd (Ed.), *Contemporary rhetoric: A conceptual background with readings*. New York: Harcourt Brace Jovanovich, 1975.

Britton, J., Burgess, T., Martin, N., McLeod, A., & Rosen, H. *The development of writing abilities (11–18)*. London: Macmillan, 1975.

Cazden, C. The neglected situation in child language research and education. In F. Williams (Ed.), *Language and poverty*. Chicago: Rand McNally, 1970.

Cooper, C. R., & Odell, L. Considerations of sound in the composing process of published writers. *Research in the Teaching of English*, 1976, *10*, 103–115.

Crowhurst, M., & Piché, G. L. Audience and mode of discourse effects on syntactic complexity in writing at two grade levels. *Research in the Teaching of English*, 1979, *13*, 101–110.

Flower, L. S., & Hayes, J. R. The cognition of discovery: Defining a rhetorical problem. *College Composition and Communication*, 1980, *31*, 21–32.

Gibson, W. *Persona*. New York: Random House, 1969.

Goswami, D. *Rhetorical occurrences in occupational writing*. Paper presented at the annual meeting of the National Council of Teachers of English, Kansas City, November 1978.

Kinneavy, J. *A theory of discourse*. New York: W. W. Norton, 1980.

Knoblauch, C. H. Intentionality in the writing process: A case study. *College Composition and Communication*, 1980, *31*, 153–159.

Labov, W. *The study of nonstandard English*. Champaign, Ill.: National Council of Teachers of English, 1970.

Lloyd-Jones, R. Primary trait scoring. In C. R. Cooper & L. Odell (Eds.). *Evaluating writing: Describing, measuring, judging*. Urbana, Ill.: National Council of Teachers of English, 1977.

Moffett, J. *Teaching the universe of discourse*. Boston: Houghton Mifflin, 1968.

Odell, L., & Goswami, D. Writing in a non-academic setting. *Research in the Teaching of English,* 1982, *16,* 201–224.

Polanyi, M., & Prosch, H. *Meaning*. Chicago: University of Chicago Press, 1975.

Rubin, D. L., & Piché, G. L. Development in syntactic and strategic aspects of audience adaptation skills in written persuasive communication. *Research in the Teaching of English*, 1979, *13*, 293–316.

Scribner, S., & Cole, M. Literacy without schooling: Testing for intellectual effects. *Harvard Educational Review*, 1978, *48*, 448–461.

Smith, E. R., & Miller, F. D. Theoretical note: Limits on perception of cognitive processes: A reply to Nisbett and Wilson. *Psychological Review*, 1978, *85*, 355–361.

Van Dyck, B. *Partial taxonomy of writing demands on bank executives*. Paper presented at the annual conference on College Composition and Communication, Washington, D.C., March 1980.

9

Understanding Writing Instruction: Issues of Theory and Method

Christopher M. Clark and Susan Florio
with
Janis L. Elmore, June Martin, and Rhoda Maxwell[1]
Michigan State University

BACKGROUND OF THE RESEARCH PROBLEM

Written literacy is an acknowledged and valued outcome of schooling in our society, yet it has been lamented that writing is the most neglected expressive mode in both research and teaching. The social and cognitive complexities of writing make it a difficult activity to study. But writing instruction continues to be a thorny responsibility of teachers, and the economic and social futures of children rest, in part, on their mastery of some set of writing skills. For these reasons, it is fitting that teachers and researchers with diverse skills and interests invest energy and creativity in the study of writing in schools.

Frustration with past efforts marks the current state of research on writing in fields as diverse as psychology, anthropology, and educational research. In psychology, for example, difficulties have been encountered in attempting to test the relation between writing and mental abilities in societies that lack formal schooling. This has prompted a call for research on the acquisition of written literacy to focus not on the incremental development of a set of generalizable mental capabilities, but on literacy as a repertoire of context-related expressive behaviors that is, to a large extent, imparted and acquired by means of cultural membership (e.g., Scribner & Cole, 1978).

Similarly, in anthropology, years of modest interest in writing as merely an index of cultural development and as a symbol system divorced from daily expressive activity in a culture has given way to a call for an "ethonography of writing"—a study of writing and its meanings as part of the "total communicative economy of the society under study" (Basso, 1974, p. 432). This research focus is particularly appropriate because anthropology is increasingly applied to questions of educational equity and cultural difference in our own society.

Finally, in educational research, contemporary studies of classroom organization and teacher decision making highlight the classroom as a special place that both constitutes a small community in its own right and is linked in important ways to the larger socio cultural milieu. The classroom community is special because it is one in which one individual is empowered to think and plan self-consciously for the structuring of many interactional activities that take place within it. This structuring is thought to be important in light of the community's valuing of growth and beneficial change over time for each individual member. Such insights derived from naturalistic study of classroom life have fueled interest in the investigation of writing in school, not as the 'outcome' of teaching behavior per se, but as an integral activity in the establishment and maintenance of the classroom as a learning community and as one measure of that community's power as a socializing force (Florio, 1979; Clark & Yinger, 1979).

Thus, the interests of psychologists, anthropologists, and educators have converged on questions of writing in use—on its expressive functions, on the ways in which literacy is acquired in the course of social life, and on the range of cognitive skills that ought to be considered when documenting or planning for instruction in writing. Questions about the acquisition of skilled performance and its relation to social context lend themselves particularly well to investigation by naturalistic means. One of the best ways to learn about writing is to watch people navigating their daily lives, noting occassions on which writing is the chosen mode of expression, listening to the language people have about writing, considering the nature of the writings they produce, and observing the ways in which writing works for people as functional communication. This strategy seems useful not only to the ethnographer who hopes to locate writing meaningfully in his or her portrayal of a society, or to the psychologist who observes the repertoire of skilled performances in a group of literate but unschooled people, but also to researchers, who are interested in the current state of the art in the teaching of writing, and to practitioners who seek ways to support and nurture the process of becoming literate.

LITERACY AND COMMUNITY

When we investigate the acquisition of written literacy by children both in and out of school, we are asking fundamental questions about the individual pyschological development of those children and about their membership in a community. Although children acquire many skills as a part of development, writing is one skilled performance that epitomizes the profound connections between personal development and the development of the community. The learning of systems of signs and symbols in speaking, reading, and writing is a stunning example of the interconnection between the growth of the individual and that of the society. In this spirit, Vygotsky (1978) cites writing as a

> particular system of symbols and signs whose mastery heralds a critical turning point in the entire cultural development of the child. (p. 106)

Not only does writing, like speaking, provide entrée into community for the individual, but community is, in fact, able to exist to the extent that people are able to share their thoughts and feelings by means of communicative symbols. In this regard, Schwab (1975) asserts that:

> Our beginning personness, as children, consists first of a world of perceived and felt significances that we have made from things seen. It is when another —adult or child—signals recognition that we have such a world, seeks to know it, and tries to give us a glimpse of his private world that one-to-one community begins. This is done in one and only one way—through speech, by talk. (pp. 31–32)

Speech and writing are both instances of the use of cultural tools—they are systems created and passed on in societies so that the members of those societies can live and work meaningfully together (Scribner & Cole, 1978).

The problem with studying the acquisition of any such communicative system in a society is that, for the most part, the process happens gradually, informally, and without much explicit instruction. This phenomenon has been documented in speech by Cook-Gumperz (1975): "the appearance of competence in daily life is given more by the activities that are not singled out for attention by the actors than by those activities that are singled out" (p. 138). The process of acquisition of literacy, even in school where such acquisition is an explicit and valued aim, is equally opaque. Although we can develop curricula and organize classroom activities around the practice of reading or writing, we are, finally, not able to render a full account of becoming a reader or becoming a writer simply by listing requisite skills to be acquired (see Wittgenstein, 1953/1968). Evidence of this problem is the great difficulty with which we make decisions about how to assess student performance in such areas as expressive writing or the appreciation of literature (Elmore, 1979).

In our pilot naturalistic research in the classroom (Florio, 1979), we have seen that the acquisition of written literacy in one second-grade classroom resembles the acquisition of speech in some important ways. We know that as children acquire a first language they are welcomed into the family as communicators even before their first words are uttered. Early on, children find that moves and sounds are expressive in that they elicit action from other people. Children in effect *practice* the use of language not as preparation for social life, but as social life itself. In that process, grammatical skills are seldom taught directly to children by the adults who are expert in their use. Rather, by means of the practice that comes from use, children gradually approximate the matures forms of speech in stages that appear to be developmental (e.g., Brown, 1973; Cazden, 1972). Similarly, in the classrooms we have studied, children did not receive much direct instruction in the process of writing unless or until there was a breach in the normal order of things. We observed considerable practice of writing and gradual approximation of the mature forms, but only occasional remediation. If all went well, the process of becoming a writer, although a remarkable one in the life of the child, went unremarked in the classroom. We observed the developing writer coming "to know a world in common with others and in common with others to be taken for granted" (Garfinkel, 1967, p. 139).

In attempting to account for what we have seen in the classroom, we assume with Goody, Cole, and Scribner (1977) that the occasion for mastery of written symbols, like the occasion for mastery of speech, arises in the course of social life and is supported by the community in which it occurs. People begin to write because within their communities they need to be able to perform the operations that literacy makes possible. They need to engage in commerce or to keep records, they need to remind themselves of the thoughts they have had (Brooks, 1978). Again, in our pilot work, we have found that children in one second-grade classroom—in which a small community was created in microcosm during the course of the school year—wrote in the greatest volume and complexity when working on the correspondence and record keeping required to maintain their classroom town. All other writing of worksheets, test papers, compositions, and the like was considered to be merely work 'for school.'

Like so many other forms of tacit cultural knowledge, writing, its uses, and the process of its acquisition are difficult for participants fully to describe or reflect upon. Rather, considerable insight into the writing process can be gained by "investigating the activity of writing as a dynamic component in the conduct and organization of social relations" (Basso, 1977, p. 431). The insight that mastery of communicative systems arises in the midst of social life is not a new one. In language arts, the point of view has been argued, for example, by Moffett (1968). We see evidence of this point of view in the writings of Bettelheim (1967) as well of Dewey (1956), and Freire (1970). The implications of this insight for research and practice are straightforward. In coming to understand individual development, it is necessary to consider that development in the context of community. As educators, we need to know more about such development, not because it would fail to arise without direct instruction and schooling, but because, in schools, we have a potential opportunity to enhance the process. Furthermore, in schools many children from diverse communities come to be taught and evaluated by us. We are responsible to approach the individual stylistic differences in communication arising from differences in community membership with insight and respect (Philips, 1972; Shultz, Florio, & Erickson, in press).

TEACHER THOUGHT AND ACTION

In addition to the assumption that the acquisition of written literacy in schools serves multiple social and communicative functions, the present inquiry was also informed by a model of the teacher as a rational agent who takes an influential and proactive role in planning, initiating, maintaining, and integrating classroom interaction in general and occasions for writing in particular. This view of the teacher derives from the cognitive information processing approach to research on teaching (Clark, 1980; Shulman & Elstein, 1975). From this perspective, the teacher is seen as bringing his or her thoughts into action through the information processing sequence depicted in Figure 9.1.

The leftmost section of Figure 9.1 represents the professional memory of a teacher; it includes a teacher's implicit theories about the commonplaces of education (subject matter, learners, teacher, and context) and his or her expectations and commitments concerning the particular

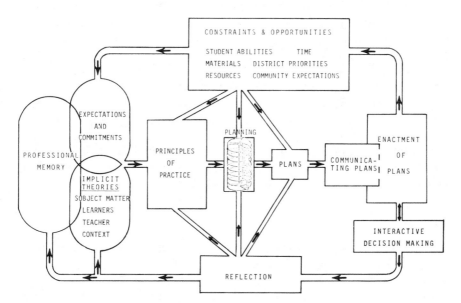

FIGURE 9.1   A Model of Teacher Thought and Action.

class and task of interest. In this model, the teacher's implicit theories about each of the commonplaces of education interact with his or her hopes, expectations, and commitments for writing instruction at a particular time to produce and rationalize a set of principles of practice. These principles of practice may be explicit or implicit. Taken together, they constitute a teacher's set of criteria for effective writing instruction. That is, if a teacher can be faithful to the set of principles of practice, he or she has every reason to believe that the teaching of writing will succeed. Particular successes and failures are explained largely in terms of maintenance of, or violation of, these principles of practice. It has been argued elsewhere (Clark & Yinger, 1980) that the essence of what is professional about teaching is the translation of principles of practice into action.

Teacher planning, the next step in Figure 9.1, is the process of combining constraints and opportunites with principles of practice to produce a plan for action. The plan consists of particular writing activities that have been created, adopted, or modified to be consistent with a teacher's principles of practice and, at the same time, practical within the limits of constraints and opportunities as the teacher sees them.

Next, the teacher communicates the plan to his or her students and they jointly enact the plan. This is the most visible part of teaching—what one can see during a visit to a classroom in full operation. All that has gone before, and that which follows, constitutes the hidden world of teaching. Almost inevitably, there is a difference between a plan and the enactment of that plan. Classrooms are characterized by interruption and unpredictability. Spontaneity is often valued by teachers and students alike. Because writing activities are joint productions of teacher and students, a teacher's plan often serves mainly to get the process started, with full enactment a divergent process. Teacher interactive decision making is the process of adjusting the plan to fit reality.

As a writing activity is enacted (and afterward as well), the teacher and the students gain experience of several sorts, and the teacher has an opportunity to evaluate and reflect on these experiences. This set of processes is represented in the teacher experience and reflection section of Figure 9.1. Experience and reflection can lead to confirmation, explanation, explication, or change in any or all of the earlier mentioned parts of the model. Thus, we have come full circle in this preliminary model of teacher thought and action in writing instruction.

Summary

There are important theoretical reasons why the authors of this study have chosen to analyze both (1) the functions that writing can be observed to perform in the classroom and (2) teachers' implicit theories about writing in the same study. Previous research in both the ethnographic/sociolinguistic tradition and in the tradition of cognitive psychology has been incomplete and has left us with questions that require the merging of perspectives. First, by documenting classroom interaction without attention to the intentionality of teacher (and students), little insight into the rationales for the observed social structuring can be gained. Classrooms are not like any other community. They exist for purposeful change in their members. They are organized by teachers whose responsibility it is to articulate the plans for activity and to structure the environments in which that activity occurs. However, to consider only the planning that underlies social life in the classroom is to miss both the spontaneity of the plans enacted and to encounter serious problems of interpreting the self-reports of teachers about their plans.

In an effort to increase understanding of how teacher beliefs and values about writing (implicit or explicit) manifest themselves in the classroom on the one hand and simultaneously to make better sense of those beliefs and values on the other hand, research perspectives are combined in this study. The combination of a cognitive psychological approach to research on teaching with an ethnographic/sociolinguistic approach to the study of classroom life is a particularly powerful and appropriate way to achieve the stated research aims. Cognitive psychological research can explore the thoughts, intentions, and decisions of the teacher as he or she conceives, initiates, and maintains writing activities.

The theoretical orientations with which we began our study helped to determine our methods of data collection, reduction, and analysis. In general, our methods were descriptive. Using such techniques as participant observation, journal keeping, interview, and collection of documents, we hoped to develop theoretically grounded descriptions of writing and its instruction in two classrooms. More will be said about our methods in the next section.

ISSUES OF THEORY AND METHOD

A description of writing in two classrooms is the heart of this study. That description is intended to illuminate both occasions for writing in the classroom as well as the teacher beliefs and plans that help to shape them. The descriptions of school writing have been derived by observing everyday life in these two classrooms and by asking teachers to share, in the course of their regular efforts, their beliefs and plans about writing and its use. What follows is a discussion of important theoretical and methodological issues that arose in our efforts to understand writing and its instruction in school.

Theoretical Assumptions and Working Hypotheses

Because no observation is unbiased, it is important to mention at the outset several kinds of information that contributed to the sense made of what was seen, read, and heard in the classrooms under study. Information about theoretical presuppositions, methodological decisions, and the frames for interpretation that were applied to the data should help the reader to locate the descriptions and analyses offered here in an intellectual context and should stimulate discussion and criticism of the findings.

Perhaps the key assumption of this research on written literacy is that writing is a form of social action, one way in which the members of a community transact across time and distance to accomplish social life and work. That assumption has implications for how one studies writing. For example, on the basis of that assumption, this study emphasizes the process and use of writing in classrooms rather than the written products isolated from and artifactual to that process. Important to the study of writing in use is the analyst's ability to document the social conditions out of which writing arises and the grounds on which participants select writing as the appropriate expressive alternative on any given occasion. To gain this kind of insight into social action and its meaning in the research reported here, additional assumptions and attendant methodological decisions were made. It was assumed, for example, that it would be crucial to understand the subjective point of view of the classroom participants. The hypotheses subsequently generated and tested, and the means of testing them, pertained to the nature of this point of view and its relation to the classroom events observed.

The study was further limited in significant ways in that it highlighted the teacher as purveyor and planner of the learning environment in which writing takes place. Clearly one could have elected to focus instead on the students as writers or on the functions of writing in other social contexts in children's lives. Selecting the teacher as the focus for study was deliberate and rooted in a concern that the research illuminate writing instruction as one of the important pedagogical responsibilities of teachers in our culture. It also reflects a bias that the classroom is a significant place in the child's universe where writing is learned and used.

To understand the point of view of the teacher and its relation to writing as social action in the classroom, it is necessary to consider what is observable in classroom behavior and what is inferable about the mental life of the teacher.

> To understand human action we must not take the position of an outside observer who "sees" only the physical manifestation of these acts; rather we must develop categories for understanding what the actor—from his point of view—"means" in his actions (Schutz, 1967, quoted in Bernstein, 1976, p. 139).

There are many ways to move beyond mere observation of phenomena to an understanding of their meanings to participants. Sometimes people can give words to the meanings they hold; sometimes they reveal their meaning systems in patterns of action. The design of this study contains the eclecticism and methodological pragmatism of fieldwork research to obtain and validate information about the meanings held by teachers with respect to writing, its functions, and its pedagogy (Schatzman & Strauss, 1973). Thus, the researchers asked the teachers participating in the study to share (in both writing and conversation) what they thought about writing in their classrooms. In addition, by means of participant observation, the researchers lived some part of the teachers' lives with them. This primary experience of their world informed the researchers' questioning of the teachers and aided in the interpretation of the self-reports of the teachers. Finally, the teachers were engaged directly in the deliberative process at monthly meetings where they joined the researchers in developing ideas from data by generating hypotheses and by relating variables in meaningful ways to explain classroom observations. In short, the teachers joined the researchers in generating theory about practice.

The decision to undertake this study (Clark, Florio, Elmore, Martin, Maxwell, & Methany, 1982) was the result of pilot work by the principal investigators on writing instruction and of review of the research on writing extant in the fields of anthropology, psychology, and sociolinguistics. Thus, the researchers did not enter the field without a conceptual orientation. Just as the initial questions of the study reflect that orientation, early working hypotheses developed in initial stages of data collection reflect the study's theoretical orientation. They are set out here because they served not only to constrain what the researchers noticed out of the myriad of observable classroom behaviors but also because they provided initial frames for interpretation of what was observed.

The researchers began data collection with the following limited working hypotheses:

1. There is an important relation between the acquisition of written literacy and membership in a community.
2. The classroom constitutes a community for learning in its own right and it is part of the wider community.
3. Many occasions for writing arise in a community. In the classroom, these occasions arise both as teachers and students develop a classroom community and as they transact with the wider community.
4. Across social occasions, writing serves a variety of expressive functions. Thus, the cognitive and social demands of writing tasks may differ from occasion to occasion.
5. The teacher is chiefly responsible for conceiving, initiating, and maintaining writing occasions within the classroom community; but the enactment of those occasions and the writing produced therein are consequences of the interaction between teachers and students.

Despite these conceptual organizers, the complex nature of the research problem and the methods used to address it enabled the generation of many new hypotheses, not a priori, but in terms of, and as a consequence of, the life observed unfolding in the classrooms, interviews, and journals. Therefore, additional working hypotheses were generated that were grounded in observation and tested in short and long-range ways against subsequent observation. As a result, the researchers tested and refined or rejected some initial hunches about writing instruction and learned many other things not dreamed of in the original research proposal. The work reported here, therefore, reflects the influence of both the theoretical constructs antecedent to the research (limiting its focus and locating it in an intellectual tradition), and the researchers' efforts to make disciplined sense of their own observations and the insights of their teacher informants.

Data Collection

Four methods were used to collect data about writing and its instruction in the two classrooms of interest:

1. *Participant observation* in which researchers spent extended periods of time in the classroom taking field notes and attempting to understand the classroom as a community for learning and the functions of writing within it.
2. *Elicitations of teacher thinking* about writing in the classroom:
   a. Weekly journals in which the teachers recorded their plans for, and reflections on, teaching in general and writing instruction in particular.
   b. Weekly interviews in which each teacher discussed her journal entries with a researcher.
   c. Monthly meetings in which the teachers and the research staff discussed patterns emerging in the data and other research-related issues.
   d. Viewing sessions in which teachers viewed videotapes that were occasionally made in their rooms and discussed the videotape content.
3. *Audiovisual recordings* of naturally occurring classroom life in which researchers attempted periodically to capture—for later analysis and for discussion with the teachers—those classroom interactions that appeared to be related to writing and its use.
4. *Writing samples* produced by both students and teachers in naturally occurring classroom activity that were used to illuminate and supplement analysis of classroom writing activities and teacher plans.

Data were collected throughout the entire 1979–80 school year. For purposes of both collection and preliminary analysis, the year was divided into four periods: September, October-December, January-March, and April-June. Previous classroom research indicated that this demarcation might be consistent with teachers' views of the functionally different parts of the school year (Clark & Yinger, 1980; Shultz & Florio, 1979).

The intention of the study was to document writing and its instruction in two schools and classrooms—one, a second/third-grade elementary school classroom and one, a sixth-grade middle school classroom. In each classroom, there was a two-person team of teachers. One member of each team was the focal teacher-informant for that class. For the bulk of observation and interview, therefore, these two teachers worked closely with the researchers. The other teammate in each room, however, quickly became interested and involved in the study and attended the monthly meetings and other project-related functions.

An initial interview with each focal teacher took place shortly before the beginning of the school year. This interview provided background information and was related significantly to the establishment of entry both into the school and the classroom and the establishment of rapport with each teacher.

The first month of the school year was a particularly important time in the study. The researchers anticipated that much of the interactional work needed to establish the classroom community would go on during that time (Shultz & Florio, 1979). For this reason, participant observation took place five days per week during the first month of school. These early ethnographic observations of the classrooms and schools were useful in characterizing the social context in which occasions for writing happened.

For the remainder of the school year, participant observers spent whole days in the classroom approximately three times each week. Because of the discovery-oriented nature of this study, it was decided not to limit observation to times of the day explicitly set aside for reading or language arts or to limit fieldworkers' presence in the classroom to particular days, weeks, or terms. The nature of classroom writing and its instruction mandated the extensive presence of fieldworkers in the classroom and required them to be flexible about the kinds and amounts of their participation.

Elicitation of teacher thinking was another important aspect of data collection. The two participating teachers kept weekly journals in which they each described their thoughts and plans about the week in general and about school writing in particular. This journal-keeping technique was previously used successfully in studies of teacher planning that had been undertaken by cognitive psychologists (Clark & Yinger, 1979). Field notes from participant observation and teacher journals augmented one another in the production of a rich description of classroom writing. In addition, an analysis of either the field notes or the teachers' journals provided useful interpretive frameworks to apply to the other one; inferences drawn about writing from analysis of one source of data could be cross-checked with data from other sources (Gorden, 1975).

Expansion and clarification of the journal entries were made possible by the addition of weekly interviews of the focal teachers. Once each week a researcher visited the school and talked with the focal teacher about the contents of her journal. These interviews not only provided the researchers with another source of information but also provided encouragement and support to the teachers for their journal-keeping efforts and alerted the researchers to forthcoming classroom activities that might be appropriate for special notice.

Two kinds of data were collected periodically to amplify the documentation of writing and its instruction. Teachers normally collected many of the student writings that were produced in a variety of activities in their rooms. These pieces of student work would later be shared by the teachers with parents to document student progress in language arts and other skill areas. Researchers copied many of these teacher-collected student writings and, because they frequently were accompanied by field notes describing the circumstances in which they were produced, the writings could be examined both in their own right with reference to the circumstances of their production and used to supplement analysis and description arising in the observational notes, journals, and interviews.

Originally, the researchers intended to supplement fieldwork and journal keeping further by one day of videotaping in each of the four segments of the year. These tapes were to be analyzed by both the researchers and the teachers in periodic viewing sessions. Deviating from the original plan, videotaping was undertaken for only three days in each classroom and one viewing session was held with each teacher. Periodic videotaping of isolated classroom writing activities was a decision made before beginning the study. Once the research was underway, it became evident that the meaningful unit of analysis for writing instruction and planning might not be the isolated lesson but rather a series of socially and thematically linked writing activities separated from one another in time and space and often difficult to predict in advance. This realization made periodically collected videotape data and their analysis less prominent parts of the study than originally anticipated. This methodological insight is an important one for future studies of the enactment of writing. There appears to be a relationship between the research questions and the specific level of analysis that they imply and the data-collection strategies used to greatest advantage by the researchers.

Although it was unanticipated that videotaped lessons would be a less than efficient and optimum source of data, the methodological pragmatism of fieldwork and its responsiveness to research questions arising inductively in the field led serendipitously to one unanticipated form of data that illuminated the study considerably. Originally, weekly meetings were to be held among the researchers and focal teachers to talk about the progress of the study. However, consultants convinced the researchers that to require such meetings was to place undue demands on the time and energies of the teachers. As an alternative, monthly dinner meetings were held throughout the year of fieldwork. These meetings provided for the sociability that is important to continued negotiation of entry and to establishment and maintenance of rapport between the researcher and the informant. Held in a congenial location in the workplace of neither the teachers nor the researchers, the dinners provided a context in which open discourse was more likely to transpire. These meetings were audiotaped and transcribed. The researchers also documented them in field notes. They were the catalyst for some major insights in the study and citations from the transcripts and notes from those meetings appear throughout the full technical report of the study in testament of this fact.

Data Reduction and Analysis

The processes of reduction and analysis of the descriptive data would have been unwieldy, if not impossible, if we had waited until the completion of data collection to begin them. The data set included field notes, videotapes, teacher journals, interviews, and student work samples. Working with data that are collected naturalistically over time can present problems and provide advantages. To get the most from our data set, it was necessary to plan for the gradual reduction and analysis of information gathered while still in the field.

The data collected had the following features bearing on reduction and analysis:

1. Some of the data were collected in relatively *unstructured* ways in that an attempt was made to limit the imposition of a priori analytic categories on what was seen, heard, and read—for example, field notes, continuous videotapes of naturally occurring classroom activity, writing samples, open-ended journal keeping.
2. Some of the data were collected by more *structured* means, for example, scheduled interviews with teachers.

For the most part, categories for analysis were arrived at inductively, as participants sifted the naturalistic data for patterns of meaningful activity in writing and writing instruction. In addition, insights from previous research literature on both the writing and teaching processes, and the experience of participating teachers provided potential "conceptual levers" that we used to make sense of our data (Schatzman & Strauss, 1973, p. 117).

The study's interdisciplinary research staff worked together in the development of a series of descriptions of the acquisition of written literacy in the two classrooms studied. This collaborative working relationship was important for two reasons. First, because of ongoing contact among participating teachers and the interdisciplinary team, it was possible to engage collaboratively in a cyclic process that involved the formation of working hypotheses about what was happening in planning and instruction, the testing of those hypotheses in subsequent data collected, and the refinement of the working hypotheses. Such a design made it possible for the project staff to test and refine descriptive models of the process of writing instruction in the two classrooms that were grounded in the observed phenomena. In short, the goal was to render descriptions that were able to be "based on an accumulation of data, [to] predict an event or state that people will behave in special ways under certain conditions" (Geer, 1969, p. 152). The ability to build such a predictive model is one of the strongest tests of the adequacy of a descriptive case study (Erickson, 1978).

The second advantage of such a research design for the processes of data reduction and analysis was that it fostered the process of triangulation. We recognized that the social and cognitive phenomena of interest in our study were very complex and we acknowledged, in Gorden's terms (1975, p. 46), that:

> Often the nature of the problem under investigation demands a multimethod approach because the various methods give totally different kinds of information that can supplement each other, because we do not know how to interpret some of the information unless we can couple it with other information, or because we need a cross-check to verify the validity of our observations.

By examining written, oral, and observational data with varying degrees of structure and from the perspectives of various investigators, we had the opportunity to accomplish such triangulation. We intended that our study reflect as validly as possible the perspectives of the participating teachers. By means of multiple methods and opportunities for the researchers and teachers to cross-check their inferences about the data, both as they were collected and retrospectively, we hoped to maximize our coverage and understanding of writing and its instruction in the two classrooms of interest.

The processes described here yielded the following three-step procedure for reporting the research:

1. Define a descriptive unit of analysis that makes sense to all the participants in the research. (We termed this unit an occasion for writing.)
2. Identify a manageably small number of such occasions for writing that are of theoretical importance and of significance to the classroom participants.
3. Describe the genesis, unfolding, and fate of these occasions for writing, both individually and in relation to one another, using

multiple data sources to enrich the descriptions and to cross-check inferences about their meaning.

The following case study of an occasion for writing in the second/third grade classroom that we studied is offered to give the reader a feeling for the kinds of data and analytic approaches typical of the study at large. The case study illustrates the diversity of the data collected and one way that data can be interwoven in the presentation of a descriptive analysis.[2]

The Safety Posters: An Illustrative Case Study

The following paragraph is an excerpt from notes taken during an interview of Ms. Donovan,[3] the teacher of a combined second/third grade, on Monday, 9/17/79, the eighth school day of the school year:

> In our interview, Ms. Donovan described how she used an unexpected traffic-safety assembly as an opportunity to do a writing exercise. The assembly included a film on bicycle and pedestrian safety and a talk on the same subject. After Ms. Donovan and her students returned to Room 12, she asked them to recall some of the safety rules that they had just heard about. Ms. Donovan said that she was very surprised at the terrific difficulty that the children had in remembering the safety rules. At first, they could remember only the general topic of the assembly. With some coaching and reminding, several of the rules were recalled. Then Ms. Donovan asked the students to each choose one safety rule and draw a picture illustrating the rule. These poster-size pictures, with the safety rules as captions, will be posted in the hallways as a service and a reminder to the other students in the school. (Interview notes, 9/17/79, p. 1)

The Safety Posters Activity is an early and telling example of occasions for writing in this primary-grade classroom. It began with the unexpected, a schoolwide assembly of which Ms. Donovan learned only on arrival at school Monday morning. What began as an unexpected interruption of the school day grew into an elaborate series of learning experiences that extended over several days and, to some degree, involved children and adults throughout the entire school. What happened and how did it come about? To answer this question, it is useful to unpack the above paragraph from the interview notes of 9/17/79:

> (1) *In our interview, Ms. Donovan described how she used an unexpected traffic-safety assembly as an opportunity to do a writing exercise.*

Commentary: This assembly was a schoolwide event presented in the gymnasium by two uniformed young women employed by the local police department. Some of the children knew the young women because the women's summer jobs had involved monitoring bicycle safety. The assembly is a clear example of formal contact between the larger community and the school population. Bicycle and pedestrian safety are topics that are quite relevant to elementary school children, and responsibility for the safety of school children is shared by school personnel, parents, public safety officers, and the community at large. Safety is a fundamental issue, and, in this case, a safety assembly took priority over classroom and academic issues. The fact that the assembly was unexpected but easily incorporated into the morning was due, in part, to the flexibility of the early weeks of school when the daily and weekly schedules were not yet fully developed into relatively fixed routines. Ms. Donovan learned about the safety assembly before the children arrived and she included it as the first entry in the daily schedule that was written on the chalkboard (Field notes, 9/17/79):

Today is September 17, 1979

9:20–10:05	11:30–12:15	2:15–2:45
Assembly	Language Arts	Science (2) Soc. St. (3)
10:05–10:30	12:15–12:50	
Gym	Lunch	2:45–3:00 Clean up
10:30–11:00	12:55–1:15	
Reading	Centers	
		3:00–3:10
11:00–11:15	1:15–1:55	Diaries
Recess	Math	
11:15–11:30	1:55–2:10	
USR	Recess	

---

(2) *The assembly included a film on bicycle and pedestrian safety and a talk on the same subject.*

Commentary: The 9/17/79 field notes describe the assembly differently: "The young women talked about and showed several filmstrips about safety in walking or bicycling to school." The fieldworker who attended the assembly also remembered that this was the first schoolwide assembly of the year, that some students were loud and disorderly and were brought back to order by the school principal, and that the safety presentation was not smooth and spellbinding. One of the filmstrips actually burned up as it was being projected. In short, this assembly had as much to do with learning how to behave at an assembly as it did with safety rules.

It was during the assembly that Ms. Donovan had the idea of using this experience as the basis for a writing activity to be assigned later in the morning. Although the data do not reveal what triggered the idea, earlier interviews and observations suggest that Ms. Donovan was predisposed to make the most of the unexpected. She valued writing and believed that school writing activities must have a clear purpose if they were to be successful. On the second day of school, Ms. Donovan and her students did another writing activity that began with the common experience of a film. She described this activity in her journal entry:

> I was pleased with Friday's writing lesson. Motivation was movie on word families, then students wrote and illustrated sentences utilizing a word family (e.g., Tim *Rice* slid on *ice* and landed in *lice*.) This type of open-ended lesson seems to be the most effective. Children with differing abilities can be as simplistic or sophisticated (as they want to) depending upon their creativity. Instruction is to the group, but the results are individualized without isolation from the total group. (Teacher journal, 9/9/79)

As will become apparent as the Safety Posters Activity unfolds, the structure of this occasion for writing includes an initial shared experience (the safety assembly), a clear purpose and audience, and the open-ended opportunity for children to produce something that reflects their ability, creativity, and sophistication. The most advanced students are not held back, and the least advanced students can still achieve a measure of success. In short, the safety assembly probably triggered the plan for the Safety Posters Activity because the assembly fit Ms. Donovan's pattern, or set of criteria, for a good writing activity. It seems that this 'spontaneous planning' in which Ms. Donovan engaged is more frequently seen in such curriculum areas as language arts—where there are few published series or kits—than in subjects like mathematics, reading, and science—areas that are largely structured by published materials.

(3) *After Ms. Donovan and her students returned to Room 12, she asked them to recall the safety rules that they had just heard about. Ms. Donovan said that she was very surprised at the terrific difficulty that the children had in remembering the safety rules.*

Commentary: Again, the field notes give a clearer picture of what actually happened on that Monday morning. Ms. Donovan's students stayed in the gymnasium after the safety assembly for physical education (10:05—10:30 A.M.). When the children returned to Room 12, they worked on reading worksheets, went to recess, then did fifteen minutes of silent reading. It was not until 11:35 A.M. (language arts time) that the children were asked to recall the safety rules taught in the assembly. Given so many interpolated activities, that the assembly itself was full of interruptions and distractions, and that the children did not know in advance that they would be expected to remember the specific wording of the safety rules, it is not surprising that they had difficulty. The safety assembly was an experience removed in space and time from the classroom. The children had no props or memory aids to stimulate their recall.

(4) *At first, they could remember only the general topic of the assembly. With some coaching and reminding, several of the rules were recalled.*

Commentary: In attempting to bring her plan into action, Ms. Donovan had to take on the role of 'class memory' and 'memory coach.' She had assumed that the safety assembly experience would be sufficiently recent and vivid to serve as the common experience basis for the language arts activity. When Ms. Donovan discovered (to her surprise) that the children did not remember the specific safety rules, she changed her plan on the spot. The teacher's task now became to recreate the common experience in a form, place, and time so that all the students had this experience available to them for use in the next part of the activity. The field notes show how this was done:

> As part of language arts, Ms. Donovan asks students to "re-run" this morning's safety program and recall what they learned. On a piece of large white paper up front, Ms. Donovan prints what they recall. The format is that an individual raises her/his hand. Ms. Donovan writes down what (s)he says. Another student is asked to read it back.
> Ms. Donovan writes down what students say in multicolor magic markers:
> 1. Don't run on the street without looking.
> 2. Don't take shortcuts you don't know.
> 3. Don't cross the street when the light is red.
> 4. When you ride your bike, keep your hands on the handlebars.*
> *This formulation arrived at after several revisions. Ms. Donovan has said, "Take your time and restate it, how you want to say it." In coming up with this one, students chime in with alternatives; Ms. Donovan asks them to let her restate it.
> (This activity resembles others that have been observed so far. It is the generation of general information posters by the whole group, with Ms. Donovan acting as scribe.)
> In coming up with sentences, Ms. Donovan says, "Sometimes does it take a couple of times to get out what you want to say? That's OK." The person who offers the original idea has the final say as to how it is written down. (Field notes, 9/17/79, p. 3)

This process continues until ten safety rules are recorded. Notice that Ms. Donovan goes to some length to see that every student has a chance to be actively involved in the rule-generation part of this process. Oral editing, friendly amendments, and reading aloud are all used to produce a document in which every child has had a hand and understands. Mechanics, such as spelling and penmanship, are taken care of by the teacher acting as scribe. The use of a rough draft is foreshadowed by Ms. Donovan's statement, "Sometimes does it take a couple of times to get out what you want to say? That's OK." In short, this part of the Safety Posters Activity constitutes a collective and largely oral preparation for writing that makes visible how the solitary, silent author could prepare to write (and it is an activity in which even kids who have 'forgotten how to write' over the summer can compose).

(5) *Then Ms. Donovan asked the students to each choose one safety rule and draw a picture illustrating the rule. These poster-size pictures, with the safety rules as captions, will be posted in the hallways as a service and a reminder to the other students in the school.*

Commentary: This was the point at which the full plan was first communicated to the children, that is, the part of the plan that had to do with transforming what the students 'knew' into graphic form. The students were given a choice, within a clear and limited set of alternatives, and this element of student choice seems to have been an important part of Ms. Donovan's beliefs about effective learning activities, particularly in writing. The combination of drawing and writing is also a striking aspect of this task. Other researchers (Clay, 1975; Cook-Gumperz & Gumperz, 1978; Ervin-Tripp & Mitchell-Kernan, 1977; Graves, 1978) have commented on the close and mutually supportive relationship between drawing and writing, especially in the early grades. The field notes give a vivid and more complete portrayal of the writing/drawing phase of the Safety Posters Activity:

Next Ms. Donovan asks students to think of ways to help remind the rest of the school of these rules.* The students suggest the following:
   "take them around"
   "put them up on the hallway"
   "tell them not to do it"
*This is in response to Ms. Donovan's question: "How could each one of you help remind them of one rule?"
(It is interesting to note that, in response to the charge, the students do not generate any means that are specifically writing related. They *do* offer symbolic alternatives that are largely visual.)
After the students make their suggestions, Ms. Donovan says, "I had an idea, too. Each person could make a poster with one rule and put it in the hallway."
The students say, "Yeah!"
Ms. Donovan: "Do a picture and write the rule on the bottom."
Before getting started an additional rule is generated:
   11. Don't ride a bike too big for you.
At 11:50, as students go to their seats to start, Ms. Donovan says, "At the end I'll write the rule for you or you can write it yourself in marker. The picture has to be done in crayon."
The students sit quietly at first. Overheard is the following exchange:
   S: "What are you going to do?"
   S: "I don't know; I'm still thinking."
Some students prefer to write the rule first; others make pictures first. Several students found the task difficult for several reasons: e.g., they did not want

to do a rule that they found out a lot of other students were doing; they couldn't draw what they needed to illustrate the rule (such as a bicycle). The upshot of these difficulties was that by the end of the available time, some students were completely finished while others were just getting started. (Field notes, 9/17/79. pp. 4–5)

Notice that both the purpose of the posters and the audience for the posters are specified before crayon touches paper. The students are guided by their teacher to participate in 'coming up with the idea' of drawing safety posters. All of the necessary elements are now in place: the list of rules on 'experience paper,' crayons, poster paper, an opportunity for choice and originality, a sense of shared ownership of the project, and the dual motivation of having one's work displayed in the hallway (a place of honor) and of doing good (perhaps even saving a life) by reminding other schoolmates of the safety rules. Ms. Donovan took a further step to minimize threat by offering to write the rule herself on the bottom of the posters of those students who wanted or needed that help.

The time allowed for drawing and safety-rule writing was about forty-five minutes (11:30–12:15). As the field notes indicate, there were wide individual differences in task completion. This is an issue that Ms. Donovan returns to again and again during the course of the year. For example, the issue was first raised in the 9/17/79 interview:

In discussing planning and diagnostic testing, Ms. Donovan raised a perennial problem for teachers: how to deal with the relatively large differences in the speed at which children work when they are working independently. "What should I do with the kids who finish fast? When I give them fun and extension activities to do I feel that the children who finish more slowly are being gypped. I like closure— everyone must finish. I don't want the slower students to get farther and farther behind."

(It is interesting to note that this problem of individual differences in working speed has shown up so early in the year. We should take care to note the ways in which Ms. Donovan deals with this issue as she tries to resolve an apparent conflict between her personal philosophy and value on equal opportunity and the practical realities of a mixed-ability class. She seems to recognize that faster is not always better. This might be especially true in writing.) (Interview notes 9/17/79 p. 4)

EPILOGUE: The Safety Poster Activity continued to develop as though it had a life of its own. By Wednesday, 9/19/79 (two days after the safety assembly) all of the posters were finished. That day, in a conversation at lunch with Mr. Brown, the kindergarten teacher, Ms. Donovan had the idea that her students should make small group presentations of their posters to the kindergarten children as a prelude to displaying the posters in the school hallways. Arrangements were made to do this on Thursday, 9/20. During the morning and afternoon that day, groups of three or four of Ms. Donovan's students were sent to the kindergarten room to show their posters and teach the younger children the safety rules. The field notes for 9/20 and 9/21 show how this process developed:

(9/20/79): At 9:20, students gather in the center. Ms. Donovan says, "The kindergarteners are just learning to get along together." This comment is prelude to her sending several students to kindergarten to hang posters and tell about them. (Yesterday at lunch, Ms. Donovan negotiated the time and purpose of the safety-poster sharing with Mr. Brown, the kindergarten teacher.) (p. 1)

(9/20/79): Dani returns from the kindergarten and says that she was scared to read her poster to the children. She says that, "the kids didn't even listen," but that she read it and showed them her drawing anyway. (p. 1)

(9/20/79): [At about 11:00] Before the students left for pictures, they began to talk about their experiences of sharing the safety posters with the kindergarten earlier this morning. Some said they found it "embarrassing" and "scary." Some students said they thought it might have helped to practice beforehand. They agree that students who will go this afternoon should practice first. Ms. Donovan tells the other students to help them practice by asking questions "that you think the first graders would ask." As a few students stand up to do it, their peers applaud their efforts. (p. 3)

(9/20/79): At 12:55 the students reconvene in the center. Ms. Donovan, who has had a chance to talk to Mr. Brown (the kindergarten teacher) at lunch, says, "Mr. Brown said that you guys did a good job this morning, even if you were nervous." Then five students leave with their posters to talk to Mr. Brown's afternoon class, saying they are nervous (Lea has a stomachache). (p. 4)

(9/21/79): At 12:55, after lunch, the students gather in the center. Afternoon roll is taken and one of the students reads the "afternoon plans." Three students leave for the kindergarten with their safety posters. Ms. Donovan asks them, "Do you know what yours say?" She has them read back what's written on the posters before leaving. (p. 3)

(9/21/79): At 1:05, students return from kindergarten.
    JD: "How'd it go?"
    S: "Terrific."
    S: "Not very many questions, though." (p. 3)

Oral presentation of the safety posters to the kindergarten children added a number of things to the Safety Posters Activity. The second and third-grade authors' sense of audience was undoubtedly heightened. They saw very clearly that it is useful to reexamine, edit, and rehearse what they have written if an audience is expected to understand their messages. They learned that writing and drawing can be used to focus oral communication (in this case, teaching) and that a graphic product can serve the author as a reminder and illustration of his or her teaching. Ms. Donovan's students also learned from one another's experience and served as a constructively critical audience for the dress rehearsals. Finally, this phase of the project served as a meaningful connection between two groups of children within the school, showing on a small scale how writing can contribute to the building of a social system when members are separated in space and time.

This has been a lengthy description and analysis of the Safety Posters Activity, one of literally hundreds of occasions for writing that took place in the two classrooms under study during a full school year. The analysis of, and commentary on, the Safety Posters Activity have raised a number of issues about how, why, and under what circumstances written literacy is acquired in schools and have shown what roles the teacher and students play in this process.

IN CONCLUSION: PICTURES OF A PROCESS

This study was conceived and conducted in the spirit of discovery. Its aim was to describe the writing undertaken in two classrooms and the teaching attendant to it. The combination of anthropological, psychological, and practical perspectives was found to be a powerful and flexible way of working to craft these descriptions. This work represents only one of many useful approaches to research on writing and writing instruction. Correlational studies, surveys, and experiments can also make contributions to knowledge about the acquisition of written literacy. As the corpus of research grows and is shared and reviewed, we shall come closer to the goal of understanding writing in school.

In concluding this chapter, one caution is warranted. This caution applies to all educational research that is broadly descriptive, whether that research be ethnographic or correlational in nature. The caution pertains to the tendency in educational research to draw implications for teaching and policy uncritically from descriptions of current practice. The potential strength of descriptive research lies in its rendering of analytic portrayals of the complex activities of teaching and learning and of the thought processes of participants in those activities. But descriptions are not uncomplicated. They are static attempts to represent processes that change in time. They are, in addition, neither value-neutral renderings of what is, nor are they facile roadmaps for what ought to be.

When we study schooling, we describe everyday life and practice within the context of a social institution governed by shared norms and values. Thus, statements of fact about life in such settings as schools and classrooms are statements meaningful in terms of the norms and values held there. Our descriptions of teaching and learning in school settings thus presuppose the institution in which the behaviors arise and the rules that regulate those behaviors and make them meaningful. It is in virtue of this state of affairs that our mere descriptions are already somewhat evaluative even as we render them and are turned so conveniently into prescriptions for practice (Searle, 1964).

Critics of mainstream educational research have pointed out that failure to recognize the normative nature of the descriptions we devise can lead to uncritical acceptance of the underlying rules that presently govern practice and hence to their unreflective perpetuation by the very act of studying them (Cherryholmes, 1980). From description we may be tempted to offer heavy-handed recommendations for practice. But the principles of practice documented in one educational setting may be inappropriate to the local and particular perspective of participants in another (Hymes, 1976). If handled unreflectively, our accumulating corpus of research on instruction is unlikely ever to lead to a normative theory of education, one that stands back from research findings and asks questions ultimately about what it is worth knowing (Fenstermacher, 1978).

At a time when we are just beginning extensive research on the teaching and learning of writing, it is worth asking ourselves what we mean by literacy. What are we willing to count as writing? What do we assume is the teacher's role in the process of acquisition of writing? What resources are available, and for whom, in enabling the process? Descriptive research cannot answer fundamental value questions for parents, teachers, or policy makers beyond reification of the status quo. Nor can it offer simple and direct prescriptions for practice. What it can offer are pictures of the complex processes at work in schooling and the acquisition of written literacy (Wittgenstein, 1953/1968). These pictures are, of course, limited because they are abstractions. As such they freeze ongoing action to describe it. In addition, to be sensible, they must be constructed like caricatures, delineating certain features and demonstrating overall patterns. Thus, they must be drawn from one particular point of view and not another (Erickson, 1978). But, like pictures, they are of value despite their limitations. For the inexperienced, they share situations that may be heretofore unknown or difficult to observe at firsthand. For the experienced, they provide much food for thought, a chance to examine their own unique but related experiences.

In this study, we have attempted to draw such pictures of processes. We have not focused on products. We have not, for example, regarded student writing as a product in isolation from the social and academic processes that engendered it. Nor have we regarded teaching behavior as a mere product or output. We have considered teacher actions in light of teacher thought and in the context of classroom life. We have looked at instruction as a process, the dynamic and collaborative creation of teacher and students in a particular setting. Thus, our study has reflected truly local norms that govern writing and its instruction. But by examining our pictures of writing and its instruction, the reader may learn about a process heretofore obscure or may find the opportunity to think about her or his own situation. She or he may be surprised that her or his experience is quite different, not recognizing a familiar episode, agree or disagree with our interpretations, find our renderings satisfying or incomplete. In short, the reader may find these descriptions the occasion for reflection on her or his own work. And, with the gradual accumulation of such local portrayals, by means of comparison and contrast, the generic may be illuminated in the particular.

IMPLICATIONS FOR FURTHER RESEARCH

In this chapter, we have described our view of school writing as a complex social, psychological, and practical enterprise and have illustrated the methods we have used to do research on school writing. Our reflections on the data and experiences of this study of two classrooms leads us to recommend three types of studies for future research:

1. Descriptive studies of school writing in settings different from those documented here.
2. More focused descriptive, correlational, or experimental studies of specific factors identified in this study as important elements in school writing.
3. Inquiry into ways of relating research on written literacy (its processes and findings) to the practice of teaching.

The first suggestion for future research is a call for more thick description of children's writing in context. Before the field can put together the beginnings of a developmental picture of the the acquisition of written literacy, it needs to document the teaching and learning of writing at grade levels other than second, third, and sixth. Other potentially important setting differences include bilingual classes, inner-city schools, and special teacher training and background (e.g., the Bay Area Writing Project or one of its progeny). Furthermore, future descriptive research should attempt to observe and describe those events and experiences outside the school, at home, and in the neighborhood and community that provide opportunities for children to learn, practice, and apply writing as a means and as an end in itself.

Several of the factors identified in the present study as important in the teaching and learning of writing deserve more focused attention. These include the role of audience, the use of process and product models in writing assignments, the influence of teachers' conceptions of the writing process on their planning and teaching, form and timing of constructive criticism of students' written work, motivation for writing, and the setting of expectations for writing performance. We are reasonably convinced that these factors are important to successful school writing. Understanding precisely how and why they are important will have to await additional descriptive, correlational, or experimental research.

Our final suggestion for future study concerns the process of relating research to practice. By and large, the research on teaching of the last fifteen years has not had dramatic effects on the practice of teaching. In part, this is because accumulating research findings is a slow and deliberate business, whereas the demands of the classroom do not wait patiently for researchers to come up with precise answers to precise questions. Furthermore, much of research on teaching addresses questions that are of little practical interest to practitioners.

But even when research on teaching is timely and addresses questions of real interest to practicing teachers, the problem of putting research into practice is not solved. Because every classroom situation is unique, a list of prescriptions for teaching will miss the mark more often than not or be couched in such general terms as to constitute a set of mere slogans. Furthermore, teachers are thinking professionals and not mere technicians. They deserve and need to have a sense of ownership over what, why, and how they teach. Both the processes of inquiry and the findings of research on teaching must be subjected to careful deliberation by all interested parties to ground recommendations for the practice of teaching in the wisdom and experience of practitioners.

In the context of applying research on the teaching of writing, we have proposed the creation of a Written Literacy Forum. The purpose of this Forum is to build on our research on written literacy in schools and on our experiences in meaningful collaboration with practicing teachers to create a new and powerful way to bring research into practice. Specifically, we will organize a Written Literacy Forum comprised of researchers, practicing teachers, and teacher educators (a working group of about twelve people). Forum participants will develop and try out answers to the question, What does research on writing mean for teachers and teacher educators? Forum members will have access to a rich corpus of descriptive data on the teaching and learning of writing in schools. Consultants with special expertise will be called on from time to time. Pairs or small groups of Forum members will identify issues of particular interest to them and pursue these issues, producing analytic papers, syntheses of knowledge about some aspect of written literacy, and materials useful in teacher training and development. Deliberation within the Written Literacy Forum will be documented and carefully described. In short, the Written Literacy Forum will be a serious attempt to study and analyze research on writing so that interpretation and adaptation of the research can be employed in ways truly likely to make a difference in schools. Documentation of the development of the Written Literacy Forum may also produce a model for relating research to practice that can be adapted for use by other researcher-practitioner teams.

NOTES

1. The major authors of this paper are named in alphabetical order. As co-principal investigators in the study reported here, they have contributed equally.

This study was funded by the National Institute of Education, U.S. Department of Education (Grant No. 90840). The opinions expressed in this paper do not necessarily reflect the position, policy, or endorsement of the National Institute of Education.

2. This case study also appears in Florio and Clark (1982), where it is reported in greater detail.

3. The names of the teachers, children, schools, and school district used in this report are pseudonyms.

REFERENCES

Basso, K. H. The ethnography of writing. In R. Bauman & J. Sherzer (Eds.), *Explorations in the ethnography of speaking*. Cambridge: University Press, 1977.

Bernstein, R. J. *The restructuring of social and political theory*. New York: Harcourt Brace Jovanovich, 1976.

Bettelheim, B. *The empty fortress*. New York: Free Press, 1967.

Brooks, N. *Hypothetical face-to-face interaction: Letter writing as a mediation process between private and public ways of knowing*. Unpublished special qualifying paper, Harvard University, 1978.

Brown, R. *A first language: The early stages*. Cambridge, Mass.: Harvard University Press, 1973.

Cazden, C. B. *Child language and education*. New York: Holt, Rinehart & Winston, 1972.

Cherryholmes, C. H. *Theory and practice: Issues in reflective theory and reflective practice*. Paper presented at the annual meeting of the American Educational Research Association, Los Angeles, April 1980.

Clark, C. M. Choice of a model for research on teacher thinking. *Journal of Curriculum Studies*, 1980, *12*, 41–47.

Clark, C. M., Florio, S., Elmore, J. L., Martin, J., Maxwell, R. J., & Metheny, W. *Understanding writing in school: A descriptive study of writing and its instruction in two classrooms*. (Research Series No. 104). East Lansing: Institute for the Research on Teaching, Michigan State University, 1982.

Clark, C. M., & Yinger, R. J. *The hidden world of teaching: Implications of research on teacher planning* (Research Series No. 77). East Lansing: Institute for Research on Teaching, Michigan State University, 1980.

Clark, C. M., & Yinger, R. J. *Three studies of teacher planning*. (Research Series No. 55). East Lansing: Institute for Research on Teaching, Michigan State University, 1979.

Clay, M. M. *What did I write?* Auckland, N. Z.: Heinemann, 1975.

Cook-Gumperz, J. The child as practical reasoner. In M. Sanches & B. C. Blount (Eds.), *Sociocultural dimensions of language use*. New York: Academic Press, 1975.

Cook-Gumperz, J., & Gumperz, J. From oral to written culture: The transition to literacy. In M. F. Whiteman (Ed.), *Variation in writing*. New York: Erlbaum, 1978.

Dewey, J. *The child and the curriculum and the school and society*. Chicago: University of Chicago Press, 1956.

Elmore, J. *Teacher planning for reading and writing instruction.* Paper presented to the annual meeting of the Michigan Reading Association, Grand Rapids, April 1979.

Erickson, R. *On standards of descriptive validity in studies of classroom activity.* Paper presented at the annual meeting of the American Educational Research Association, Toronto, March 1978.

Ervin-Tripp, S., & Mitchell-Kernan, D. *Child discourse.* New York: Academic Press, 1977.

Fenstermacher, G. D. A philosophical consideration of research on teacher effectiveness. In L. S. Shulman (Ed.), *Review of research in education.* Itasca, Ill: F. E. Peacock, 1978.

Florio, S. The problem of dead letters: Social perspectives on the teaching of writing. *Elementary School Journal,* 1979, *80,* 1–7.

Florio, S., & Clark, C. M. What is writing for? Writing in the first weeks of school in a second/third grade classroom. In L. Cherry-Wilkinson (Ed.), *Communicating in the classroom.* New York: Academic Press, 1982.

Freire, P. The adult literacy process as cultural action for freedom. *Harvard Educational Review,* 1970, *40,* 205–225.

Garfinkel, H. *Studies in ethnomethodology.* New York: Prentice-Hall, 1967.

Geer, B. First days in the field: A chronicle of research in progress. In G. J. McCall & J. L. Simmons (eds.), *Issues in participant observation.* Reading, Mass.: Addison-Wesley, 1969.

Goody, J., Cole, M., & Scribner, S. Writing and formal operations: A case among the Vai. *Africa,* 1977, *47,* 289–304.

Gorden, R. L. *Interviewing: Strategies, techniques, and tactics.* Homewood, Ill.: Dorsey Press, 1975.

Graves, D. H. *Balance the basics: Let them write.* New York: Ford Foundation, 1978.

Hymes, D. H. *Ethnographic monitoring.* Paper presented at the symposium on Language Development in a Bilingual Setting at the Multicultural/Multilingual Materials Development Center, California State Polytechnic University, Pomona, March 1976.

Moffett, J. *Teaching the universe of discourse.* New York: Houghton Mifflin, 1968.

Philips, S. Participant structures and communicative competence: Warm Springs children in community and classroom. In C. B. Cazden, V. J. Hymes, & D. H. Hymes (Eds.), *Functions of language in the classroom.* New York: Teachers College Press, 1972.

Schatzman, L., & Strauss, A. *Field research: Strategies for a natural sociology.* Englewood Cliffs, N. J.: Prentice-Hall, 1973.

Schwab, J. J. Learning community. *Center Magazine,* 1975, *8,* 30–44.

Scribner, S., & Cole, M. Literacy without schooling: Testing for intellectual effects. *Harvard Educational Review,* 1978, *48,* 448–461.

Searle, J. R. How to derive "ought" from "is." *Philosophical Review,* 1964, *63,* 44–58.

Shulman, L. S., & Elstein, A. S. Studies of problem solving, judgment, and decision making. In F. N. Kerlinger (Ed.), *Review of research in education,* (Vol. 3). Itasca, Ill.: Peacock, 1975.

Shultz, J., & Florio, S. Stop and freeze: The negotiation of social and physical space in a kindergarten/first grade classroom. *Anthroplogy and Education Quarterly*, 1979, *10*, 166–181.

Shultz, J., Florio, S., & Erickson, R. Where's the floor? Aspects of the cultural organization of social relationships in communication at home and at school. In P. Gilmore & A. Glatthorn (Eds.), *Ethnography and education: Children in and out of school*. Washington, D.C.: Center for Applied Linguistics, in press.

Vygotsky, L. S. Mind in society: *The development of higher psychological processes*. In M. Cole, V. John-Steiner, S. Scribner, & E. Souberman (Eds.), Cambridge, Mass.: Harvard University Press, 1978.

Wittgenstein, L. *Philosophical investigations*. New York: Macmillan, 1953/1968.

Part IV

Other Approaches

10

Writing Disability

Sean A. Walmsley
State University of New York at Albany

If this volume's title were "Research on Reading: Principles and Methods," a chapter on reading disability would not seem out of place—if anything its absence would be noted—but a chapter on writing disability in a book on writing research methodology is likely to trigger quite varied reactions, depending on the reader's orientation.

Medical researchers and specialists in the field of learning disabilities and special education are least likely to object to such a chapter because most of the literature on writing disabilities is confined to journals and books read by these professionals and used in preparing instruction in writing for the various populations under their supervision (e.g., children with various language handicaps, such as agraphia, dyslexia, and so on).

Reading researchers and practitioners, particularly if they have training in diagnosis and remediation of reading disorders, are also not likely to object to a chapter on writing disability, although their enthusiasm will probably depend on how much they embrace the notion of literacy as including equal parts of reading and writing. Until quite recently, the reading field has defined literacy almost exclusively in terms of reading while regarding writing either as penmanship and spelling or as a language art with the same status as drama and speaking. When James Allen, former U.S. Commissioner of Education, launched the national Right-to-Read effort in 1969, he spoke of achieving national literacy by 1980, but he meant achievement in reading (see Carroll & Chall, 1975). Until 1978, the National Institute of Education (NIE) defined its basic skills research program solely in terms of reading and arithmetic. Right-to-Read has now been converted to Basic Skills and includes equal attention to reading, writing, and arithmetic. In fact, several of the chapters in this volume derive from research funded as a result of NIE's recent shift in emphasis. The passage of Public Law 94–142 (which mandates special programs for children identified as having reading and writing disorders) and the requirement of many states that students demonstrate competence in reading and writing to graduate from high school (see Lawlor, 1979) has jolted the reading profession, partly because attention now has to be given to a "basic" literacy skill other than reading and partly because, in many instances, it is reading teachers who must take responsibility for writing instruction, particularly remedial writing for students who exhibit writing difficulties.

Some reading teachers embrace this expanded view of literacy because they have long wondered why writing was any less important than reading. Others would like to embrace it but have so little knowledge of the writing process and are so ill prepared to teach writing (in contrast to what they know about reading theory and pedagogy) that they are reluctant to proceed without better preparation (Walmsley, 1980), and they turn in vain to their university catalogs for courses in writing theory and pedagogy (Graves, 1978). In either case, reading professionals generally are comfortable with the term disability because it is widely used in the teaching of reading, and it is supported by a large research and pedagogical literature, which includes, incidentally, some of the early work on writing done by such reading researchers as Gray (1956) and Orton (1937).

A less enthusiastic reception is to be expected from what might loosely be termed the writing field—a loose federation of composition teachers in secondary schools and colleges and researchers drawn from several disciplines, such as cognitive psychology, rhetoric and communication, linguistics, and sociology. In the writing field, only those who deal with what Shaughnessy (1977) has termed basic writers are likely to be intrigued by the notion of writing disability because so many secondary schools and colleges have instituted remedial writing programs in response to competency tests in writing and complaints by secondary teachers and college professors that students do not write well. Cognitive psychologists, linguists, and sociologists are skeptical about the notion of disability, especially when used in relation to a skill like writing about which so little is known. How, they argue, can we talk about writing disabilities when we know so little about writing abilities? (They are, of course, similarly critical of the notion of reading disabilities).

Because the various literatures rarely overlap, the term writing disability has become firmly established in elementary and secondary schools (mostly as a consequence of competency testing and the federal mandate of Public Law 94–142) and accepted by a body of researchers investigating language disorders. Yet, little communication has been established between these two groups or between either of them and the writing field. Thus, although writing researchers frequently scoff at the idea of writing disabilities, there is a growing practice of diagnosing and remediating writing disabilities as well as a growing literature on the nature and cause of these disabilities.

The purpose of this chapter is an attempt to bridge the gap between these viewpoints by examining what is meant by the term writing disability, focusing particularly on the domains of writing used in defining the term and on the theoretical perspectives from which the definitions derive. Following this review, some alternative perspectives on writing disability will be discussed. The argument to be made in this chapter is that current definitions of writing disability are too restrictive and that there are some important methodological shortcomings in the research on writing-disabled populations that need to be overcome.

DEFINITIONS OF WRITING DISABILITY

Historical Perspective

Until the end of the nineteenth century, in the United States, writing was defined largely in terms of penmanship, spelling, and knowledge of grammatical principles and used texts from England (e.g., Hodges, 1653/1968; Watts, 1721/1972). Hodges (1653/1968), for example, presents his "most plain directions" for true writing, which comprise a series of spelling rules:

> Take heed that you never put a double consonant with an "e" at the end of a word; for there is no necessitie thereof; and the rather wee may bee bold so to doo, because the Learned, both in Printing and Writing doo daily practise it. (p. 42)

Despite attempts (e.g., Eliot, 1894) to shift the emphasis toward actual composition, a definition of writing that more closely fits our current conception did not emerge until the 1930s (Burrows, 1977). Consequently, one should not be surprised to learn that the first definitions of writing disability were concerned exclusively with handwriting and spelling. Orton (1937), for example, defines the manifestations of what he calls developmental agraphia as either slow (but otherwise neat and acceptable) or illegible handwriting (whether rapidly or slowly executed). The samples of writing used to determine the severity of the writing disability are taken from exercises in which children copied information from chalkboards. The notion that writing disability primarily comprises handwriting and spelling problems has persisted ever since (see Critchley & Critchley, 1978; Kinsbourne & Warrington, 1966), although more recently it has been broadened to include the full range of what might be termed transcription aspects of writing. These are features of text that a copyeditor could ensure were correct without needing to know anything about the communicative intent of the writer or the topic about which the writer was writing (Tamor, Bond, & Matz, 1980). In addition to purely mechanical features, such as spelling, handwriting, punctuation, and capitalization, transcription also includes usage aspects (i.e., the use of standard written English conventions for subject-verb agreement, tense markers, personal and possessive pronouns, plurals, adverbs and so on) as well as what Shaughnessy (1977) calls the dialect of formal writing, which dictates appropriate syntax and style particularly at the sentence level. Shaughnessy (1977) provides examples of problems with the dialect of formal writing in her basic writers:

> Most of the more demanding jobs have many people at which their financial status is very low or about average.
> (The jobs that are easy to get don't pay much).
>
> His ability to cope with people around him will be on a better basis.
> (He will cope better with other people). (p. 45)

This preoccupation with transcription aspects of writing arises from at least four sources. First, researchers interested in developmental dyslexia (or, more loosely, learning disabilities) have shown that learning disabled children frequently have handwriting and spelling difficulties that accompany their reading problems. Newton and Thomson's (1976) observation of a dyslexic's writing is typical:

> His written work was marked by reversals, mirror-image writing, omissions, random use of capital letters, no punctuation and bizarre spelling. (p. 3)

Many similar examples can be found in the standard texts on learning disabilities (Critchley, 1970), although many current texts make little or no reference to writing (e.g., Baren, Liebl, & Smith, 1978; Lerner, 1971). Until quite recently, compositional or communicative aspects of dyslexics' writing have been almost totally ignored (Silverman, Zigmond, Zimmerman, & Vallecorsa, 1981). It is hardly surprising, then, that researchers whose primary interest is in the reading difficulties of learning disabled children should emphasize only transcription aspects of writing when they attempt to characterize children's writing difficulties (e.g., Alley & Deshler, 1979; Andolina, 1980; Vellutino, 1979).

Second, there is a long tradition of inquiry and debate into the nature of the orthography that focuses researchers' attention on children's understanding of the orthography (e.g., Gelb, 1965; Havelock, 1976), particularly as manifested by children's spelling (e.g., Beers & Henderson, 1977; Chomsky, 1971; Read, 1975). Given this tradition, it is not difficult to understand how writing might be viewed primarily as a method of representing the orthography and therefore conceptualize writing disability primarily as an inability to learn the orthographic principles of a particular language (Lebrun & Van de Craen, 1975). Boder (1971) has gone so far as to suggest that bizarre spelling is the key to diagnosis of learning disabilities.

Third, the notion that children with learning disabilities have impairments in the development of their motoric system, particularly in the fine motor coordination required for writing (Kephart, 1971) has enjoyed considerable popularity over the years, although nowadays the idea of a central motoric imbalance is not widely held. Nevertheless, examining a child's handwriting is one way to detect problems in the motoric system; consequently, learning disabled children's handwriting ability has been the object of much attention, spurred particularly by the work of de Ajuriaguerra and his colleagues (de Ajuriaguerra & Azuias, 1975) on developmental issues in motoric growth. As with spelling, learning disabled children's handwriting is so frequently illegible or bizarre that inevitably it attracts researchers' attention (e.g., Critchley & Critchley, 1978).

Finally, researchers from the medical profession (particularly neurologists) have been interested in the effects of aphasia and other neurological disorders or diseases on the language production and reception of their patients. Perhaps because of the historical emphasis on transcription but also because they are easier to measure, only manifestations of transcription aspects of writing have generally been examined in this literature (e.g., Weigl & Fradis, 1977).

Domains of Writing Disabilities

In the various literatures on writing disability, the domain of writing examined by researchers appears to be restricted almost exclusively to transcription aspects of writing. By way of illustration, consider first the content of the most widely used measures of writing ability for disabled populations. There are two types of writing tests. One measures students' knowledge of written conventions (e.g., punctuation, capitalization, word usage, spelling) in a paper-and-pencil, multiple-choice format; the other elicits a sample of writing and applies specific criteria for its analysis. Examples of the former include the writing subtest of the *Sequential Tests of Educational Progress* (*STEP*) (Educational Testing Service, 1972) and the written expression subtest of the *Tests of Achievement and Proficiency* (*TAP*) (Scannell, Haugh, Schild, & Ulmer, 1978); examples of the latter include the *Picture Story Language Test* (*PSLT*) (Myklebust, 1965), the *Test of Written Language* (*TOWL*) (Hammill & Larsen, 1978), and the *Diagnostic Evaluation of Writing Skills* (*DEWS*) (Weiner, 1980).

Measures such as the *STEP* and the *TAP* are restricted by their response format (true/false and multiple choice) to purely transcription aspects of writing. Essentially, these tests measure students' ability to recognize standard English usage, correct punctuation and capitalization, and proper spelling, although the *STEP* claims to be testing organization, written conventions (syntax and sentence structure, etc.), critical thinking, effectiveness, and appropriateness in written expression. The following is a typical example of the *STEP*'s approach—students are shown a written sample (in this case, a letter written by a girl to a classmate who is sick) and asked questions about it:

> Dear Betty;
> I was sick too. And I know how you feel. It's not much fun to have nothing to do is it. I had the flu. We have to write this letter dureing English. . . .

Sample Questions:
1. How should "Dear Betty;" be punctuated?
   (Student chooses from alternatives.)
2. What is the best thing to do with the first two sentences?
   (a) leave them alone.
   (b) omit them.
   (c) change them to: "I have been sick, too, and I know just how you feel."
   (d) change them to: "I was sick, too, and I knew just how you felt."

The student's ability to produce standard English in a legible handwritten form is rarely assessed in these standardized measures.

The Diagnostic Evaluation of Writing Skills (*DEWS*) (Weiner, 1980) requires students to write an autobiography (within a class period). The writing sample is then analyzed to determine graphic problems (e.g., excessive pencil pressure, ambiguities in letter formation, mixture of upper and lower case); orthographic problems (e.g., letter sequence, misuse of spelling rules such as doubling the final consonant, changing y to i); phonologic problems (e.g., nonphonetic or strictly phonetic spelling, letter or syllable omissions, words run together); syntactic problems (e.g., subject and predicate agreement, word order, punctuation, subordination); semantic problems (e.g., coherence, logical sequencing, distinction between major and minor points); and problems in self-monitoring skills (e.g., self-correction, improvement through revision). With the possible exception of the semantic and self-monitoring categories (although even here, the examples given appear to be more structural than semantic), the *DEWS* is a measure of transcription skills.

The Test of Written Language (*TOWL*) (Hammil & Larsen, 1978) is one of the most up to date of the normed measures of writing ability. Because it is currently the only writing test (other than writing-competency tests) with recent norms, its use is widespread in assessing written-language difficulties, especially among learning disabled and special education populations. The *TOWL* comprises objective measures of word usage, style, and spelling; it also elicits a writing sample based on three cartoon pictures (about a space adventure). From this sample, assessments are made of vocabulary sophistication (assessed by comparing a sample of the student's vocabulary to a word-frequency list); thought units (essentially the same as Hunt's T-units); thematic maturity (an assessment by the scorer of the relevance of the writing sample to the rhetorical demands of the task); and handwriting (judged by a comparison to a model, but only when the child has written cursively). The thematic maturity category clearly relates to compositional aspects of writing, although, as I shall discuss presently, it does so in a somewhat restricted fashion. All other categories are transcription related.

The Picture Story Language Test (*PSLT*) (Myklebust, 1965) is the earliest of the normed measures of writing ability; it was developed, according to Myklebust, as a "measure of effective written communication." Comprising a stimulus photograph of a young boy playing with miniature dolls and furniture, the test asks the student to write "the best story you can" about the picture. The resulting story is analyzed to determine its quality in three categories: productivity, syntax, and abstract-concreteness of its content. The productivity scale includes the length of the sample in words and the number and average length of sentences (defined roughly as T-units). The syntax scale is a measure of the correctness of word usage, word endings, and punctuation, with errors in word usage weighted more heavily than errors in word endings and punctuation. The abstract-concreteness scale represents the degree of abstractness achieved by the student in describing the picture. Descriptions that merely list the items in the photograph are assessed as concrete descriptive, whereas those that tell a coherent story, involving a plot, motivation of characters, and so on, are assessed as abstract-imaginative. Despite the fact that neither handwriting nor spelling are assessed by the PSLT, most of the test is concerned with transcription aspects of writing. The exception, of course, is the abstract-concreteness scale.

The TOWL's notion of thematic maturity and the PSLT's abstract-concreteness scale reflect particular assumptions about the compositional facet of writing. The TOWL, for example, defines thematic maturity as demonstrating (in a pass/fail judgment by the scorer) the following: (1) writes in paragraphs; (2) mentions any object in the picture; (3) gives personal names to main characters; (4) gives proper names to robots, spaceships, etc; (5) indicates why the planet's environment is becoming hostile to life; (6) writes an integrated story about all three pictures; (7) writes a story as part of a dream sequence; (8) writes a story that has a definite ending; (9) mentions that the characters are building a new life; (10) explains the role of the spacelings; (11) gives personal names to the spacelings; (12) tells or implies where the spacelings come from; (13) states or implies that humans and spacelings have a harmonious relationship; (14) uses some futuristic or space language; (15) expresses some philosophic or moral theme; (16) has a title, whether related or irrelevant; (17) uses dialogue; (18) attempts humor; (19) relates plots not directly implied in the pictures; and (20) attempts to develop personalities of one or more characters.

Some of these categories clearly deal with the student's ability to grapple with the rhetorical problem posed by the sequence of the three pictures (e.g., mentions objects in pictures, indicates why planet environment is hostile, writes integrated story about all three pictures, mentions that characters are building new life, and so on). These look very much like Lloyd-Jones's (1977) primary traits although there does not seem to be a coherent rationale for the traits selected. Others appear to be structural (e.g., writes in paragraphs, writes story with definite ending). A few seem irrelevant to the task at hand; if they are indices of thematic maturity, they need to be justified as such. Writing the story as part of a dream sequence is not required nor is it easily suggested by the pictures; using dialogue and attempting humor may be inappropriate, given the particular way in which the child chooses to write a story. How writing a story without dialogue or attempts at humor indicate thematic immaturity is unclear. In general, however, a high thematic maturity score on the TOWL will indicate that the student has addressed the rhetorical task (to write a story integrating all three pictures), although the degree to which he or she has been successful is only roughly estimated, given the all-or-nothing nature of the scoring.

The Myklebust (1965) *PSLT*'s abstract-concreteness scale has much finer gradations in the scoring than the *TOWL*'s (a total of 25 points, spread across five levels), and its approach is very different from the *TOWL*'s. This is so partly because there is no explicit or implied story sequence in the picture of the boy playing with the miniature dolls and furniture (in contrast to the *TOWL*'s three space pictures). One suspects that the lack of story sequence was a conscious decision by Myklebust to construct a stimulus with little or no embedded direction or structure to test the child's ability to impose a structure. The levels of the abstract-concreteness scale reflect the cognitive distance placed by the child between the stimulus and the story and his or her control over the story's plot. Level I is Meaningless Language (a category in which stories with either meaningless collections of words or samples that bear no relation to the stimulus are placed). Level II is Concrete-Descriptive (in which the child essentially lists objects from the picture). Level III is Concrete-Imaginative (in which the child describes the objects in the picture and tells a rudimentary story involving them). Level IV is Abstract-Descriptive (in which the child demonstrates some use of plot, describes the whole picture in such a way as to relate characters to a central theme, or even introduces characters from outside). Level V is Abstract-Imaginative (in which the child writes a coherent story—not necessarily tied to the observable events in the picture—using highly abstract ideas, extrapolating into the future, or developing moral themes). As a measure of the child's ability to compose effectively, the abstract-concreteness scale can be misleading. As with items on intelligence tests (e.g., Stanford-Binet), the child has to understand that what is expected (i.e., Level V writing) is not what is asked for (i.e., "write the best story you can about this picture"). We may be confident that the *PSLT* is an estimate of the child's minimum writing capabilities, but we must be skeptical of its ability to measure optimal written expression, particularly given the datedness of the norms and the stimulus (few boys have crew cuts any more, and older children complain about the childish nature of the activity depicted). In additional, the examples given by Myklebust to train scorers in attributing appropriate scores are highly ambiguous; in practice, a sample can be scored levels apart by raters.

Quite recently, writing-competency tests have been developed by several state education departments. Although they were designed primarily to determine writing abilities of entire school populations at the secondary level, they are quickly becoming a means by which school-writing difficulties are determined and the basis on which remediation is to be carried out (see New York State Education Department, 1979; New York State Bureau of English Education, 1980). The New York State minimum competency test in writing is unusual among these measures in that it attempts to measure students' communicative effectiveness in several tasks: a business letter in which the student has to conduct some specific business task (e.g., return unwanted goods for a refund); an academic task in which jumbled notes from a presentation have to be rearranged into a coherent account; and a persuasive task (e.g., persuading one's school principal to adopt a suggestion for an improvement in school life). Students' essays are scored generally according to the degree to which they achieve the purpose of the task, with more emphasis placed on the student's ability to solve the particular rhetorical problem (i.e., Would this letter actually result in the student getting his refund? Would the suggestion for an improvement in school life convince the principal?) than on transcription aspects, such as syntax, spelling, and handwriting. Such tests are rare, however; most states who have adopted minimum writing standards tend to emphasize transcription aspects of writing (Lawlor, 1979).

One can illustrate this emphasis on transcription aspects of writing by referring to another literature, that of the writing difficulties of agraphics and aphasics. Researchers in this field rarely use standardized measures of writing, preferring to borrow subtests from reading- and language-test batteries or using samples of writing given to them by patients. In a case study of a patient suffering from dyslexia and dysgraphia (Mohr, 1976), the domain of writing is restricted to handwriting, spelling, and words written in response to a spoken or spelled stimulus by an examiner. Ferguson and Boller (1977) extend this domain to include problems in syntax in a case study of agraphic patients; a more thorough examination of the written syntax of patients with neurological dysfunctions can be found in Lawrence (1979). In this study, two patients were asked to write three short papers on any subject; many unusual syntactic errors were made in these papers (e.g., auxiliary verb either absent or redundant; copula verb or preposition absent; and so on). Dennis, Lovett, & Wiegel-Crump (1981), in a study that attempts to analyze how the skills of reading, writing, and spelling are acquired by three children with only one hemisphere of the brain intact, define the domain of writing in terms of spelling nonsense words and understanding orthographic principles. A slightly different approach is taken by Weigl & Fradis (1977), who examine the processes involved in writing to dictation by agraphic patients. In reviewing the neurological literature, not one study investigating the compositional difficulties of aphasic or agraphic patients could be found, despite the fact that in several studies, researchers claimed to be investigating reading, spelling, and writing impairments.

Although transcription aspects of writing permeate these literatures, there are some recent indications of an interest in compositional aspects. Critchley & Critchley (1978) provide an insightful description of the many transcription difficulties of dyslexic children, but they also hint at compositional problems. Using examples of the writing of accomplished writers, illiterate adults, and dyslexics, they argue that although the diversity of vocabulary (as measured by type-token ratios) of dyslexics is relatively restricted, there are significant numbers of narremes (words or combinations of words carrying a definite idea or message) in their writing. Critchley and Critchley also suggest that dyslexics are able to express themselves in verse comparatively well and take pleasure in doing so. Although these are interesting speculations, the data offered is so anecdotal and the concept of a narreme so thinly defined that it is difficult to interpret the findings. Another study (Bain, 1976) examines the writing of five dyslexic adolescents on the Myklebust PSLT. Bain (1976) comments on how the subjects were able—despite numerous punctuation, syntax, and spelling problems—to sustain ideas in succinct paragraphs, to demonstrate a sharp sense of humor, and to write clear logical stories. For example, a 14.7-year-old wrote the following in response to the Myklebust stimulus.

The Avige Business Man
This picture shows an avridge business Man hard at work on hos coffee hour. This bussiness Man has the finest eagipmint under his contrul. When I asked him what brand of eagipmint he uses, in his on words ke said "bab:ow" Trans lative it is Play Tell. With this eagipment he made dining rooms living rooms and maba more.

Although Bain's comments on her dyslexic's written samples are insightful, they still only hint at compositional aspects of writing. Similarly, Jansky's (1980) case study of a dyslexic's language difficulties is a sensitive portrait of some of the youngster's compositional problems, yet the particular problems are only vaguely described.

To recapitulate, writing behaviors considered appropriate for inclusion in a definition of writing disability appear largely to be restricted to transcription aspects of writing. Although applauding the few studies that have investigated compositional aspects of learning disabled students' writing, I see several methodological problems in these studies. First, the samples of writing elicited from subjects are much too narrow in focus. Researchers either use the Myklebust PSLT or TOWL picture stimuli (both of which elicit stories) or merely gather previously written papers. No attempt is made to elicit writing that samples a variety of topics, audiences, and functions. Second, the scoring procedures for the compositional categories on the major writing tests (e.g., the abstract-concreteness scale in the PSLT;

thematic maturity in the TOWL) appear arbitrary and suffer from a lack of construct validity. Similarly, in case studies of compositional difficulties (e.g., Critchley & Critchley, 1978; Jansky, 1980), compositional problems are vaguely defined. Third, in almost all studies, compositional problems have been investigated through the analysis of written products, not by examining the process of writing. As such, most of what is known about writing disabilities is inferred from the result of composing, not from an analysis of the act of composing.

ALTERNATIVE PERSPECTIVES ON WRITING DISABILITIES

A theme that runs through the writing disability literature, one that probably originates from Johnson (1968) and Myklebust (1973), is that writing is the last language skill acquired and is dependent on adequate development of the other language skills (i.e., listening, speaking, and reading), which are themselves dependent on the proper development of central and peripheral nervous systems in a stable and supportive emotional and cultural climate. Writing disability is, therefore, typically viewed as a result of inadequate or delayed development in listening, speaking, or reading; or as a result of central nervous system impairments, such as agraphia (a total inability to write because of brain dysfunction) or dysgraphia (a partial inability to write); or as a result of peripheral nervous system impairments, such as hearing loss, partial sightedness, and so on. Emotional disturbance and cultural deprivation may also cause writing difficulties. Authors vary in what they regard as essential prerequisites for writing, some (like Myklebust) stressing visual and auditory processes (e.g., for seeing and storing stimuli for writing, for sounding out words before writing them), others emphasizing knowledge of orthographic principles (Lebrun & Van de Craen, 1975). This view of writing is characterized by its assumption that the ability to write is made possible by adequately developed prerequisite skills (whatever they may be) and that writing disability can be traced to problems in these other skills. Writing is thus seen as the last skill acquired in a sequence of language skills, each one of which makes possible the next in the hierarchy. This view of writing seems to imply that composition is a general language skill and that writing comprises, therefore, only those skills necessary for transcribing what has already been thought out and articulated orally. In other words, the only writing skills that need to be learned after the other language skills have been mastered are those aspects of writing unique to transcription, such as spelling, handwriting, and syntactic conventions, which are not typically found in oral language.

This view of writing disability can be criticized from several perspectives. First, although it is a frequent observation that children learn to listen and speak before they read and write, it is also quite a general claim. We note, generally, that children are able to understand language long before they can utter it, but this is not to say that children do not utter language until they fully understand it. The newborn infant is quite capable of communicating feelings of pain and hunger long before he or she understands even quite simple referents, such as "Mummy" and "ball"; similarly, the three-year-old is often quite capable of writing messages long before he or she is able to read (Clay, 1975). Rather than one skill having to be developed to a particular point before another can be acquired, it is more likely that each skill develops as a consequence of, and in conjunction with, development in the others. For example, considerable amounts of reading will expose a child to semantic and syntactic written conventions (e.g., style, format, punctuation, etc.), which probably—but not necessarily—will assist in the development of writing ability. But to what extent is reading prerequisite to writing? How good a reader must a child be to be a good writer? Except in very general terms, we are quite unable to specify how much a child needs to know about reading or to be proficient as a reader to satisfy the reading prerequisite for mature writing. Some authors (e.g., Ashton-Warner, 1953; Chomsky, 1971) have successfully demonstrated that children can begin to write before they read because they have acquired sufficient knowledge of the orthography (albeit not necessarily the standard version) to produce comprehensible written stories well in advance of their ability to read conventional text. Although language hierarchies have never been established with any degree of specificity, many researchers and practitioners act as though they had been. This often leads to an insistence (e.g., in the diagnosis of writing disorders) of an examination of prerequisite skills (e.g., Cicci, 1980; Litowitz, 1981) and, in the classroom (sometimes), of a requirement that kindergartners speak in complete grammatical sentences as a prerequisite for writing complete sentences in grade 1. Similar practices in reading (e.g., insisting that children's auditory and visual discrimination abilities be properly developed as prerequisites for reading) have been shown to be ineffective, particularly when compared to the simple practice of having children read more frequently (Coles, 1978; Vellutino, 1979). Unless specific hierarchies (as opposed to mere correlations) can be established for normal writers as well as disabled writers, the question of which language skills have to be mastered and in what order must remain open.

A second problem derives from the view of writing disability as comprising primarily transcription difficulties. Because transcription aspects of writing can be assessed from almost any sample of writing (although one will never be sure that the child has displayed the full range of his or her transcription skills), it makes little difference what topics about which the child has written or the conditions under which the writing was elicited. One does not need to know much about the content of a piece of writing to discover mechanical errors. In fact, transcription problems can be tested quite well without having children write connected text at all. For example, a spelling test may reveal more about a child's spelling abilities than an analysis of a sample of the child's writing, particularly if the child tries to avoid using words he or she cannot spell. The writing-disability literature appears insensitive to the fact that writing, like reading, is a means to an end, not an end in itself (with the possible exception of calligraphy); consequently, proficiency in writing should not only be viewed solely in terms of the mechanical production of text but also in terms of its purpose. Similarly, we need to consider that writing disability is not merely an inability to transcribe but is an inability to accomplish the various purposes of writing. These purposes can be thought of simply as the range of writing tasks typically encountered in school (i.e., taking notes and writing short answers, essays, stories, journals, etc.). Even a rudimentary sampling of writing tasks typically given in schools would provide researchers with a rational basis for selection of experimental writing tasks. Similarly, a sampling of typical adult writing tasks (e.g., constructing shopping lists, writing social and business letters, keeping a diary, filling in forms) would considerably enhance the quality of the research on adult agraphics and dysgraphics. For a more comprehensive analysis of writing tasks, however, schemes such as Kinneavy's (1971), Moffett's (1968), or Britton's (1975) could be used to generate writing tasks that represent both the range of writing functions (e.g., poetic, expressive, transactional) and the distance one wanted subjects to place between themselves and the stimulus (e.g., Moffett's, 1968, recording, reporting, generalizing, and theorizing). The problem with using Kinneavy (1971) or Moffett (1968) as the basis for constructing writing tasks is that either of their schemes can result in setting tasks that are consistent with the theoretical framework but that are impractical, given the particular population under study. However, a careful integration of the kinds of writing tasks typically encountered by one's population and, say, Kinneavy's (1971) communication triangle (writer-audience-function), will result in the selection of suitable tasks.

Another important consideration is that once one begins to sample the range of writing purposes, it is difficult to think of the notion of writing disability as being applicable to all of them. To illustrate this point, I need to introduce a framework for writing purposes derived from an analysis of purposes for reading (Walmsley, 1981). Briefly, I have suggested that purposes for reading can be conceived as reflections of four educational ideologies—cultural reproduction, romantic, cognitive-developmental, and emancipatory. Cultural reproduction has as its primary educational goal the transmission of knowledge, values, and skills that are deemed appropriate by the dominant culture of a society to pass on to succeeding generations. Kohlberg and Mayer (1972) distinguish between two branches of this ideology, the academic and the utilitarian. The academic branch stresses the transmission of those skills and values appropriate to an intellectually oriented education, whereas the utilitarian stresses skills appropriate to a vocationally oriented career that prepares students for coping with a complex technological society. In terms of writing, the academic branch places particular emphasis on students' ability to learn the conventions of formal writing (of the type and range necessary for college entrance), whereas the utilitarian branch teaches students how to master practical writing tasks imposed on them by school and society. Northcutt (1975), for example, has suggested that competence in writing in the areas of consumer economics (e.g., writing checks, business letters), health (e.g., filling out health-related forms, writing for health information), government and law (e.g., completing tax forms), occupational knowledge (e.g., writing applications, memoranda), and community resources (e.g., taking written driver's license examinations) are necessary for survival in society. The recent upsurge of interest in texts for training college students and corporate employees in technical writing (e.g., Pearsall, 1978) is evidence that utilitarian purposes for writing are highly regarded. To conceive of difficulties in any of these tasks is not difficult. But difficulties arising in writing generated by other ideologies are problematic.

A romantic ideology for education stresses the development of the individual's autonomy or ownership of self (Spring, 1975). Derived principally from the philosopher Rousseau, it emphasizes the need for children's education to be free from the pressures and beliefs of the outside world to maximize the development of the child's own set of values and beliefs. Romantic ideologies have always had a stronger influence on the writing than the reading field, and they continue to play a major role in writing instruction, both at the elementary and college levels. Romantics place particular importance on the need for children to write from their own experiences in a form as untrammeled by the requirements of standard English as possible (especially for beginning writers) and allowing them to dictate their own pace in learning (e.g., Graves, 1976). In addition, the romantic ideologies tend to emphasize expressive rather than transactional writing. The notion of writing disability is difficult to conceive from a romantic perspective because children are ipso facto at a level of writing proficiency commensurate to their development. How can one say that a child has drawn inadequately or improperly from his or her experiences? If there are writing problems, they are either those that the child himself or herself has declared as such or they are impediments placed in the student's way by an unsupportive academic environment.

The cognitive-developmental ideology has as its educational goal the nourishment of intellectual growth through the interaction of the child's natural curiosity and the challenges of the external world (Kohlberg & Mayer, 1972). Writing, of course, plays a crucial role in this development, particularly in the middle-school and secondary-school curriculum where the solution of problems is made possible, in part, by writing about them (e.g., Emig, 1971; Smith, 1982). A cognitive-developmental approach to writing essentially consists of working through writing tasks on various topics and for various purposes, the consequence of which (through a continuous succession of assimilations and accommodations) is the development of new mental structures that allow the child to write more sophisticatedly

(Moffett, 1973). Although some important aspects of the development have been identified (e.g., Bereiter's, 1980, notion of possible stages in writing development), no one is yet ready to specify exactly how the stages of development are to be operationalized; consequently, one cannot assess with precision whether a child is at a particular stage or whether he or she is behind.

Finally, an emancipatory ideology for education has as its goal the sociopolitical transformation of a society by oppressed people. Derived principally from the work of Freire (1970), the emancipatory ideology places great emphasis on the skills of reading, writing, and discussion (dialectic) as the means by which oppressed people can emerge from their culture of silence and transform the relationship between them and their oppressors. Giroux (1978a) has argued that writing as an activity cannot be divorced from the larger sociopolitical realities that students bring to their classrooms and that writing should be a liberating, not a repressive, process. He has developed a social studies writing curriculum that embodies some of Freire's principles (Giroux, 1978b). Again, how does one define a writing disability from an emancipatory perspective? Only to the extent that a student is not participating in the sociopolitical transformation (i.e., is becoming freed from his culture of silence) can one even hint at the notion of a disability.

It is interesting that the concept of writing disability is easy to define in a cultural reproduction ideology and very hard to define in other ideologies. One reason for this is that cultural-reproduction ideologies have a writer-as-object approach in that the writing tasks, domains, and even the order in which writing skills are to be learned are imposed on the student from outside (by the school, employers, society); romantic ideologies, in contrast, have a writer-as-subject approach in that the writers themselves determine the task and domains. Cognitive-developmental and emancipatory ideologies are essentially interactive in that they attach almost equal weight to internal (writer-as-subject) and external (writer-as-object) approaches. As a consequence, it is easy to establish agreed-on writing tasks and domains for the cultural-reproduction ideology—one merely lists the academic and utilitarian writing demands. But where the student initiates his or her own writing (romantic) or where writing occurs as a result of an interaction between the student and his or her environment (cognitive-developmental, emancipatory), it is difficult to agree on particular tasks and domains because, in these latter ideologies, it is the process of writing (in the service of personal growth, intellectual growth, or sociopolitical transformation) not the product that is important.

CONCLUSION

It is the intent of this chapter to show that research on writing disability is quite extensive and crosses several disciplines. As schools begin to identify children with writing disorders under the mandate of Public Law 94–142 and as states develop minimum competencies in writing as part of the requirements for high school graduation, the term writing disability will become as familiar as the term reading disability already is.

Research in writing disabilities over the past fifty years has provided a fair description of the handwriting, spelling, and orthographic and grammatical knowledge of children identified as having writing problems. There exists an extensive account of some of the transcription difficulties of patients suffering from various central and peripheral nervous system disorders (e.g. agraphia, dysgraphia). The compositional difficulties of these populations, in contrast, are much less well documented and understood. In particular, researchers need to assess writing proficiency over a much wider range of writing tasks, especially those derived from the kinds of writing normally expected in the real world of classrooms, home, and workplace. In addition, there is a need to adopt or adapt current techniques for compositional analysis (e.g., Lloyd-Jones's 1977 primary trait analysis, or the communicative efficacy of Tamor et al. [1980]; see also Cooper & Odell, 1977).

Although these techniques may improve the quality of analyses of written samples of children with writing disorders, researchers should also consider the possibility that observing the act of writing itself may provide important evidence that analyzing written products cannot. There are several approaches to observing the act of writing, ranging from the least obtrusive observation (Graves, 1981) to a combination of observing and having the student think aloud about the decisions he or she is making (e.g., Hayes & Flower, 1980) to experimental manipulation of particular writer and task variables (e.g., Bereiter & Scardamalia, 1980; Bracewell, 1980; Tamor et al., 1980). Because none of these approaches have been used so far to observe the writing processes of children with writing disorders, it is hard to predict the kinds of methodological problems that will emerge as techniques are pressed into service. Nevertheless, one would expect that what we have learned about normal readers from examining the reading processes of disabled readers will hold true for examining the writing processes of disabled writers.

Finally, researchers should not underestimate the importance of examining different instructional approaches to remediation of writing problems, particularly because schools are now compelled to provide such remediation for children who fail competency tests or who are identified as writing disabled under PL 94–142. Very little research is currently being conducted to identify promising instructional approaches to remediation, despite a growing commercial market for remedial writing programs at both elementary and secondary levels.

At the beginning of this chapter, I alluded to the skepticism shown by many members of the writing field about the concept of writing disability. It was not my purpose to convert these skeptics but rather to show how researchers in other fields define the term and to attempt to bridge the gap somewhat between the two groups. What emerges from this review is that current conceptions of writing disability are much too narrow in their focus and too vague in their descriptions of compositional difficulties. In addition, if one views writing from a romantic, cognitive-developmental or emancipatory perspective, it is difficult not to be skeptical about the concept of writing disability, particularly in terms of describing the particular compositional difficulties. Researchers in the writing disability field have so far avoided this issue by largely restricting their definition of writing to transcription aspects and by taking only a cultural reproduction perspective on writing. If progress is to be made in the etiology, diagnosis, and remediation of writing disorders, an accommodation of these alternative perspectives will have to be made.

REFERENCES

Alley, G., & Deshler, D. *Teaching the learning disabled adolescent: Strategies and materials*. Denver, Colo: Love, 1979.

Andolina, C. Syntactic maturity and vocabulary richness of learning disabled children at four levels. *Journal of Learning Disabilities*, 1980, *13*, 27–32.

Ashton-Warner, S. *Teacher*. New York: Simon & Schuster, 1963.

Bain, A. M. Written expression—The last skill acquired. *Bulletin of the Orton Society*, 1976, *26*, 79–95.

Baren, M., Liebl, R., & Smith, L. *Overcoming learning disabilities: A team approach*. Reston, Va.: Reston, 1978.

Beers, J. W., & Henderson, E. H. A study of developing orthographic concepts among first graders. *Research in the Teaching of English*, 1977, *11*, 133–148.

Bereiter, C. Development in writing. In L. W. Gregg & E. R. Steinberg (Eds.), *Cognitive processes in writing*. Hillsdale, N.J.: Erlbaum, 1980.

Bereiter, C., & Scardamalia, M. From conversation to composition: The role of instruction in a developmental process. In R. Glaser (Ed.), *Advances in instructional psychology* (Vol. 2). Hillsdale, N.J.: Erlbaum, 1982.

Boder, E. Developmental dyslexia: Prevailing diagnostic concepts and a new diagnostic approach. In H. R. Myklebust (Ed.), *Progress in learning disabilities*. New York: Grune & Stratton, 1971.

Bracewell, R. J. Writing as a cognitive activity. *Visible Language*, 1980, *14*, 400–422.

Britton, J., Burgess, T., Martin, N., McLeod, A., & Rosen, H. *The development of writing abilities (11–18)*. London: Macmillian, 1975.

Burrows, A. T. Composition: Prospect and retrospect. In H. A. Robinson (Ed.), *Reading and writing instruction in the United States: Historial trends*. Urbana, Ill.: International Reading Association, 1977.

Carroll, J. B., & Chall, J. S. *Toward a literate society*. New York: McGraw-Hill, 1975.

Cicci, R. Written language disorders. *Bulletin of the Orton Society*, 1980, *30*, 240–251.

Chomsky, C. Write first, read later. *Childhood Education*, 1971, *47*, 296–299.

Clay, M. M. *What did I write?* Auckland, N.Z.: Heinemann, 1975.

Coles, G. S. The learning-disabilities test battery: Empirical and social issues. *Harvard Educational Review*, 1978, *48*, 313–340.

Cooper, C., & Odell, L. (Eds.), *Evaluating writing*. Urbana, Ill.: National Council of Teachers of English, 1977.

Critchley, M. *The dyslexic child*. London: Heinemann, 1970.

Critchley, M., & Critchley, E. A. *Dyslexia defined*. Springfield, Ill.: Charles C. Thomas, 1978.

de Ajuriaguerra, J., & Azuias, M. Preconditions for the development of writing in the child. In, E. E. Lenneberg & E. Lenneberg (Eds.), *Foundations of language development* (Vol. 2). New York: Academic Press, 1975.

Dennis, M., Lovett, M, & Wiegel-Crump, C. A. Written language acquisition after left or right hemidecortication in infancy. *Brain and Language*, 1981, *12*, 54–91.

Educational Testing Service. *Sequential Tests of Educational Progress*. Princeton, N.J.: Educational Testing Service, 1972.

Eliot, C. W. *Report of the committee of ten on secondary school studies with reports of the conferences arranged by the committee*. New York: American Book, 1894.

Emig, J. Writing as a mode of learning. *College Composition and Communication*, 1977, *28*, 122–128.

Ferguson, J. H., & Boller, F. A different form of agraphia: Syntactic writing errors in patients with motor speech and movement disorders. *Brain and Language*, 1977, *4*, 382–389.

Freire, P. *Pedagogy of the oppressed*. New York: Seabury, 1970.

Gelb, I. *A study of writing*. Chicago: University of Chicago Press, 1965.

Giroux, H. A. Beyond the writing crisis. *Journal of Education*, 1978, *160*, 40–49. (a)

Giroux, H. A. Writing and critical thinking in the social studies. *Curriculum Inquiry*, 1978, *8*, 291–310. (b)

Graves, D. H. Let's get rid of the welfare mess in the teaching of writing. *Language Arts*, 1976, *53*, 645–651.

Graves, D. H. *Balance the basics: Let them write*. New York: Ford Foundation, 1978.

Graves, D. H. A new look at research on writing. In S. Haley-James (Ed.), *Perspectives on writing in grades 1–8*. Urbana, Ill.: National Council of Teachers of English, 1981.

Gray, W. S. The teaching of reading and writing. Chicago, Ill.: UNESCO/Scott Foresman, 1956.

Hammill, D. D., & Larsen, S. C. *Test of Written Language*. Austin, Tex.: Pro-Ed, 1978.

Havelock, E. A. *Origins of western literacy*. Toronto: Ontario Institute for Studies in Education, 1976.

Hayes, J. R., & Flower, L. S. Identifying the organization of writing processes. In L. W. Gregg & E. R. Steinberg (Eds.), *Cognitive processes in writing*. Hillsdale, N.J.: Erlbaum, 1980.

Hodges, R. Most plain directions for true writing. (Originally published, 1653). In

R. C. Alston (Ed.), *English linguistics, 1500–1800: A collection of facsimile reprints*. Menston, England: Scolar Press, 1968.

Jansky, J. J. Language disability: A case study. *Bulletin of the Orton Society*, 1980, *30*, 252–267.

Johnson, D. The language continuum. *Bulletin of the Orton Society*, 1968, *18*, 1–11.

Kepart, N. C. *The slow learner in the classroom* (2nd ed.) Columbus, Ohio: Charles E. Merrill, 1971.

Kinneavy, J. L. *A theory of discourse*. New York: W. W. Norton, 1971.

Kinsbourne, M., & Warrington, E. K. Developmental factors in reading and writing backwardness. In J. Money (Ed.), *The disabled reader: Education of the dyslexic child*. Baltimore: The Johns Hopkins University Press, 1966.

Kohlberg, L., & Mayer, R. Development as the aim of education. *Harvard Educational Review*, 1972, *42*, 449–496.

Lawlor, J. *State requirements for high school graduation: Communication skills* (Report No. TN 3–79–04). Los Alamitos, Calif.: South West Regional Laboratory, 1979.

Lawrence, B. Writing patterns of the congenitally neurologically impaired adult. *Brain and Language*, 1979, *7*, 252–263.

Lebrun, Y., & van de Craen, P. Developmental writing disorders and their prevention. *Journal of Special Education*, 1975, *9*, 201–207.

Lerner, J. W. *Children with learning disabilities*. Boston: Houghton Mifflin, 1971.

Litowitz, B. E. Developmental issues in writing language. *Topics in Language Disorders*, 1981, *1*, 73–89.

Lloyd-Jones, R. Primary trait scoring. In C. Cooper & L. Odell (Eds.), *Evaluating writing*. Urbana, Ill.: National Council of Teachers of English, 1977.

Moffett, J. *Teaching the universe of discourse*. Boston: Houghton Mifflin, 1968.

Moffett, J. *A student-centered language arts curriculum, grades K–13*. Boston: Houghton Mifflin, 1973.

Mohr, J. P. An unusual case of dyslexia with dysgraphia. *Brain and Language*, 1976, *3*, 324–334.

Myklebust, H. R. *Development and disorders of written language* (Vol. 1). New York: Grune & Stratton, 1965.

Myklebust, H. R. *Development and disorders of written language* (Vol. 2). New York: Grune & Stratton, 1973.

Newton, M. A., & Thomson, M. E. *Dyslexia as a phenomenon of written language*. Unpublished paper, University of Aston (Birmingham, England), 1976.

New York State Education Department. *Competency test in writing*. Albany: New York State Education Department, 1979.

New York State Bureau of English Education. *Helping student writers, grades 7–12*. Albany: New York State Education Department, 1980.

Northcutt, N. *Adult functional competence: A summary*. Austin: University of Texas Press, 1975.

Orton, S. T. *Reading, writing and speech problems in children*. New York: W. W. Norton, 1937.

Pearsall, T. E. *How to write for the world of work*. New York: Holt, Rinehart & Winston, 1978.

Read, C. Pre-school children's knowledge of English orthography. *Harvard Educational Review*, 1971, *41*, 1–34.

Scannel, D. P., Haugh, O. M., Schild, A. H., & Ulmer, G. *Tests of achievement and proficiency*. Boston: Houghton Mifflin, 1978.

Shaughnessy, M. P. *Errors and expectations: A guide for the teacher of basic writing*. New York: Oxford University Press, 1977.

Silverman, R., Zigmand, N., Zimmerman, J. M., & Vallecorsa, A. Improving written expression in learning disabled students. *Topics in Language Disorders*, 1981, *1*, 91–99.

Smith, F. *Writing and the writer*. New York: Holt, Rinehart & Winston, 1982.

Spring, J. H. *A primer of libertarian education*. New York: Free Life Editions, 1975.

Tamor, L., Bond, J. T., & Matz, R. D. *Instruction writing: A promising approach to the study and teaching of written composition*. Paper presented at the annual meeting of the American Educational Research Association, Boston, April 1980.

Vellutino, F. *Dyslexia: Theory and research*. Boston: MIT Press, 1979.

Walmsley, S. A. What elementary teachers know about writing. *Language Arts*, 1980, *57*, 732–734.

Walmsley, S. A. On the purpose and content of secondary reading programs: An educational ideological perspective. *Curriculum Inquiry*, 1981, *11*, 73–93.

Watts, I. The art of reading and writing English. (Originally published, 1721.) In R. C. Alston (ed.), *English linguistics, 1500–1800: A collection of facsimile reprints*. Menston, England: Scolar Press, 1972.

Weigl, E., & Fradis, A. The transcoding processes of patients with agraphia to dictation. *Brain and Language*, 1977, *4*, 11–22.

Weiner, E. S. Diagnostic evaluation of writing skills. *Journal of Learning Disabilities*, 1980, *13*, 48–53.

11

Procedures for Describing Written Texts

Charles R. Cooper
University of California at San Diego

There is much to learn about written texts and the processes that produce them. Almost any linguistic, psychological, or rhetorical perspective can yield richly significant information. Producing written language is such a complex activity, integrating so many diverse cognitions and performances going on simultaneously, that it can be informed by studies of memory and consciousness and of fine-motor coordination as well. Written texts themselves contain so many different features that are related to each other in such a variety of complex ways (linearly, recursively, hierarchically, lexically, and rhythmically; or by embedding, reference, collocation, repetition, forecasting, and summary; as well as in relationships of given information to new information, topic to comment, generalization to particular) and in ways that shift noticeably from one writing situation to the next. Thus, we can analyze these features from perspectives as diverse as invented spellings, stylistics, or story grammars.

In this chapter, I want to survey a number of procedures for describing the written texts of novices and professionals. And I want to argue that these procedures—most of them quite new—make possible an important kind of basic research in our field, that is, the abstract characterization or schematization of whole texts. This research will take us beyond the sentence, to which we have been bound in developmental studies for over sixty years, and it will give us a completely new perspective on the development of written-discourse competence. Indeed, this research will provide for the first time a description of writing competence as it develops from children's earliest written messages in invented spellings to the elaborate variations and refinements in the writing of skilled college students.

Because I am doing this kind of research myself, I am very enthusiastic about it. Although I am an advocate, I recognize fully that it is only one of several productive areas for basic research, the other principal ones being, in my view, research into the composing process and into the practices of expert teachers. It does seem to me, however, that text descriptions and the analytic procedures that produce them, will enrich other areas of basic research and have important implications for teaching and evaluation as well. The more we know about the semantic patterning and structural specifications of written texts, the more we shall learn from process studies and the more confidently we shall teach writing and evaluate the results of our teaching.

The procedures I am recommending come from linguistics, structuralism (in literary theory), and rhetorical theory. They are gradually being gathered up into a new field called textlinguistics or discourse analysis. Useful introductions to this new field are de Beaugrande (1980), de Beaugrande and Dressler (1981), Dressler (1978), Morgan and Sellner (1980), and van Dijk (1977, 1980). Two new journals to watch are *Discourse Processes* and *Text*. The references at the end of this chapter will indicate the interdisciplinary nature of this new venture.

ESSENTIAL BACKGROUND INFORMATION

For the researcher on writing, the important background and context for the studies I shall propose are in current discourse theory. The basic references here remain Britton (1978); Britton, Burgess, Martin, McLeod, and Rosen (1978); Kinneavy (1971); Kinneavy, Cope, and Campbell (1975, 1976); and Moffett (1968, 1981). Secondary, but still useful references are D'Angelo (1975) and Odell, Cooper, and Courts (1978). A useful brief review of current discourse theory is D'Angelo (1976).

The seminal studies of Kinneavy, Britton, and Moffett have given us a comprehensive discourse theory, a way of classifying the modes and types of writing. In a global way, these theorists have characterized the patterns and movements in the various kinds of writing. They have already demonstrated conclusively that there are essential, substantive structural differences among the many types of prose nonfiction writing, not just differences between subdiscourse writing strategies (compare/contrast vs. process description for example), but major whole-discourse differences between explanation and persuasion or even between writing about oneself and writing about others. These distinctions remind us that text descriptions will have to be discourse specific; for example, nine-year-olds' narratives and arguments will require different analytic procedures. It is the case that certain text features of between-sentence cohesion and between-sentence semantic and structural relationships are common features of all texts—indeed, they make text possible; I shall present several ways of describing these in-common features. However, even with these descriptions of in-common text features, I shall demonstrate that an important use for them in research on discourse development is to reveal to us how such features pattern differently in different kinds of writing. In this way, we shall begin to discover precisely how different kinds of texts differ as texts and indirectly test certain claims in current discourse theory. In longitudinal or cross-sectional studies, we may learn just when certain text-creating strategies become available to young writers. My point here is that we already know enough from current discourse theory to know that nonfiction prose texts differ from each other in substantive ways structurally, not just functionally. The procedures I shall describe will permit us to begin specifying these structural differences at a level of detail and exactness currently not available in discourse theory.

SOME CURRENT APPROACHES TO WRITTEN TEXTS

Although the procedures I recommend are new, I do not want to give the impression that I believe no one has ever before engaged in close description of written texts. The poem, the story, the novel, and the play have received centuries of attention from literary critics and theorists. One strand of that work—formalist or structuralist analysis of narratives—will be helpful to us later in this chapter. Occasionally, as far back as Aristotle, nonfiction prose texts have received attention in terms of their parts and structures. Anyone who has ever analyzed the structure of text in terms of large patterns characteristic of the whole has engaged in discourse analysis.

We are not presently lacking concepts and terms for discussing nonfiction texts. English teachers talk about topic sentences, introductions and conclusions, forecasts and summaries, and patterns for comparing and contrasting. They sometimes use essay outlines. But none of this is done with any great precision, and some of it is downright misleading; for example, insistence that paragraph topic sentences are essential or that one outline format will do for all forms of explanatory and persuasive writing. Nearly all of these concepts and terms have been with us, with little refinement or development, since the nineteenth century. Still, anyone concerned with text structures and patterns is doing a form of discourse analysis.

Beyond these practical but unsophisticated current pedagogical uses of discourse analysis, there are interesting and instructive examples of discourse analysis in research on composition. I shall mention two here. We are all familiar with collections of the writing of children and adolescents that seek to demonstrate the range of their talents, the surprising and original work of which they are capable, or even just the variety of their ordinary work at school. Recently, we have begun to see a different sort of collection of child writing, one that goes beyond mere presentation to arrangement and analysis, usually for the purpose of demonstrating some features of writing development. Good examples are Marie M. Clay's *What Did I Write* (1975) and Glenda L. Bissex's *GNYS AT WRK: A Child Learns to Read and Write* (1980). Clay illustrates the early development of writing with a large number of examples from New Zealand children between the ages of four and seven. Bissex traces in detail the writing and reading development of her son Paul from age five to eleven. The book contains dozens of examples of Paul's writing, from his earliest invented spellings to a long story. I mention these two studies in particular because they are full of real writing, attractively presented and insightfully analyzed. The reader never loses sight of the human importance of the act of writing. For the new studies that I wish to propose, even though the analysis will be much more technical, I want to recommend strongly that published reports should seek to emulate the attractive features of the Clay and Bissex reports. I am tired of reading reports of language research, especially studies of syntactic development, that contain no actual discourse. The Clay and Bissex reports could have told us a good deal more had some of the writing been analyzed with the procedures I describe below, but they are, nevertheless, models for us to emulate.

Another example of discourse analysis in recent composition research is in studies of paragraph structure and development. These studies, too, remind us of familiar strands of research from which the discourse studies I recommend will be the next major development. Research on paragraph development is an interesting case history in our field. It argues better than any claims I might make for the procedures and the new research I want to recommend. In the middle of the nineteenth century, Alexander Bain proposed a classification of paragraph types based on logical development. In one form or another, his classification and his general principles of paragraph development can be seen in most current school and college composition handbooks. We are told that each paragraph should be regarded as a "miniature composition" (McCrimmon, 1972) and that each should have a topic sentence. We are exhorted to strive for unity, coherence, and completeness in each of these explicitly topicalized miniature compositions. Usually, other specialized types of paragraphs are illustrated—introductory, transitional, concluding—but it is clear that the most important paragraphs, those in the body, must fulfill the basic principles outlined above. We are, then, assured that these principles apply to all of the paragraphs in a comprehensive classification of types: narrative, process, cause/effect, description, comparison, contrast, definition, analysis, classification, examples, analogy, reasons. Often the student is asked to practice each of these in turn after examining examples of each. The student is then told that extended discourse is made up of such paragraphs.

The problem with all of this is that it is not true. The research that demonstrates it is not true is a prototype of the careful descriptive studies I want to recommend, but before I review it briefly, I want to mention a peculiar current version of this flawed paragraph rhetoric. Some popular new writing texts (Cowan and Cowan, 1980; D'Angelo, 1980; Winterowd, 1981) claim that the paragraph types in the list above are actually essay types, that writers write essays of definition, analysis, comparison, cause/ effect, or classification. Even when such texts point out that essays can be of a 'mixed type,' that is, can contain several of these types, each type is still carefully illustrated and then assigned. Current discourse theory and a little reflection illustrates the contradictions in such an approach. Analysis is not a kind of writing but a way of thinking or problem solving. Discourse that is the result of analysis may be organized and developed as written text in a variety of ways. Definition is a useful short-term strategy but not a way to develop extended discourse. An analogy may provide the central theme in an essay, but written text is not developed by analogy. The basic problem seems to be a confusion of ways of thinking or of logical systems with actual forms of written texts. The assumption about teaching seems to be that high school and college students need to practice simple thinking strategies that are already as familiar to them as breathing or dreaming.

What real writers actually do, of course, is attempt to achieve a global discourse purpose by choosing a variety of appropriate writing strategies. Writing for a real and meaningful purpose engages thought: writing *is* thinking. This thinking process leads the writer to choose appropriate strategies and forms for presenting the outcomes of thought *as written text*. In real writing, this text is invariably a 'mixed type.' And its paragraphs hardly ever resemble those in current handbooks.

How do we know this? Two simple studies were carried out by writing teachers unbiased toward empiricism, teachers who had the good sense to match textbook prescriptions against published professional writing. Although no older than 1970, both studies have become minor classics. I shall not review all the features of their designs and writing samples here but, instead, just note briefly the major findings. Meade and Ellis (1970) learned that 56 percent of the professionals' paragraphs in their sample could not be classified with any of the most-often-cited methods of paragraph development in secondary-school textbooks of the 1960s. Of the remaining paragraphs in their sample, 23 percent were developed by examples, 9 percent by reasons, and 6 percent by chronology. No other textbook classification accounted for more than 2 percent of professionals' paragraphs. In the second study, Braddock (1974) learned that only about half the professionals' paragraphs he examined contained topic sentences and only 13 percent *began* with a topic sentence.

Even the work of the best paragraph theorists of the 1960s (Becker, 1965; Christensen, 1965) implies or claims that paragraphs develop from an initial top-level statement. Clearly, though, these pronouncements are contradicted by Braddock's (1974) results, which suggest that if teachers do insist on topic sentences, they should show students how to place them most of the time some place *besides* the beginning of the paragraph. View-ing all of this research in the context of current discourse theory, I think we can see that concern about paragraphs and their structure is misplaced. The real issue is discourse, not paragraphs. Certainly the starting point in discourse analysis should not be paragraphing or paragraph structure. What is really interesting in written discourse—and what can be discovered from the procedures I shall outline—seems to be both smaller than a para-graph and larger than a paragraph.

NEW PROCEDURES FOR DESCRIBING WRITTEN TEXT

In the remainder of this chapter I shall outline several promising new approaches to the analysis of written texts. I shall first describe modes of analysis that may be useful in describing a text of any discourse type or genre: cohesion analysis, information management, thematic structure, sentence roles, and abstraction levels. Although these are generally useful with any text, their use will inform us about distinctions among types of texts; for example, the thematic structure of personal narrative will differ from that of argument. The work on text-type distinctions has barely begun. Then, I shall describe modes of analysis developed solely to describe pattern and structure in descriptions, in narratives, and in argu-ments. With the length limitations of a book chapter, I cannot offer a com-plete handbook for carrying out all these forms of discourse analysis. That is a needed project, but a much more expansive one. Instead, I shall try to say enough about each procedure for the reader to see its possibilities. I shall also mention all the necessary references. What follows, then, is something like a bibliographic essay on new developments in analyzing written texts. My concern all along in my own research has been to seek out procedures that may inform us about the development of discourse competence, procedures useful for analyzing the texts of children and older novice writers.

Cohesion Analysis

We say that good writing hangs together, that it flows, that it has coher-ence. We say that in good writing the sentences are logically related to each other. We feel a strong sense of momentum and direction. Everything seems connected. All of the procedures I want to recommend can help us account for these intuitions about good writing because we recognize that this connection is created by multiple overlapping structural and semantic relationships at many levels in the text, from the relation of specific words across sentences to abstract, global thematic and structural patterns. One relationship that is fundamental is that of the cohesive ties across sen-tences. Cohesion is not all of coherence, but it is a big part of it and an essential part.

Fortunately, we have a recent book that accounts comprehensively for the cohesive system in English—Halliday and Hasan's *Cohesion in English* (1976). With a good grammar handbook nearby, like that of Quirk and Greenbaum (1973), a nonlinguist will find *Cohesion in English* perfectly accessible. Even more important for researchers in composition, *Cohesion in English* offers a detailed coding scheme as well as models for organizing the results of a cohesion analysis into tables. Several different kinds of texts are fully analyzed as examples. Halliday and Hasan (1976) describe five types of cohesive ties: reference, substitution, ellipsis, conjunction, and lexical. The precision in their work comes from an exhaustive classification of all possible subtypes of these five main types. For example, lexical ties can be the same items repeated, synonyms or near synonyms, superordinate terms, general terms, or collocation. In written texts, lexical ties and reference ties occur far more often than the others. *Cohesion in English* offers one further research tool: a way of plotting the distance between ties that indicates whether the ties are immediate or remote, and if remote, whether they leap over intervening sentences or are mediated back through related items.

Instead of attempting to define and exemplify all of the parts of this elaborate and sophisticated analytic procedure, let me illustrate how cohesion analysis might be applied to a brief part of one text.[1] The text that follows is the first eight T-units[2] (each T-unit is indicated by a superscript number) of a thirty-one–T-unit text that describes a favorite place. The discourse aim is explanatory; the audience is the writer's peers (seventeen-year-olds) who have never seen the place. The principal mode of development is description.[3]

In this text, there are examples only of lexical and referential ties. Only two types of reference occur: the definite article "the" (Rdef) and the personal pronoun (Rex), which Halliday and Hasan regard as exophoric (referring outside the text), but which we have chosen to count as a cohesive tie in our research. The lexical ties are of two types: reiteration (L) and collocation (LC). Collocational lexical ties are those in which the cohering item is part of the same domain of experience or knowledge as the presupposed item. These are words we are not surprised to find together in the same text: "hotel" in a text describing a resort vacation. (For each collocational tie, the presupposed word is in parentheses.) In addition to these referential ties, I have indicated whether the tie is immediate or remote by underlining once all immediate ties with words in the just-previous T-unit and underlining twice all ties that jump over a T-unit. The subscript number following each double underlining indicates the number of intervening T-units between the two words forming the tie. To avoid overcomplexity, I have not tried to indicate mediated ties. I shall point out just one example however: the word "small" in T-unit 4 forms a reiterated lexical tie with the same word in T-unit 1, but after leaping over T-unit 3, it is mediated through the collocation "twenty-one miles long and fourteen miles wide" in T-unit 2.

Last summer our family went on a vacation to a small island country in

                      Rdef   L   LC (small)
the Caribbean called Barbados.[1]/ The country is only twenty-one miles long,

                  Rex   LC (vacation) Rdef LC (long and
and fourteen miles wide.[2]/ We[1] stayed at a resort hotel[1] on the   southern

wide) Rdef L   Rex L   L LC (island) Rdef L
side of the island[1].[3]/ Our hotel had its own small[1]   beach. [4]/ The beach it-

             LC (twenty-one and fourteen) L   Rex   L
self was only about   two hundred yards[2]   long.[5]/ Our[1] hotel[1] was on

Rdef LC (southernside) Rdef L
the   eastern end[2]   of the beach surrounded by coconut[4], almond[4],

           LC (Carribbian)
papaya[4], and other tropical trees[4].[6]/

      Rdef LC (beach) Rdef L   LC (beach)
      The   sand   on the beach was pure   white   just like on a televi-

          Rdef L   L   Rdef L
sion show about the South[3] Sea islands[2].[7]/ The sand was formed from broken

  L   LC (beach)
white   coral.   [8]/

For now I shall mention a few obvious features of the cohesive system in this brief text. For lack of space, much must go unmentioned. We can notice the density of cohesive ties. Even though the long verb phrase in T-unit 6 contains all new information, nearly every word in the T-unit contributes in some way to cohesion with what has come before. Coding the lexical ties in this brief text indicates the lexical chains that are central to this text. The main chain is Barbados–country–island–beach–beach–beach–beach–sand (one item from each T-unit). One minor chain is the one for orientation: long and wide–southern side–eastern end. There is a good deal of rich collocation throughout the text. Every T-unit has immediate ties with the preceding T-unit; yet, there are a good many remote ties, some leaping over as many as four intervening T-units.

Even if the analysis of the cohesion in this brief text were complete and comprehensive, it would still not explain fully the *coherence* of the text. But this is not a limitation of cohesion analysis in comparative studies; where individuals or groups are compared in their deployment of the available text-creating cohesive strategies. In those cases; the researcher is not claiming to provide a full accounting of the coherence—or even the cohesion—in each text. He or she is simply looking for differences that may emerge in the analysis of texts of various kinds: those from younger writers and those from older writers; those from poor writers and those from skilled writers; those from one discourse type and those from another type; those from normal writers and those brain-damaged or psychotic writers.

The first few published studies using cohesion analysis provide examples. Rochester and Martin (1979) studied the cohesion of retold narratives and interviews of thought-disordered and nonthought-disordered schizophrenics as well as normal speakers. All their subjects were adults. Except for clause length; they found no differences among these subjects in grammatical or syntactic control at the sentence level. There were, however, noticeable differences in the texts revealed by cohesion analysis. The thought-disordered speakers used fewer cohesive ties in narratives, relied more on lexical cohesion in interviews, and were less effective at creating full verbal contexts for their utterances, relying instead on references to the immediate situation outside the text itself. Witte and Faigley (1981) compared the cohesive ties in poor and good writing by college freshmen. They found that good writers created a much richer, denser texture of ties and relied more on immediate and mediated ties. Crowhurst (1981) analyzed the cohesive ties in the argumentative writing of students in grades six, ten, and twelve. She found that older students used more lexical ties per T-unit and were better able to manage remote ties. King and Rentel (1981) traced the earliest developments in control of the cohesive system in the narrative writing of children in grades one and two. They found that as the children grew older, they reduced the amount of exophoric reference in their stories and came to rely increasingly on conjunction and lexical ties. By the end of grade two, both boys and girls from vernacular-speaking lower-class families and from nonvernacular-speaking middle-class families had developed strong control of the cohesive system in narrative writing.

These few early studies reveal that cohesive ties are a powerful and reliable index of difference in writing samples. Lexical ties appear to be particularly telling, and it may be that future studies could focus here. One caution for researchers is to be aware of the high positive correlation between T-unit length and number of cohesive ties—as T-units increase so do the number of ties per T-unit. Consequently, unless covariance analysis is used, it may be better to calculate number of ties per one hundred words (see Witte and Faigley, 1981) rather than number of ties per T-unit.

Information Management

Another text-creating system available to writers is one for managing or staging the flow of information in the next. It is not independent of the cohesive system (as we shall see), but it can be analyzed separately and it promises to teach us a great deal about the development of writing ability.

Managing the information flow involves two critical decisions, deciding in each clause (1) what to treat as new and old information and (2) what to treat as theme or topic. The Prague School linguists (Danes, 1974; Palkova & Palek, 1978) were the first to study systematically this crucial part of discourse. Others have written about the same concepts (Chafe, 1975; Halliday, 1967; Grimes, 1975). Each clause in a written text can be considered along two independent dimensions: (1) old/new or given/new and (2) theme/theme or topic/comment (linguists have not yet agreed on what to call the two dimensions). What is old in a clause of written discourse is what the reader can be expected to remember from what has appeared previously in the text. What is new is what the writer has decided now to add to what the reader already knows. The decision about old/new is made solely to accomodate the reader. Usually, old information comes first in a clause, new information last. Often what is new at the end of one clause is the old information at the beginning of the next clause. In this way, lexical and referential cohesion—the nouns and pronouns of this old/new alternation—are entwined with managing information. The theme in a clause is what the writer wishes to emphasize. It is the first element in the clause, sometimes the grammatical subject, but not always. Although the theme is usually old information, it can, through a small set of syntactic options that are now well known, contain new information and thereby shift the information focus to the front of the clause. These three features of text—old/new, theme/comment, information focus—interact in subtle and complex ways. As with cohesion, there is not space enough here to present such a complex system. Instead, I shall assert that the nonlinguist can understand how all this works with some patient reading in the sources I have mentioned. Then I shall demonstrate how it looks in a brief text, this time the fifteen clauses comprising the first three paragraphs of the text we have seen earlier. Repeating the first two paragraphs in the cohesion analysis above will enable the reader to make a careful comparison of the interdependence of cohesion and information management.

This time, the theme in each clause is in capital letters. Just above each theme I indicate whether it contains old or new information and what the abstraction level (Nold and Davis, 1980, see below) of the information might be. Again, we classify a theme as new if it has not been specifically mentioned previously in the text or if it is one of a small class of syntactic fronting strategies I will identify shortly. If it makes a cohesive tie with the same word, a near synonym, or a general or superordinate term, we consider it new. However, if the tie is only one of collocation, we consider it old.

       Old 1   Old 1
LAST SUMMER/OUR FAMILY went on a vacation to a small island

                     Old 2
country in the Caribbean called Barbados.[1]/THE COUNTRY is only twenty-

Old 2
one miles long, and fourteen miles wide.[2]/ WE stayed at a resort hotel on the

Old 2
southern side of the island.[3]/ OUR HOTEL had its own small beach.[4]/ THE

Old 3   Old 2
BEACH ITSELF was only about two hundred yards long.[5]/ OUR HOTEL

was on the eastern end of the beach, surrounded by coconut, almond,

papaya, and other tropical trees.[6]/

New 2
THE SAND ON THE BEACH was pure white, just like on a television

Old 3
show about the South sea islands.[7]/ THE SAND was formed by broken white

coral.[8]

New 4
THE FIRST THIRTY YARDS OF THE BEACH CLOSEST TO OUR

New 4   Old 5
HOTEL was quite rocky.[9]/ AND THE WATER was shallow.[10]/ IN THIS

New
SHALLOW WATER/YOU were bound to find coral, sea urchins and a

countless variety of small marine tropical fish[11]/ THE FISH HAD A VARIE-

New 5 (Existential "have")
TY OF COLORS, FROM BLACK TO A DULL GREEN TO A

FLUORESCENT YELLOW, BLUE AND GREEN.[12]/ THERE WERE

New 4 (Existential "there")
ALSO MANY CRABS IN THE SHALLOWS.[13]/ THE ONLY PROBLEM

New 5 (Transposed)
IN WALKING THROUGH THE SHALLOWS, BESIDES THE ROUGH

ROCKS, were the thousands of black and white sea urchins.[14]/ IT WAS DIF-

New 6 (Extraposed)
FICULT WALKING AND TRYING TO AVOID THE URCHINS AT

THE SAME TIME.[15]/

A good way to approach our brief analysis of these paragraphs is to begin by contrasting the information management in the first paragraph with that in the second and third paragraphs. In the first paragraph, all of the themes (in capital letters) present old information with the new information and hence the information focus coming at the end of each clause. In the clause sequence, we see the familiar pattern of new information at the end of one clause becoming the old information at the beginning of the next clause; for example, in clause 4 the new information "beach" at the end becomes the old information "beach" at the beginning of clause 5. By contrast, in the second and third paragraphs, nearly all of the themes present new information. The writer has intentionally shifted the information focus to the front of the clause. How does he do this? Sometimes, he simply places the new information in the position of grammatical subject of the clause (clauses 7, 9, 10, and 11), but usually he relies on some special syntactic strategy (clauses 12, 13, 14, and 15, where the strategy is indicated in parentheses above each new theme. Existential "have," existential "there," and extraposed clauses are considered by linguists to be predicateless and, therefore, all theme [Clements, 1979; Quirk & Greenbaum, 1973].).

Why does the writer shift the information focus in this way? We can make several conjectures. Recall that the theme in each clause points the discourse in the way the writer wants it to go. The theme announces his interests and goals. Notice, then, that the writer signals the new emphasis of paragraphs 2 (sand) and 3 (the beach near his hotel) by beginning with new information. Notice, also, that themes with new information predominate as the abstraction level in the text shifts to lower and lower levels when the writer begins providing specific details of the scene (clauses 9 to 15). Finally, we can note that when the emphasis in clauses 14 and 15 shifts away from features of the scene toward the writer's actions in the scene, he front-shifts the new information identifying these actions. In research, Anne Gray and I have underway (Cooper & Gray, in preparation), we have found that the information-management strategies our seventeen-year-old writer uses are quite consistent with those used by highly regarded published writers like John McPhee.

Now that we have a general notion of how the information system operates in texts, we can conjecture about its uses in research. The linguistic specifications of the system (dividing clauses into old/new and theme/comment, and identifying the information focus and the syntactic strategies for shifting it) are highly reliable as analytic procedures. For both this system and cohesion analysis, researchers report high agreement among analysts. Nearly all of the research so far based on information management (or on staging, packaging, pragmatics—as it is variously identified) has been of three types: (1) the difficulty of understanding pairs of sentences and brief texts in which the expected old/new pattern is violated in various ways (see Clark & Haviland, 1977, for a review); (2) the effects of various staging arrangements on comprehension of extended text (Clements, 1979; Pratt, Krane, & Kendall, 1981); and (3) explorations into the earliest period of language development in young children (Bates, 1976; Bates & MacWhinney, 1979; Gruber, 1967).

For researchers in writing, this analytic procedure can help us answer a number of important questions. Perhaps the most important is how young writers gradually develop control of the information system. We need to inquire into the strategies that writers have for shifting the information focus in writing. Are these strategies dependent on certain syntactic options? At what points in a text is fronted new information advantageous? In general, what function does fronting serve throughout a text? (See Jones, 1977, for useful conjectures on this question.) What are the exact relations between the rich system for signaling information focus in conversation and the lean system for signaling it in written texts? We also need to study variations in the information system across various types of texts. In addition, we could examine information management as one aspect of the style of published writers. The only published study in English that I am aware of that uses theme and comment analysis compares the "distribution of theme-dynamic patterns" in the writing of several prominent writers (Enkvist, 1973). Finally, I think we need to inquire carefully into the relation of information-management strategies to cohesion and to all the other text-analysis procedures I propose in this chapter. Although they will tell us a good deal separately, they are all related in complex ways. They are all interdependent. For some research questions, one may be better than another, whereas for others, some combination of procedures may work best. Both Clements (1979) and Cooper and Gray (in preparation) provide formats for arranging and tabulating the results of clause-level analysis of the information system.

At this point in my review of procedures for analyzing written texts, I can suggest that these ways of describing texts may inform us about the composing process itself. Ann Matsuhashi and I (Cooper & Matsuhashi, in press) have tried to demonstrate that the cohesive and information systems in text comprise a set of crucial decisions a writer must make to produce each clause. We have argued that an adequate theory of the composing process must finally include an accounting of these clause-level plans and decisions.

Sentence Roles

For a long time, composition theorists and teachers have been concerned with the structural and functional relationships of sentences. This concern grew mainly out of an interest in the rhetoric of paragraphs. Every writing teacher knows that some sentences are generalizations, some particulars; but we have not known very much about the exact nature of general to particular, of abstract to concrete, of claim to support. Although we do not have it yet, I think there may be a way to achieve a good description of the functional or semantic roles sentences (or clauses or T-units) play in text. In my view, we shall need a separate system of roles for each major discourse type or genre. Devising such a system will teach us a great deal about the pattern and movement in the various types and genres, and it should provide a useful research procedure for developmental studies as well. Because it is more global than analysis of cohesion and information management, it will have less precision. But I believe a carefully refined system of sentence-roles analysis can eventually be used with enough reliability to justify its use in research studies where descriptions of writing samples are required.

Little work has been done so far on sentence-semantic roles, either by linguists or composition theorists. Most of what has been done by composition theorists has been for the purpose of instructing novice writers about paragraph development. Winterowd (1970) has proposed seven roles that sentences can play: coordination (and), obversativity (but), causativity (for), conclusivity (so), alternativity (or), inclusivity (expressed with a colon), and sequential (first, second, third). Larson (1967) has offered a much more comprehensive set of relationships: state, restate, expand, particularize, exemplify, define, describe, narrate, qualify, concede, support, refute, evaluate, identify a cause or result, compare or contrast, summarize, conclude. Two further studies are important to note, even though their approach to content relations is not limited to units of sentence size. It may be that content or functional relations are so complex within certain clauses that the sentence is too large a unit for charting the pattern of functional relations in text. At any rate, studies like these two will be essential in informing further work on sentence roles. Grimes (1975) outlines a set of 'rhetorical predicates' that account for all the organizing relations in text. Meyer (1975) has proposed a way of identifying and diagramming Grimes's rhetorical predicates. Here is an abbreviated list of Grimes's content relations (adapted from Meyer, 1975, pp. 33–34):

Alternative: Equal weighted alternative options.

Response: Equal weighted question(s) and answer(s), remark and reply, or problem(s) and solution(s).

Attribution: Describes qualities of a proposition.

Equivalent: Restates same information in a different way.

Specific: Gives more specific information about something that was stated in a general manner.

Explanation: Previously stated information is explained in a more abstract manner (e.g., relating the information to a general principle) or more concrete manner.

Evidence: Evidence through perception of a situation to support some idea.

Analogy: Analogy given to support an idea.

Manner: Way an event or event complex is performed (e.g., slowly, carefully).

Adversative: Relates what did not happen to what did happen.

Setting time: Gives time of setting in which information being related occurs (often in narratives).

Setting location: Gives location of setting in which information being related occurs (used particularly in narratives).

Setting trajectory: Gives changing background of location and time that occurs in a narrative when characters travel through various places.

Representative identification: Singles out one element of a group and makes it stand for the group as a whole.

Replacement identification: One thing standing for something else.

Constituency identification: Identifies a part in relation to some whole.

Collection: List of elements related in some unspecified manner.

Covariance: Relation often referred to as condition, result, or purpose, with one argument serving as the antecedent and the other as the consequent or result of the antecedent.

Pitkin (1977, pp. 664–672) has described the functional relations within clauses and sentences in terms of binary relations:

Coordinate/coordinate: Coordinate units at the same hierarchial level; can be arranged in any order.

Includer/included: A distinction based on level of semantic inclusiveness; includes classification, structure analysis, operation analysis, and component analysis.

Cause/effect: Includes both physical and logical cause.

Contrast/contrast: Concerned with differences; includes contrasts between positive/negative, concession/assertion, potential/actual, ideal/real.

Comparison/comparison: Concerned with similarities.

Assertion/intensification: The second term is a more extreme expression of the first.

Assertion/regression: The second term softens or tempers the first.

Time/assertion: Locating an assertion in time.

Place/assertion: Locating an assertion in space.

Manner/assertion: The manner in which something occurs.

Evaluation/assertion: An evaluation of the assertion.

Assertion/significance: What is significant or important about the assertion.

Term/categorization: Offering an interpretation or categorization of a key term in the assertion.

There are exasperating differences in the above four lists of roles, yet, there are intriguing similarities as well. What seems to be needed is some helpful categorization of roles and some further research to learn whether certain roles are characteristic of a particular discourse type or of short-range writing strategies within a discourse type.

For her research on temporal features of the composing process (Matsuhashi, 1981) and as part of a theory of the writing process we have developed together (Cooper & Matsuhashi, in press), Matsuhashi and I developed a system for analyzing sentence roles. Larson's (1967) work was our starting point. We also included unique narrative roles from Labov's work on unrehearsed oral narratives (Labov, 1972). Working with the writing of seventeen-year-olds in several discourse types, we attempted to devise a comprehensive scheme that would be useful with any type of writing. Here are our sentence roles—T-unit roles really—grouped into five organizing categories:

1. Generalizing roles: High level T-units that assert the thesis or controlling idea of a text.
   (a) State: Presents the theme, thesis, or controlling idea; includes what Labov (1972) calls the abstraction role in personal narrative.
   (b) Restate: A restatement of state role, usually for clarification or emphasis.
2. Rhetorical roles: T-units that summarize or conclude.
   (a) Summarize: Summarizes what has gone before.
   (b) Conclude: Draws a specific conclusion or serves as an exit from the text; includes what Labov (1972) calls coda in personal narrative.
3. Sequencing roles: T-units that add information at the same level of generality as the previous T-unit.
   (a) Add: Adding one assertion at the same level of generality or abstraction.
   (b) Replace: The role of reformulation or alternatives (different from restate, which must always follow a state T-unit).
   (c) Narrate: Naming an event or series of events in a time sequence.
4. Relationship roles: T-units that have a particular logical relationship to the previous T-unit.

    (a) Contrast/compare: A comparison or contrast with the assertion in the previous T-unit.

    (b) Infer: An explicit inference drawn from the preceding T-unit or sequence of them.

    (c) Evaluate: Makes a judgment of, or reflects on, assertions in previous T-units; plays an important role in personal narrative.

    (d) Cause/result: Expresses the cause or result of what has just been said.

    (e) Qualify: Restricts the meaning of an earlier assertion.

5. Development roles: T-units provide examples, facts, details at a lower level of generality than the preceding T-unit.

    (a) Exemplify: Provides examples, facts, and illustrations for the previous assertion.

    (b) Define: Offers a definition for a word or concept in a previous assertion.

    (c) Describe: Presents details of an object or person.

Analyzing a number of papers with this system, we reached 97% agreement in our decisions for the T-units in personal narrative but only 67% in explanation (a generalization supported by illustrations and anecdotes). The low agreement in explanation reflects the great variety of sentence roles in that discourse type, but it also suggests that an adequate system of sentence-roles analysis would have to be discourse-specific.

Two brief sections from longer pieces of our seventeen-year-old writer will illustrate how this system works in actual text and how different the sentence-roles sequencing is from one type of writing to the next. Each T-unit is marked and numbered. The first piece is a personal narrative. It reveals the very great prominence of evaluation in some narratives. These evaluative clauses and T-units function much like inference in explanatory or persuasive writing.

        Narrate   Describe
I was walking down the hall.[1]/ I saw my friend and this other person in

           Evaluate   Evaluate
front of me.[2]/ I knew my friend had stopped talking to me[3]/ and I began to

                                      Evaluate
wonder if they would say anything or do anything to me.[4]/ I wondered if they

                             Describe
would be friendly or if they would be mean.[5]/ I decided that I would play it

           Evaluate   Evaluate
their way.[6]/ If they were friendly, I would be friendly.[7]/ If they weren't, neith-

          Describe
er would I.[8]/ I was very cautious.[9]/

Narrate
As I passed them, I heard their laughing and their mumbling,[10]/ and I

Evaluate
knew they were talking about me.[11]/

The second piece is explanatory writing. The second paragraph reveals novice writers' extraordinary persistence in repeating a high-level generalization again and again.

State   Exemplify
The first form of competition was in the field of athletics.[1]/ In athletics,

individuals or groups of individuals (teams) try to become better than the

Replace
people they are going against.[2]/ In other words they try to do better than

Exemplify   Result
their competition.[3]/ Some people run against other people.[4]/ The object is to

Definition
be the first person across the finish line and be a winner.[5]/ The people you

run against are known as your competition.[6]/

State   Restate
Other forms of competition are in the field of business.[7]/ The businesses,

factories and corporations that produce manufactured goods are in competi-

Restate
tion with each other.[8]/ Companies that produce the same items are in

Restate
competition.[9]/ They try to get the people to buy their products and not the

products of the other companies.[10]/

One specialized form of sentence-roles analysis has been developed for classifying the functions of sentences in writing about literature (Odell and Cooper, 1976; Purves, 1968). This system has proven to be a reliable analytic procedure in many studies of response to literature and film (see Applebee, 1977, for a review).

An adequate system of sentence roles analysis will provide a quite special kind of information in all the various types of studies we have mentioned so far: comparative stylistics, developmental studies, discourse comparisons. Indeed, they may help us develop paradigms of the various discourse types and of the available strategies for presenting information and experience in text. The may point the way to an adequate paragraph rhetoric.

Abstraction Levels

Sentence roles analysis informs us about the *functional* or semantic relations of sentences or T-units. Another way to view sentence relations is in terms of their abstraction level in the content hierarchy of a text. This approach reveals the *structural* roles of sentences. Both a structural analysis and a functional analysis are, of course, interrelated—a sentence which provides an example for a generalization will always be at a lower level of abstraction than the generalization itself; if a new generalization appears part way through a text, it will always be at a higher level of abstraction than the preceding sentences of exemplification for a prior generalization.

Since the mid-1960s a particular form of structural analysis proposed by Francis Christensen (1965) has attracted considerable attention among composition teachers because it has promised to illustrate for students the structural requirements of adequately-developed writing. Teachers were already quite familiar with certain forms of structural analysis. For example, nearly all composition handbooks illustrate two basic ways to organize a comparison or contrast: either contrast each feature of the contrasted items in turn (1A-B, 2A-B, 3A-B, etc.) or describe all the features of one item first (1A, 2A, 3A, etc.) before taking up the contrasting features, usually in the same order, of the other item (1B, 2B, 3B, etc.). Since the structural analysis proposed by Christensen was equally apparent and just as accessible, it became widely known. Christensen, who was interested in the structure of paragraphs, defined a paragraph as "a sequence of structurally related sentences." He claimed that all sentences in a paragraph stood in a relation of coordination and subordination to a topic sentence and to each other. He demonstrated how to diagram paragraphs to reveal these structural relationships. Most important, he proposed a number of useful principles of paragraph development: addition, direction of movement or modification, level of generality (or abstraction level), and texture. Other researchers (e.g., Grimes, 1975) have confirmed the correctness of Christensen's analysis.

More recently, Ellen Nold and Brent Davis (1980) have refined Christensen's analysis by demonstrating that it is important to allow for the possibility of superordinate up-shifting as a text develops, not just at the beginnings of new paragraphs, as Christensen's analysis would accept by implication, but also within paragraphs. Their system of analysis produces a three-dimensional "discourse matrix," which has several important new features. For example, it defines constraints on producing coherent paragraphs, predicts points of greatest difficulty in writing or reading a paragraph, and isolates the important generalizations which contain the gist of a text.

At least two studies have used abstraction levels analysis, one to examine the time required to produce sentences at different abstraction levels (Matsuhashi, 1981), the other to contrast the incidence of high-level abstractions in the typical and superior writing of high school students (Dilworth, Reising, and Wolfe, 1978).

To illustrate this sort of analysis we refer to the student piece on page 297. Each theme in capital letters is numbered for information level (or abstraction level). The piece opens with its most general statement, at Level 1. T-units 2, 3, 4, and 6 are one level lower in abstraction and are all coordinate with each other, that is, all at about the same level of abstraction. T-unit 5, at Level 3, is subordinate to T-unit 4. T-unit 6 is a superordinate upshift to Level 2 after T-unit 5. The abstraction level moves lower and lower as the writer presents more and more specific details of the scene.

For further illustration look at the student piece on page 303. Here we can see the close relationship of T-unit functional and structural roles. In the first paragraph there is a consistent down-shifting of abstraction level as the writer provides examples, results, and definitions. In the second paragraph, a high level of abstraction is sustained as the writer continues to restate the opening generalization. Either analysis—structural or functional—confirms the problem any reader would sense in that paragraph.

All of the procedures for describing written texts discussed so far—cohesion analysis, information management, sentence roles, abstraction levels—are accessible to any serious student of writing development or to any composition teacher. All are powerful text analysis procedures. Taken together they would enable us to say much more than we have been able about the characteristics of professional writing. Singly and in combination, they can tell us much that we need to know about the development of writing ability and the differences among the major types and genres of writing. Though the procedures begin with labeling and enumeration of text features, they can take us well beyond pointing and counting. They provide a sound, linguistics-based description from which we may more confidently interpret differences we find in discourse types and in writers at various stages of development. What we want to know is what these text features mean—for the individual writer, for the constraints and possibilities in written text, for cognition in general and for problem-solving and planning in composing in particular, and for the culture. We can achieve these insights only with adequate, comprehensive text descriptions as a starting point.

Thematic Structure

I want to mention briefly one further descriptive procedure which might be used with all kinds of written texts. It is a procedure for specifying the network of propositions and meanings and displaying the hierarchical relationships among them. This is a very complex procedure based in propositional analysis (Kintsch, 1974) and case grammar (Fillmore, 1958) or in tagmemic theory (Pike & Pike, 1977). Though several linguists and psychologists have proposed ways to specify what I call here the thematic structure of text, I recommend three proposals as starting points. Jones (1977) has used concepts in tagmemic theory as well as notions of theme and information focus in order to devise a way of identifying the thematic development in a text. Her "blocking charts" present the text as a sequence of propositions (essentially clauses in their surface forms from the text). She then identifies the key concepts in the propositions along with the grammatical devices which link them. From the key concepts the text can be blocked into thematically related segments. Finally, Jones proposes a "dominance chart" as a way of diagramming the thematic hierarchy in the text.

In a procedure which accounts even more fully for the content structure in text, Meyer (1975) relies on Grimes' (1975) semantic grammar of propositions, which is based in part on case grammar. Her procedure specifies both the case role relationships in each clause and also the rhetorical strategies by which they are related across clauses. This detailed specification of meanings and relationships can then be diagrammed to reveal the hierarchical thematic structure of a text. De Beaugrande and Dressler (1981) propose an alternative scheme for displaying the thematic structure, a scheme they call a "conceptual network."

Good work of this kind is informed by all the descriptive procedures I have discussed so far in this chapter. An adequate thematic chart or diagram or network will result from a close analysis of the text not only in terms of its underlying propositions and its case roles but also in terms of its cohesive ties, old/new patterning, theme and information focus, sentence semantic roles, and abstraction levels. Jones (1977) is particularly helpful in showing how some of these features, along with certain syntactic patterns, may contribute to an analysis of thematic structure. The Jones and Meyers schemes were developed to analyze published writing in order to carry out studies of reading comprehension. I am claiming that their schemes, or some version of them, can be used to analyze and display the thematic structure of novices' writing. Such abstract structural displays will enable us to achieve new insights about text type differences and about the gradual growth toward discourse competence.

In the remainder of this chapter I mention some possibilities for analysis and description of three types or genres of writing: description, personal narrative, and persuasion. As I have already noted, an important goal for the studies I recommend is a fuller understanding of the features and structures of the major discourse types and genres. Presently we know much less than the confident tone of many composition handbooks suggest.

Description

Descriptive writing is not so much a special type or genre as it is a particular writing strategy a writer of prose fiction or non-fiction may choose in order to accomplish a larger discourse purpose. Description presents a number of special problems to writers, for example, choice of vantage point for presenting the scene, whether to shift from panorama to close-up, and which particular details to include. In terms of the structure of descriptions, writers must decide how to order and relate the details they wish to include. In a well-known study of oral descriptions, Linde and Labov (1975) found that when asked to describe the layout of their apartments, adults nearly always took the listener on a tour beginning at the front door, rather than beginning with a more general overview as if viewing an architect's drawing. The tour was organized in a surprisingly consistent way depending on whether the room was major or minor, to be entered and toured or merely looked into from the door.

Stahl (1974) has studied written descriptions from a similar task: School children were asked to describe their homes so that someone who had not seen them could have an idea of how they look. He devised a detailed scoring guide for the papers based on how well students forecast the order of their descriptions (implicit, explicit) and the relation of that forecast to the organization of the paper (consistent, inconsistent), the ways students chose details to include, and the methods of arranging the details (comprehensive, surveying, associative, egocentric, enumerating). He used this descriptive scheme for studying the writing development of groups of Israeli school children between Grades 2 and 8 (Stahl, 1977).

Narrative

The structure and features of fictional and personal narrative have been studied for so long a time and from so many perspectives that it is difficult to know how to advise a composition researcher new to this work. For my own research I have found it helpful to organize various schemes for analyzing narrative into three categories: (1) contributions from structuralism in literary theory; (2) story grammars from cognitive psychologists studying memory structure, thinking processes, and reading comprehension; and (3) linguistic analyses of the strategies available to storytellers for evaluating the experiences they present in personal narratives. I will provide references to central readings in the first two categories and then give more attention to the very promising work of Labov (1972) in the third category. My concern with this work on narrative structure has been to find a comprehensive and productive scheme for analyzing the personal experience narratives of school and college writers.

A readable, brief introduction to structuralism is John Sturrock's *Structuralism and Since: From Levi-Strauss to Derrida* (1979). Readers wishing to go immediately to examples of specific proposals for structures of narratives might want to begin with Barthes (1977), Todorov (1977), and Holloway (1979). Good places to start in cognitive science studies of narratives are Warren, Nicholas, and Trabasso (1979), Johnson and Mandler (1980), and de Beaugrande and Colby (1979).

Labov's work on the features, structure, and evaluative strategies in personal narrative is of great importance to composition researchers. Studying the unrehearsed oral narratives of dialect speakers (adolescents and adults) Labov noticed the importance of evaluations of experience in the narratives. This led him to a detailed examination of the various syntactic strategies available to embed evaluation into ongoing narratives. His procedures provide an immediately useful scheme for describing a crucially important and previously slighted aspect of narrative. Labov titles the chapter of the book in which he reports this work (1972) "The Transformation of Experience in Narrative Syntax." In this same chapter Labov reports results of a study comparing evaluative strategies of preadolescents, adolescents, and adults. In a series of pilot studies, Rita Gerber, Ronda Fox, Nancy Martin, and I have confirmed the usefulness of Labov's scheme for both developmental studies and evaluation studies of written narratives. Labov also offers a useful way to identify the central features of narratives. He calls these features abstract, orientation, complicating action, evaluation, result, and coda.

Quite clearly, there are rich resources already available for studying the oral and written narratives of school and college writers. I am particularly surprised that studies using these new resources have not begun to appear in the journals.

Persuasion

Since persuasion and argument have been studied since classical times, we might assume that we know more about the structure of argument than about the structure of narrative. Such is not the case. There are compelling new theories of persuasion which identify its major features or requirements (Toulmin, 1958; Kneupper, 1978, for an introduction to Toulmin), but very little careful analysis of the structure of argument. Probably the best current work describing persuasion is being done in studies of audience awareness in persuasive writing (Rubin and Piché, 1979). My own view is that there are so many different kinds of persuasion and so many strategies for developing arguments that it may be difficult if not impossible to arrive at one way of describing the structure of persuasion. Rieke and Sillars (1975) have demonstrated that even so straightforward a type of persuasion as problem-solution may take different forms, depending on how much the readers know and how much opposition the writer might expect from them.

CONCLUSION

The descriptive procedures I have recommended are only starting points. Except for Labov's scheme of evaluating strategies in narrative and for cohesion analysis, none of the procedures is well enough tested and refined to be put to use right away in studies of writing development. The procedures do provide the basis for a great deal of productive new work, however. My hope is that the urgent need for descriptive procedures by composition researchers will result in major contributions to textlinguistics, cognitive science, and rhetoric. At the least, the new work I am encouraging will give us the kinds of descriptions of published writing we need in order to move beyond outdated and inappropriate nineteenth century notions about text patterns. It should also help us begin to see how the forms and constraints in a written text explaining the results of an analysis are different from the thinking process itself—that descriptions of intellectual processes are not good labels for written texts. Of great importance for developmental studies will be new descriptions of children's and adolescents' writing on its own terms, in a way which accepts the cognitive, linguistic, and rhetorical constraints in development. We will learn what school and college writers are truly capable of, and we will also be able to accept realistically their limits. There can be little question that this new work will have an immediately beneficial result in classroom teaching and the design of writing programs.

NOTES

1. This text and all others in this chapter are from the Cross-Sectional Study of Writing Performance. Planned as a data base for descriptive studies of writing performance, this study was designed in early 1976 by Charles R. Cooper, Lee Odell, and Cynthia Watson, who together devised the sampling plan and the writing tasks. During the 1976–1977 school year, Cooper and Watson coordinated the gathering of the sample from school districts in New York, Michigan, and Illinois. Subsequently, Cooper and Odell supervised the primary-trait scoring of the sample.

2. A T-unit is one independent clause with all its modifying phrases or clauses.

3. All the texts in this chapter are from the same writer, an unusually competent seventeen-year-old.

REFERENCES

Applebee, A. N. The elements of response to a literary work: What we have learned. *Research in the Teaching of English*, 1977, 11, 255–271.

Barthes, R. Introduction to the structural analysis of narratives. In *Image, music, text*. New York: Hill & Wang, 1977.

Bates, E. *Language and context: The acquisition of pragmatics*. New York: Academic Press, 1976.

Bates, E., & MacWhinney, B. A functionalist approach to the acquisition of grammar. In E. Ochs & B. B. Schieffelin (Eds.), *Developmental pragmatics*. New York: Academic Press, 1979.

Becker, A. L. A tagnemic approach to paragraph analysis. *College Composition and Communication*, 1965, *16*, 237–242.

Bissex, G. L. *GNYS AT WRK: A child learns to read and write*. Cambridge, Mass.: Harvard University Press, 1980.

Braddock, R. The frequency and placement of topic sentences in expository prose. *Research in the Teaching of English*, 1974, *8*, 287–302.

Britton, J., Burgess, T., Martin, N., McLeod, A., & Rosen, H. *The development of writing abilities (11–18)*. London: Macmillan, 1975.

Britton, J. The composing process and the functions of writing. In C. R. Cooper & L. Odell (Eds.), *Research on composing: Points of departure*. Urbana, Ill.: National Council of Teachers of English, 1978.

Chafe, W. L. Givenness, contrastiveness, definiteness, subjects, topics, and point of view. In C. N. Li (Ed.), *Subject and topic*. New York: Academic Press, 1975.

Christensen, F. A generative rhetoric of the paragraph, *College Composition and Communication*, 1965, *16*, 144–156.

Clark, H. H., & Haviland, S. E. Comprehension and the given-new contract. In R. O. Freedle (Ed.) *Discourse production and comprehension* (Vol. 1) Norwood, N. J.: Ablex: 1977.

Clay, M. M. *What did I write?* Edinburgh: Heinemann, 1975.

Clements, P. The effects of staging on recall from prose. In R. O. Freedle (Ed.), *New directions in discourse processing* (Vol. 2). Norwood, N.J.: Ablex, 1979.

Cooper, C. R., & Gray, A. *Sequencing and staging information in explanatory discourse: A developmental study*. University of California, San Diego (in preparation).

Cooper, C. R., & Matsuhashi, A. A theory of the writing process. In E. Martlew (Ed.), *The psychology of writing*. London: Wiley, in press.

Cowan, G., & Cowan C. *Writing*. New York: Wiley, 1980.

Crowhurst, M. *Cohesion in argumentative prose written by sixth-, tenth-, and twelfth-graders*. Paper presented at the annual meeting of the American Educational Research Association, Los Angeles, March 1981.

Danes, F., (Ed.) *Papers on functional sentence perspective*. The Hague: Mouton, 1974.

D'Angelo, F. J. *A conceptual theory of rhetoric*. Cambridge, Mass.: Winthrop, 1975.

D'Angelo, F. J. Modes of discourse. In G. Tate (Ed.), *Teaching composition: 10 bibliographic essays*. Fort Worth: Texas Christian University Press, 1976.

D'Angelo, F. J. *Process and thought in composition* (2nd ed.). Cambridge, Mass.: Winthrop, 1980.

de Beaugrande, R. *Text, discourse, and process: Toward a multidisciplinary science of texts*. Norwood, N.J.: Ablex, 1980.

de Beaugrande, R., & Colby, B. N. Narrative models of action and interaction. *Cognitive Science*, 1979, *3*, 43–66.

de Beaugrande, R., & Dressler, W. U. *Introduction to text linguistics*. London: Longman, 1981.

Dilworth, C. B., Jr., Reising, R. W., & Wolfe, D. T. Language structure and thought in written composition: Certain relationships. *Research in the Teaching of English*, 1978, *12*, 97–106.

Dressler, W. U. *Current trends in textlinguistics*. Berlin: DeGruyter, 1978.

Enkvist, N. E. "Theme dynamics" and style: An experiment. *Studia Anglia Posnaniensa*, 1973, *5*, 127–135.

Fillmore, C. J. The case for case. In E. Bach and R. Harms (Eds.), *Universals in linguistic theory*. New York: Holt, Rinehart and Winston, 1968.

Grimes, J. E. *The thread of discourse*. The Hague: Mouton, 1975.

Gruber, J. S. Topicalization in child language, *Foundations of Language*, 1967, *3*, 37–65.

Halliday, M. A. K. Notes on transitivity and theme (Part II). *Journal of Linguistics*, 1967, *3*, 199–244.

Halliday, M. A. K., & Hasan, R. *Cohesion in English*. London: Longman, 1976.

Holloway, J. *Narrative and structure: Exploratory essays*. Cambridge: At the University Press, 1979.

Johnson, N. S., & Mandler, J. M. A tale of two structures: Underlying and surface forms in stories. *Poetics*, 1980, *9*, 51–86.

Jones, L. K. *Theme in English expository discourse*. Lake Bluff, Ill.: Jupiter, 1977.

King, M. F., & Rentel, V. M. *How children learn to write: A longitudinal study*. Columbus: The Ohio State University Research Foundation, 1981.

Kinneavy, J. L. *A theory of discourse*. Englewood Cliffs, N. J.: Prentice-Hall, 1971. (Available in paperback, W. W. Norton.)

Kinneavy, J. L., Cope, J. Q., & Campbell, J. W. *Aims and audiences in writing*. Dubuque, Iowa: Kendall Hunt, 1975.

Kinneavy, J. L., Cope, J. Q., & Campbell, J. W. *Writing—basic modes of organization*. Dubuque, Iowa: Kendall Hunt, 1976.

Kintsch, W. *The representation of meaning in memory*. Hillsdale, N.J.: Erlbaum, 1974.

Kneupper, C. W. Teaching argument: An introduction to the Toulmin model. *College Composition and Communication*, 1978, *29*, 237–241.

Labov, W. *Language in the inner city: Studies in the black English vernacular*. Philadelphia: University of Pennsylvania Press, 1972.

Larson, R. L. Sentences in action: A technique for analyzing paragraphs. *College Composition and Communication*, 1967, *18*, 16–22.

Linde, C. & Labov, W. Spatial networks as a site for the study of language and thought. *Language*, 1975, *51*, 924–939.

Matsuhashi, A. Pausing and planning: The tempo of written discourse production. *Research in the Teaching of English*, 1981, *15*, 113–134.

McCrimmon, J. M. *Writing with a purpose*. New York: Houghton Mifflin, 1972.

Meade, R. A., & Ellis, W. G. Paragraph development in the modern age of rhetoric. *English Journal*, 1970, *59*, 219–226.

Meyer, B. J. F. *The organization of prose and its effects on memory*. Amsterdam: North-Holland, 1975.

Moffett, J. *Teaching the universe of discourse*. Boston: Houghton Mifflin, 1968.

Moffett, J. *Active voice*. Montclair, N.J.: Boynton Cook, 1981.

Morgan, J. L., & Sellner, M. B. Discourse and linguistic theory. In R. J. Spiro, B. C. Bruce, & W. F. Brewer (Eds.), *Theoretical issues in reading comprehension*. Hillsdale, N. J.: Erlbaum, 1980.

Nold, E. W., & Davis, B. E. The discourse matrix. *College Composition and Communication*, 1980, *31*, 141–152.

Odell, L., & Cooper, C. R. Describing responses to works ot nction. *Research in the Teaching of English*, 1976, *10*, 203–225.

Odell, L., Cooper, C. R., & Courts, C. Discourse theory: Implications for research in composing in C. R. Cooper & L. Odell (Eds.), *Research on composing: Points of departure*. Urbana, Ill.: National Council of Teachers of English, 1978.

Palkova, Z., & Palek, B. Functional sentence perspective and textlinguistics. In W. U. Dressler (Ed.), *Current trends in textlinguistics*. Berlin: deGruyter, 1978.

Pike, K. L. and Pike, E. G. *Grammatical analysis*. Summer Institute of Linguistics, 1977.

Pitkin, W. L. X/Y: Some basic strategies of discourse. *College English*, 1977, *38*, 660–672.

Pratt, M. W., Krane, A. R., & Kendall, J. R. Triggering a schema: The role of italics and intonation in the interpretation of ambiguous discourse. *American Educational Research Journal*, 1981, *18*, 303–315.

Purves, A. C. *Elements of writing about a literary work: A study of response to literature*. Urbana, Ill.: National Council of Teachers of English, 1968.

Quirk, R., & Greenbaum, S. *A concise grammar of contemporary English*. New York: Harcourt Brace Jovanovich, 1973.

Rieke, R. D., & Sillars, M. O. *Argumentation and the decision making process*. New York: Wiley, 1975.

Rochester, S. R., & Martin, J. R. *Crazy talk: A study of the discourse of schizophrenic speakers*. New York: Plenum, 1979.

Rubin, D. L. and Piché, G. L. Development in syntactic and strategic aspects of audience adaptation skills in written persuasive communication. *Research in the Teaching of English*, 1979, *13*, 293–316.

Stahl, A. Structural analysis of children's compositions. *Research in the Teaching of English*, 1974, *8*, 184–205.

Stahl, A. The structure of children's compositions. Developmental and ethnic differences. *Research in the Teaching of English*, 1977, *11*, 156–163.

Sturrock, J., (Ed.), *Structuralism and since: From Levi-Strauss to Derrida*. New York; Oxford University Press, 1979.

Todorov, T. The poetics of prose (Richard Howard, trans.). Ithaca, N. Y.: Cornell University Press, 1977. (Originally published, 1971.)

Toulmin, S. *The uses of argument*. Cambridge: At the University Press, 1958.

Van Dijk, T. A. *Text and context: Explorations in the semantics and pragmatics of discourse*. London: Longman, 1977.

Van Dijk, T. A. *Macrostructures: An interdisciplinary study of global structures in discourse, interaction, and cognition*. Hillsdale, N.J.: Erlbaum, 1980.

Warren, W. H., Nicholas, D. W., & Trabasso, T. Event chains and inferences in understanding narratives. In R. O. Freedle (Ed.), *New directions in discourse processing*, (Vol. 2). Norwood, N. J.: Ablex, 1979.

Winterowd, W. R. The grammar of coherence, *College English*, 1970, *21*, 828–835.

Winterowd, W. R. *The contemporary writer* (2nd ed.). New York: Harcourt Brace Jovanovich, 1981.

Witte, S. and Faigley, L. Coherence, cohesion, and writing quality. *College Composition and Communication*, 1981, *32*, 189–204.

Author Index

Subject Index

Abstraction levels, 292, 305–306
Accessibility, 182
Accommodation, 44, 57
Acquisition of written literacy, 236,
    238–240, 257–258
Affective states, 107
Agraphia, 267, 275, 277, 282
    developmental, 269
Aphasia, 270, 276
Artificial intelligence technology, 17
Assimilation, 44
Audience awareness, 309
Audience for evaluation, 94, 96, 140
Automaticity, 182, 190
    Interpretation, 196, 199

"Basic" literacy skill, 268
Beginning situation, 162–163
Bottom-up inquiry, 14
Bridge principles, 27, 29, 30, 34, 38, 44, 45,
    49, 64, 65

Case grammar, 307
Case role relationships, 307
Case study, 250
Categorizing, 140, 170
Change of initial state, 149
Children's manipulation of simple
    sentences, 183, 191
Children's oral text, 141–142, 170
Children's written text, 141–142
Clinical-experimental interviews, 4, 12, 14
Cognitive information processing approach
    to research on teaching, 240
Cognitive psychological approach to
    research on teaching, 242
Cognitive style, 110
Cognitive system information processing
    constraints, 108
Coherence, 293–294
Cohesion, 10, 140–141, 143–145, 150,
    164–165, 171, 288, 292–296, 299
    Conjunction, 140, 144–145, 165, 170,
    183, 293, 299

Ellipsis, 140, 144, 164, 293
    Lexical cohesion, 140, 145, 165, 293
    Reference, 140, 143–144, 170, 293
    Substitution, 140, 144, 164–165, 293
Cohesive ties, 139, 170, 292, 294, 295, 307
    (*See also* Cohesion)
    number of, 295
Collocation, 145, 292–293, 296
    (*See also* Lexical cohesion)
Combinatorial explosion, 9, 10
Comment, 296, 298
Comparatives, 144
Competence
    Linguistic, 46, 47 (*See also* Linguistic
    performance)
    Psycholinguistic, 47
Competitive proofreading exercise, 183–186
Complication of initial state, 149
Composing aloud, 230–234
Conceptual levers, 248
Conceptual network, 307
Concurrent verbal protocols, 212
Confounding, 89
Conscious thought, 13
Constraints and opportunities, 240–242
Context Pyramid Model of Writing, 30–33,
    35, 38, 39, 49, 50, 51
    (*See also* Full context model of writing)
Control of writing processes, 192
Conversational exchange, 15
Cooper and Matsuhashi's sentence roles,
    302
Coordination, 190
Coordination level, 188
    Intermediate, 189
    Higher, 189
Credit assignment problem, 217
Criterion, 198, 201
Cultural deprivation, 277

Decomposable hierarchy, 91
Degradation of initial state, 149
    (*See also* Complication of initial state)
Degrees of freedom, 81